THE JUSTICE GAME

Geoffrey Robertson QC is Head of Doughty Street
Chambers and the author of textbooks on constitutional and media law. He has appeared as counsel in
many landmark cases in Britain and the Commonwealth and in the European Court of Human Rights,
and has conducted missions for the Bar and for
Amnesty International. He has received a number of
awards for his writing and broadcasting, and is
currently a visiting Professor at Birkbeck College. he
helped to found Charter 88 and is an executive
member of JUSTICE and the Institute of Contemporary Arts. He is married to the author Kathy
Lette; they live in London with their two children.

ALSO BY GEOFFREY ROBERTSON

Reluctant Judas
Obscenity
People Against the Press
Geoffrey Robertson's Hypotheticals
Does Dracula Have Aids?
Freedom, the Individual and the Law
Media Law (with A. Nicol)

Geoffrey Robertson

THE JUSTICE GAME

VINTAGE

Published by Vintage 1999

2 4 6 8 10 9 7 5 3 1

Copyright © Geoffrey Robertson 1998

First published in Great Britain by Chatto & Windus in 1998

Vintage
Random House, 20 Vauxhall Bridge Road, London SW1V 2SA

Random House Australia (Pty) Limited
20 Alfred Street, Milsons Point, Sydney,
New South Wales 2061, Australia

Random House New Zealand Limited
18 Poland Road, Glenfield,
Auckland 10, New Zealand

Random House South Africa (Pty) Limited
Endulini, 5A Jubilee Road, Parktown 2193, South Africa

Random House UK Limited Reg. No. 954009

A CIP catalogue record for this book
is available from the British Library

ISBN 0099581914

Papers used by Random House UK Limited are natural,
recyclable products made from wood grown in sustainable forests.
The manufacturing processes conform to the environmental
regulations of the country of origin.

Typeset by SX Composing DTP, Rayleigh, Essex
Printed and bound in Great Britain by
Cox & Wyman Ltd, Reading, Berkshire

For my mother and father

Contents

Preface

> I could tell you a lot about the law . . . we got a man
> to argue for me tomorrow who wouldn't have me
> to dinner in his house. But I have paid his price and
> he will be at my side for as long as it takes.
>
> Mr Schultz, *Billy Bathgate*, E. L. Docterow

In 1989, on an Amnesty International mission to Vietnam, I was told in several villages the same story, about a farmer who one day vanished. The local communist party chief had the farmer's enemy arrested and executed for murder. Years later, the farmer was found tending ducks in another village. This story was repeated as a parable for political change – a demand, if not for democracy, at least for a legal system independent of the State. In the same year in England, where such a system had existed for centuries, its justice was being called into question by the dawning realisation of the wrongfulness of the convictions of the 'Birmingham Six', the 'Guildford Four', Judith Ward and others. The message of these miscarriages was more complicated, but essentially the same: they had been caused by State agencies – police and prosecutors and Home Office scientists – who had been so blind to the possibility of innocence that they had withheld, as irrelevant, information consistent with it.

This book is an attempt to explain why justice matters. It matters because we have an elemental need for reassurance that there is some chance of winning a legal contest against the powers that be. Most of us will never find ourselves accused of crimes we did not commit, or oppressed by Whitehall or by the most mighty in the land, or wish to publish something so shocking that public opinion will want to string us up. What we need to feel is that should this (heaven forbid) ever happen, we can turn to a legal system which will give us a reasonable chance of victory –

preferably not posthumously. Justice is *the* great game precisely because its rules provide the opportunity of winning against the most powerful, and against the State itself. This does not mean that David will necessarily slay Goliath, but that laws of battle will prevent Goliath from sidling up and hitting him on the head. They arm David with a slingshot, a *possibility* of victory.

I have sought to explain this by recounting actual cases, the method by which law itself develops as it narrows down from precedent to precedent. These were hard cases, although some made good law and others exemplify the need to make law better. No human trial system is infallible: compromises must be made, in doing the best we can. The minimum which the law must offer is a possibility of success to those up against it, irrespective of their wealth or indeed their guilt. That applies to all defendants on criminal charges, especially when those charges are brought to protect the State in the name of national security or national morality. It must apply to those who challenge the State to obtain 'rights' which have been denied them – rights as basic as to know how their children have died or as paradoxical as to be treated with decency on the way to the gallows. Law is erroneously regarded as a tool for oppression: in this book I have tried to show how it can serve as a lever for liberation.

That was not what I had been taught at Law School, which dunned into me that law was a system for applying rules made by legislators or by judges to facts elucidated by evidence, through which process a just result would be achieved. We were dubious enough in the sixties about this 'slot machine jurisprudence' to be taken in by a most charismatic and controversial judge, Lord Denning, whose slogan was 'I must do justice, whatever the law may be'. His invitation to tear up the rule book in order to reach popular results suited the iconoclasm of the time. That it was dangerously simplistic only became evident years later, as I sat in courtrooms in Singapore and Kenya and South Africa, listening to his idiosyncratic judgments being quoted by State prosecutors as warrant for locking up dissidents without trial, as threats to national security. Denning played Prospero to lawyers of his generation, creating the result his own opinionated mind believed 'just' through the alchemy of obscure precedents he found in the common law: his prejudices were his principles. 'Trust the judges' became his motto, and although my cases show that judges usually favour liberty more than governments do, they need advocates to push them and principles to protect them.

'Law is the wisdom of the old,' says Auden, but neither law nor lawyers strike me as repositories of any sort of wisdom at all. What we normally distil is convenient sagacity: ways around statutes, the likely outcome of precedents, the tactics which may triumph at trial. At a functional workaday level, the law is a mechanism for reducing the level of grievance in a society. It serves to let blood, mostly with clinical skill although sometimes by leeches whose conduct has inspired most of the lawyer jokes through the ages. We get results for clients by constructing arguments which win the day because they are judged better than the arguments offered by the other side. If that seems a weary, jobbing definition, it is less cynical than the one offered by the American realist school of jurisprudence, that 'law is what officials do in fact'. The whole point of law, it seems to me, is that it offers the possibility of establishing that what officials do is, in fact, wrong. The value we call 'justice' is the description applied to (or withheld from) the result of an actual case, although it more accurately describes the rules by which the case was decided or settled. These rules are ordained by the State: whether they are just depends on whether they provide for the possibility of beating the State at its own game.

This book begins in 1970, with the State's first cack-handed attempts to punish some excesses of the sixties, such as the crude effusions of the underground press. This political use of the law culminated in the sledgehammer prosecution of Duncan Campbell under the Official Secrets Act and the wrongful conviction for blasphemy of *Gay News*. More extreme examples of repression I later observed in South Africa and Malawi, and fought against in Prague and Singapore, but all derived from the same error: the perception that laws can and should silence subversive people and ideas. The government learned a lesson from the ABC Trial, but the powerful private prosecutors of the artist Stephen Boggs and the director of *The Romans in Britain* had to be taught it as well. It was the adversary system that gave these dissidents a chance: there was always the jury, the 'gang of twelve', its constitutional power to cause an upset confirmed, curiously enough, by the case of runaway MP John Stonehouse. But juries do not always do justice to unpopular people. That task calls for unflinching appellate judges, like those who freed the man convicted of supplying 'nuclear triggers' to Saddam Hussein, because his trial was unfair.

The book chronicles a sea change in the attitudes of judges, partly generational and partly through the influence of human rights treaties. This can be seen most markedly in the decisions on the death penalty made by the Privy Council and described in Chapter 4, between the judgment which hanged Michael X in 1975 and the decision which saved the lives of Earl Pratt and Ivan Morgan and hundreds more in 1993. A reminder that justice is reasonably demanded by *victims* of crime and can take precedence over the interests of the State is found in the battles of Ron Smith to establish how his daughter Helen died in Saudi Arabia and in the similar crusade of the 'Friendly Fire' parents to penetrate the army's all-purpose excuse that their sons were killed in the 'fog of war'. As a further reminder, in 'Fantasy Island' I describe some international efforts on behalf of the innocent victims of drug cartels, the honest judges and journalists whose killers were helped by irresponsible bankers and businessmen and politicians. In contrast, 'Diana in the Dock' is a tribute to one would-be plaintiff who was partly the author of her own misfortune, but whose claim for privacy does need to be weighed with the value (heavily supported in other chapters) of freedom of expression.

Although British culture and history sustain a rhetorical commitment to 'fair play', decisions taken behind the closed doors of Whitehall may nonetheless lack consistency and sometimes honesty – as the Matrix Churchill trial revealed. That case was important not only as an example of how the justice game can be played against the State, but for setting the sleaze ball rolling towards the 1997 general election. This picked up speed with the collapse of another trial – Neil Hamilton's libel action against *The Guardian*, a game won in the teeth of odds which the Lords and Commons had stacked in the plaintiff's favour by tinkering with the Constitution. Although Sir Humphrey Appleby and the *Yes Minister* brigade regard open government as a contradiction in terms ('You can be open, or you can have government'), my point in these chapters is that openness is conducive to better government, part of which entails respect for the value of justice.

All these case histories serve as jumping-off points for a wider argument about the role of law in guaranteeing individual liberty. Considered in isolation, they demonstrate how this has been achieved, variously and haphazardly – sometimes by strokes of advocacy, occasionally by an ingrained sense of fairness in the trial judge; more often by politic bargains in the jury room or by proper application of precedent in appellate courts. Taken together, I believe they make an overwhelming case for a return to first principles, for approaching all these problems not just with a grab-bag of precedents and a sentimental faith in the jury or the adversary system, but from the bedrock of a Bill of Rights. The absence of human rights as a starting point for legal argument is the great and glaring defect of the common law tradition, in England which developed it and Australia which inherited it. Studying and practising law in these two countries over the past quarter-century has often felt like worshipping scientology rather than true religion, a search for artificial arguments to win cases which should be decided by appreciation of basic values. In Australia, progressive-minded judges have sought to import these values from inter-national human rights treaties (somewhat to the discomfort of politicians who signed them without thinking they would have any real effect). In Britain at last we have a government prepared, at the time of writing, to make the European Convention on Human Rights a part of domestic law, thereby willing to have its exercises of arbitrary power controlled by independent arbiters of fairness. For many reasons – enumerated in the last chapter – I believe that this will lift the justice game to First Division level. It will not mean that the best team will always win, but the match will be worth watching.

The book argues for freedom of information and libel law changes, for abolition of blasphemy, for proper inquiries into violent deaths, for a privacy law, for an Independent Commission Against Corruption, and for an end to that great British confidence trick, 'voluntary self-regulation', as it is deployed to excuse the misbehaviour of politicians and newspaper editors. These populists are the first to cry 'let's kill all the lawyers' when the law does not conform to their expectations, although their 'Privileges Committee' and 'Press Complaints Commission' are fraudulent bodies through which they contrive to avoid conforming to law. It is a great mistake for lawyers to want to be loved: their job is to ensure that the value of fair adversarial trial is recognised as a guarantee for civil liberty of importance equal to a free press and a democratically elected Parliament. The advent of a Bill of Rights will make this role both explicit and worthwhile. They must prepare themselves to perform it in return for more satisfaction and less money.

The chapters come chronologically rather than logically, spanning twenty-five years. Some of the earlier forensic flashpoints could not happen now (which is some measure of progress) while others have done something to penetrate the secrecy and upset the complacency which have been the abiding features of British Governance over the period. The book offers a view from the robing room, a place as important as the jury room and the police canteen in the hidden culture of the English adversary system. Yet however objective an advocate tries to be, you cannot cut psychologically adrift from that obsessive commitment to the side you were on at the time, no matter how many years have elapsed, and these histories should be read with that caveat. For that reason too, the reader is owed some explanation of where I am coming from – hence the accounts of Sydney and Oxford and of early days qualifying for the Bar. This is not intended as an autobiography and is probably too argumentative to qualify as a memoir. It is a chart of some cases which I look back on in the way airline pilots think of radio beacons – they call them 'way points', aids to work out how far they have come, and how far they have yet to go.

It remains to thank those clients who have entrusted me with their battles and encouraged me to write about them. For editing, my thanks to Jenny Uglow and Jonathan Burnham, and for preparing the manuscript to Anthony Hudson, Jane Mulholland and Christopher Whitehouse. My colleagues at Doughty Street Chambers have suffered my distraction over this book in silence, unlike my wife whose support has, as ever, been critical. Most of these cases can be found in skewed perspective in the press clippings and in the more circumspect pages of the law reports. I have tried to show how they really happened and for what they stood or fell in the long march for human rights.

Geoffrey Robertson
Doughty Street Chambers
November 1997

I

Sounds of the Seventies

Chapter 1

Who is Mr Abbie Hoffman?

'That was Abbie Hoffman – he's catching the nine o'clock flight from Paris, and he wants a lawyer at Heathrow in case they try to deport him.' Richard Neville, the editor of *Oz* magazine, put down the telephone and looked at the only lawyer immediately available to the English underground press on a Sunday night in March, 1971. Not really a lawyer – a 24-year-old postgraduate whose thesis on freedom of speech had provided the excuse for descending from Oxford at weekends to Richard's basement flat in Notting Hill, scene of the crime of conspiracy to corrupt public morals for which he was shortly to stand trial at the Old Bailey. I was a strait-laced, short-haired, pedantic Rhodes Scholar; Richard was London's latest Peter Pan, a charming chat-show revolutionary whose basement served as a crash-pad for the lost boys and girls of *fin de sixties* England. This never-never land had Tinkerbells, I noticed, who rolled fairy dust and evinced a mixture of dread and contempt for the pirates moored at Scotland Yard, who made regular raids to spoil their fun.

Richard's eyes gleamed at the prospect of meeting the star of the Chicago conspiracy trial, who had defied a reactionary judge and turned a prosecution for disrupting the 1968 Democratic Convention into an epic courtroom clash between the American protest movement and the establishment. But there was a dab of caution beneath his bravado. The *Oz* editors had been committed for trial for an offence carrying a maximum sentence of imprisonment for life. After Richard's arrest, Scotland Yard had objected to bail, and even objected to his surety, a long-haired television producer of apparent good character named John Birt. Abbie Hoffman, he suspected, would be banned from entering Britain as

3

the result of an escapade the previous year involving his co-conspirator Jerry Rubin, whose appearance on *The David Frost Show* had been interrupted by 'yippies', led by Richard and *Oz* co-editor Felix Dennis, squirting water-pistols. Frost had become hysterical, and the government had overreacted by placing all the Chicago conspirators on a 'stop-list', as persons whose presence in the United Kingdom was 'not conducive to the public good'. As an Australian, Richard too was liable to deportation if convicted (although the journalist Anna Wintour had graciously offered her hand should he need to avoid transportation).

These were strange Buñuel-type times, before the IRA's resurgence, when secret policing of young radicals was justified less by their anti-Vietnam protests than by the small bombs which sporadically exploded at 'Miss World' contests and outside Spanish tourist offices, planted by Cambridge graduates calling themselves 'The Angry Brigade'. Every time I walked along Palace Gardens Terrace and descended into Richard's basement at No. 11A, I was captured on film by the Special Branch, who were (I discovered many years later) occupying an entire floor of the Edwardian house opposite. What they made of a clean-cut Australian law student in an unfashionable brown suit and tie I shall find out only if I live long enough for a Freedom of Information Act which allows me to see my file. (They certainly must have recorded a decline in dress sense, as my hair lengthened and I changed into compost-coloured corduroys and finally acquired the mandatory velvet suit.) Had I known 'they' were watching, I would probably have caught the next train back to Oxford. But at the time, I did not think twice: I had not been in this town long enough to realise how limited was its tolerance. Abbie Hoffman was a celebrated defendant who might be in need of a lawyer. Excited at the prospect of standing in momentarily for William Kunstler, the 'movement' lawyer who had defended the Chicago conspirators, I agreed to go and meet him.

Richard had acquired a chauffeur – a crippled New Zealander named Stan, who hinted darkly on the way to Heathrow at his qualifications for driving get-away cars. He parked directly outside the arrival hall, idling his souped-up engine while Richard and I waited for the flight from Paris to empty. To our surprise, it was not long before Abbie Hoffman sailed through – there is no other metaphor to describe the passage of a person so resplendently rigged with billowing black hair. 'It's Sunday night. They got dozy' he laughed, embracing his English acolyte. 'I brought my attorney,' said Richard with some pride: the best-selling hip adventurer Hunter S Thompson never travelled without one, so having a lawyer in tow had become a desirable fashion accessory for the well-groomed revolutionary of the period. Hoffman eyed me for a moment, with ill-concealed disdain for my youth and my haircut; his broken Brooklyn nose actually crinkled at my olfactory *faux pas* – Old Spice aftershave. 'I need to go down to Pan Am to check my ticket through to Northern Ireland,' he said breezily. 'I'd advise you to do that tomorrow,' I whispered, mindful of the stoplist, but Hoffman surged downstairs to the Pan Am counter, where we were promptly intercepted by three immigration officials.

'We're sorry, Mr Hoffman, we need your passport back for one moment,' said the largest, with an embarrassed smile. 'We just need to put another stamp in it before you go. Please.' Richard, ever polite, said 'Sure' and Abbie, like most Americans a sucker for English good manners, reached for the vital document. That was when, to everyone's surprise and especially my own, I intervened. 'Actually, Mr Hoffman will not surrender his passport. He's been lawfully admitted to the United Kingdom, and you have no power to detain him or require him to give you his passport again. As his legal advisor, I assure you he will abide by his conditions of entry. Gentlemen, good night.' Then, undermining the majesty of this message, I muttered, 'I think we'd better run for it' – and we did, leaving the officers standing, legally powerless to pursue us. Stan's get-away car was still waiting outside, and just in case my advice was wrong, he gunned it at break-neck speed towards the lights of London.

Abbie Hoffman's motor-mouth went just as fast, and I sank into silent reflection. Hoffman seemed arrogant and self-obsessed, with nothing much to say in England and even less in Northern Ireland. His presence was, in fact, not particularly conducive to the public good and certainly not conducive to mine, if I wanted to stay after my student visa expired. What had made me intervene, to abort the process whereby officialdom would simply have cancelled his entry visa and put him on the next flight to New York? Perhaps I was a lawyer by nature, as well as by training? I had realised that these pleasant officials were lying, in the good cause of retrieving their mistake (the fact that they said 'please', and said it nervously, was the giveaway). They were abusing their power, or at least asserting a power they did not have, once they had given Hoffman leave to enter. The rights or wrongs of Abbie Hoffman being banned from Britain did not enter into the calculation: he was entitled to know his rights, even a right which had accrued through an oversight. It struck me, miserably, on that high-speed, white-knuckled journey, that the sooner I found a rationale for defending people as meretricious as Abbie Hoffman, the better.

The rationale was found for me a few days later. I had retreated to the safety of the postgraduate common room at University College, where homesick American Rhodes Scholars mooched behind copies of the *Herald Tribune*. (Bill Clinton from Arkansas was one of them at 'Univ', where it had not been thought he would amount to much. The ambitious American we middle-commoners voted 'most likely to succeed' was Paul Gambaccini.) Taking my place behind *The Times*, I read with astonishment how my first piece of legal advice in Britain had caused a rumpus in Parliament:

Mr Fell (Yarmouth, Conservative) asked what were the circumstances under which Mr Abbie Hoffman was allowed into Great Britain.

Mr Sharples (Minister of State, Home Office, Conservative): Mr Hoffman was inadvertently admitted as a visitor on March 21st.

Mr Fell: Is it not rather serious, as hippies are perfectly well known to the Home Office and have stated that they support the National Liberation Front in Vietnam, the Black Panther Movement, and the Irish Republican Army. What is the Minister to do to prevent inadvertently letting in people of this type?

Mr Sharples: The immigration officers do an extremely good job. A mistake was made in this case and steps have been taken to see that it will not happen again.

Mr Merlyn Rees (Leeds South, Labour): Who is Mr Abbie Hoffman? (*Laughter*)

Mr Sharples: There is a long description of Mr Hoffman. Perhaps I had better write to Mr Rees. (*Renewed laughter*)

Reading these inane exchanges gave me the first inkling of the fallacy that Parliament is the true guardian of civil liberties. Abbie Hoffman's three days in England had been uneventful, yet here were MPs and ministers contriving to keep others like him out, for no reason other than their lifestyle and political opinions. They were supported by the Shadow Home Secretary. (A few years later Merlyn Rees welshed on Labour's commitment to introduce a Freedom of Information Act, explaining to a disappointed MP that 'only two or three of your constituents would be interested'.) So I had the retrospective satisfaction of realising that I had given legal advice that was correct and which had contributed to freedom of speech. And, of course, that had caused 'steps to be taken' to ensure such a contribution could not be made again. I tossed the newspaper onto the table, dimly aware that I had discovered in it the first evidence for what over the next quarter-century would harden into my only unshakeable belief; namely that it is to the law and the courts, rather than to politicians and Parliament, that we have no alternative but to turn if civil liberties are to be protected.

What struck me more immediately was the irony that I had so recently left a country which *did* regularly refuse entry to people and books and films that its government did not like, in order to enjoy the liberty I had learned about from reading the *New Statesman* and Penguin Specials. Growing up in Sydney in the fifties and sixties had been the cultural equivalent of living in a suburb of the Isle of Wight, without the pop festivals. We had studied only English history ('Australian history' being a short course in British penology, circa 1788); we listened to recycled BBC radio programmes and had swooned, quite literally, over the young Queen. (The first atrocity I observed, at the age of nine, was the sight of hundreds of small children collapsing from heat exhaustion after waiting hours in the boiling sun at Sydney Showground for a limp wave from the passing monarch.) One result of this cultural obeisance was that from afar England sounded increasingly attractive as it progressed from the *Lady Chatterley* trial through the Beatles to the liberal reforms of Harold Wilson: Australia did not enter the sixties until it was dragged into them by Gough Whitlam's Labour government in 1972. That was two years after I arrived in what Australians still called, and with fondness, 'the mother country'.

In the post-war diaspora of displaced Australians, I arrived with the second wave – less witty, more political as a result of Vietnam. The first surge had left while I was at school (a boy's comprehensive) in Sydney. I would sneak off to watch Barry Humphries trying out Edna Everage, whose cringing self-abasement was originally the joke. I arrived at Sydney University in 1964: the revue was still using scripts left behind by Clive James, and a tear-stained tutor arrived very late for my first philosophy seminar, explaining through sniffles, 'I've just come from the airport. *Germaine* is gone forever.' The office I soon occupied as the President of the Student Council had traces – kicked over, I suspect – of these and other expatriates who honed their wit on a country run in small-minded and ridiculous ways. They left before being required to die for it, in the Vietnam War, to stop the 'yellow peril' which was waiting to descend, as if by gravity, on its whites-only civilisation.

Conscription was conducted as fairly as a lottery: only those twenty-year-olds whose birth-dates were drawn out of a barrel were called up. Old schoolfriends who had not made it to university and draft exemption started to go missing, presumed dead, in unpronounceable provinces of South Vietnam, fighting people of a colour they would never have seen at school. This gave student politics a kind of steel – if we were old enough to fight an unjust war, we were no longer prepared to be treated like children. 'Student power' required our participation at every level of university government: I became the first 'student proctor', sitting in judgment on friends accused of pelting reactionary politicians with rotten tomatoes, secretly wishing I had the gumption to commit the same crime. But on every occasion that tempted towards heroism or hedonism, I had this albatross around my neck, what my mother called 'your legal career to think of'. It led to a reserve, a detached and slightly puritanical outlook, a sense that I would always be last to join the orgy.

I had first thought of a legal career at school, as the result of a bizarre act of Antipodean censorship. The acquittal of *Lady Chatterley's Lover* at the Old Bailey, by a jury which had been asked 'Would you allow your wife or even your servants to read this book?', had horrified the repressive Australian establishment. The Prime Minister, Robert Menzies, announced in Cabinet that the book must remain on the banned list because he would never allow his wife to read it; zealous customs officials, in an excess of wife protection (Australians, at least, did not worry about their servants), banned C H Rolph's edited account of the trial as well, which had been published as a Penguin Special, on the grounds that it too might 'tend to deprave and corrupt'. This idiocy provoked one courageous Sydney bookseller to arrange for friends in England to transcribe by hand every word of Rolph's book onto thirty-two tightly spaced air letters, which entered the country as personal mail and so eluded the censor. *The Trial of Lady Chatterley* was then reconstituted and printed in a *Samizdat* edition, which fell into my schoolboy hands. Endowed with the thrill of forbidden fruit, it was this book which must first have aroused in me the corrupting desire to practise at the Old Bailey like D.H. Lawrence's defenders, Gerald Gardiner and Jeremy Hutchinson.

At Sydney University, the ideals of the time demanded we should learn a different kind of law to that which regulated conveyancing and commerce. We wanted to understand how it impacted upon the poor, so we could use it to improve their lot. There were bloody fights with the Faculty to force it to offer a course in 'poverty law', a battle won only after we promised to change the title to 'Law and Social Justice'. In these years, much affected by Martin Luther King's example, we organised 'freedom rides' to outback towns to break down the colour bans which were everywhere, from pubs to swimming-pools, a petty apartheid as entrenched as it was in South Africa. I became a Board member of an organisation for the advancement of Aborigines and Torres Strait Islanders, and began to act for blacks – usually on minor criminal charges. There was a problem in bringing them back to the prestigious commercial law firm where I worked as an articled clerk and then as a solicitor: it never dirtied its hands with crime. I took this up with the senior partner: why couldn't we defend clients on criminal charges? He sucked his pipe for a moment and looked on me rather like a fond father called upon to tell his son the facts of life. 'Why, lad, it's like this. We just couldn't have *criminals* sitting alongside clients like Mr Packer and Mr Murdoch in our waiting room.'

Australians of my generation are haunted by the treatment meted out to Aborigines in the past, the more so as these persecuted people were the first to break down the 'Englishness' in the national character: they taught us to dream, to be easy-going, and to find our way through the bush. Acting for them, however, was not a matter of sentiment: no other group suffered such injustice. The first case we took up was that of Nancy Young, a mother who had been jailed for the manslaughter of her baby who had died, so the police doctor said, from malnutrition. She lived in abject poverty on an unsanitary Aboriginal reserve behind a prosperous country town in Queensland: her all-white, all-male jury ignored expert evidence that the child had died from disease rather than neglect, and so did the local Court of Appeal. There were student protests, a television programme and my first articles for serious newspapers about this wrongful conviction. The Queensland authorities found a pretext to reconsider the case and quash the conviction on a technicality, without any apology or any misgivings: the next time it happened they hoped that nobody would notice. It was my first inkling about how often justice only gets done when someone does notice.

In law, Australia was still a colony, its final court of appeal made up of English judges – the Law Lords – who sat in the Privy Council in London. This was despite the fact that the Australian High Court boasted the best judge in the common-law world, Sir Owen Dixon. His was a great legal mind with a curious pathology – he discouraged the Privy Council developing as a true Commonwealth Court because he was physically revolted by the prospect of sitting alongside a black judge. Dixon's successor as Chief Justice was Garfield Barwick, who had been the pre-eminent advocate of his day, much admired by the Privy Council. I would dine with him occasionally, and he would tell of his exploits in that far-off battlefield in Downing Street before the Lords of English justice. The best story, or so he regarded it, was the one about the 'thirteen little Malaysians'. All were communist subversives who had appealed to Her Majesty's Privy Council against their death sentences, but only twelve had the sense to retain Barwick. He took a very short and very technical point about the validity of the execution warrant, which the barrister for the thirteenth man had not noticed and did not take. In due course the Lords of English justice delivered their verdict: Barwick's argument succeeded and the lives of his twelve clients would be spared. The thirteenth, whose case was the same in every way, had his appeal rejected and was hanged. The moral of this story, I suppose, was that lawyers best serve the cause of human rights by attention to detail, rather than by waxing passionate about evils like capital punishment. As a student, I found it shocking rather than amusing.

The lawyer who seemed most to epitomise progress was Gerald Gardiner, the defender of *Lady Chatterley*, who had only taken the job of Lord Chancellor in the British Labour government on condition that the death penalty be abolished. Under his guidance the government had put homosexuality and abortion outside the reach of criminal law, had abolished censorship of the theatre, passed a law against incitement to racial hated and had begun, by establishing a Law Commission and appointing Leslie Scarman to it, to reform the archaic common law. When I left Sydney, Bill Deane, the city's leading silk, kindly gave me *QB VII* to read on the boat. This is Leon Uris's fictionalised account of the libel action brought against him by one of the Auschwitz doctors he had exposed in *Exodus*. There I found the most glowing literary tribute ever paid to a member of the Bar. The worried author, walking in the Temple late at night, sees the lights still burning in the room of his advocate, and is filled with awe that a man could so relentlessly dedicate himself to another's cause. Gardiner was that counsel – his room was known as 'the lighthouse' long before Uris saw its beam and identified the obsessive commitment which is a barrister's most admirable (and most overlooked) quality.

Lord Gardiner had gone, along with the Labour government, by the time I reached Britain. It was not until 1985 that I was provided with an excuse to meet him, to invite his help in what was probably an unlawful conspiracy to publish a book called *Spycatcher*. Mrs Thatcher had got wind of an embittered ex-MI5 officer penning his memoirs in Tasmania, and her Cabinet Secretary, Sir Robert Armstrong, had sworn an affidavit to stop him in the Australian courts. He claimed that Gardiner, as Lord Chancellor in 1967, made a blanket prohibition on the release of any document making reference to the security services. By now, Lord Gardiner was in an advanced stage of Hodgkinson's disease, but his mind and his memory were as precise as ever. The electric blue eyes, which had once terrified witnesses like torches shone on rabbits at night, switched on as they burned through the Cabinet Secretary's claim. Gardiner told me he would be happy to testify that a blanket ban was not what he had meant at all. As I was leaving he said, 'By the way, I seem to remember a convention that former Lord Chancellors should notify the incumbent if they are going to breach the Official Secrets Act: would you like me to drop a warning note to Quintin Hailsham?' The eyes flickered for a second – a momentary loss of voltage, or a twinkle? It occurred to me then that one essential characteristic of a great advocate is the ability to control an instinctive sense of mischief.

Lord Gardiner died in 1990, a few weeks after he had the pleasure of hearing *Lady Chatterley's Lover* read as a 'Book at Bedtime' on the BBC. His performance in defending that work I knew almost by heart, as the result of my schoolboy reading, but by the time I received a Rhodes Scholarship I had no intention of practising law at the Old Bailey. I was already a solicitor, and had begun to specialise in setting up tax havens for the corporate beneficiaries of Australia's mining boom. Oxford, I thought, would be a pleasant diversion where I could briefly pursue a passing interest in liberal jurisprudence, so I chose to spend it at University College, where the exemplars of that philosophy, Professor H L A Hart and his successor Ronald Dworkin, were Fellows. I was, however, just beginning a doctoral dissertation on 'blue sky laws' over international stockmarkets and contemplating a respectable future at the Sydney Bar, when a small bear with a large penis came along and changed my career trajectory.

Oz began in Sydney in 1963 as an Antipodean equivalent of *Private Eye*. I had been recruited to write for the magazine when two of its founders – Richard Neville and the artist Martin Sharp – left to take the yellow brick road which led, via Kathmandu, to the basements of swinging London. Here, in the late sixties, *Oz* was reborn in a blaze of local colour which rendered much of it unreadable, although Richard attracted contributions from his Australian friends like Robert Hughes, Clive James, Colin MacInnes and Germaine Greer, and his new English ones such as David Hockney, David Widgery, Auberon Waugh and John Peel. Their articles, washed in day-glo, appeared flush against borrowings from the crude cartoons of Robert Crumb and Gilbert Sheldon and the hippie manifestos of the anti-Vietnam movement in the US (such was the idealism of the times that the 'underground press' proudly waived all copyright), interspersed with personal advertisements for sexual partners, all jumbled between the covers of Martin Sharpe's Todd-AO coloured imagination. The magazine's philosophy was later alleged by its prosecutors to be a glorification of 'dope, rock and roll and fucking in the streets', and it may be that the attraction for more credulous readers was to be made to feel that it was possible to achieve all three at once, but the notion of the 'philosophy of *Oz*' was a contradiction in terms. It was a coffee-table magazine for a revolution which would never happen – unless someone in authority took it seriously.

A few months after arriving in Oxford, I caught up with Richard Neville. We met in the Balliol common room, where he was holding a seminar on the underground press with Tony Palmer (once famous for five minutes for comparing the Beatles to Schubert) and Caroline Coon, the beautiful and passionate dancer who had left the Royal Ballet to found 'Release', an organisation which helped drug victims and victims of drug laws. The student audience was large, but its curiosity languid: in privileged Oxford, the Thames Valley police were a good deal more respectful of young gentlemen than the drugs squad at Notting Hill. University life looked in and up itself: the Law Faculty seemed unaware that 'rights' might be conferred on anything other than property. A New Zealand don at New College called a meeting to set up a legal advice centre for unemployed car workers at Cowley: I attended but no one else bothered, and so Bryan Gould abandoned the idea. Many Rhodes Scholars regarded the university as little more than a five-star refuge from the draft: a place for post-coital punting and a base for touring Europe. It was not that we lacked all awareness: when we discovered that not a single black had ever been selected as a Rhodes Scholar from South Africa or Rhodesia, many of my year were so outraged we threatened to resign our scholarships (the Beatles, by returning their OBEs in protest against Vietnam, had made this kind of gesture fashionable). Yet it had not occurred to any of us, in 1970, that *women* had never been eligible for selection, or that such discrimination against them might be in any way objectionable. We had a lot to learn, and it would not be taught at Oxford.

So we listened condescendingly to Richard Neville and Caroline Coon talk of busts in London basements and of police brutality, much as one might hear missionaries recount tribal behaviour in lower Volta, until Richard mentioned that the editors of *Oz* had just been hit with a conspiracy charge – something called 'conspiracy to corrupt public morals'. Now this really was a hot topic of conversation in Oxford common rooms, if nowhere else in the world. Our liberal jurisprudes, under Hart and Dworkin, argued that conspiracy to corrupt public morals was a crime which should not exist. Their opponents, led by Patrick Devlin, found elegant reasons for a law so vague that it permitted the judges (as one of them had declaimed) 'to guard the moral welfare of the State against attacks which may be more insidious because they are novel and unprepared for'. Hence my postgraduate excitement at surveying a member of this academically significant species, a real-life conspirator to debauch and corrupt the morals of the realm. That the crime is charged no more is largely due to Richard Neville, but in 1970 the debate over its existence was truly at the cutting edge, or the interface, between academic and practical law (and scholarly dialogue was happily free of phrases like 'cutting edge' and 'interface').

The crime of corrupting public morals had been created by the King's judges in 1663 to punish the drunken poet Sir Charles Sedley for urinating from a Covent Garden balcony over a crowd below. The law reports, the last to be written in Norman French, are not unanimous on the nature of Sir Charles's momentous act. One contemporary translation has him 'inflamed by strong liquors, throwing down bottles, piss'd in' whilst another avers that 'pulling down his breeches, he excrementaliz'd into the street'. The poet claimed 'benefit of clergy' – his right to be tried in the over-merciful ecclesiastical courts, which were run by the Church and had, up to that time, a monopoly over morals, but the King's judges refused: only they had the power to punish 'offences against good manners and decency'. The poet was heavily fined and set in the pillory, as a health warning to others inclined to rain on Covent Garden parades.

On any view of 1663, this was progressive law reform. As the centuries passed, however, Parliament got around to defining fairly comprehensively in statutes the kind of conduct which offended morals and decency. Sedley's case remained an historical footnote for three hundred years, until in 1961 the Law Lords needed a precedent to punish a man named Shaw, for publishing *The Ladies Directory*, a 'Who's Who' of London prostitutes. No doubt Mr Shaw thought he was serving the public as well as the prostitutes and indeed himself, but the judges had become alarmed at the slowness of Parliament to legislate against such depraved initiatives. So they dramatically arrogated to themselves a power to turn conduct they did not like into a criminal offence, whenever they thought it showed a 'tendency to corrupt public morals'. One dissenting judge aptly remarked, 'where Parliament fears to tread, it is not for the courts to rush in'. But rush in they did, with increasing fervour as the sixties began to swing. Club-owner Paul Raymond was jailed in order to discourage what the Court of Appeal described as 'this new craze for what we are told is called strip-tease', and he was soon followed by the proprietors of shops in Soho selling appliances the uses for which the judges did not wish to imagine. The high-watermark of 'swinging London' came with the conviction, for corrupting public morals, of a man who was advertising chastity belts.

For prosecutors, using this conspiracy device was a neat way of side-stepping the 'public good' defence which had saved *Lady Chatterley* and other books from conviction on obscenity charges. In 1969 the Law Lords refused to heed academic criticism, and upheld the conspiracy conviction of the editors of *International Times* (*IT*), an underground competitor of *Oz*. It had more Marxism and less wit, and lots of personal advertisements for homosexual partners – a 'Gentlemen's Directory'. This decision outraged the legal philosophers of Oxford, but for policemen and prosecutors it was the sledgehammer they needed to crack nuts like *Oz*. The offence carried a maximum sentence of life imprisonment – a fact of which Richard Neville seemed only dimly aware before I reminded him of it at Balliol. He offered me the job, then and there, of preparing his defence, against the accusation of: 'Conspiring to produce a magazine containing divers lewd, indecent and sexually perverted articles, cartoons, drawings and illustrations with intent thereby to debauch and corrupt the morals of children and young persons within the Realm and to arouse and implant in their minds lustful and perverted desires'.

The magazine which inspired this condemnation – *Oz: The*

Schoolkids' Edition – was a piece of late sixties juvenilia, put together by two dozen bright but bored teenagers from London comprehensives. Quite a few of them grew up to work for *The Sunday Times*, before moving in middle age to the *Independent*, but at this precocious stage, aged between fifteen and eighteen, they were alleged to be co-conspirators in a plot to undermine the nation's morals, with older flower children whose fun was over, and who were to be punished for having it.

Richard showed me the page which had caused all the fuss, a cartoon of Rupert Bear with an erection, and I wondered whether it might not be too late to change my thesis topic from regulation of stock exchanges to freedom of speech. It is never too late to do anything at Oxford, and so I read up on free speech philosophy and sought to do some practical research by descending into the underworld of alternative London.

The first step was a seat in a solicitor's office in Old Bond Street, which featured in that summer of the mini-skirt more flesh than I had seen since leaving Bondi Beach. Here was the fashionable apotheosis of the sixties revolution, the *Revolt into Style* identified in the title of George Melly's new book, presaging a revolt into money. Offenbach and Co was a family firm which had for many years looked after the tax and probate requirements of Harry Offenbach's neighbours and golfing partners in Harrow, until his son David, down from the LSE, had turned it into a legal aid factory for the defence of drug-takers and dissident pornographers. Harry was uncomfortable at first, but after the *Oz* trial had pioneered the defence of pornography, some of the golfers went into that business and paid for the firm's services. But for the present I was given the run of David's office and his permission (subject to legal aid limits) to turn the case of *Regina v Neville, Anderson, Dennis and Oz Publications Ink* into the trial of *Lady Chatterley*, part II.

Richard expressed the hope that it would become 'the English version of the Chicago conspiracy trial'. But the Chicago trial, in 1969, had been presided over by an angry and reactionary judge, who ordered one defendant, Bobby Seale, to sit bound and gagged in a court which was routinely disrupted by the antics of 'yippie' co-conspirators. It had been difficult to decide who was the more provocative – the judge or the defendants – and it must have been obvious (I thought) that any 'English equivalent' of such a circus would be out of the question. Richard Neville had the boarding-school mannerisms of Prince Charles, Jim Anderson was a gentle, gay ex-barrister and Felix Dennis, despite a South London abrasiveness, had all the makings of the multi-millionaire mogul he later became. The 'English equivalent', I had no doubt, would be a trial in which the jury would be taught, if not to love the lifestyles of the defendants, at least to extend that toleration for which their nation was celebrated. But then, I was quite literally an innocent abroad. I had been in the country a few months, with a cargo-cult view of the Old Bailey as the citadel of fair trial and of Scotland Yard as a model of honest policing. I had, as I have said, a lot to learn.

In mounting a defence to the conspiracy charge it would be necessary to destroy its theoretical basis – the notion that there is one moral standard to which all right-thinking persons must subscribe. Philosophers could give expert evidence that the times were a-changing and how the 'alternative society' had values as morally principled as the mainstream. I had scoured the Bodleian law library at Oxford and could find no compelling reason for excluding such evidence. There was no precedent: Sir Charles Sedley had not sought to justify the ethics of public urination, nor Mr Shaw the morality of prostitution; but the first rule of creative lawyering is that if something has not been done before, that means there is no precedent to stop you from trying to do it for the first time. (The second rule is that there soon will be.)

The three months before the trial were a mad scramble for expert witnesses. I interviewed over one hundred, dictating their statements to Marsha Rowe, the good-humoured secretary assigned me by *Oz*, whom I treated so much like a secretary that she later started the feminist magazine *Spare Rib*. In the universities and research institutes there was eager support from dons under thirty, while a few distinguished professors with principles – like Hans Eysenck, Ronald Dworkin and Richard Wollheim – were willing to stand behind the logic of their own beliefs, even for such a wretched article as *Oz 28*. It was at the mid-life redbrick lecturer and pontificating left-wing journalist level that nervousness set in: my first lesson was that many of these English liberals, who exuded tolerance in speeches on campus and in letters to the *Guardian*, were too worried about what funding institutions or neighbours might think to stand up and be counted in the witness box. We invited Richard Crossman, the luminous Labour intellectual, to take the stand: instead he gave us an hour-long lecture on how to conduct the defence. Would he testify? I asked at the end. 'Of course not. But if you follow my advice you will most certainly be acquitted.' The man's arrogance was breathtaking: he had missed his true vocation as a Queen's Counsel.

There was the delicate matter of Germaine Greer's tax break. Germaine was without doubt Mother Superior to those who had taken vows of poverty, promiscuity and disobedience during the sixties: she had written for *Oz*, and her powers of explication were awesome and cross-examination proof. If anyone could make others understand what *Oz* was about, it was she. Unfortunately, Germaine was out of the country. I was referred to her accountant, who explained that under the crazy tax laws which then prevailed, the only way she could receive more than a tiny fraction of her royalties from the paperback of *The Female Eunuch* was not to set foot in Britain for the entire year. If she came back to give evidence at the Old Bailey she would be ruined. I explored alternatives – the BBC was prepared to let us use their satellite link from New York with a feed to the Old Bailey courtroom: her evidence would be admissible by this means if she were very ill, or too nervously disposed to travel. I had a feeling that fear of landing rather than fear of flying would not be good enough.

Should I ask Germaine to play cuckoo to her nest egg? When I caught up with her by telephone, at some mid-western campus on an extended book tour, I have to say she actually relished the dilemma. 'This is all the money I've made from slaving in libraries for years. But I'd do anything to save Richard, Jim and Felix from prison. Tell me, is there any real chance they will go to prison?' I told her that there was a real chance if someone like Judge Argyle tried the case. 'Will I make a difference? Can you assure me that my absence from the trial could mean their conviction?' It is a tribute to Germaine that she actually seemed to want this re-assurance in order to forgo her life savings. I was sure she would make a formidable witness, but what made the lawyer in me hesitate was the small matter of her anus which had appeared in a joke photograph published by the notorious European 'sexpaper' called *Suck*, depicting her grinning face upside-down between her legs. Scotland Yard was well aware of it (they showed it to visitors as an example of the filth they were fighting from abroad) and I did not want to give the prosecution an excuse to show it to the jury as the downside of Dr Greer. So I thanked her for offering to give up her money for the sake of her friends, and decided that on balance I would not ask her to make the sacrifice.

By the time the trial date loomed, we had mustered an impressive collection of expert witnesses. All we needed now was a barrister who would accomplish the difficult forensic task of persuading a judge that their evidence was relevant and admissible. This would not be easy: English judges distrust 'experts', and the law relating to expert evidence is pretty much a list of reasons for not allowing it. The notion that defending *Oz* might be regarded as anything other than a privilege had not occurred to me. The QC who had originally been booked pulled out eleven days before the trial began, claiming other commitments, so the brief was sent to the silk who seemed, from reading the newspapers, to be the doughtiest defender in the land. He accepted it, or so we thought. We all had a two-hour conference with him on the Thursday before the trial, but just half an hour later, when we returned to Bond Street, he called to say he was returning the brief. 'He says he can't take the risk,' our solicitor David Offenbach explained, dropping the phone in disgust. 'What risk?' I innocently enquired. David shrugged. 'Maybe he thinks it will stop him becoming a High Court Judge.'

This was my first experience of the British Bar. Renowned as an independent and courageous profession, here it was quailing at the prospect of defending the editors of *Oz*. We had only four days to find a QC: the next morning someone mentioned that John Mortimer was defending an axe-murderer at the Old Bailey. He had successfully argued the appeal for the publishers of *Last Exit to Brooklyn*, and was our only and last hope. Richard and I tracked him down, lunching with two young women of my own age. 'What exactly is the case all about?' he enquired. Nervously, and somewhat shamefacedly, we unfurled Rupert the Bare, shielding him self-consciously from the ladies. To our enormous relief, John giggled – and showed it to them. Penny (later Mrs Mortimer) and her sister laughed, too. I produced the brief, crossed out the names of the QCs who had become mysteriously unavailable and inserted his. 'Goody,' he said. 'When do we start?' On Tuesday. 'I must just finish my poor axe-murderer,' he cautioned. 'The blood-stains are not running our way.' He left us to his dessert and his companions, and he shuffled over the road to cross-examine a forensic scientist on a subject he – and years later his fictional character Horace Rumpole – knew everything about: how to deduce a reasonable doubt from the pattern made by splashes of blood.

It was some achievement, creating in Rumpole a lawyer the world could love. It was also, and to my surprise, an achievement in 1971 to find a QC prepared to defend *Oz* magazine. I suspect John Mortimer thought of sex as an amusing but bemusing fact of life, not to be taken entirely seriously. 'The whole business has been overestimated by the poets,' as his own father, played by Alec Guinness, put it in the play (*A Voyage Round My Father*) that John was preparing for its West End opening in two months' time.

> Father: No brilliance is needed in the law. Nothing but common sense and relatively clean fingernails . . . Learn a little law, won't you? Just to please me.
>
> Son: It was my father's way to offer the law to me – the great stone column of authority which has been dragged by an adulterous, careless, negligent and half-criminal humanity down the ages – as if it were a small mechanical toy which might occupy half an hour on a rainy afternoon.

In time, John would become my own forensic father, teaching by example that the art of cross-examination is not to examine crossly and that it is a fearful thing to have responsibility for another's fate. For the present, his willingness to sacrifice his precious writing time to save these provocateurs from prison gave reason to hope that there was yet some life left in old liberal England.

Chapter 2

The Trials of *Oz*

These accused men agreed to publish a magazine
which would carry, as it had carried before, the
banner of the alternative society. Look at that
magazine and ask yourselves: 'What alternatives
are there?' Dropping out of society. Expecting the
State to provide – and by the State I mean nothing
more than you and me – those of us who don't
mind working, who think it's right to work, those
of us whom advocates of the alternative society
might describe as 'those foolish enough to work'. It
puts forward as a way of life, does this alternative
society, sex as being something to be worshipped
for itself until you reach the ultimate state called
'fucking in the streets'. You won't, I know,
members of the jury, sneer at accepted values, or
reject that viewpoint of *Oz* which holds that it is
not right to be too ready to sneer at accepted values
and to destroy everything we believed until now.

This was how treasury counsel Brian Leary put the Crown's
case against the three editors of *Oz* magazine, at their trial
in the Old Bailey in the summer of 1971. Richard Neville
defended himself, and John Mortimer appeared for Jim Anderson
and Felix Dennis. I was in the well of the court throughout, as
stage-hand for the defence. I knew all about the law – but nothing
about justice, and I was looking forward to seeing it done.

The prosecution explained how the defendants had conspired to
publish the twenty-eighth edition of *Oz* – the 'Schoolkids' Edition'.
The conspiracy had begun quite genteelly, with a story in the *Daily
Telegraph* that the editors of *Oz* were feeling so old and boring that
they wanted to give editorial control of one edition to school-

children. As a result some two-dozen teenagers, cited as co-conspirators, had come to a basement in Notting Hill and compiled this magazine. The jurors would be required to read it in the privacy of their jury room, to decide whether it was (in order of importance) a conspiracy to corrupt public morals (Count 1), an obscene article (Count 2), or merely an indecent object sent to a few subscribers through the post (Count 3).

It is a notable feature of obscenity trials that they seldom involve great works of art or literature. *Lady Chatterley's Lover* was among the least impressive of Lawrence's novels, and *Last Exit to Brooklyn* is hardly a classic. *Oz 28* would have contributed substantially to 'the worst of Oz' – its most enduring merit came from its borrowings from American cartoonists Robert Crumb and Gilbert Sheldon (*The Fabulous Furry Freak Brothers*) and its precocious music reviews by Charles Shaar Murray. There were of course the 'small ads' for what was delicately termed 'erotic minorities', among which with the help of a magnifying glass (the print was minute) might be descried an advertisement for that Amsterdam paper, *Suck*, describing an act of oral sex. Then there were the front and back covers, featuring female silhouettes later described by the Lord Chief Justice as 'extremely attractively drawn and appearing to be a simple piece of artistic work . . . closer inspection however shows that the women are indulging in lesbian activities . . . attention has not unnaturally been drawn to that as an example of material which might deprave or corrupt'. Not unnaturally in 1971, although as the Chief Justice conceded, there were also 'a great many serious and wholly innocuous articles and a great many illustrations, some of them charming and humorous, which would not cause the slightest flutter in any well-conducted Victorian household. Others, however, are quite different . . .' by which he meant the Rupert Bear strip. The prosecution had a witness statement from the Secretary of the National Union of Teachers, complaining that the magazine would tend to undermine the authority of teachers. Did that amount to a subversion of public morals? It was all a matter for the jury, applying the law as directed by the judge, Michael Argyle QC.

As Recorder of Birmingham, Judge Argyle had become famous for his catch-cry 'we just don't do this sort of thing in Birmingham', uttered when imposing heavy deterrent sentences.

He sent delinquents who vandalised public telephone boxes to prison for three years, and boasted that the result was to extinguish this particular crime in Birmingham, although the local press pointed out the consequential upsurge in telephone vandalism in Coventry, just outside his jurisdiction. Then he announced a novel campaign to end burglary by sentencing burglars to prison for life: 'If you come, boys, we are waiting for you,' he trumpeted from the Bench. The Court of Appeal was sufficiently concerned to call for a transcript of his remarks. His judgeship was a career consolation for the Tory MP he had tried several times to become, and a platform from which to inveigh against what he saw as the evils of the permissive society. His sentences on the *Oz* editors would be severe – if the jury convicted.

Oz was one of the last cases tried by a jury which was not randomly selected. Until 1972, every juror had to own property – a qualification which at this time meant they were mainly male, and generally middle-aged or elderly. This did not of itself worry the defendants; they had spent many evenings fantasising about the elderly gay actor, the middle-aged polytechnic lecturer and the successful graphic designer who would be summoned to the Old Bailey to hold the scales between *Oz* and the State. The night before the trial they saw the list of names, addresses and occupations of the jury panel and their faces fell: 'Boilermaker, Driver, Ganger, Foreman, Crane Driver, Salesman, Supervisor . . .' They had drawn a hard-hat panel from the building sites of Kent and E15: the very class of person who would loathe *Oz* the most. There was not a single member occupationally predisposed to youthful iconoclasm. I noticed that one juror, a builder from Bexleyheath, was named William Blake, so in deference to the poet we determined not to challenge him. However, he turned out to be a severe sixty-something who looked with such horror at the long-haired defendants that they had to object. The defendants (the three editors and the company, Oz Publications Ink) mustered twenty-eight challenges between them, and each was used in an increasingly frantic attempt to obtain younger jurors. The final panel comprised ten men and two women, all lower-middle-class artisans of average age about sixty. A jury of peers it was not, but the marketing man in Felix Dennis loved the challenge: if he could persuade this lot to like *Oz*, the magazine's future was assured. In his opening speech, Richard tried a small joke: 'We have had a *Transsexual Oz*, a *Female Liberation Oz*, a *Homosexual Oz*, a *Flying Saucer Oz* and a *Schoolkids' Oz*. At the end of the trial, we'll invite you to edit a *Jurors' Oz*.' Ominously, no juror smiled.

The prosecution case was brief. The only exhibit was the magazine itself. Detective Superintendent Luff told of his frequent raids on the *Oz* office, seizing the contents of filing cabinets and even the pictures on the walls. He told the court that his interview with Felix Dennis had ended with the suspect exclaiming 'Right on!' Judge Argyle, taking down the evidence longhand, looked up, puzzled. 'Write on . . . but you had finished the interview?' 'Not write on – W - R - I -T - E, my Lord – but R - I - G - H - T on. It's a *revolutionary* expression,' Luff added darkly. He pronounced the magazine 'unacceptable from the family point of view'. He was followed into the witness box by a co-conspirator from an unacceptable Hampstead family: Viv Berger, the fifteen-year-old son of Grace Berger, Chair of the National Council for Civil Liberties. It had been Viv's idea to produce a collage using a six-panel cartoon by Robert Crumb and a page from his childhood *Rupert Annual*. 'Subconsciously,' he told John Mortimer, 'I wanted to shock your generation.' He succeeded: half of the six-week trial was devoted to 'the Rupert Bear strip'. The forensic effect of young Berger's art may be gathered from this passage in editor Jim Anderson's cross-examination:

Leary (*reading from Anderson's editorial*): '*Oz* was hit with its biggest dose of creative energy for a long time. Have a look at the Rupert Bear strip. Youthful Genius.' Did you write this, Mr Anderson?
Anderson: Yes, I did.
Leary: Is it still your opinion that Vivien Berger's cartoon of Rupert Bear is the work of 'youthful genius'?
Anderson: Yes, I think it was an extremely clever and funny idea.
Leary: Did it amount to youthful genius?
Anderson: Well . . . maybe I was a little bit generous in my praise but . . .
Leary: The youthful genius set to work by snipping out of the *Rupert Annual* the head of the bear. That's right?
Anderson: Yes . . . er . . . I suppose that's what he did.
Leary: And then if we were keen to watch a genius at work, we

would see him sticking it on the cartoon already drawn for him?
Anderson: Yes.
Leary: Wherein lies the genius?
Anderson: I think it's in the juxtaposition of the two ideas, the childhood symbol of innocence . . .
Leary (*shouts*): MAKING RUPERT BEAR FUCK?
Anderson (*after a long pause*): . . . Er . . . Yes.
Leary: Is that what you consider youthful genius?
Anderson: Yes, I thought it was extraordinary, even brilliant.
Leary: Extraordinary it may be, but whatever it is, it's not genius, is it?

This fine example of Old Bailey cross-examination deserves a place in the advocacy courses which now affect to teach a trade which comes instinctively or not at all. It is the demolition of the overstatement, cleverly achieved by having the witness endorse it without qualification before it is taken apart. It was accomplished with perfect timing and a dramatic climax: a quarter of a century later, I can still hear Brian Leary – who questions in a soft, insinuating voice – producing an electrifying shock for everyone in court by shouting the unthinkable.

Jim Anderson crumpled quickly, but the cross-examiner hardly needed more subtlety to undermine the eminent artist Felix Topolski, who also began overconfidently:

Topolski: This to me is a tremendously clever, tremendously witty putting together of the opposite elements in the comic culture, and creating a riotous clash. I think it is a great invention if one accepts its satirical basis.
Leary: What we're looking at here is a new Andy Warhol?
Topolski: Well, it works in that direction. There's a statement by Arthur Koestler that comes to mind, 'unexpected elements brought together produce an act of creation'.
Leary: I fully understand what you mean about bringing the two things together. I want to separate them for a moment . . .
Topolski: But that's unfair to the situation on this page.
Leary: Do you agree that Rupert as he appears in the comic strip in a national daily and in the *Rupert Annual* is not art?
Topolski: Not to me.

Leary: But you say that bringing the two together makes it different?
Topolski: Yes.
Leary: Does it make it art with a capital 'A' in your opinion?
Topolski: It makes it satirical art.
Leary: Satirical art. I see.

In cross-examining experts on artistic merit, sarcasm will get you everywhere. Topolski can describe Warhol's genius, but cannot explain why Rupert is art when he has an erection, but non-art without any organ at all. Where the cross-examiner tended to come unstuck was with the defence psychologists, who were not asserting that the sight of Rupert rampant was art with a capital 'A', but that it would not have a depraving and corrupting effect on the beholder. He failed to confuse the popular 'lateral thinker' Dr Edward de Bono:

Leary: What do you suppose the effect is intended to be of equipping Rupert Bear with such a large-sized organ?
De Bono: I don't know enough about bears to know their exact proportions; I imagine their organs are hidden in their fur. But if you had a realistic drawing I think you would miss the point of the drawing entirely.
Leary (*angrily*): Mr de Bono, why is Rupert Bear equipped with a large organ?
De Bono: What size do *you* think would be natural?
Judge: Well, forgive me, but you mustn't ask counsel questions.
Leary (*another tack*): A success, do you think this lavatory drawing?
De Bono: If one considers it a success to have it published in *Oz* then I dare say it would be a certain measure of success.
Leary: The success being this. That the lavatory wall is only available to those people who use the lavatory for the purpose of nature and this particular magazine has, as we are told, a circulation of up to 40,000.
De Bono: I find that question difficult to answer, Mr Leary, unless I knew the turnover of a normal lavatory wall, which I would expect to be in the region of 30,000.
Judge: What, one lavatory, 30,000?
De Bono: If you stop to calculate it, I expect so.

De Bono's analogy, like 'lateral thinking', does not bear too much examination, but cross-examiners do not have time to think on their feet and Leary was thrown by the mathematics. As the trial wore on, it was interesting to observe (a common phenomenon, this, in obscenity cases) that the subject matter of the art developed a life of its own, and ended up in the dock. The *Lady Chatterley* trial was less of D H Lawrence as a writer than of Connie Chatterley as a wife taken in adultery. In Rupert Bear's case, he was in the dock of a juvenile court, on a charge of indecent behaviour while truanting. Dr Michael Schofield had written many books about the effect of verbal and visual stimuli on young humans, but not on young animals:

Leary: What sort of *age* would you think Rupert is, to your mind? What sort of aged bear?

Schofield: Oh, I'm very sorry – I'm not up to date with bears.

Leary: You don't have to be because he doesn't change, Rupert, does he? (*Witness shakes his head – in disbelief, but judge assumes ignorance.*)

Judge: I think the question is: what age do you think Rupert is intended to be, a child, an adult, or what?

Schofield: It's an unreal question: you might as well ask me how old is Jupiter.

Leary: He's a young bear, isn't he? He goes to school – that's right, isn't it?

Schofield: I don't know whether he goes to school or not. I'm sorry but I'm obviously not as well informed as you are about little bears. I'm a psychologist.

In this way was battle joined at the Old Bailey for six weeks of the hot summer of 1971. It seemed at times that we were all serving the interests of entertainment: American lawyers in London over for their Bar conference would jostle for seats in the public gallery as they might at a theatre, their roars of laughter silenced by ushers' booming cries of 'Silence!' followed by the judge's regular threat to clear the public gallery. 'This is a courtroom, not a theatre,' he would remind them repeatedly. John Mortimer would leave the courtroom each afternoon for the Vaudeville Theatre (where *A Voyage Round My Father* was being rehearsed) with a sense that he was returning to real life.

The case continued. George Melly, sociologist and jazz singer, was asked whether he thought it acceptable 'in this day and age' for a magazine to describe oral sex attractively. He did: 'I don't think cunnilingus could do actual harm if you believe that sexuality is a wide thing in which one can do a large number of things as long as they don't hurt the opposite partner.'

'Well, pardon me,' Judge Argyle was ineffably polite. 'For those of us who did not have a classical education, what do you mean by this word "*cunnilinctus*"?' He had misheard, as if the reference had been to a cough medicine. Melly beamed, thinking he was being asked to be less formal: 'I'm sorry, my Lord, I've been a bit inhibited by the architecture. I will try to use better known expressions in the future. "*Sucking*" or "*blowing*", your Lordship. Or "*going down*" or "*gobbling*" is another alternative. Another expression used in my naval days, your Lordship, was "*yodelling in the canyon*".'

This brought more laughter and cries of 'Silence!' and threats to clear the gallery. Twenty-six years later, it inspired the title of the 1997 British Eurovision song entry, 'Yodelling in the Canyon of Love'. For Judge Argyle, however, oral sex was always unthinkable and invariably dangerous. Whenever any witness made the point that it was not harmful, he would intervene: 'Well, just excuse me. Have you ever heard of the case of Mr Fatty Arbuckle?'

The witness would answer 'yes' or 'no', and the matter would be left hanging, as a clear judicial indication that the case of Mr Fatty Arbuckle proved beyond reasonable doubt that oral sex did harm. I rushed to a library to discover that whatever implement did cause the fatal internal injuries to starlet Virginia Rappe in a hotel bedroom in San Francisco in 1917, it was neither a tongue nor Mr Arbuckle (as a jury finally made clear by acquitting him). Somehow, rumours about the case had been filed in the judge's mental data-bank as proof that oral sex can kill. The most telling insight into Argyle's mind came from an article he wrote in the *Spectator* in 1995, extravagantly attacking the defendants and their witnesses. He revealed that he had felt it necessary to have a glass of water smashed to pieces, after disc jockey John Peel had taken a sip from it in the witness box. He apparently believed it might be infected because some years before the witness had picked up a brief venereal infection. This bizarre action (his usher did in fact destroy the glass) came about in the following way:

Leary: Look at the article by Master Charles Shaar Murray which refers to 'straightforward fuck music' . . . Sexuality was one of the elements introduced into music on the pop scene by Mr Elvis Presley, in the rock 'n' roll era, wasn't it?

Peel: I'm sure that sex has always been an important part of music since the earliest dance days, because a lot of early music was for things like fertility ceremonies.

Leary: Yes, but you have not yet heard of a criticism, have you, of Mozart or Beethoven, which deals with somebody having an orgasm over it?

Peel: Well, I must admit that I never read sexual climaxes into the music of Mozart or Beethoven. If I were to write music I should be very flattered to think people were making love to that music.

Leary: Yes. I see you used the expression 'making love'.

Peel: Yes.

Leary: So we take it that you would consider it bad taste to use the word 'fuck' rather than 'making love'? Which would you prefer?

Peel: The expressions are not different. I just felt because I was in court I should say 'make love' but everybody else seems to say 'fuck' so I will say 'fuck' as well.

(*Laughter.*)

Judge: Once again I have to remind people that this is not a theatre, but a court.

Leary (*having paused to study a note passed to prosecution from a court reporter*): Are you married?

Peel: Yes.

Leary: Have you had venereal disease?

Peel: Yes.

Leary: Am I right in suggesting that you thought it right to announce over the air, so that anyone listening in could hear, the fact that unhappily you had contracted venereal disease?

Peel: Yes, and I would do the same thing today. I had it and wish I didn't, but the BBC had prepared a programme for broadcasting on Radio 4 about venereal disease and the fact that some people were not prepared to admit that they had got it and I was asked to participate. I mean, I wouldn't be surprised to learn that quite a few people in the courtroom have had venereal disease. Whether they would admit it or not I don't know.

Judge: Well, just forgive me for a moment. It is so terribly easy to say a thing like that but *what does it mean?*

Peel: Well, according to the doctors who did the programme, a great number of people in all walks of society suffer from venereal disease and the main problem they have in trying to combat the disease is that people are not prepared to discuss it openly . . .

Leary: When you made the comment that you dare say a number of people in this court have had it and never mentioned it, which *part* of the courtroom had you in mind?

Peel (*looks at the dock, the barristers' rows, the press box, the jury box* . . .): I would say all parts of the courtroom.

Leary: You were serious?

Peel: Yes, I mean it is a very common disease.

Judge: Let's go on to another topic, Mr Leary.

Leary: Do you mind if I ask a few more questions?

Judge: I don't think so. A very great accusation about the people in this court has been made. I can't see any point in pursuing it. If the witness wishes to persist in it, he is perfectly entitled to do so, I suppose.

Peel: I didn't bring it up in the first place.

Twenty-five years later, the long-retired Argyle went on to tell *Spectator* readers how he still switches off his bedside radio when he hears Peel's familiar, flat voice. The episode is typical of a trial which became a collision of cultural incomprehension. Even the court reporters took sides: the seedy regulars, 'Old Bailey hacks' in shabby pinstripe suits, occupied the press benches and curried favour with the police by feeding them titbits of information (such as Peel's broadcast, years before, about his VD). These court correspondents were a sad bunch of 'Lunchtime O'Boozes', who perceived themselves as press officers for the police. One morning, hidden behind a pillar in the antechamber, I overheard several of them boasting about how they had kept reports of Richard Neville's closing speech out of their newspapers. 'Except the *Guardian*, of course. We can't do anything about that.' They refused to accommodate on their press bench specialist writers, such as Nicholas de Jongh from the *Guardian* and Jonathan

Dimbleby for the *New Statesman* – they had to sit with *Oz* supporters in the back row of the stalls.

The tension of the trial was tightened by its ritual. The oak panels of the old court, the fancy-dress parades each Monday with retainers brandishing swords to usher in the judge, who carried a nosegay (once clutched by judges to ward off prison fever), all impressed with the weight of history, and with the expectation of a conviction. We had, somehow, to defuse the tension, to encourage the jury to think differently – even laterally – about this case. Richard and I spent a long evening with Edward de Bono pondering how this might be achieved. He assured us that he had the answer, which worked at his seminars to jolt executives out of their mind-sets. It was a brightly coloured wind-up toy bird, which he offered to produce (ready-wound) from his inside pocket at an appropriate moment, and have it flap across the court. 'It always helps on solemn occasions,' he assured us. 'I'll explain to the judge and jury how the surprise has worked to unlock their thinking processes, to enable them to look at the evidence with a more open mind.' De Bono gave evidence for several hours, but the atmosphere was not conducive to take-off. The bird did not fly. 'Just as well,' I consoled the crestfallen Richard. 'We would all have been jailed for contempt.'

Like the squalor behind the splendour of the stage at Covent Garden, so the solemn ritual of an Old Bailey trial disguised the fact that it was produced in greasepaint and chaos. The solicitors' clerks who stage-managed the shows would meet to rehearse the cast for the day around the formica tables of the Rex Café opposite the court. Each morning, over fried bacon and beans, the bottle-blondes would be coached to recite their alibis about the defendant being in her bed at the time the bank was robbed. This was amateur hour – the police delivered their lines like professionals, in a loud voice from a script in their pocket notebook. It was a strange system, the English criminal justice I observed in the other courts and precincts of this fabled building. A serious crime would be committed and the police would be told – usually correctly, by a paid informant – who did it. The criminal would then be arrested and 'verballed' – i.e. a confession which he never made would be recorded in police notebooks. This would in due course be 'challenged' for weeks by his barrister (paid lavishly on legal aid) while he would, with the help of his solicitor's clerk, have invented an alibi. More or less everyone committed perjury. Many police were bent and so were some solicitors' clerks; but the conviction rates were reasonable, white-collar criminals were rarely troubled, and the public was happy watching *Dixon of Dock Green* on the box and believing it reflected reality.

Another discovery was what can only be described as the plodding orality of the English criminal trial. The judge is expected to take down all the spoken evidence in longhand, in a large red book, and then with Olympian impartiality to remind the jury of such of it as will be crucial to their verdict. In the theatre of the courtroom, a small spotlight is trained throughout on 'his Lordship's pen'. This has the effect of emphasising what the judge thinks is important. It was a technique which Argyle employed as if trained by Stanislavsky: if during the trial he regarded evidence as irrelevant he would put his pen down with a clatter, fold his arms and lean back in his seat. 'Watch his Lordship's pen' counsel always say, to witnesses who speak too quickly: the jury watch it too, as a sign of whether they should pay attention. The ritual dance of his Lordship's pen not only slows and directs proceedings: it conduces to mistakes in every summing up. Evidence not taken down will not feature, and evidence which has been taken down inaccurately will be regurgitated to the jury inaccurately. In other countries courts arrange for palentype transcripts to be available a few hours after the evidence has been given. But in Britain although shorthand writers take down every word of evidence, they are only asked to type it up if there is a conviction and it is relevant to a point of appeal. Thus most of their work is pointless: it is not available to enable an accurate summing-up. This is as true in 1997 as it was in 1971, when it produced some of the mistakes Judge Argyle made when he came to sum the case up to the jury.

The *Oz* trial was serving as my induction into English criminal law as practised at the Old Bailey, a world removed from law as taught in the lecture halls of Oxford. Judge Argyle glared at my star witness – Ronald Dworkin, the Professor of Jurisprudence at Oxford – as if upset at the thought that an academic lawyer (and an American, at that) could teach an Old Bailey judge anything. 'You succeeded to the jurisprudence chair of the renowned Professor H

L A Hart . . .' The judge broke in as Richard was reciting Dworkin's qualifications. 'Who? H L A who?' 'Er, I'm sorry, I thought he was well known,' stammered Richard. 'Spell this name,' snapped the judge. He did not take many notes of Dworkin's answers, narrowing his eyes and occasionally interrupting, 'This is a courtroom, Professor, not a *lecture* theatre.'

Then there was the notorious appearance of Marty Feldman, who had agreed to testify to the merits of the humour in *Oz*. He thought Rupert was genuinely funny and came to say why. The problem began because of the unnecessary ritual then surrounding witnesses who did not wish to take an oath on the New Testament. 'Witness does not wish to take the oath, my Lord,' the usher would loudly say, as the cue for Argyle (a devout Christian) to look pained and ask, 'Why? Why do you want to affirm?' Feldman, taken aback by the unnecessary question, took this as an insult. 'Because I think there are more obscene things in the Bible than in this issue of *Oz*.' 'That's not what I wanted to hear. The answer is that you don't have any religion,' said the judge, firmly. 'I have my own religion. It's not one that you would understand,' Feldman shot back. Things could only get worse, and they did. 'I don't know if it matters,' Argyle interjected a few minutes later, 'but I can't hear anything the witness is saying.' 'I think it matters,' Feldman answered, and then he raised his voice. 'Shall I say it louder?' Argyle put down his pen, folded his arms and turned his back on the witness. 'Sorry, Judge,' said the comedian, no longer funny. 'Am I waking you up?' His evidence completed, Feldman walked to the court door, muttering to the defendants as he passed the dock, 'He's a boring old fart.' This whisper was heard by a *Times* reporter, and was front-page news the next day. It was an unedifying episode, provoked by a procedure (now abandoned) which assumed that an oath not taken on the Bible needed explanation. Argyle relived the incident in his summing-up, reminding the jury that according to the Bible that Feldman had declined, those who led children astray deserved to be 'drowned in the depths of the sea' with millstones around their necks. It seemed, the way he said it, a matter of regret that his own sentencing powers over the defendants were more limited.

There was a paranoia around these proceedings which I was not alone in failing to understand. The *Oz* trial was held under tight security, in a courtroom with a dock specially designed to hold vicious East End gangsters like the Krays and the Richardsons. Judge Argyle has since revealed that behind the scenes in the court corridor were four armed Special Branch officers and two alsatian dogs and their handlers, guarding him twenty-four hours a day. At night, they took up their positions in a suite in the Savoy, rented for his use at public expense. Yet these defendants were incapable of hurting the proverbial fly, and their supporters were too spaced out or peaced out to pose any threat to anyone. The judge believed (he still did, when he wrote about these security arrangements in 1995) that he was dealing with dangerous criminals. The sad truth lay in the deranged mind of the wife of his court clerk, a Mrs Blackaller. She busied herself throughout the trial sending threats to murder the judge, her husband and even herself, pretending to be 'a friend of *Oz*'. So seriously were they taken that *twelve hundred* hours of police time were wasted on investigating them, for which the woman was later prosecuted and sentenced for psychiatric treatment.

As the trial drew to a close, I felt the defence was in fairly good shape on two of the three charges. 'Your defendants are all so *nice*,' Brian Leary said to me at the time, and later. Our witnesses were mainly professors with short hair and happy marriages, and the most Brian could extract from them was a confession that George Melly swore in front of his children ('You are trying to make me out to be some kind of NW1 monster') and that Grace Berger had taken her son to see *Hair*. 'Well just pardon me,' interjected the judge. 'But is *Hair* an article?' '*Hair* is a play,' sighed John Mortimer wearily. 'It's been running in the West End for the last five years.'

The conspiracy charge (Count 1) was the big worry, because it gave the judge unlimited sentencing power. Obscenity (Count 2), which carried a maximum of three years, was a more focused question, namely whether *Oz* tended to deprave and corrupt a significant proportion of its readership. The law was clear that 'deprave and corrupt' meant to make 'morally bad' rather than simply to shock and disgust, but the latter was enough for a conviction on the third charge (Count 3) of sending an indecent article through Her Majesty's mails. This was a minor offence, for which even Argyle would be hard-pressed to pass a jail sentence – just as well, since we were hard-pressed to find any defence. Some of the satirical cartoons were, in a word, indecent. But they were not obscene in the legal sense, because they did not tend to deprave and corrupt, in the opinion of ten of the country's leading psychologists, psychiatrists and educationalists who had testified. At times, this argument came perilously close to contending that nothing – at least, neither the written word nor illustrations – could deprave and corrupt. There was a novel argument here, since pornography had been freely available for the past decade in Scandinavia without causing any obvious increase in depravity. Moreover, in America, a Presidential Commission had just reported, after spending millions on research, that pornography did not cause anti-social behaviour. Pornographic films had been shown to college students and married couples who were none the worse for the experience. 'What, thirty hours of oral sex and still no detrimental effect!' John Mortimer declaimed. 'Zis is right,' Professor Hans Eysenck would nod his head sagely.

I always wonder about the ethics of such studies, and indeed, the validity of their conclusions. In the years after *Oz*, barristers would take the *US Presidential Commission Report* around the country for obscenity defences, proclaiming this research as the revealed truth. My favourite was one study which concluded that 'pornography enhances marital communication'. That clinched it for juries: porn was now pro-family. Many years later, a follow-up study was done with the married couples who had participated in the original experiment. They explained that what had enhanced their marital communication was not watching the pornography, but their shared amusement at filling in the researchers' absurd question-naires afterwards.

As a matter of law, obscenity requires some glamorisation, titillation, or other inducement to behave badly, and *Oz 28* was one of the least seductive pieces of literature ever published. The real problem was the indecency charge, to which the only obvious defence I could find was the one which the European Court of Justice would uphold fifteen years later (see page 156), namely that it was wrong to have a more stringent standard for what was sent through the post than for what was sold over the counter. At the trial, we settled on the causative argument that there was a difference between an indecent act, and the depiction of an indecent act which might itself not be indecent – if it were clothed with humour or satire or some other redeeming quality. But Judge Argyle had the last word, and his direction to the jury on indecency was as follows:

> Indecent is less than obscene. It refers to matters which are unbecoming and immodest. If you are on the beach with your children and a woman comes along and takes off all her clothes, and proceeds to walk about on the beach and then to swim, this is immodest or indecent in our society on a crowded beach: we just don't do this kind of thing in this country. Another example to help you with indecency is this: let us say you attend an athletic event, and the athletes – beautiful physical specimens, male or female – haven't got clothing which fits properly and as they compete, you can see their private parts, it is immodest and it is indecent in this country.

We just don't do this kind of thing in Birmingham.

Before the summing-up came the final speeches. Brian Leary's closing remark was insinuatingly effective:

> The question which you may like to ask yourselves when you go out to consider your verdict in this case, is not 'Would I like *my* children to see it', because no doubt your own children come from very nice homes where they can discuss properly questions about love and sex and the dangers of taking drugs. Ask yourselves rather, 'Would I like *my neighbour's children* to see this particular magazine'. Because, when all is said and done, morality is essential to the health of a community such as ours and it is for you, ladies and gentlemen of the jury, to set the moral standard by which we shall continue to live in this country.

After this seductive invitation, John Mortimer abandoned rehearsals for *A Voyage Round My Father* to produce a speech which would read in perfect cadences on the stage:

> Ladies and gentlemen of the jury, we have sat here while the best

part of the summer has passed us by. Wimbledon tournaments have come and gone, the Royal Birkdale has passed us, and we have almost entered the Common Market, whilst we have turned over and over and over again the pages of a little underground magazine and done it so often that we may feel the Fabulous Furry Freak Brothers have entered our sleeping as well as our waking hours. A huge quantity of public time and money has been spent in the ardent and eager pursuit of what? A schoolboy prank. In pursuit of that prank, ladies and gentlemen of the jury, to squash this rather unsuccessful number of a little underground magazine, to gag a little cheeky criticism, to suppress some lavatory humour and some adolescent discussion of sex and drugs, we have had rolled out before us the great majestic engine of the Criminal Law. The threat to our nation of forty-eight blurred pages of schoolboy ebullience has been countered by the rolling prose of Count 1 of the indictment, by the tireless researches of Inspector Luff and the inexhaustible cross-examination of Mr Leary, and by the deep, carefully preserved sonorous solemnity of a great criminal trial. One may be tempted to feel that the prosecution is like some nervous public official who, when a child puts out a tongue at him in the street, calls out the army.

As the final speaker, Richard Neville had to argue for his liberty. The remarkable fact is that his argument needed to be made at all, in the year AD 1971, by a defendant on trial for conspiracy to corrupt public morals, carrying a maximum penalty of imprisonment for life:

One of the strangest and most menacing allegations levelled throughout this trial is that we are part of a community without love. 'Sex is worshipped for its own sake,' said Mr Leary, who went on to ask: 'why have we heard nothing of love?' The sort of love I suspect Mr Leary was searching for in *Oz* consists of violins, moonlit terraces, tuxedos, lace hankies and E-type Jaguars – the sort of world characterised by the novels of Barbara Cartland, where dashing young bucks cannot afford to kiss the satined debutante until marriage. To reject that sort of love is not to reject love at all, but to reject a myth or an image of love, which is not only unattainable, but, in the guise of ennobling women, actually enslaves them. I think that what *Oz* tries to do, or at least the community of which *Oz* is a part, is to redefine love, to broaden it, extend it, revitalise it, so it can be a force of release and not one of entrapment . . . I remember ten years ago Bob Dylan sang about the danger that tension between the generations would become so extreme that it will lead to a breakdown of communication.

> You mothers and fathers throughout the land
> Don't criticise what you can't understand
> Your sons and daughters are beyond your command
> Your old road is rapidly ageing
> Please get out of the new one if you can't lend a hand
> For the times they are a-changing.

Will you lend a hand, members of the jury?

Richard Neville's own hand extended towards them, from the high wall of the security dock. They seemed receptive. Then their heads swivelled in unison in the opposite direction as the judge cleared his throat to begin his summing-up.

Judge Argyle's views were unconsciously signalled to the jury through *tone* of voice and body language, which did not show up on the transcript for the Court of Appeal. Whenever he dealt with the defence his tone could not help but be scathing and contemptuous: the prosecution arguments he repeated with respect. Frequently, he expressed his own opinion – usually to the detriment of the defence, but always followed by the appeal-proof formula '. . . but it's a matter entirely for you, members of the jury'. He would recite a piece of evidence favourable to the defence, in somewhat surprised tones, then turn to the jury: 'Well, there it is!' At this point he might hold up the magazine, and slowly let it drop – thump – onto the desk, as if it were a thing of infinite toxicity. He could hardly have made his views more clear had he actually held his nose and raised his arm as if pulling a toilet chain. Jonathan Dimbleby reported:

> The judge's summing-up was stunning. Suddenly the defence witnesses became 'so-called defence experts, who you may think either had to admit they were wrong or tell a lie'. If *Oz* was a window

on the hippie world – 'well, windows sometimes need cleaning, don't they?' As he finished with a witness, he would toss his copy of *Oz* disdainfully down onto the table, and with it, one felt, the case for the defence.

The jury was out for several hours, before returning to ask the judge for a definition of 'obscene'. He read to them from the Oxford English Dictionary, which said it meant, amongst other things, 'indecent'. In law, that is precisely what obscene does not mean, as the Court of Appeal had repeatedly emphasised. I knew this schoolboy howler should lead the Court of Appeal to invalidate any conviction on Count 2: everything (or at least, the defendants' liberty for the next ten years) hinged on the verdict on the conspiracy to corrupt public morals charge. Would the jury be moved by Bob Dylan to lend a hand? 'On Count 1, do you find the defendants guilty or not guilty?' asked the court clerk. 'Not guilty,' said the foreman. The sighs of relief from the gallery, and from the counsel's row, were audible.

Anti-climactically but predictably, the foreman went on to announce 'guilty' verdicts on the obscenity and indecency counts. The judge could hardly wait to ask, 'Have deportation papers been served on Richard Neville?' They had, said Inspector Luff – neither knew that Anna Wintour was still prepared to extend her own hand in convenient matrimony, although the wedding might now have to be at Wormwood Scrubs Prison. The three editors tensed for the sentences, but Judge Argyle announced that he was remanding them in custody for 'medical and psychiatric reports'. John jumped up: 'It really is inhuman to keep them in suspense any longer,' but the judge turned to the prison officers and said, with the relief of a man making a bowel movement after weeks of constipation, 'Gaoler, take them down!'

I could not believe it. Where were we – the Soviet Union? These dissidents were stark-staring sane, yet were being imprisoned for three weeks to have their heads examined. It was the next development, however, which threw the media into a frenzy. When I visited the defendants after their first night in prison I did not at first recognise, in the gloom of the cell, the three crew-cut, disinfected figures who were laughing at me. 'Surprise!' they chorused. Prison regulations, like those of the armed forces, required short back and sides: the State had wreaked its atavistic revenge by stripping them of their hippie symbol of insolence. That they were long-hairs no longer should not be kept secret: the next morning every newspaper led with 'artist's impressions' of the new-look *Oz* trio. At breakfast tables throughout the land, generation gaps widened as the old exulted and the young exploded. At this breaking point, something happened. Something very English, really: an unspoken recognition that things had gone too far, that it was time for moderation to reassert itself. At last the forces of reason, notably silent before the trial, began to make themselves heard. Michael Foot, Tony Benn and many other MPs put down early-day motions condemning the judge for sending them to prison for psychiatric reports, and Bernard Levin (who had refused point-blank to give evidence for the defence) produced for *The Times* one of his finest polemics against the prosecution. The Home Secretary made a quick change to the prison rules, which would henceforth allow remand prisoners to keep their hair on.

Judge Argyle, however, was unmoved. On the day of the sentences, the psychiatric report he had ordered on the defendants was read: 'They are of high intelligence and lack interest in material gain. They are polite and courteous. There are aspects of society that appal them and they edited *Oz* to show the urgent need of reform.' At first the judge railed against the defence experts and their liberal, lateral thinking. He continued: 'As these three accused are over twenty-one, probation would be totally inappropriate' (there is no appropriate age for a probation order); 'They are comparatively poor men, therefore a fine is inappropriate' (judges should never decide that prison is the only alternative because a person is too poor to pay a fine); and 'It follows therefore, that the sentence of the court should be a custodial one' (it did not – the sentence could have been suspended for first-time offenders). In the result, he 'had no option' but to jail Neville for fifteen months; Anderson received three months less, apparently because he had once been a barrister, while Dennis, 'because you are very much less intelligent than the other two', received a dullard's discount and went down for merely nine months. Each was made to stand in turn, for Argyle to incant 'take him down', before disappearing in a swarm of prison officers to the dungeons. There were a few cries of horror at Richard's sentence, from his girlfriend Louise Ferrier and the journalist Carol Sarler – with the decorum of cement trucks the heavily built Old Bailey attendants, waiting for this moment, seized both women and carried them from the court. The judge complimented the Obscene Publications Squad for their 'extremely unpleasant task' in raiding and reading *Oz*, before making a stately exit with his ruffed-up aldermen toting the sword and the mace of his office.

With Marcel Berlins, a friend working at *The Times*, I stood on the court steps to watch as hundreds of demonstrators, encircled by as many policemen, lit a bonfire: an effigy of the judge was going up in flames. British justice (Marcel studied law in South Africa) had been a lodestar for us both: it now seemed there might be more justice on offer back in the colonies than at the Old Bailey. In search of some kind of sanity I took a taxi to the offices of *Private Eye* where Paul Foot was foaming at the mouth and comparing the infamy of the day to that on which Shelley was sent down from 'Univ' for blasphemy. He ushered me into the presence of an ashen-faced Lord Gnome – at least that was how the proprietor, Peter Cook, introduced himself. 'I always believed they would get *me*, that I would be the one they would put inside. Now it's happened to Richard Neville. I feel I should be in his shoes.' I left the licensed jesters at work on their *Oz* trial edition (the cover was a savage caricature of the judge by Gerald Scarfe, captioned: 'This justice must be seen to be done') and went off to prepare a bail application. Bail pending appeal was (and still is) almost impossible to obtain, but failure would mean that the editors would remain in prison for four months before their appeal could be heard.

The application was heard at 2 p.m. the next day, a Friday, before the 'vacation judge' – the most recent appointment to the High Court Bench, given the short straw of working over the summer holiday. Mr Justice Griffiths was a kind but cautious man, who needed to be convinced this was an exceptional case. John used all the legal arguments – ever so lightly dressed with emotion – for so regarding it, and the judge said he would think about 'this very difficult matter' over the weekend. 'He wants to read the Sunday editorials first,' came the cynical whisper from David Offenbach. These were divided about *Oz* and I could offer no great hope to Richard when I saw him at the prison on Sunday afternoon. For the first time in this whole saga, I sensed he was afraid. 'You've got to get me out tomorrow . . .' Would he, I wondered, go so far as to admit to the fear of every handsome heterosexual, of being raped in prison? No, not even to me? 'It's . . . er . . . got to the stage where I really can't stand the smell of Felix's socks.'

At 9.55 a.m. the next morning, in the High Court, we were truly anxious. I scarcely noticed a young blonde in a denim jacket and jeans emerge from the judge's entrance. She came swiftly down the steps to seat herself beside John Mortimer. He looked up from his papers and blinked owlishly at this lovely apparition, who seemed to have hitched a star in Carnaby Street and landed in the row reserved for Queen's Counsel in Court 13 in the Royal Court of Justice. 'Ah, excuse me, but this is counsel's row,' I heard John murmur reluctantly. 'The judge wouldn't like it if he saw you sitting here.' There was a beat, and a tight smile. 'I don't think Dad would mind.' What was happening then dawned: the judge came in, made conventional noises about how rare it is for bail to be granted pending appeal, and then, his daughter's gaze upon him, granted bail to all the defendants. He had not adjourned to read the editorials, but to listen to his children. Bob Dylan did not get it quite right: in some of our better homes, the daughters were not beyond command, they were in command.

The court clerk filled out the release forms, which I grabbed and rushed into the Strand to hail a taxi to Wormwood Scrubs, followed by the world's press. By the time the *Oz* editors were processed there were a hundred journalists and photographers milling about the prison gate, clamouring for pictures of their short-haired craniums. The transformation *was* remarkable: Richard, who two weeks before had resembled the young Oscar Wilde, now had the profile of a Lombroso criminal type. He was not so overcome with joy as to forget that 'the Scrubs' is handily situated for Television Centre: that night he was accorded a respectful half-hour interview by David Dimbleby on BBC2. At this ripe moment, no doubt, he could have mounted the barricades and led some sort of revolution, but to the disappointment of his acolytes Richard in his humble heart was a journalist, with the lizard of *Oz* in his genes: all he wanted now was to lie with friends in the sun. *Oz* had not been about either lust or emancipation: it was about pointing derisive fingers at emperors who had no clothes, without having the slightest inclination to tailor new ones. The Empire had made the mistake of striking back.

It had one last strike. The Lord Chief Justice presided over the three-day appeal in November, hearing our seventy-eight grounds of appeal against Judge Argyle's summing-up. Lord Widgery had an exact legal mind, and by the third day he was convinced that although many of the factual mistakes did not amount to much, there had been several serious errors which had to derail the obscenity conviction. Unless . . . There is always, in criminal appeals, this 'unless' – called in those days 'the proviso'. The judge has erred so fundamentally that the conviction must be quashed, *unless* the Court of Appeal is satisfied that the evidence is so overwhelming that the conviction would have been inevitable had the error not been made. On the last morning, the Chief made his reservation plain: he just could not imagine how the tiny advertisement for *Suck* magazine, which he described as 'a written account of the joys from the female aspect of an act of oral sexual intercourse', could be anything other than obscene. 'There is nothing here,' he said plaintively, 'which could induce people *not* to conduct the activity described.'

By lunchtime, the defendants were in a state of panic, and John and I were at a loss, even with the help of Professor Dworkin, to think of anything more that might be said as to why they should not go back to prison for publishing the fact that women might find cunnilingus an enjoyable experience. John's face was sagging badly as we returned for the normal 2 p.m. start. Surprisingly, there was no sign of the three judges. We waited and waited, until at 3.15 they returned with minds that had clearly been made up. 'You need not address us further about the proviso,' said the Chief in his clipped voice, before launching into a long judgment. The off-the-judicial-cuff decision is one of the lost glories of the English appeal courts now that judges all use word-processors, and Lord Widgery was the Laurence Olivier of the impromptu judgment. Suddenly his voice switched off, he bowed and exited, and we realised that the obscenity convictions and the prison sentences and the deportation order had all vanished into thin air.

The Lord Chief Justice had said that he was deeply troubled by the judge's constant denigration of the expert witnesses. Moreover, he had not understood the defence. One of its main planks was that the effect of *Oz* was emetic rather than erotic, aversive rather than titillating: it would not lure people into emulating the conduct that it satirised or depicted unpleasantly, but rather cause them revulsion. Somehow Judge Argyle managed to reinvent this argument in his own mind: he told the jury that it would only have this aversive effect on readers who were mentally ill. This proved fatal to the conviction, and so was his direction that obscenity meant what the dictionary said were its synonyms: 'filthy, disgusting, indecent, loathsome, lewd'.

But what was it that had, over the extended lunch-hour, persuaded the Chief Justice not to apply the proviso? The explanation which went around the Bar was that like many judges of his age and rectitude, whose reading matter was largely confined to law reports and *The Times*, Lord Widgery could envisage nothing more obscene than publishing the possibility that women might enjoy oral sex. For this appeal, fortuitously, he was flanked by two men of the world. Unable to convince the Chief by argument, one sent his clerk, a former able seaman, to Soho with £20 and a direction to acquire some 'up and down the wicket' examples of the pornography there on open sale. He returned at lunchtime with magazines which consumed their Lordships until 3.15 p.m. and served to persuade the Lord Chief Justice that *Oz* paled by comparison. That was why, in the course of his judgment, he issued a resounding call for pornographers to be jailed. He was oblivious to the fact that the shops from which the samples had been acquired were being run in partnership with the Metropolitan Police.

This was the crowning irony of the *Oz* trial: it was a fig leaf to cover up the deep and vicious corruption in Scotland Yard. This corruption spiralled downwards from Assistant Commissioner level to encompass the Obscene Publications Squad. These policemen had for some years been in the handsome pay of Soho pornographers. They called ahead before 'raiding' their shops, and seized lorry-loads of porn which would be totted up for the crime statistics and then surreptitiously returned to its owners. (One senior commander was so breast-high with the porn merchants that he actually edited one of their 'spanking' magazines.) As a pretence that the police really were concerned with the nation's morals, the much-publicised raids and trials of the underground press served as the perfect decoy. Indeed, even as the *Oz* trial was drawing to a close, the camouflage for the following year was being prepared. A team of eight police officers and two sniffer dogs walked the length of Berwick Street in Soho, passing eight bookshops they 'licensed' to sell pornography of the hardest core. They entered a decrepit building and climbed rickety stairs to the attic, where they pounced on the singer Mick Farren and several dazed artists working on the production of the underground comic *Nasty Tales* (more Crumb and Shelton, interspersed with the work of local cartoonists). The artists were arrested on obscenity charges, and marched in handcuffs down the stairs and past all the porn shops to the police vans. Too honest to pay for police protection, too political to be prurient, they were to be the next convenient scapegoats.

Detective Inspector Frederick Luff was one policeman not motivated by money. He was religiously committed to the closure of *Oz* and throughout the trial he worked as if his life depended on the outcome. On its last day, he had taken me to lunch at The Magpie and Stump. So why, I asked as he threw back his head to suck at a burnt pub sausage, was he persecuting *Oz* and not the real pornographers? He took a deep breath and almost pleaded, 'I *know* those boys in Soho. You have to believe me, I know them, and they would not – on their mother's grave – those boys would not sell that stuff to a kid. But Richard Neville and these underground people . . . That Isle of Wight pop festival, that was part of it, it's all organised, you see. I believe in God, and I'm doing this for our children . . .' Luff's eyes were blazing, on behalf of the kids my clients were Pied-Piping to their moral doom, and I believe he was sincere: several years later he gave a long witness statement to the investigators who came in with Robert Mark to clean up Scotland Yard. He was allowed to go off and do missionary work, while a dozen of his colleagues were prosecuted and jailed for – as Mr Justice Mars-Jones said – 'turning the Obscene Publications Squad into a vast protection racket'. Porn may not deprave and corrupt its readers, but it certainly corrupted some of those charged with enforcing laws against it.

And that was the end of *Oz*. This quintessentially sixties magazine, having proved its point in the law courts, lay down and died from an overdose of publicity. The editors went their separate ways – Richard returned to Sydney to raise children in a house called 'Happy Daze' by a waterfall in the Blue Mountains; Jim became a waiter at a gay restaurant in Sausalito and then wrote well-received novels; Felix, driven to refute the slur on his intelligence, built up an empire of art and land and computer magazines worth over £170 million by 1995. In that year Michael Argyle, now President of Restore the Death Penalty International Inc, wrote his own recollections of the *Oz* trial for the *Spectator*. He accused the defendants of importing drugs and selling them to schoolchildren and threatening his life. I advised Richard against suing the magazine, on the grounds that free speech was what the *Oz* trial was all about and that such evidence of the judge's mentality had historical merit. Felix took less nostalgic advice from George Carman and hit the *Spectator* with a claim for exemplary damages. The magazine published a full-page apology to this leading British businessman and paid a substantial sum to a children's charity of his choice.

Finally, what good came of it at last? The Court of Appeal decision, by declaring that 'obscenity' was much more than something shocking and disgusting – that it required some seductive invitation to depravity – has served as a bulwark against the resurgence of political censorship by way of criminal trials. Artists and writers who obey Kafka's injunction to 'use your pen like an ice-pick, to smash the frozen sea inside us' are in consequence unharassed, as are those whose shocking work is experimental or downright bad. The written word, certainly, is now beyond the long arm of the law, thanks to what was practically a replay of the *Oz* trial in 1976 – Brian Leary prosecuting, with John and myself and the ever-principled Professor Dworkin defending a shoddy little book called *Inside Linda Lovelace*. A jury of twenty-somethings acquitted without hesitation, after the judge had directed them, 'If this is not obscene, you may ask yourselves "what is?"' That acquittal, I suspect, was also a result, culturally rather than legally, of the *Oz* trial, which had aroused the hostility of the younger generation of jurors to a law which could apparently be used for political purposes. Ironically, in this way it may have proved a windfall for those involved in the commercial exploitation of sex – most notably for Rupert Murdoch, whose nudes began their appearance on page 3 of *The Sun* just after the *Oz* decision made clear that bad taste was not a crime.

Perhaps the best thing about *Oz* is that they just don't have trials like that any more. The last one of note was when John and I were enlisted to defend a particularly polite and studious young university graduate who sung under the sobriquet of 'Johnny Rotten'. Virgin had just launched a new Sex Pistols album: *Never Mind the Bollocks, Here's the Sex Pistols*. Display of the cover in shop windows was alleged to be an indecent exhibition and a test case was taken before the magistrates in Leicester. The justices made no attempt to hide their disapproval, so we called a Professor of English from Leicester University to trace for the court the etymology of the allegedly indecent word 'bollocks'. He explained that it was in common usage in the Middle Ages as the word for testicles, but had altered its meaning in the late eighteenth century because of a character in popular literature called 'Bollocks', a parson. From this association with parsonical canting, it developed the meaning of 'cant' and its modern slang sense, 'rubbish' or 'nonsense'. But it undoubtedly had respectable origins: indeed, the professor emphasised, Caxton in his Bible used the word 'bollocks' to mean 'testicles', and it had been republished in that sense until the King James edition, when it was replaced by the word 'stones'. At this point Johnny Rotten passed me a note. It read: 'Don't worry. If we lose the case, we'll retitle the album *Never Mind the Stones, Here's the Sex Pistols*.'

Soon after, the magistrates faced a courtroom packed with tabloid journalists. 'We have to find, unfortunately, that this charge is not made out,' grumbled the chairman, 'but don't think you are going to get any costs out of us.' John Mortimer, who belonged to that old school of advocates which thought that applying for costs slightly lowered the tone of a victory, had no intention of asking. Richard Branson was already leading the press-pack to a priceless front-page photo opportunity outside a record shop festooned with the acquitted cover: publicity over this would turn the Sex Pistols' heavy metal into gold. This is the abiding irony of all censorship, what might be termed 'the *Spycatcher* effect' – attempt to ban by law any form of artistic expression, and the publicity you bestow upon it will only serve to promote massive sales.

We seem to have laughed 'lifestyle' prosecutions out of court – even out of magistrates' courts. For authors, the accolade of an Old

Bailey trial is unavailable and the testimony of that once familiar figure, the 'expert on literature', is no longer heard in the land. For ten years, between 1987 and 1997, I was a director of the Institute of Contemporary Art, and not once did we suffer a police raid. I did stop one show by an HIV-positive performance artist whose idea of attaining empathy with his audience was to splatter them with infected blood (his own). This was not censorship, it was applying health regulations.

In 1992 the BBC produced my play re-enacting the *Oz* trial. In the direction box high in the cavernous studios at Television Centre, I looked down on the cardboard courtroom set as the actors took their place: there was one person missing. There was no postgraduate student at the solicitors' table in front of John Mortimer, looking appalled at the realities of English justice, *circa* 1971. I pointed out the omission, and hopefully added that I could always play myself. The producer and director – both were in nappies in 1971 – smiled and let me down politely. 'OK, but we'll get a young extra. You are – well, too old to be credible, really. What was that *Oz* slogan – never trust anyone over thirty.'

As I watched, the sentence of imprisonment and deportation of Richard Neville still fell with a shock, even though it was falling on the head of Hugh Grant, bowed in the dock to take the dramatic blow from a judge played by Leslie Phillips. I watch the extra recruited to play myself turn in distress to Simon Callow's John Mortimer. Simon's face, like John's, collapses to that precise level of weary resignation at which the barrister's emotion must bottom out, for below it lies tears, and further down, fury. The camera does not pan through the walls of the Old Bailey to the hundreds of angry demonstrators on the street outside, who burned the effigy and then formed what the *Daily Express* described as 'a wailing wall of weirdies' trying to levitate the foundation-stones. BBC2 did not have the budget. When the play was first performed by the Royal Shakespeare Company, I wanted the judge to have a magnifying glass, through which he would peer at Rupert. The director demurred. 'But he did. I was there,' I insisted. 'Of course it happened – in court. In a theatre, the audience won't believe it happened in court.' The most difficult thing about re-creating the *Oz* trial is that it was the sort of life which art cannot imitate.

Chapter 3

One of Our MPs is Missing

Gerald Gardiner started his career on the stage: he switched to the Bar because he wanted to deliver his own lines. In 1972 that yellow brick road beckoned briefly, when my *Oz* play attracted an off-Broadway production as a musical. Despite inspired direction by Jim Sharman, my theatrical career was short-lived: the *New York Times* critic, the Englishman Clive Barnes, hated the ridicule it heaped on his homeland. So I returned to Oxford to complete my thesis – and to find another friend in peril in the Old Bailey. This time it was twenty-two-year-old Peter Hain, who was being prosecuted on a blunderbuss conspiracy charge for organising the anti-apartheid demonstrations which had forced the MCC to cancel the 1970 test series against South Africa. His defence was being organised by the NCCL's solicitor, Larry Grant, who invited me to spend the summer of 1972 playing the justice game against the supporters of apartheid in sport. My acceptance was made possible – ironically – by Cecil Rhodes, whose Trust extended my scholarship for another year so that I could move to London to qualify for the Bar – and join Peter's legal team.

Peter Hain was the world's least likely law-breaker: he was excruciatingly polite, with hair the most conscientious prison barber would not have dared to touch. He had led the Young Liberals, and had come to stand for peacefulish protest (i.e. protest that was peaceful until the police arrived). He advocated 'direct action tactics' which meant running onto sportsgrounds during play and being carried off without a struggle: this, alleged his prosecutors, amounted to 'conspiracy to trespass', another obscure offence against the common law which carried a maximum sentence of life imprisonment. He faced four conspiracy charges, three of them serious, in a prosecution funded by a company – 'Freedom Under Law Limited' – which had raised money in South Africa under the slogan 'Pain for Hain'. In that country, they had no doubt that when football and cricket matches were disrupted in England, 'Hain stopped play'. But Peter had really been the spokesperson for mass protests in which tens of thousands of people had demonstrated in different ways their abhorrence of apartheid. The mistake his private prosecutors made was to claim that the rule of law required him to be convicted and jailed, when the law they relied upon – conspiracy to trespass – had never been approved by Parliament and was so vague in its definition and uncertain in its scope that some criminal textbooks denied its very existence. It was, in any event, irrational that an action (trespass) which if done by one person was merely a civil matter should be turned into a serious crime by the fact that it was done by agreement with others.

Hain's judge did not think that way, however, and the trial lasted for five weeks: for most of it, Peter defended himself with Larry and myself as his advisers. The prosecution Q.C. called sports stars (including Dawie de Villiers, South African football captain) and a journalist who later admitted working undercover for BOSS, the South African secret police. We countered with bishops and Liberal MPs. The jury was out for seven-and-a-half hours, and it was terrifying to think that they might return a verdict which would put Peter in prison and lead to dancing in the streets and segregated sporting clubs of Johannesburg. In the *Oz* case the jury had done their best to help without actually disobeying the judge's instructions; Peter's jury made in the end an acceptable bargain between the law and their consciences. They convicted him by a majority verdict only on the most minor count (of disrupting a Davis Cup tie for five minutes) and he was fined £200 – a disappointing dividend for investors in 'Freedom Under Law Limited'. The crime of 'conspiracy to trespass' was soon abolished by Parliament following a Law Commission report that it offended against the fundamental principle of certainty in the criminal law. Peter Hain's defence had, I think, a small part to play in preventing the rule of law being misinterpreted to mean the rule of lawyers.

My student summers had been spent as script-writer for two

notable self-defenders, and as Larry Grant observed, 'it's always your contributions that provoke the judge'. In 1973 I finally qualified to speak for myself. The law exams were easy compared to the statutory ordeal of dining – not well, but very often – with fellow students at the Middle Temple. I suffered thirty-five boarding-school meals, washed down by cheap Spanish wine and a non-vintage port which we learned to pass in a direction I now forget. On my ceremonial 'call' to the Bar the authorities discovered that I had eaten one dinner less than I should as the result of wishfully thinking I could count that night's dinner as part of my tally. 'This is an appalling way to begin a career at the Bar,' said Mr Justice Milmo, in the tone of voice he normally reserved for sentencing offenders to long periods of imprisonment. I offered to return to Australia, where communal dining was not a vital professional qualification, but at the last moment he relented: 'I think I may – just may – have a discretion to lift the requirements of the statutes.' With a grimace as painful as Samson's when he held up the pillars of the Temple, the judge lifted an ancient statute and I crawled from underneath it to a career at the Bar.

There were other obstacles. Australians were not unwelcome, but some of us – those who could not claim new-fangled 'patriality' by possessing a grandparent born in Britain – had to be sacrificed so that the government could stop black settlement. My Surrey ancestors had lost the family fortune at Paris gaming tables and had been reduced to commissions in the navy, leaving on convict escort duty in 1837. They had been too long gone to make me a true Brit, so my application for a permanent residence permit would depend on whether I could maintain myself without becoming a burden on the rates, which in turn depended upon whether I could practise at the Bar. The Council for Legal Education had a monopoly on that decision, and under Home Office made it depend on attending a course of 'practical exercises', which foreign students were not allowed to undertake unless they had permanent residence permits. This catch-22 had the effect (and the intention) of preventing a lot of black barristers from working in Britain. The pretence that it was not a racist rule was that it would catch a few whites, like me. My old tutor Lennie Hoffman, a brilliant Chancery barrister, found a way around the impasse: he explained to the credulous council that I should be allowed to do the practical exercises '*de bene esse*' (i.e.

'just in case'). If my residence application was eventually granted, then I would have been qualified to practise all along. But if it wasn't, then I would not have done the course at all. The result of Lennie's sophistry was that my hypothetical presence was permitted in the drab rooms of various down-at-heel barristers, imbibing their sweet sherry and their approach to cross-examination.

I began pupillage in chambers and acquired a clerk named Arthur (clerks are always referred to by their Christian name, which is usually Arthur) who refused to pass on telephone messages from the National Council for Civil Liberties. When I taxed him with this, Arthur replied elliptically, 'It's for your own good, sir.' 'Why is that, Arthur?' I asked innocently. 'Because it's a fucking communist front, innit sir?' I begged to differ, and suggested that the NCCL was precisely the sort of organisation which might put impecunious young barristers in the way of interesting and ultimately lucrative briefs. Arthur's eyes rotated in their sockets. 'I will now give you a piece of advice, sir, that you should never forget if you want a career in this profession. Take my Guv'nor. He's the best fucking silk there is. And why is he never going to be made a fucking High Court judge? Just answer me that. I will tell you why he's never going to be made a High Court judge. Because when he was a young barrister, he took telephone calls from the National fucking Council for Civil fucking Liberties.'

I had been warned. Arthur's 'Guv'nor' was Lewis Hawser QC, and he was indeed one of the best silks in practice, but he had acted for civil liberties causes many years before, and he never was made a High Court judge. He became an Official Referee, of great distinction, but the prize he sorely wanted and surely deserved was never vouchsafed him. Many years later, and shortly before his death, he invited me to speak at a weekend he organised for Bar students, and he took me aside and asked if I knew why he had never been appointed. I knew nothing more than Arthur had told me. Nor did he.

I was elected in 1974 to the NCCL's executive council, deepening Arthur's despair. Fellow members ranged from young Tory Clive Landa, who eventually married into the Thatcher Ministry, to youngish Trotskyite Paul Foot, whom I enjoyed embarrassing at meetings by pointing out that *Private Eye* in those days accepted 'D' notices, directives from government forbidding publication of official secrets. Monthly meetings were dull affairs, at which Arthur's communist front did little more than give retrospective approval to the actions of its General Secretary, Patricia Hewitt (daughter of Australia's Cabinet Secretary) and her legal officer, the beautiful and bossy Harriet Harman, niece to Lord Longford. This eclectic mix was secretly dubbed subversive by MI5, which took the liberty of tapping our telephones. Many years later when this was confirmed by Cathy Massiter – an MI5 official who spent so much time listening to the intercepts on the Campaign for Nuclear Disarmament that she resigned in order to join it – I took the case for Pat and Hattie to the European Court, which condemned the UK government for invading their privacy. (The government did not put up much of a defence, since it was still pretending that MI5 did not exist.) It was of course ridiculous for MI5 to behave in this way, as I said to its former Assistant Director, Peter Wright, during the *Spycatcher* saga. To my surprise, this most paranoid of spooks actually agreed. 'Of course it was a scandal, but – don't you see – it proves my point that the communists were in control of MI5 by 1974. They actually took resources away from bugging their friends the Soviets, and deliberately wasted them on bugging insignificant organisations like the NCCL. Do you see?' Wright had lived for too long in a Little Buttercup world, believing that things are the opposite of what they seem. The MI5 bosses who decided to waste taxpayers' money on targeting the NCCL were not Russian spies; unlike the KGB, they thought the NCCL a significant organisation.

My stipend from the Rhodes Trust ran out so I tried a second career in journalism to tide me through the unpaid period of pupillage. I joined C H Rolph as a commentator on legal matters for *The New Statesman*. Tom Baistow, the kindly and painstaking deputy editor, would sub my prose, blue-pencilling any *double entendres*. ('The editor's father is a clergyman, remember'.) I was thrilled to be invited to lunch – which I attended straight from court, in wing-collar and white bands – and to be seated beside the entertaining Tom Driberg, with Christopher Hitchens (a more beautiful youth) on his other side. I was unaware of Driberg's real appetites and did not understand the joke, until afterwards I overheard someone say, 'Tom couldn't believe his luck – he didn't know which knee to stroke first.'

One of my *New Statesman* investigations was expanded into a book – *Reluctant Judas* – about an Irishman shot through the head on Easter Sunday 1974. Two organisations had a motive for eliminating him: one was the IRA, the other was British Intelligence. Kenneth Lennon had been a Sinn Fein supporter turned Special Branch informant, responsible for long jail sentences imposed on three members of an IRA cell in Luton. He was arrested with another member while 'casing' the prison where the men were held; to maintain his cover both men were prosecuted, but the case against Lennon was 'massaged' to ensure his acquittal. On the day of his release, however, he claimed to have a flash of conscience: he sought out George Melly, in a break between his performances at Ronnie Scott's nightclub in Soho, and confessed to 'setting up' innocent men. The next day he turned up at the NCCL, repeating these allegations and dictating to Larry Grant details of how the police had given false but favourable evidence at his trial to secure his acquittal. He concluded by predicting his own death: 'the Special Branch may do me in and try to make it look like an IRA job'.

It did look like an IRA job when Lennon's body was found in a ditch near Gatwick Airport a few days later, but once his confession was published it seemed to many that his prediction may have come true. Court records confirmed that his trial had been 'rigged' to the extent that damaging evidence against him had been withheld and police witnesses had given untruthful testimony in his favour. So favourable, indeed, that it made his accomplice look guilty: he was found so, and sentenced to five years in prison, while Lennon was acquitted. A police report ordered by Home Secretary Roy Jenkins admitted that this had been done to protect an important informer, without the knowledge of judge or counsel but with the approval of the DPP. The IRA bombs in Birmingham had just killed twenty-one people, and no proper inquiry was deemed appropriate by the government or by the media. The *Daily Express* spoke for Fleet Street: 'It is absurd and dangerous to apply Queensberry rules to measures taken by the authorities. In this context there is no "right" or "wrong" – all that matters is success.' This was the moral mind-set, in courtroom and press room and police interview room, as the cases against Irish Sinn Fein sympathisers wrongfully accused of planting bombs – the Birmingham

Six, the Guildford Four and Judith Ward – were prepared and tried, like Lennon, in 1974–5. It shaped the thinking of policemen who fabricated interview notes with some of them, and forensic scientists who dissembled in their evidence to assist the prosecution, and government lawyers who withheld evidence which would have been vital to the defence. They were behaving as the *Daily Express* had urged – 'there is no "right" or "wrong" – all that matters is success'.

Notwithstanding my view that Lennon, who was being paid by results, may have incited crime to achieve them acting as an *agent provocateur*, there was soon no doubt in my mind about who killed him. Lennon had been 'arrested' by the IRA after his acquittal, and brought before a kangaroo court. He was promised an 'amnesty' if he confessed in an appropriately public way to the NCCL, foretelling his death at Special Branch hands. But the hand that pulled the trigger of the gun held at his head was not serving the British State. He was executed by the IRA. This conclusion was not the one my Sinn Fein sources would wish or expect, and after publication of *Reluctant Judas* I waited with some trepidation for their call. It soon came, and the first words made me gulp: 'I want you to know, your book's been proscribed'. My knees started knocking, as if to remind me of the fact that they had caps. 'Proscribed – what do you mean?' ('Proscribed' was what the Catholic Church used to do to books it did not like, before burning their authors.) 'Yes, you know, it's been banned. By the Governor of Long Kesh. They won't let it through the wire. It's the truth they can't take, isn't it?' I breathed a silent 'thank you' to the Governor of Long Kesh, whose act of prison censorship had convinced the IRA that my book must be on their side, and so relieved them from reading it.

Investigative journalism, clearly, was a more dangerous career than barristering. And it lacked the law's long-term advantage, that the older you get the more distinguished you are presumed to have become. So I cleaned my fingernails and cleared my throat for my first solo appearance in a courtroom. I still spoke with Australian irritable vowels, which lend a different and more nasal aspect to words like 'France' and 'branch'. My debut was at Knightsbridge Crown Court, appearing for a company accused of manufacturing indecent T-shirts. It fell to me to explain the nature of the offending logo to a judge renowned for his rectitude and propriety. Nervously, I ventured that it read 'Fuck Art, Let's Dance'. There was a shocked silence in court. The judge's eyebrows narrowed with irritation. 'Fuck art let's *what*, Mr Robertson?' 'Let's dance, Your Honour.' 'Oh, you're an *Australian*,' he muttered. 'What you mean to say is "Fuck art, let's *darn*ce".'

My next brief was a four-week committal proceeding at Watford Magistrates' Court, concerning a conspiracy to make blue movies in divers fields, barns and houses in the suburb of Rickmansworth. I was representing two of the actors, a spray-painter and his girlfriend: he appeared with some thirty partners in the course of the making of dozens of short films, but she refused to have sex with any partner but him. Their *pièce de non-résistance* was entitled *Santa's Coming*, in which he emerged in Father Christmas attire from the chimney to kiss and copulate beneath the mistletoe. They married shortly before the committal, and held hands every day in court. I could not resist asking the police officer in charge of the case whether he would accept that my clients were very much in love. He accepted it, just before the deadline for the final edition of the *Evening Standard*, where I made my first reported appearance as counsel under the head-line 'Porn Couple "Very Much In Love"'. In court next day, a man in a grubby raincoat sidled up to me and pressed a calling card into my hand. 'I'm from the *News of the World*,' he explained. 'We'll be hearing more of you.'

They did, but only because in my first year of practice masturbation was an endless preoccupation of policemen and lawyers. The Old Bailey at times resembled a pornographic cinema complex as judges came to grips with this new form of entertainment. Jurors, solemnly empanelled for what they imagined would be a murder or a robbery, could be in for a surprise. At the trial of the first importer of the film *Deep Throat*, the all-male jury were told no more by the prosecutor's opening but that they would be shown a film, and it would be their task to say whether it constituted an indecent import. The courtroom lights were then dimmed, and Ms Linda Lovelace appeared. Some ninety minutes later the lights went up and the judge adjourned for lunch, making his exit in a crouching position. The jurors, red-faced and saucer-eyed, remained seated in their jury box. 'Come along now,' urged the prim lady usher. Not one of them moved. 'It's lunchtime,' she exclaimed, 'I've got to lock the court.' She could not understand why still there was no movement. It took some minutes for them to stand upright and shuffle out, on the only occasion on which I have been forced to acknowledge the benefit of wearing a gown.

These early adventures in the skin trade brought an invitation from Clive Landa to speak at the Young Conservatives 1974 Annual Conference. They wanted to open proceedings with a bang, by having me ignite Mrs Mary Whitehouse, a Colchester housewife who billed herself as leader of the 'moral majority' and was developing formidable political skills. The Young Conservatives were an engaging and libertarian lot in these days: Mary's thesis, that pornography was a communist plot to destabilise Western society, met with their free-market mirth. That evening, as the band struck up at the Young Conservatives Ball, I asked Mrs Whitehouse for a 'darnce'. 'This could be the start of a long relationship, Geoffrey,' she warned, as I trod on her toes.

To Mary's chagrin, jurors were now much younger than at the time of the *Oz* trial because the property qualification had been abolished, and they looked more cynically on obscenity prosecutions. This led them to acquit, or at least fail to agree, thereby mirroring the community confusion about sexual explicitness. The police resorted to raiding bookshops and delivering their contents to strait-laced lay justices who, unlike jurors, could be relied upon to reject my arguments and order the burning of magazines like *Forum*. My lectures on the jurisprudential subtleties of obscenity law were too much for one magistrate, David Hopkin, with whom I spent a day at Bow Street contemplating several hundred 'spanking' magazines. 'I've had enough,' he interjected, a few hours into my speech. 'If the gels are being spanked with their pants off, that's obscene. If their pants are on, then it's not obscene. Sort it out between yourselves – I'm going home.' Others were less robust, like Mr Pugh, the very old stipendiary in Liverpool, to whom I had to address an argument about Alex Comfort's book *The Joy of Sex*, which had been seized from the local W H Smith. 'But it is about perversion,' he complained, 'it has pages on . . .' he whispered, 'oral sex.' I produced an expert's report, which showed that by now, three years on from *Oz*, a majority of married couples in Britain were admitting some indulgence in the practice. Mr Pugh sighed, and said in a voice of infinite sadness, 'If that is really so,

Mr Robertson, I'm glad I do not have long to live.'

I turned with some relief to real crime, and began to spend much of my time 'down the Bailey', restoring many a burglar to his friends and relations. The Old Bailey in 1974 was a kind of Jurassic Park, in which judicial dinosaurs still roamed. There was Judge Mervyn Griffith-Jones, a footnote in history for prosecuting *Lady Chatterley's Lover* and asking a lower-middle-class jury whether they would allow their wives or their servants to read the book. He was a burned-out case by the time I came to do a trial before him. 'He's had twenty-two acquittals in a row,' whispered my co-defender. His main concern was that counsel should sit up straight and not slouch in their chairs, and the jury soon added a twenty-third. Justice Melford Stevenson, however, was in full flight. He caused consternation at the defence bar by cutting the fees of barristers who had dared to waste the court's time by accusing police of 'planting' fingerprint evidence against a group of Irish defendants: 'Counsel has no duty,' he intoned in his gravel-pit voice, 'to be a loudspeaker to a maladjusted set'. It was Melford who gave my career its first boost, by insisting that I appear without a leader in a complex and serious case of industrial espionage. Sensing reporters in court when I made the application for a Q.C. on behalf of the penniless defendants, he delivered them a sound-bite about the need to empty 'the bottomless cornucopia of legal aid'.

My career had till then been stuck at the very bottom of Melford's alleged cornucopia. Legal aid paid solicitors to prepare cases, but not to attend them: they would instead send 'outdoor clerks', usually 'resting' actresses or 'retired' policemen (i.e. police who had been given the option of retiring rather than being prosecuted for corruption). I had a strange experience one day at Bow Street, where the client I had been sent to represent demanded a change of solicitor, and the officer on custody duty seemed to understand why. I didn't, and asked the solicitor's clerk, a kindly old ex-copper with sad eyes, what the problem was. 'It's me, sir,' he confided. 'This is the third villain that's turned me down. I'll lose my job, now.' The custody officer did not seem sorry: '*We* don't want him down here, either. We can forgive what *he* did, but we can't forgive what he did to those young police officers. They went down for five years, and Challoner wasn't even tried!'

I realised then that my sorry old solicitor's clerk was the single most significant contributor to the national awareness of civil liberties. Detective Inspector Harry Challoner had been in charge of West End Central in the early sixties, when police officers could, in the public mind, do no wrong. The wrong he did – with the assistance of his junior officers – was to arrest political demonstrators, force their fingers around builder's bricks, and then have them and the bricks fingerprinted. They were invariably convicted and imprisoned, and Challoner's crimes were covered up by his superior officers – until they realised he was not just overzealous, he was a paranoid schizophrenic. The younger policemen were convicted of perverting the course of justice, while Harry was found to be too mentally ill to stand trial. That day at Bow Street I took him for a coffee, with which he took his medication. Delicately, I touched upon his dealings with protesters, and he told me how his voices had directed him to plant the bricks and fabricate the evidence. His pills now helped him to lead a normal life, but he missed his days in the force. Did he regret sending innocent people to prison? He looked at me with astonishment, and the sadness in his eyes lifted for one moment. 'Of course not. My voices were right. They were all guilty.'

A man who would have understood Challoner was my next client, Professor R D Laing, whose work had opened so many minds to the illnesses in them. He had been licensed to prescribe LSD to patients, and when that drug was eventually banned, he had left some capsules forgotten at the back of his fridge where they were discovered one night by some very thorough burglars. Ronnie called the police and was gratified when they made a quick arrest, but less pleased when they prosecuted him for possession of the illegal drugs which had been stolen from him. The charges were finally dropped, with Hampstead justices awarding Ronnie his costs as a mark of displeasure that they should ever have been brought: the scene of his non-crime is now the well-adjusted home of Helena Kennedy and her family.

That case was a success, but the day had to come when I first lost a client to prison. He was a man of my age – twenty-six – who had no previous convictions and who on my advice pleaded guilty to stealing an almost out-of-date tax disc from a car which was nearly – but not quite – abandoned. He was crippled by polio in one leg – a matter to which I was warming in my mitigation until I noticed that the judge had only one arm and was becoming impatient with this line of pleading. He jailed the man for twelve months, and in the cells later the probation officer thought it more necessary to counsel me than my client. I continued to feel a personal responsibility for the young man whose plight, I believed, was due to my own inadequacy and inexperience. After days of self-doubt I took myself off to the theatre, where providentially I saw the Mortimers. I must have been in a bad way, because John, who always teaches by example, gave me the only lecture I can recall ever receiving from him. He told me I would destroy myself if I became emotionally involved in the fate of my clients. And he asked whether I had yet found chambers.

This was the final milestone: to find a 'seat' – a permanent place – in a set of chambers. For a few heady months I had planned, with Tony 'Lord' Gifford and others, to take the revolutionary step of establishing chambers outside the rabbit-warren of the Temple. Because no barrister had done this for centuries, we wondered whether it was even ethically possible, so we sought an audience with the legendary Mr Boulton, General Secretary of the Bar Council and author of at least five editions of *Boulton on Ethics*, a slim volume of biblical stature solemnly presented to all barristers on their call to the Bar.

For all the fear that his written words had instilled, Mr Boulton of *Boulton on Ethics* was a kindly, owlish man whose advice was limited to the numbered paragraphs of his textbook, which he kept at his fingertips. Tony and I visited him, with all the trepidation of those ancient messengers who approached the shrine at Delphi, to enquire as to the propriety of establishing chambers outside the boundaries of the four Inns of Court. Mr Boulton picked up his book and slowly and carefully thumbed through its pages, as if reading them for the first time. Eventually, he pronounced judgment: 'I find nothing in *Boulton on Ethics* against a set of chambers located outside the Temple.' This ruling in our favour emboldened us to seek another breach in tradition: would it be proper to employ a clerk *on a salary*, rather than on the universal percentage? Again, the sage consulted his book, from front to back cover. 'There is nothing in *Boulton on Ethics* against a barrister employing a clerk on a salary.' Tony tried our luck a third time, with the most radical proposal ever to emanate from an English barrister. Could we share our fees equally? Mr Boulton's eyebrows raised imperceptibly at this Marxist idea, but he followed the same course before at length declaring, 'There is nothing to be found in *Boulton on Ethics* which precludes fee-sharing arrangements'. We left his office, feeling as excited as Lenin on leaving the Finland Station: permission had been given for the revolution to begin. (Had we asked permission to make bombs in the basement, I imagine Mr Boulton would have gone through the same procedure, and declared that there was nothing in *Boulton on Ethics* against the making of explosive substances in barristers' chambers.)

This was heady stuff in 1974; now even the Bar Council has moved from woodwormy gloom and over-priced tenancies in the Temple, and many chambers have put their clerks on salaries. Fee-sharing, like Marxism, never worked and I bailed out as soon as some colleagues made clear that it was my fees they wanted to share. The best argument for the Bar is that it produces lawyers who are independent of pressure, whether from partners or principals or fellow-members of a fee-sharing collective. I wanted to give that argument a chance, if only I could find a chambers that would take someone already labelled on the clerks' grapevine as a 'radical barrister' (a concept I still reckon to be a contradiction in terms). I called on Emlyn Hooson, the wise and humane head of John Mortimer's chambers at No. 1 Dr Johnson's Buildings, to seek a tenancy. It was offered – because, I suspect, John made one of his rare attendances at a chambers meeting in order to support it.

So I took up professional residence for the next fifteen years at the building which bore the name of Dr Samuel Johnson, London's most illustrious lawyer-baiter. My historic first-floor room overlooked the Temple church. There was dry rot in the walls and mice in the skirting-boards: it was cold enough in winter for clients to keep their overcoats on, and shadows fell eerily from a gas lamp, romantically lit each evening by a Temple retainer. My conferences were regularly interrupted by loud lectures from guides who brought American tourists to stand beneath the windows, looking up to envision the good doctor at verbal play with his pipe and his port and his faithful Boswell. These declamations, I could not help but hear, were designed to leave tourists gasping in awe and admiration at the character and traditions of English lawyers. They were far removed from the true spirit of Dr Samuel Johnson. 'I don't care to speak ill of any man behind his back,' he once said, possibly in my room, 'but I believe the person who has just taken his departure to be an attorney.'

With a seat in chambers, I could now open my vowels and close my mind to journalism. I had eaten thirty-five dinners (and one *de bene esse*); I had relatively clean fingernails and a contact on *News of the World*. Christmas 1974 I spent dutifully with my grandmother in a coastal village north of Sydney where, on fishing expeditions, I dreamed of landing what barristers called 'a big case'. On Christmas Eve, my grandmother ran a mile along the breakwater to tell me some exciting news . . .

'They've caught the cabinet minister who murdered his nanny!' She was as confused as most Australians when they heard of the arrest by the Melbourne vice squad of John Stonehouse MP, the former Postmaster-General. He had last been seen five weeks before, walking into the water off Miami Beach. His clothes, money and passport had been left in a hotel locker, to help the five life insurance companies with whom he had recently taken out policies to deduce that he had drowned. Stonehouse's disappearance had come shortly after that of Lord Lucan, whose car was found abandoned near an English beach, inviting the presumption that he had committed suicide after battering to death his nanny, mistaking her for his wife. The British press was busy scouring the exotic locations of the world for both men: the last place they suspected was the unremarkable Melbourne suburb where every morning an elegant Englishman would collect his airmail edition of *The Times* and then wander off to open bank accounts in the names of Clive Muldoon and Joseph Markham. The local police, alerted to this curious behaviour by a suspicious bank clerk, cabled Scotland Yard to ask laconically whether England was missing any members of its establishment. The Yard cabled back that the mysterious man might be Lucan or might be Stonehouse, and that the former had a six-inch scar on his inside right thigh.

That is why Australia's most celebrated arrest began with the order 'Pull down your trousers'. The absence of any scar came as a disappointment to the coppers, who had been hoping their mystery man would turn out to be the bloody aristocrat rather than the runaway MP. Stonehouse had served in the sixties as a minister in the Wilson government but when the Labour Party was returned to power in 1974 he had decided to return to the back benches to go into business in his spare time. His companies soon ran into as much trouble as his marriage – his obsessive dedication to causes had left him insensitive to the needs of others, whether they were creditors or members of his family. (As one psychiatrist later put it, in evidence at the Old Bailey, John Stonehouse 'had been reared as a socialist rather than as a person'.) In Melbourne, the arresting officers invited him to telephone his wife and children, who had for the past five weeks genuinely believed him to be dead. They secretly recorded the call, in which his astonished wife Barbara was told, 'I decided I would be like thunder and lightning and just drop out of my old identity. It was some sort of brainstorm . . . now, how have you been?' As she listened to him announcing his intention to settle permanently in Australia, two airline tickets to Melbourne were thrust through her front door by a *News of the World* reporter. Barbara told him of this, and asked, 'Do you want me to come?' 'Yes,' he replied imperiously. 'Do come immediately. And bring Sheila Buckley with you.'

Thus began the media circus, which over the next two years carried this over-maligned man inexorably to his doom. By the time I joined as his counsel, on his extradited return to Britain in July of 1975, he had become the most derided person in the country. This was only partly the fault of the British press, which had thrown his right to a fair trial to the winds in their lubricious delight over the 'love triangle' with wife Barbara and secretary Sheila, which they spiced with false allegations that he had been a paid agent of the Czech secret police. Although the charges were comparatively minor (two false passports; theft of £29,000 of his own company's money, and an 'attempt' to leave £125,000 in insurance policies payable to his family), these were treated as if they amounted to the fraud of the century. But John was in some ways the author of his own media misfortune: he played up to press prejudices by ranting against Britain, by blaming everyone but himself for his business problems, and by instantly writing a book, *Death of an Idealist*, declaring his innocence. His dubious argument boiled down to every good boy deserving a favour: he had been such a devoted public servant for twenty-five years that he was entitled to have a breakdown and start a new life. Worst of all, from the public's point of view, was his insistence on remaining an MP for the bewildered constituents of Walsall North, even when he was in Melbourne declaring his wish to live the rest of his life 12,000 miles away from them.

Acquiring an ex-cabinet minister as a client made a welcome change from the minor drug dealers and porn merchants with whom I had spent my first year in practice. By the time he agreed to come home rather than contest extradition proceedings, John had convinced himself that he was the victim of a political prosecution, and was reassured by the fact that I had defended *Oz* and Peter Hain. The first thing he said to me when we met in Brixton Prison was that he wanted bail so that he could get back to the House of Commons. He did have a right to bail, together with ample sureties: there was no prospect that he would interfere with witnesses or flee the country again. 'This is the face that has launched a thousand headlines!' I exclaimed in exasperation when the sour-faced chief magistrate at Bow Street predicted that John would abscond.

The court was crammed with a hundred reporters, who had no intention of letting John Stonehouse out of their sight if he gained his liberty. But until Parliament recessed, the Bow Street magistrate was determined that this honourable member should not disgrace it with his presence. So the Stonehouse bail show played every Monday to the press, much to the delight of the court's regular customers arrested in Covent Garden on Saturday nights for 'drunk and disorderly behaviour'. On 'Stonehouse days', these vagrants and prostitutes were *sober* and disorderly, as they played to the packed press gallery, competing with each other to draw the loudest laughs (and the heaviest fine) by abusing the beak. After repeated rejections of my increasingly florid bail applications, I decided one week not to bother: that was when, to everyone's amazement, the magistrate announced he was granting bail, whether we asked for it or not. It was 3 August 1975, and it was finally safe to apply the law correctly: Parliament had just risen for its summer recess.

It was a summer I spent preparing for the committal proceedings, which took place in October at Horseferry Road Magistrates' Court. The prosecution had been entrusted to Dai Tudor-Price, a deceptively low-key (and for that reason, highly effective) treasury counsel. Before he stood up to open the case, he showed me the instruction he had written to himself, ten times over, on the first page of his notebook: 'Say nothing to provoke Mr Stonehouse'. John for his part threw himself into the task of establishing his innocence. He would rise at 5 a.m. and prepare a list of several hundred questions for me to ask the day's witnesses. At 9 a.m. I would meet him at court and go through them (they would be neatly written by hand in green ink on House of Commons notepaper) to explain why many were irrelevant. At lunchtime we would retire to our room to feast on the contents of a picnic basket provided each day by the much-forgiving Barbara, replete with silver cutlery and silk napkins. In court, I would occasionally manage to elicit a favourable answer from a prosecution witness – like the kindly manager of a Lloyds Bank branch who had accepted John's personal guarantee for an overdraft, and still believed it to be of value 'because I think Mr Stonehouse has a good life ahead of him, and is a potential force for good'. When the afternoon session concluded, the potential force for good would march ministerially out of the courtroom and along the embankment to the House of Commons.

John returned to his parliamentary duties as if nothing had happened, although he took a new interest in issues which touched on criminal justice. My main concern in this period was to persuade him to resign his seat. This was a vital step, I believed, towards obtaining a fair trial at the Old Bailey the following year. By strutting and fretting on the Commons stage, flourishing his MP's privileges while facing serious criminal charges, he was simply inviting the media to stoke up the prejudice against him. John was prepared to resign, but only after making a 'personal explanation' to the House. I sat in the parliamentary gallery and watched while he nervously tried to explain his mental breakdown in an anodyne text which had been pre-censored by the Speaker. It was a dignified performance on a somewhat melancholy occasion: *Private Eye*'s next cover showed him brandishing a newspaper:

'TOTALLY INNOCENT MP WRONGLY ACCUSED!' This was funny only to those who presumed that Stonehouse was totally guilty. Everyone in London, the geographic pool from which his jurors would be drawn, seemed to find it uproarious.

One person determined that the media circus should pass well outside his court was the magistrate. Mr Harrington SM, impervious to the public loathing of my client (or, perhaps, only too aware of it), bent over backwards to be fair, actually dismissing the most serious charges (the insurance frauds) which pivoted upon the allegation that Stonehouse, having taken out the policies, had attempted to defraud the insurers by faking his death. There were two problems of a technical nature with these charges. In the first place, the power of English courts to punish crime depends on where that crime is committed, and Stonehouse's 'attempt' was made outside the jurisdiction, in Miami. In the second place, to be found guilty of 'attempt' to commit crime you must have had a real go at pulling it off: the legal test is whether the act charged as an attempt (the disappearing act in Miami) was 'sufficiently proximate' to the notional completed crime (the eventual payment of the insurance moneys to Barbara in England). Since Stonehouse, in order to achieve this objective, would have to remain hidden for years, and in Melbourne (then one of the world's dullest cities), my argument was that what he had done by faking his death was not close enough to the anticipated insurance claim to be punished as an 'attempt'. Mr Harrington agreed, and threw out the insurance charges.

The unsought consequence of the magistrate's fair-mindedness was to kindle a belief in John that he could beat all raps. With this new-found confidence he decided that he would not resign from Parliament after his 'personal explanation' speech. He was shunned by the Labour Party, but that did not disturb him one whit: he had reached that stage, familiar to many socialist MPs, of disbelief in socialism – a condition provided for, a few years later, by the foundation of the SDP. But John had become a social democrat before there was a social democrat party, so he cast around for an alternative and ended up joining the 'English National Party'. They were a collection of fairly harmless oddballs, who dressed up in Robin Hood costumes and held tea-parties before jousting on the green sward – not much in evidence amongst the tower-blocks of Walsall North, whose electors were now represented by the one MP who stood for Merrie England.

While John jousted in Parliament, I had the problem of preparing his defence. Now that he was no longer resigned to losing, he thought it sensible to enhance his chances by retaining a leading counsel. His first choice, F Lee Bailey, was not admitted to practise at the English Bar, so he called Lord Hailsham, the once and future Tory Lord Chancellor. Hailsham graciously declined the proffered brief, explaining the convention that out-of-office Lord Chancellors should not return to the Bar, but wishing him the best of luck – a politeness from which John took great heart. He decided he would shop around for his silk, leaving to me the task of shortlisting the best candidates and asking them if they would mind undergoing an audition for the role, to take place over tea with their prospective client. London's top criminal silks submitted themselves with good humour to this novel beauty contest: much Temple tea was consumed until the winner was declared, on BBC news, to be Richard du Cann QC. Stonehouse much admired his elder brother Edward, whose ability to make large amounts of money as a director of Lonhro while representing constituents as an MP had served as a role-model for his own, rather less successful, business ventures.

Dick du Cann was an advocate's advocate, a saturnine and sardonic prosecutor now turned defender, who threw himself into the case with a commitment his client was never able to recognise. John later complained that Dick never, over many months of conferences, gave the slightest hint that he thought him innocent. Given the evidence this was not entirely surprising, but in any event Dick firmly belonged to that school of advocacy which suspends moral judgment and leaves guilt and innocence to the jury. He never descended to first-name terms with a client, and insisted upon a personal distance which gave a false impression of disdain: his early death from cancer was attributable to the cartons of cigarettes he burned in an all-consuming anxiety to concentrate on cases like John's. He was the epitome of professional conduct, and it took me aback when he proposed that we should interview Barbara Stonehouse. 'But she's a potential witness,' I objected, directing him to the paragraph in *Boulton on Ethics* which laid down the rule that barristers should never interview witnesses of fact. 'I think my back is broad enough to bear any criticism,' he said with a smile. 'It's essential to our conduct of this case to decide whether the wife was party to an insurance swindle.' Dick's judgment after we subjected her to a searching inquisition was that she knew absolutely nothing about John's intention to disappear. Barbara's conduct, from the moment she flew to his side, taking Sheila with her, was magnificent. She stood by her husband throughout two years of abject humiliation, protested forcefully at his over-severe sentence, and then quietly and quickly divorced him.

It was left to me, and to his doggedly devoted solicitor, Michael O'Dell, to find some sympathetic explanation for John's treatment of the lioness who loved him. If it were madness, there was too much method in it ever to convince the jury. Yet there was something unhinged about the grandiosity of his conduct which could not be explained merely by a desire to avoid business reversals or to live with a younger lover. We had evidence from Dr Maurice Miller, a GP and MP whom he consulted from time to time, that in the year before his disappearance John changed in character and frequently sank into deep anxiety states, and none of the independent experts in psychology or psychiatry we consulted had any doubt but that he had been clinically depressed. The private self lost faith in the public man: he seriously contemplated suicide, but designed instead a psychiatric equivalent: he would kill off John Stonehouse, MP, and return as Mr Markham or Mr Muldoon – anonymous and unambitious men whose ordinary joys he would savour. It was the middle-aged, *Moon and Sixpence* dream-world of pleasure free from pressure, which he pursued in his five weeks of invisibility in Melbourne by joining the Victorian Chess Club and the Victorian Jazz Club. There was, on one level, nothing crazy about this dream at all: the king who disappears to become a beggar is a fable which charms because it involves a sacrifice of power. Had Harold Wilson 'done a Stonehouse' while Prime Minister, he would be remembered with more affection and certainly more interest. John's problem was precisely that his breakdown had involved no sacrifice at all. He was out of power, out of luck, and out of money, and his desire to play chess and listen to jazz in Melbourne while living modestly with Sheila Buckley made all-too-perfect sense.

What nobody heeded was the fact that John had no crime to run away from: on the contrary, his only crimes were committed in order to run away. The passport forgeries, the £29,000 taken from his one-man company for his expenses, the insurance policies taken out to console his unwitting wife – these were crimes committed in the course of fleeing from his middle-class English existence. But why? There would have been no great difficulty about leaving his wife for Sheila, his bankers would never have forced an MP into bankruptcy and his creditors would have compromised. The genuine mystery was why he magnified his run-of-the-mill problems, and behaved as though incurring comparatively minor debts was equivalent to committing great train robberies. I had no doubt that he was mentally disordered, that his illness was triggered by mild reverses, and that it combined with a natural arrogance and self-regard to produce a state of mind which paid little or no attention to whether his behaviour was criminal. The only two problems with this analysis were (1) how did that make him different from other politicians, and (2) how could a sufferer from this form of mental illness expect to be acquitted for crafty forgery and meticulously calculated fraud?

Orthodox psychiatry offered no helpful answers, so I consulted R D Laing on the subject of my client's divided self. Much of Laing's work is controversial, although it always seemed to me that he advanced our knowledge of mental health at least by one insight, namely that the people we diagnose as paranoid usually do have something to fear. Ronnie had a dour sense of humour. His first report, after meeting Stonehouse, was written in question and answer form thus:

Question: Is his account of his mental breakdown plausible to you as a psychiatrist?
Answer: Yes.
Question: Can you say for certain whether he is lying or not?
Answer: No.

I pressed the guru for more details. How should ordinary psychiatrists describe my client? R D became more expansive:

Everyone perhaps has a breaking point. The term for this in psychiatry is a *reactive psychosis*. The mind temporarily 'boggles', the

person 'cracks' in two or three, or even more, into multiple pieces –
and dissociation, splitting, disintegration of the personality occurs.
A man in public life begins to feel desperately trapped by the life he
is in, and he reacts by acting out a weird death–rebirth fantasy.

That was the closest we came to a defence. John had passed
through some kind of 'fugue' – a journey of conscious abnormality,
driven by self-interest ('he never thought of us for a minute,' said
Barbara later), in which rules were things that applied to others; he
was not in a mental state which could be described as dishonest,
because he honestly believed that *he* could do no wrong. How, I
asked Laing, could this 'fugue' condition in Mr Stonehouse be
distinguished from that frequently encountered in other politicians
caught in law-breaking, for example Richard Nixon? 'It could not
be so distinguished,' came the answer. I reported these revelatory
developments in political psychiatry to Dick, whose reaction left
me with the distinct impression that he would leave his junior to
present this part of the defence case.

We had both been working for months on its preparation and
were deep in conference with our client on the day before the trial
was scheduled to commence, when a telephone call came through
to Dick's chambers. It was from Sheila Buckley's QC, who had
heard on the midday news that we had been sacked, and that John
had decided to defend himself. Thunderstruck, Dick repeated this
information and asked Stonehouse whether it was true. John
confirmed that it was, and actually apologised (I had never heard
him apologise before) for not telling us. There was nothing to be
done, except to tie pink tape around our briefs and wish him luck
on the morrow, when he would stand alone before a difficult judge
and a jury hugely prejudiced against him.

It was three months before I saw John again. This time, it was in
the cells beneath the Old Bailey, whence his solicitor had summoned me as the 'guilty' verdicts began to roll in. Irrepressible as
ever, he was already contemplating his appeal, for which I was re-
hired. Incredibly, he had written a 230-page book while defending
himself: it was entitled *My Trial*, and subtitled *My blow-by-blow
account and psychological reaction to trial and verdict – from the Old
Bailey dock*. It did not become a best-seller, but it was certainly a
first and probably a last. From all accounts except his own, John's

trial had been a sad affair, as he floundered in technical legal submissions in front of a disgruntled judge undisposed to help him. He had been permitted to call R D Laing and other expert witnesses as to his psychiatric state, but he had mishandled their questioning. (The noble art of self-defence is not appropriate where that defence depends on psychiatry. An accused eliciting sympathy for himself – 'Tell me, why am I mentally ill?' – is not a convincing sight.)

In one respect, the Stonehouse trial *was* unfair. The judge withdrew his bail at the close of the prosecution case, just before he was to go into the witness box in his own defence. This practice of 'no bail after half-time' was common in the seventies, and meant that the defendant was suddenly thrown into prison – with its inevitable sleeplessness and disorientation – at the very time when he needed all his wits about him. John had planned to go into the witness box, but after a night in prison he changed his mind and chose an alternative course known as making a 'dock statement'. Defendants who adopted this course normally did so because they had something to hide which they did not want to emerge in cross-examination. Instead, they would stand up in the dock and make a short speech asserting little more than their innocence. But Stonehouse used the dock as a platform for no fewer than six days – thirty hours in length, his was the longest dock statement in history. The judge who suffered it was later appointed to the Royal Commission on Criminal Procedure where he lobbied enthusiastically for its abolition. In due course he prevailed, and the ancient right to make a dock statement was extinguished by legislation. John Stonehouse had filibustered it out of existence.

In another respect, however, the Stonehouse proceedings became a bedrock of the law which protects the liberty of the subject. This came in the ultimate appeal decision by the House of Lords. The judge had been so convinced of Stonehouse's guilt on the charge which the magistrate had dismissed, of attempting to obtain insurance moneys by deception, that he had not only permitted the prosecution to reinstate it but directed the jury that Stonehouse's disappearing act in Miami was enough to constitute an 'attempt' and they had no choice but to convict, despite his plea of 'not guilty'. It had been a hallowed but vulnerable tradition of English law that the jury, and the jury alone, must be left to decide the facts: no matter how damning these are, the judge should never make their minds up for them by directing a conviction. By the narrowest majority – three votes to two – the Law Lords embedded more firmly in the common law the great principle that the jury are entitled to acquit, irrespective of how strong the prosecution evidence is. Thanks now to 'the rule in *Stonehouse*', a judge is not permitted, no matter how guilty the defendant appears on the facts, to direct the jury to convict.

This remains the most significant feature of English criminal law. It makes every trial a game, in the sense that there can be no certainty about conviction, because the judge cannot tell the jury what conclusion must be drawn from the evidence, however screamingly obvious one conclusion may seem to be. There is still something to play for, a possibility of acquittal because the law is bad or the defendant is sympathetic or the police have abused their powers. In politically motivated prosecutions judges provide the first level of protection: should they fail by overdue deference to the State, there is still the 'gang of twelve' which has the power to cause an upset. As a lawyer, I do not want such upsets to occur: it is the *possibility* that they will which makes the law (and those who practise it) acceptable.

The rule in *Stonehouse* still applies in every court where juries sit, with their constitutional entitlement to bring what the dissenting Law Lords called 'a perverse verdict' but which (even when I sit as a judge) I prefer to think of as a 'sympathy acquittal'. Clive Ponting, who supplied an MP with classified information about the sinking of the *Belgrano*, was prosecuted under the catch-all provisions of the Official Secrets Act: they did not catch *him*, because of the rule in *Stonehouse*. This verdict discouraged the Thatcher government from prosecuting more of its political enemies. But in 1990, 106 Tory MPs demanded the prosecution of Pat Pottle and Michael Randle, who had been suspected since 1970 of helping George Blake to escape from prison. I knew they were guilty – if only because they had just published a book entitled *The Blake Escape – How We Freed George Blake And Why*. So when my legal argument about the unfairness of such a long-delayed prosecution failed, I had to wish them luck and withdraw from the case – I could not ethically invite the jury to ignore a law I was sworn to uphold. Pat and Michael defended themselves and invited the jury to acquit (which it did), as a protest against the staleness of their crime and the political motive behind their delayed prosecution. In this way the rule in *Stonehouse* still ensures that the only enemies of the State who are put in prison are enemies of the people as well.

This was one comfort I took from my time with John Stonehouse. The other was that I had done my best to save him from himself. I have always refused to 'twist the arms' of clients to plead guilty, but in John's case I begged him to take this course for the sake of everyone who loved him. He had asked me to predict his length of sentence, and I told him that if he pleaded 'guilty' and showed some contrition, the punishment would be no more than three years. If he instructed Dick and myself to fight everything, professionally and to the finish, I estimated a maximum sentence of five years or less. 'But if you defend yourself and infuriate the judge, you could get seven.' I rarely make predictions, in case they do not come true: this one did. The judge decided that pride would have its fall, and an over-severe sentence of seven years' imprisonment was imposed and upheld on appeal. The Home Office refused him early parole, although he was the most harmless of inmates, and he died of a heart attack only a few years after his release. Sheila Buckley gave the lie to a lot of the nonsense written about her by reuniting and living with him in this last, broken period of his life. Inspired by the success of another disgraced ex-MP, the briefly debt-ridden Jeffrey Archer, he wrote several novels, but they lacked whatever it is that makes Archer's work sell. I received a Christmas card from him each year until his death. It was always, poignantly, a House of Commons Christmas card.

Chapter 4

Michael X on Death Row

'I'm in favour of abolishing the death penalty,' said the taxi driver to whom I had explained my reasons for visiting the Royal Gaol in Trinidad. My face brightened, until he added 'as soon as they hang Michael X'. It was Michael X I had come to see, and if possible to save. The most vocal black-power prophet in sixties Britain was now dishonoured in his own land, and awaiting execution on death row in Port of Spain. He had been convicted of killing one of his dwindling band of followers, and sentenced in consequence to hang: the Court of Appeal had unhesitatingly confirmed the conviction, and Trinidad's ultimate tribunal – the Privy Council – had found no basis for thinking that justice may have miscarried. That ruling had been delivered in November 1973, just after I qualified to practise. Michael's solicitor in London, Denis Muirhead, felt sure that something more could be done, although he had no funds left to do anything with. My overdraft amounted to an act of faith by my bank, but we both had student memories of the Australian lawyers who had taken every conceivable point to keep their clients alive, in the hope that public and political appetite for capital punishment would weary, as it finally did. Their ingenuity lives on in the law reports, which I read while sitting at Heathrow Airport for three days until a cheap stand-by ticket to Trinidad became available. I could not afford to pay the full fare, and Michael X could have been executed at any moment, while his impoverished lawyer was waiting for someone to cancel their Caribbean holiday.

Lawyers and judges cannot arrogate to themselves the power to abolish capital punishment in countries where it has been established by the will of a democratically elected Parliament. They can either refuse to play any part – by resigning rather than passing death sentences – or they can do their best to minimise casualties – if judges, by imposing the most stringent legal safeguards; if barristers, by playing every trick in the textbook to preserve the lives of their clients. Committed death-row lawyers who delay the hangman with last-minute *habeas corpus* appeals and arcane points of law are objects of irritation and alarm to any government trying to arrange a popular execution. They are likened to ingenious tax lawyers whose imaginative avoidance schemes outwit the language of the legislature. But tax lawyers are not philosophically opposed to taxation of the rich, any more than the death-house lawyers are opposed to punishment of the guilty. What the latter are opposed to is punishment by way of human sacrifice. It is their duty to take every point possible, for the sake of their clients and for the sake of countries which progress by the development of constitutional values. So I had no hesitation in ransacking the common law to find some excuse for not hanging Michael X: the problem was that the common law offered very little encouragement.

The common law which applies in the Caribbean Common-wealth is the law which has been made and handed down by English judges over the centuries – judges who were, in the past, the leading advocates of practices such as gibbeting, drawing and quartering, and hanging a dead body in chains, rituals they described as 'bulwarks of the constitution'. Until the abolition of capital punishment in Britain in 1964 the common-law judges, far from thinking up obstacles to execution, had insisted they be carried out as speedily as possible – within six weeks of conviction, even making allowance for appeals. This was to emphasise the deterrent effect of punishment which followed so soon after the exposure of the facts of the crime in court; it was also to ensure that no campaign of sympathy for the criminal had time to build up a head of steam. This unattractive reason was never admitted: it was always made out that swift execution was necessary to avoid the mental torture of a long wait on death row. Given the choice, I would prefer five years on death row to five years of death – but no State should offer that choice to men it has decided, one day, to kill. I first appreciated that when I met Michael X.

On arrival at the Royal Gaol, it was a relief to find that Michael had yet to be executed. I was taken to visit him, in the way that one might be taken by a zoo-keeper to see the rarest specimen in a monkey-house. That is the only possible – because it is the exact – analogy for death row in Trinidad's Royal Gaol. There were thirty men, sweating in the heat, fingers scratching through the wire of their concrete-floored cages, screeching and shouting at each other and at the warders. Each cell was 8' 4" by 5' 10", and contained only a mattress and a slop bucket. In them, the inmates spent twenty-three, often twenty-four, hours of the day, occasionally taken out for exercise in handcuffs. The uncovered light bulb in each cell burned all night. No work of any kind was organised, and education was not allowed: some of the prisoners were obviously mentally disturbed, while others merely raged. Michael alone was quiet and self-contained: close-shaven, wiry, light-skinned (his father was Portuguese), he looked nothing like the black-power revolutionary with face twisted in bitter defiance, a stereotype he had originated for the benefit of the media in Britain a few years before. As I leant against the wire of his cage this solemn, vulnerable member of the living dead explained what would happen.

Death warrants were always read on Thursdays, between 2 p.m. and 4 p.m. The inmates spent those hours in a state of terror, straining to hear the creak of the door through which the prison governor entered when there was a warrant to be proclaimed. He would stride up and down with his folded parchment, sometimes taking a small sadistic pleasure in stopping in front of one man whom he would torture for a moment merely by clearing his throat, and then moving across to the cage of the actual victim, where he unravelled his scroll and announced: 'In the name of Queen Elizabeth the Second by the Grace of God of Great Britain, Northern Ireland and the British Dominions beyond the seas Queen, Defender of the Faith, Greetings!'

Following this grotesque salutation from the monarch, the condemned man heard a good deal of archaic language to the effect that someone bearing his name ('the said man') must be hanged by the neck until he be dead, the execution of which remains to be done, but shall be done the following Tuesday, at 7 a.m., at the usual place of execution (a large room separated from death row only by a door). At the end of this sonorous declamation came the good news: Her Majesty had graciously allowed the condemned wretch twenty-four Trinidad dollars (about £5) to order the final meal of his choice – provided he ordered it then and there. Since a man who has just been told he will hang by the neck until he is dead is hardly in the mood to contemplate a menu, the royal largesse was usually spent on ice-cream.

From the reading of the warrant on Thursday afternoon to the breaking of the cervical vertebrae on Tuesday morning, the routine was fixed. Each day, the prisoner was weighed and measured, to enable the length of the drop to be calculated exactly so that the noose would break the neck rather than decapitate. The rope, imported from a firm in Birmingham, came packaged specially with the desired weight range for its human recipient printed on the box. (The rope was never used twice: after it performed its function, it was thoughtfully sent to the Royal Trinidad Blind Society, whose members used the sisal for weaving.) On Saturday the gallows were moved into position, and the trapdoor greased and tested: everyone on death row, including the man who was to fall through it, could hear the trap open. On Sunday the executioner came, to eye his victim and check his apparatus: he was paid the equivalent of fifteen English guineas. Monday evening brought the family for a last fifteen-minute visit during which they were not allowed to touch the loved one they would lose at dawn. Other prisoners in the cramped row endured the ordeal as relatives wailed, screamed and sometimes had to be carried out on stretchers. The hangman and the priest would arrive at midnight, and at 5.30 a.m. a dozen government officials attended as witnesses: they watched as the prisoner was led, naked, to take his last bath, then dressed in a clean white gown, soon to be stained with his bodily fluids. A white pointed hood was placed over his head, which made him look like a Ku Klux Klansman as he walked to a cell opposite the gallows for a final tranquillising prayer with the priest. He did not see the guards behind, who dragged him across the narrow corridor of death row to the gallows-room, and strung him up.

'We hear the flying of the trap – we hear it distinctly,' Michael told me, with emphasis. The rest is not silence: on death row the screaming rage begins again, at the loss of a fellow inmate whose body the meanwhile twists slowly to and fro, suspended through the open trapdoor. Around it, the official party has tea and a cooked breakfast for a macabre sixty minutes, at the end of which the body will be cut down and taken to the prison hospital for a last, secret, degradation – an orderly will slash the wrists and the tendons of the feet. Nobody quite knows why. The prison chaplain told me it was a local ritual symbolic of the 'quartering' which took place in the olden days of 'hanging, drawing, and quartering'. By this time a black flag has been hoist atop the prison gates. The body must be hastily buried in the prison grounds and the law is very particular about this: on no account may it be handed over to the family for burial. The reason lies in the British obsession with keeping awkward facts secret: the practice was insisted upon by an official commission when it realised that 'hanging . . . leaves the body with the neck elongated'. In Jamaica, they had found a more pragmatic reason for burying all their executed felons in the kitchen garden at St Catherine's Prison – it made the vegetables grow. (The former practice of communal burial in quicklime was discontinued throughout the Empire after the First World War: it had meant that when the British government returned the remains of Sir Roger Casement from Pentonville graveyard for a hero's burial in Dublin, many of the bones belonged to Dr Crippen.)

Michael discussed all this, softly and carefully, as if an observer at his own ritual slaughter. A paranoid schizophrenic trait, but as R D Laing might point out, who would not be paranoid in these circumstances? His brow was furrowed, there was fear and pleading in his eyes. There must, I thought, have been fear in Joe Skerritt's eyes, too, when this man hacked at him with a cutlass. Afterwards, when Michael X ran from arrest into the jungle of Guyana, he might justifiably have been felled with all his sins upon him. He was now a different man: four years on, the man whom the State of Trinidad planned to kill was not the same man who with angry calculation had killed another.

He now cared about others, for a start. He explained the obscene rituals of death row, and in return I explained to him how the law as I understood it applied to these facts. Trinidad has a constitution, bequeathed by the British on its independence, which protects its citizens against the infliction of 'cruel or inhuman treatment or punishment'. It also preserved the death penalty, but said nothing about how it should be carried out. It was obvious, at least obvious to me while standing on death row, that any significant period of time spent here was the cruellest of punishments.

It follows that if a State is to inflict capital punishment without unnecessary cruelty, it must do so as speedily as possible, or else abandon its efforts. Michael heard me extemporise this constitutional theory and then put a finger to his lips. 'Stop and listen. Just listen. This place is always full of noise. But listen now . . .' When I stopped listening to the sound of my own voice, I realised there was total silence. Turning, I saw that every man in that prison was pressed against the wire of his cage, leaning towards us and straining to hear. Michael smiled, for the only time during our meeting. 'You see – for them you represent hope. Their only hope. That's why they are holding on to every word you say, even though they don't understand them. But they know that if you do this case for me, it will help them. That's why you should do it, not for me but for them. They will hang me, whatever happens.'

When *The Guardian* ran a retrospective on Michael X in 1993, Darcus Howe (who had fallen out with him in the sixties) remained unforgiving: 'He made absolutely no impact on anybody.' He made an impact on me in December 1973, sufficient to make me devote a lot of spare time to realising the hope he had challenged me for kindling on that day. It took twenty years.

Michael X was the token black on board the carnival float of sex, drugs and rock 'n' roll which careened through Britain in the sixties. He is there, in the official portrait of that gypsy caravanserai on the cover of *Sergeant Pepper's Lonely Hearts Club Band*. Like so many on this particular bandwagon, he lacked a message that could sustain momentum after the first profiles in the Sunday papers. He was the half-caste son of a Barbadian woman and a Portuguese shop-keeper named de Freitas, who brought him up in Port of Spain, but after a spell as a seaman he jumped ship in Liverpool to graft a living in London as an 'enforcer' for the Notting Hill slum landlord Peter Rachman. He was not quite the ogre in these years that some of his biographers have made out: he helped to expose Rachman (which took some courage), attacked the corruption and irrelevance of high-living High Commissioners from Caribbean countries and tried to apply the 'black power' rhetoric from America to the conditions of the new urban ghettos of London and Birmingham. His approach was derivative, but useful nonetheless in raising the awareness of white liberals to the racial discrimination that black immigrants had been suffering in comparative silence. His name – Michael X – was not a breach of Malcolm's copyright so much as a legitimate bequest. When Malcolm X came to Britain he met and conversed with Michael de Freitas, and invited him to stay the night with him at a Birmingham hotel. 'My name's Malcolm X,' he said to the receptionist. 'I want a room for myself, and another for my brother Michael.' She deduced from this that Malcolm X's brother Michael must be Michael X. He liked the look of it in the hotel register, and used it thereafter, until it was taken away at the same time as his life: the law reports remember him only as *de Freitas v Attorney General of Trinidad and Tobago*.

Michael gave the media what they wanted: he played the uppity nigger with a soul on ice. Filling in at the làst moment for Stokely Carmichael, he addressed some wild rhetoric ('If you ever see a white laying hands on a black woman, kill him immediately') to a small meeting in Reading – thirty blacks and as many whites, mainly journalists hoping to make a story out of Stokely. Instead, they made one out of Michael's 'Bitter Attack on Whites' (*The Times*). The government panicked: Home Secretary Roy Jenkins announced that the presence in Britain of American black-power leaders would not be 'conducive to the public good' and they would henceforth be banned: as a reprisal for standing in for Carmichael at Reading, Michael would be the first person prosecuted for the crime of 'inciting racial hatred' created by the Race Relations Act of 1968.

Michael X became a martyr to the good intentions of his time. The crime, for which he served a full year in prison, was created to discourage white racists who had daubed 'If you want a nigger for your neighbour, vote Labour' on the hoardings during the Smethwick election campaign in 1964. It was hypocritical to use it first to deter blacks from speaking out, especially at a time when the lethal hate speech of Enoch Powell ('I seem to see the river Tiber foaming with much blood') escaped prosecution because of its classical allusions. On leaving prison Michael wrote heavy-handedly for the underground press, lent his name to fashionable causes (he was a signatory to *The Times* advertisement calling for the legalisation of cannabis) and raised enough money to found the 'Black House' – a black-consciousness commune in Islington. He was a hustler and a poseur: at best a provocateur who dared society to do something about its endemic racism before too many others began to talk like him and before anyone began to act the way he talked. He was, in other words, one minor reason behind the passage of the 1976 Race Relations Act and the establishment of the Commission for Racial Equality. He was hyped up by hubris (André Deutsch published his autobiography), by familiarity with the famous (John Lennon, Muhammad Ali and Dick Gregory lent their names to his projects) and by constant media attention. He came to believe he really was a leader, because the press said so, and he looked for a country to lead. The luckless prize was Trinidad, land of his birth.

Self-government had been bestowed on Caribbean islands by Britain in the sixties, and they had not flourished under it. Trinidad had some oil wealth which it notably failed to share with its people: in 1970, the government came under serious attack from labour unions and suffered a rebellion in the army. The time seemed propitious for Michael to put his 'black power' preaching into practice so he returned in style, with some money and retinue left over from the 'Black House', and leased a country estate just outside Port of Spain. But his soul politics cut no ice with Trinidad's tough Prime Minister and his hard-bitten left-wing opponents, and he signally failed to attract the country's apolitical youth with his confused philosophy of hard manual work and Islamic ablutions. Brief visits from John Lennon and Muhammad Ali made him a curiosity, but nothing more. By 1973 his commune at Christina Gardens was in financial and intellectual distress – his power trip was going nowhere.

What happened next is the subject of several books, none of them convincing because they mainly rely on witnesses who incriminated Michael de Freitas in order to save their own necks. I did not talk much to him about the killings at Christina Gardens – he had some criticisms of his trial, but no fresh evidence had emerged to cast real doubt upon his responsibility. He was, after all, the chief, with a few lieutenants recruited from 'black power' sects in the US. Their followers were some wide-eyed locals, and Gale Benson. She had stepped off the Kings Road into an adoring relationship with Hakim Jamal, a black Muslim from Boston who had hitched himself to Michael, but her father was a former Tory

MP so the English press portrayed her murder as if it were an horrific warning against miscegenation. In fact, her killing defies rational explanation. The lieutenants simply dug a pit one morning, beckoned her over, stabbed her mercilessly (while she pleaded 'What have I done to deserve this?') and then covered her writhing body with compost. Michael and Hakim, meanwhile, were off on an alibi tour of the island. In the paranoia that descends on portentous people as they come to recognise their own irrelevance, Gale was suspected of being an MI6 agent, foiling their fantastic schemes for black liberation. She came to be blamed for their lack of success, money, and support. Her killing was both brutal and cowardly, and all the Muslim purification rituals Michael X religiously underwent could not wash her blood from his hands, even though he was miles away at the time it was shed.

The sacrifice of Gale Benson brought no change in luck. A hanger-on named Joe Skerritt, a distant cousin of Michael's, heard about Gale's death and threatened to blackmail them, demanding money for not going to the police. So Skerritt met the same fate, this time at Michael's own hands. He was lured to his grave, dug to the clay six feet below, on the pretext that they were making a run-off for the sewage. Michael produced a cutlass, and stabbed him ferociously: he died choking on his threat – 'I go tell, I go tell'. This time, lettuce was planted above him – a fatal mistake, as it later turned out, when a policeman experienced at growing vegetables noticed the clay that had been dug out and wondered why it had been necessary to dig so deep merely for a lettuce patch. Had Michael planted trees instead, he might have eluded justice. He flew to Guyana, and was there when the bodies were discovered. He ran, quite literally, into the jungle, where he was arrested several days into a trek to Brazil.

Brought back in chains, Michael X became the cancer that the good people of Trinidad wanted cut out of their society. The most lurid stories were published: he was a devil worshipper, an obeah man, he had drunk blood before Gale's murder, he was plotting an armed revolution with the help of Algeria. In Britain, the *News of the World* headlined him as 'Michael X – the Devil on Death Row'. The Trinidad government, sensitive to the bad image he had brought to the nation, was determined to see him hanged – its Attorney General personally prosecuted and offered immunities to associates who would testify against him. The most popular calypso at that year's Carnival – 'One to Hang' – captured the Port of Spain mood. In this atmosphere, Michael felt he would not find a defender in Trinidad, so he hired the barrister from another island who had telegrammed him, 'The best lawyer in the Caribbean is prepared to defend you. I have never lost a murder trial.' (This part was true, because he had never appeared in one before.) It was an impossible task. Michael had no defence strategy, and did not even give evidence – a rambling statement from the dock, alleging a conspiracy to tell lies against him, did nothing to refute the charge that he had murdered Skerritt. On 21 August 1972, Michael X was found guilty of Skerritt's murder. The judge pronounced the only sentence provided by law, that he be hanged by the neck until he was dead. He waved to the crowd outside the courthouse as he was driven to death row, but they had gathered to cheer his departure, not from the court, but from the world.

Any prospect of preventing that departure was extinguished by the conduct of William Kunstler, the American 'radical lawyer' who had defended the Chicago conspirators. He turned up at the Trinidad Hilton for a press conference at which he announced that Michael's appeal would be safe in his famous hands. Michael, he explained, was an innocent victim of an oppressive and frightened establishment, like his other clients Bobby Seale, Abbie Hoffman, Malcolm X, and Stokely Carmichael. The trial had been unfair and he could prove it – after all, as he said, 'I only defend those I love'. Much as I have admired the work of some 'movement' lawyers (notably that of the late Leonard Boudin) in defending victims of McCarthyism and Nixonism, within a system which requires defenders to fight for their clients as much in the media as in the courts, I was never able to stomach Kunstler's egomaniacal credo. I do not, as a rule, love my clients: I serve them better by doing something more difficult, namely by suspending any personal judgment and committing a tranche of my life to establishing their presumed innocence or (if that is not possible) to explaining sympathetically the reason for their guilt. Love, in law as in life, gets in the way of sound judgment – it leads to tactical errors, to over-emotional arguments and, most dangerously, to lies.

That was the worst feature of the 'International Committee to

Save Michael X' which formed around Kunstler in 1973, starring Kate Millett ('It's the hideous combination of racism and sexism that allows these trials to happen,' she wrote), Gloria Steinem, Leonard Cohen, Judy Collins, William Burroughs, Dick Gregory, and John and Yoko. They were well intentioned, but the publicity issued under their names was riddled with factual errors and derisively dismissed in Trinidad, where the truth did matter. The only truth which could save Michael related to the manner of his execution, not to the clouding of his responsibility for Skerritt's death. I found Kunstler's behaviour offensive because it was so arrogant: the white celebrity lawyer, parachuting in to tell the dumb local blacks that they could not hold a fair trial if they tried. It is a common error, made by Western lawyers who think they know all about human rights, to descend on developing countries shooting from the lip before getting the facts straight. It was Kunstler's press conferences at the Trinidad Hilton which had convinced my Port of Spain taxi-driver that Michael was 'one to hang'.

By the time I arrived in Trinidad, these antics had so poisoned public opinion that there was no prospect that the 'mercy committee' – a group of political appointees which advises the government whether particular death sentences should be commuted – would recommend mercy for Michael. He had been convicted in August 1972; his appeal had not been dismissed until April 1973. The Privy Council turned down his application for a further appeal on 26 November 1973. At Christmas I reported to Denis Muirhead that there was a realistic constitutional argument to be made on Michael's behalf, namely that the sixteen months he had by now spent on death row constituted inhuman punishment. There was no legal aid to make it, but Louis Blom-Cooper QC was prepared to argue for free in the Trinidad courts, especially if the hearing dates could be fixed to coincide with test cricket matches. Fortunately they could, and the money for expenses, air-fares and (always the greatest burden) paying the other side's costs was provided by John Lennon, who donated the white piano on which he had composed some songs for *Sergeant Pepper*. Predictably, our motion was dismissed by the Trinidad courts, and in due course reached the Privy Council in London, where in April 1975 we made our final bid to save Michael's life.

*

The Privy Council's address is No. 7 Downing Street, a few doors before the house of the Prime Minister. Say the password 'Privy Council' to the policeman guarding the gates, and you will be ushered through them to a hall where the state of the nation's security (black, red, or yellow alert) is posted daily on a board opposite a staircase which leads to a large antechamber where portraits of long-dead Law Lords hang sombrely from the walls. Inside, and cordoned off from rectangular rows of benches occupied by counsel, is a horseshoe-shaped green baize table around which five men in lounge suits are listening, sometimes with ill-concealed impatience, to the bewigged barrister at the centre-stage lectern. One side of the amphitheatre is taken up by rows of law books, the other has high windows overlooking Whitehall. The parade of black taxis and red buses passing Big Ben reminds the visitor that he or she is located, precisely, at the epicentre of what was once the British Empire. What is bizarre, however, is that the concentrated legal minds in this room must all imagine they are in another country. If they look out this window they must see the pitted roads and slum housing of downtown Kingston, or the open sewers of Belize, or the sheep safely grazing in a New Zealand meadow. This is a court which is juris-prudentially orbiting in space, landing one day in Antigua, another in Trinidad, the day after in Brunei. This curious institution is the final court of appeal for some sixteen independent Commonwealth countries. It decides their law (even when, as is the case with Mauritius, their law is French), it interprets their constitutions and it guarantees the human rights of their citizens – often more securely than the same judges, sitting across the road in the House of Lords, can guarantee the rights of British citizens, because Britain, unlike its former colonies, has no written constitution.

Written constitutions, however, are not panaceas for human rights. They are vulnerable both to the cunning of those who draft them and the lack of imagination of those who interpret them. Michael's appeal was vulnerable on both scores. In the first place, we sought to argue that the death penalty was, in itself, a cruel and unusual punishment. We were emboldened to take this position because it was the stance of several judges in the great case of *Furman v Georgia*, recently decided by the US Supreme Court. They fortified our argument that the penalty of death 'is unique,

85

finally, in its absolute renunciation of all that is embodied in our concept of humanity' (Justice Stewart), and that 'the calculated killing of a human being by the State involves, by its very nature, a denial of the executed person's humanity . . . in comparison to all other punishments today [it] is uniquely degrading to human dignity' (Justice Brennan). But the problem which stared us in the face every time we looked at the Trinidad Constitution was that although Section 2 provided that no law shall 'impose or authorise the imposition of cruel or unusual treatment or punishment', Section 3 said 'Section 2 shall not apply in relation to any law that is in force in Trinidad at the commencement of this Constitution'. Trinidad's Constitution commenced at its independence in 1962, when death by hanging was in full swing under colonial law. In other words, what the draftsman gave with one hand in Section 2 – namely protection from inhumane treatment – he took away in Section 3, so far as the death sentence was concerned. This is the case in almost every 'Westminster model' constitution bequeathed by Britain to its former colonies. They include a Bill of Rights with its standard guarantee against inhuman punishment, but by one formula or another they slyly preserve punishments (such as whipping and hanging) which were lawful under the British colonial administration. The task that was to preoccupy me, on and off for almost twenty years, was to find a satisfactory legal way around this constitutional blockage.

The first argument which occurred was to deploy the Bill of Rights of 1688, a meagre measure which mainly protects the rights of parliamentarians, but which does prohibit the infliction of cruel and unusual punishments. Like other British laws, it was part of the law of the colony at the time of independence, and so was 'preserved' by the constitution in the same way as the law which prescribed hanging as the mandatory punishment for murder. Might one colonial law cancel the other out? The problem was that in 1688 death by hanging was not perceived as cruel, and was by no means unusual. The phrase originated from popular outrage at the treatment of Titus Oates, who was sentenced by the infamous Judge Jeffreys to life imprisonment as well as to whipping, pillorying and defrocking, for the crime of perjury in what was perceived to be a good (i.e. anti-Catholic) cause. This sentence was regarded both as 'cruel' (in the sense of over-severe) and 'unusual' (in the sense of 'unbecoming' or 'inappropriate'). Notwithstanding the barbarity of 1688, we argued that these words meant 'unbecoming to human dignity', a phrase which applied to hangings as described by a prison warden who had seen many:

> When the trap springs the prisoner dangles at the end of the rope. There are times when the neck has not been broken and the prisoner strangles to death. His eyes pop almost out of his head, his tongue swells and protrudes from his mouth, his neck may be broken, and the rope many times takes large portions of skin and flesh from the side of the face that the noose is on. He urinates, he defecates, and droppings fall to the floor while witnesses look on . . . A prison guard stands at the feet of the hanged person and holds the body steady, because during the first few minutes there is usually considerable struggling in an effort to breathe.

There may come a time when lawyers who read such descriptions are prepared to say, without rhetorical flourish or bothering to search for precedent, that by any standard of 'human rights' this is treatment by the State which irretrievably violates them. Even in America that time may come, probably when executions are televised and attract such ratings that the nation will only suppress this bread and circus barbarity by abolishing capital punishment. But in 1975, any appeal to human rights principles was regarded as the last resort of a desperate advocate, and it proved impossible even to begin to persuade five Law Lords that these death sentence rituals, in which they had themselves participated in Britain only a decade previously, were indecent and inhuman. Society does not progress quite so quickly.

The main plank of our argument was that a prolonged stay on death row amounted to cruel and unusual treatment, contrary both to the Bill of Rights and to Section 2 of the Constitution. We pointed out that in Britain execution had always been carried out quickly – the period between conviction, appeal, rejection of mercy petitions and execution averaged only six weeks. In Trinidad, prior to independence, the equivalent delay (even with an appeal to the Privy Council in London) averaged five months: by now it had risen to two years or upwards. We cited eminent psychologists, whose work united in describing death row as a 'grisly laboratory, the ultimate experimental stress, in which the condemned prisoner's personality is incredibly brutalised'. But this argument, too, came up against a glib judicial logic: if death row was a place of torture, why was Michael de Freitas so reluctant to be put out of his misery? He had delayed his death for sixteen months by appealing his conviction, and then extended his suffering for another sixteen months by taking these constitutional proceedings. The judges quite understood how a prisoner who wanted to go quietly and quickly to the scaffold might have cause for complaint if the State did not get around to executing him. He might even be entitled to bring a legal action *demanding* to be put to death. But he certainly could not complain about what the judges termed 'self-induced delay' caused by his own actions in appealing or in bringing constitutional motions like this one. It took two decades before the Privy Council saw the light, shone by Lord Scarman: 'It is no answer to say that the man will struggle to stay alive. In truth, it is this ineradicable human desire which makes prolongation inhuman and degrading.'

The case was listed for May 1975. I was led by Louis Blom-Cooper, a remarkable institution in the Temple. The door to his room was always open, where his clever mind was available to young barristers: after a session with Louis, you came away emboldened to argue the impossible (until you were on your feet making the attempt). But the Michael X hearing was an intro-duction to the Privy Council's attitude to human rights as brutal as Garfield Barwick's after-dinner stories. Louis argued valiantly, but he stood at the lectern like a condemned man in front of a firing squad before crumpling to his seat. Lord Diplock, the most accurate hitman, needed no help from the other side: he motioned the usher for the fatal card from which the presiding judge read: 'Their Lordships need not trouble the respondents, and will humbly advise Her Majesty that the appeal should be dismissed for reasons to be delivered later'.

Translated into ordinary English, this formula means that the appellant's case is so hopeless that the State need not bother to answer it. We had lost, as the judgment would in due course confirm, and Michael was once again liable to execution. Denis, Louis and I trooped along Whitehall, talking of our next trick. It was the last, and the lowest, card in the death-row defender's hand:

an application to the court to stay the hanging of our client until it was established that he was sane. Such humanity as may be found in the common law decrees that the only humans who cannot be hanged are women while they are pregnant, and lunatics until they recover their wits. This latter exception was established centuries ago, by judges who had no compunction in burning witches, but drew the line at hanging village idiots. As one Chief Justice, Edward Coke, put it: 'The execution of the offender is for example, but so it is not when a madman is executed; that should be a miserable spectacle, both against law, and of extreme inhumanity and cruelty, and be not an example to others'.

For all the craziness of the killings at Christina Gardens, and the paranoid symptoms Michael had exhibited to prison visitors, nobody had thought to check on his sanity. The Trinidad government had refused point-blank our request to permit a psychiatrist to see him, so our final hope was to ask the courts to stay his execution until this avenue was explored. The prison authorities claimed there was no evidence of mental disorder, thereby ignoring (as V S Naipaul later put it in *The Killings in Trinidad*) the obvious evidence of his life, of 'a man led to lunacy by all the ideas he had been given of who he was'. I had no hesitation in raising this issue and nor did Michael, although we knew it would be unwelcome to Kunstler and the 'International Committee to Save Michael X', whose crusade was predicated on the proposition that he was a perfectly sane 'political prisoner'. We needed time to prepare and file a new constitutional motion and believed we would have it – the Privy Council always took months before delivering its judgments, which had to be drafted, agreed by five separate judges, and then printed before being formally handed down. But we reckoned without the irony: our argument about delay, which Lord Diplock derided as hopeless, had sufficient impact for him to write the judgment immediately, and for it to be agreed and handed down in record time, just two weeks later.

That day of judgment – Thursday, 15 May – passed without incident in Trinidad. My call from London that evening to Michael's Port of Spain solicitor established that no death warrant had been read to him that afternoon for his execution the following Tuesday. He assured me we had at least a week, until the next

Thursday, before the execution countdown could commence. I had the weekend to draft the fresh constitutional motion to stay the execution and force a proper inquiry into Michael's sanity. The papers would arrive in Trinidad by courier on Tuesday (such was legal life before the advent of the fax machine) and would be filed in court on Wednesday.

Down on death row Michael too assumed he was safe for another week. But the death penalty brutalises all involved in it, including the State and its high officials. This time, the government was taking no chances. Disgracefully, it prevailed upon the Governor General to sign a warrant on Monday evening for Michael's execution a few hours later – before dawn the next morning. This warrant was rushed to the Royal Gaol, where it was read to Michael at 9 p.m. There was no time for the traditional last meal, let alone for any last-minute legal action: the Court Registry was closed at night, his lawyers were off-duty and he was not permitted to call them; my draft papers would arrive a few hours after his death. John Lennon's piano gave out no final tinkle, and Michael X was rushed to the gallows just as he had predicted, wearing the white robe and the Ku Klux Klan-style hood. Reports of his death say that he went quietly. Condemned men usually do, overpowered by the sense of relief of getting it finally over. (Albert Pierrepont, who hanged hundreds, could recall only one who struggled at the end, 'and he was a German'.) I would have preferred him to kick and scratch and curse the flunkies about to breakfast around his twisting corpse, because I believe that of all the wasteful acts of violence done in this world, the time and money and imagination invested in despatching prisoners out of it tops the bill. But the dead man walked, leaving his lawyer to keep the promise made that day in his cage on death row, when silence fell.

I believed that the argument made in Michael X's case was correct: the problem was that it had been made in *his* case. If the law is to be advanced through test-cases, the advocate's first task is to select one with a set of facts most likely to pass the test. In 1980 I flew to Jamaica to meet some like-minded local lawyers, Denis Daley and Lloyd Barnett, and together we planned another approach to the Privy Council. Five inmates were selected, all of whom had been left on death row for *five years* after the rejection of their final appeal. It could not be said of them (as of Michael) that they had delayed their own deaths by taking legal actions, because the delay in executing them had been caused by Michael Manley's government, which placed a moratorium on capital punishment while it was the subject of a commission of inquiry. Noel Riley and the four other appellants were courageous in lending their names to this appeal. It is an unhappy fact of life on death row that the best way to save your neck is to keep your head down: those selected for execution tend to be those who irritate the State by suing it. Once again, the argument would be that the constitution, which in Jamaica prohibited the infliction of 'inhuman or degrading punishment or other treatment' was infringed by keeping these men in death-row conditions for an unjustifiably prolonged period. The death-row chaplain testified to their 'frightened, animal-like reaction' when the warrants were read to them after the four-year delay, while two leading psychiatrists confirmed that all five appellants had 'clinical features of psychological disturbances related in a causative way to the mental stresses they have undergone during the time they have been under sentence of death . . . the most prominent clinical features were those of anxiety and feelings of alternating hope and despair'.

The case of *Noel Riley and others v Attorney General of Jamaica* was dismissed in the local courts, which relied on the decision in Michael X's case. I applied successfully to the Privy Council for leave to have the point re-argued, and this was done by the Jamaican lawyers at a hearing in 1981 which lasted just half a day. It was chiefly remarkable for the presence of Lord Scarman, who had a clear grasp of human rights principles, and who could not approve of leaving anyone – black or white – in degrading and inhumane conditions for five years. Could he persuade his colleagues? Behind the scenes the five judges were diametrically divided. Eventually, three of them declared that the State could execute whenever and in any way it wished, and could keep inmates on death row for as long as it liked, provided it did not use a crueller method than hanging (such as burning at the stake). Lord Scarman and a colleague eloquently dissented, but the Jamaican government rushed Noel Riley and his co-appellants to the gallows to 'serve them right' for bringing the case. They were followed over the next four years by eighty others.

In the justice game, losing by 3–2 is as bad as 5–nil. The catastrophic result of *Riley* was to remove all constitutional inhibitions on cruel treatment of death-row inmates in countries throughout the British Commonwealth. Condemned men could still petition the Privy Council for leave to appeal their conviction, if they could find a barrister to act for them free of charge in London. This was a miserable business which engaged me through the eighties: you had to scour a haystack of badly photocopied trial transcripts in the hope of finding a legal needle to prick the conscience of the Privy Council. These applications (like executions in Trinidad) took place in Downing Street on Tuesday morning; the barrister had fifteen minutes in which to persuade a panel of three Law Lords that the local courts had taken leave of their senses. These pauper petitions were watched with amazement by barristers from Australia and New Zealand, waiting to resume their lucrative cases concerning oil pipelines and insurance contracts to which the Privy Council devoted most of its time. Yet whenever I visited the Caribbean to urge the abolition of the death penalty because there was no fail-safe system to prevent execution of the innocent, I would receive the explanation: 'There is here. All our murder convictions are approved by the finest judges in the world, sitting in the Privy Council in Downing Street.' This was a cargo-cult view of our fifteen-minute flailings before a Privy Council that behaved like a relic of colonialism: between 1980 and 1987 it quashed only one conviction in a capital case. In this period I wrote editorials for the *Guardian* calling for its abolition: why should the British government make judges available to help the hangmen of the Commonwealth?

I changed my opinion because the Privy Council changed its approach. This curious court lacks a historian to explain its turn towards human rights in the late 1980s. Three influences propelled it in this direction. First, there was the impact of the European Convention on Human Rights, through rulings by the court at Strasbourg critical of the failings of English common law and English judges. These embarrassing but educative decisions provided the intellectual impetus. Then came the disastrous discovery of how justice had miscarried in serious trials: the Birmingham Six and the Guildford Four and all the rest. This was the second influence on the Law Lords: it ended the era of complacency about police behaviour and the infallibility of the adversary system. Greater attention to human rights offered some safeguards against wrongful convictions. Thirdly, in 1989 came the massacre at Tiananmen Square, ordered by a Chinese government which would, in less than a decade, come to rule Hong Kong. Prior to the massacre, the British had shown not the slightest interest in providing a Bill of Rights for Hong Kong: in its aftermath, a Bill was speedily enacted in the expectation that the Privy Council would provide vigorous legal precedents which might restrain the Chinese after the 1997 handover. Since the Privy Council was now expected to act as a human rights court for Hong Kong, it could scarcely adopt a different posture towards its other client states. They could always abolish its jurisdiction over them if they did not like the legal punches it was no longer prepared to pull – Singapore did so as soon as it criticised Lee Kuan Yew's pliant judges for jailing his political opponent, Ben Jeyaretnam. As a result of these influences, and stocked by a new generation of judges, by 1990 the Privy Council started to make constitutional guarantees of human rights mean what they said.

Among the first to benefit from the new approach were five of my clients condemned to death after convictions based on the most unreliable evidence of all – identification by a single eyewitness, after a fleeting glance at the face of the murderer. Jamaican judges had not warned their juries that eyewitness evidence was inherently unreliable and prone to cause wrongful convictions. The Privy Council ruled that this failure was a fundamental error which had made the trials miscarry, and the condemned men were set free. Bernard Simons, Denis Muirhead's partner who now handled most of the pauper petitions, was inspired by this decision to decide the time had come to invite the Privy Council to reconsider in the cases of Michael X and Noel Riley. Our first task was to find a hard case to make good law.

For test-case litigation of this most difficult kind, where a court is being asked not only to make a progressive decision but to make it by overruling its own previous judgments, it is important to select a set of facts which overwhelmingly justifies a *volte face*. We discovered that the Jamaican authorities were trying to execute two men – Earl Pratt and Ivan Morgan – for a murder committed in

1977. By 1993, when their appeal reached the Privy Council, they had spent almost fifteen years on death row – the equivalent of a sentence of life imprisonment. So determined was the State to hang them that its Governor General had on three occasions signed their death warrants, causing their removal to the special 'condemned cell' where they were weighed to ascertain the length of their 'drop' and heard the sounds of the gallows being prepared and tested for their execution. Each time – in 1987, 1988, and 1991 – they were reprieved by last-minute court action, once only forty-five minutes before they were due to hang. It was incredible that the State should persist in its wish to kill them, especially as the murder had not been for gain and there were many mitigating factors. But they had become, like Noel Riley and his colleagues before them, a target for State revenge because of the embarrassment they had caused by asserting their rights: their deaths would serve to discourage others, not from murder, but from taking legal action against the State. Our principal hope in bringing the case was to save the lives of hundreds of prisoners who had languished for years on Commonwealth death rows, but we knew for certain that Earl Pratt and Ivan Morgan would hang if their case was lost.

We did not want any new ruling to be limited to similar cases where the delay was obviously indefensible, i.e. where prisoners had spent more than ten years on death row. If that were the chosen cut-off point, the lives of twenty-three condemned Jamaicans who had by 1993 spent more than a decade in prison would be saved, but it would give the State ample time to execute the several hundred other inmates who had been there for over five years. Our purpose, since we could not abolish executions, was to make them as difficult as possible, in the hope that retentionist governments would eventually conclude that the struggle to hang was not worth the effort. For example, if the period chosen was as short as two years then executions would become virtually impossible, because delays of this length were endemic in the appeal systems of most Commonwealth countries. The Privy Council would have to choose the cut-off point, and my job as advocate was to marshal the arguments in favour of a period as short as possible.

The court had to fix a deadline which would allow a reasonable time for appeal and clemency consideration, yet which would not be so long as to permit the accumulating stress and anxiety to have taken such a toll that the prisoner may be said to have suffered inhuman or degrading treatment. The task, in *Pratt and Morgan*, was to identify that metaphysical moment by a process of reasoning which would make the choice appear neither artificial nor arbitrary. The Privy Council was, after all, making a decision which would mean the difference between life and death for hundreds of men in Trinidad and Jamaica, and in Mauritius and Barbados, and in Hong Kong and Belize: moreover, its ruling would be influential – of 'persuasive authority', albeit not binding – in other Commonwealth countries. The judgment could affect the treatment of thousands of prisoners in the future. It had to be wise and humane, but it also had to be plausible – for those unwise and inhumane States which insist on retaining capital punishment. It could not, in other words, be designed to appeal to progressive thinkers in England or Europe. It had to appeal to regressive thinkers, or at least to those whose thinking had advanced only as far as English penal policy in the late fifties, at a time when these independence constitutions were being drafted. So I had to present a proposal which I privately believed was a contradiction in terms: a civilised way to carry out the death penalty.

There was only one way to do this: to step inside a time machine and to travel back to the days and to the minds of the men who administered the British Empire. They had drafted a Constitution for Jamaica which seemed, at least to the judges in *Riley*'s case, to enshrine the death penalty forever. The key to unlock this inflexible interpretation was to make their assumptions and to follow through their logic. These imperialists thought they were bequeathing their civilisation to the natives. As they packed up at independence, they naturally had misgivings: could the black chaps really be trusted with self-government? Their notion of 'human rights', which they left behind embedded in constitutions, was really meant as a promise, especially to the whites who remained, that the locals would not abuse their new power. Viewed from this perspective, what appeared to be a clause protecting the death penalty from challenge was in fact a clause protecting citizens from suffering execution in any manner which would have been regarded as unseemly or 'just not on' by an Empire loyalist. So I argued that the object of this provision was to preserve the standards of penal administration set by the British Crown as they had evolved by the time of Jamaican independence in 1962. It set out irreducible minimum standards, guaranteeing to the people of the former colony that while their elected representatives might not succeed in raising those standards, they were prohibited by the Constitution from lowering them.

Our research showed that there never had been a delay of more than two years in the carrying out of a death sentence in the history of British colonial administration, in Jamaica or anywhere else. Indeed, when just such a delay had occurred in hanging men convicted of murder in the Gold Coast in 1947, it caused a major scandal in the UK Parliament with Winston Churchill (then leader of the opposition) roundly condemning the 'cat and mousing of men to the scaffold' and the Colonial Secretary promising that it would never happen again. This proved that colonial governors in 1962 would have balked at hanging anyone who, like Earl Pratt or Ivan Morgan, had been convicted fifteen years before. The mistake made by the judges in *Riley* was to infer from the acceptability of hanging a murderer in 1962 that the constitution preserved hanging for all purposes and in any circumstances. But what was in fact preserved was death by hanging *as it had been carried out in 1962*: any cruelty *additional* to the ritual which had by then been settled (e.g. if men were hanged by barbed wire, or in public, or after a prolonged delay) was not constitutionally protected at all. *Riley* was wrong.

It was sad to have to condemn modern black politicians for falling below the standards of decency of white colonialists thirty years before, and ironic to do so by reference not to the barbarity of hanging, but to the barbarity of keeping men waiting before they were hanged. I could truly identify with Portia, her arguments about the quality of mercy having failed (as ours did for Michael X), resorting to a safe, legalistic approach. She upheld the validity of Shylock's contractual right to cut his pound of flesh, so long as he cut not a fraction more or less of the appointed weight, or shed one drop of blood. The Shylocks of Jamaica wanted their pound of flesh, as preserved by the Constitution. Fine, they could have it. Provided they took it as the Constitution required – without an ounce of additional delay, a drop more of cruelty, than was practised by their white masters in 1962 when the Constitution came into force. This was an argument warped in time and logic but not in law: as Shakespeare realised, bad laws can only be circumvented by bad arguments. It is the death penalty, which defies the logic of human rights, which sets the level of the argument.

Having thus swept away *Riley*, the Privy Council could move on to consider the real issue: did a prolonged stay on death row amount to 'inhumane and degrading treatment'? The institution of death row originated in 1752, by 'An Act for Better Preventing the Horrid Crime of Murder': felons had to be placed immediately after conviction in solitary confinement; where they could do no work and receive no visitors other than the priest, their only solace during the ritual preparation for their death. This is the regime which is still followed on Commonwealth death rows, to the extent that condemned men are not allowed to mix with ordinary prisoners, or engage in any form of prison work, or join in educational courses or sports. The death house is a hot-house, in which mental derangement runs riot in doomed men who do not have a kill-by date. Time is measured by the days on which death warrants are read and executed. All minds are concentrated on their own extinction, not by way of contemplation of forgiveness of sin but by the ever-presence of the sordid machinery of despatch: the weighing, the greasing and testing of the trap, the shrouding and the last hooded walk of the fellow inmate. Each execution-time brings a collective terror, a crazed apprehension: some American prisons, for this reason, arrange executions at midnight and show pornographic movies to the other inmates in order that they might masturbate their mental anguish away. It is facile to say, with Lord Diplock in Michael's case, 'while there's life, there's hope': the quality of a life which constantly envisages its end, and emotionally fluctuates between optimism and despair, is so reduced by mental torture that it cannot be permitted to continue, year in and year out. At some point, either the torture or the life must be stopped.

The chief curiosity of this case was why after fifteen years a civilised nation like Jamaica still wanted to kill Earl Pratt and Ivan Morgan. Their execution was urged by the Solicitor General, the Director of Public Prosecutions, the Senior Assistant Attorney General, the Assistant Attorney General, and the Senior Deputy Director of Public Prosecutions, who were all staying for many weeks at one of London's more expensive hotels while arguing that

Jamaica was an impoverished and under-developed country which could not afford the cost of close attention to human rights. Pratt and Morgan should be grateful for the delay in carrying out their sentence – it had prolonged their life, like a remission of cancer in the body of a terminally diseased patient. 'Don't blame us,' these high officials said in effect, 'Jamaica is just a poor country where life is hard and people are vengeful and delay in everything is endemic. Those who commit murder we can execute when we choose and how we choose: the government is merely carrying out the will of the people, the supreme law.'

Kenneth Rattray, the Solicitor General, put the case for non-intervention in Jamaica's domestic affairs as if he were addressing a UN assembly. He was using the sort of arguments which appeal to diplomats, who trade in State prestige and advantage, not in justice. Dressed up in decayed jurisprudence, it was simply a claim that independent countries were not to be held responsible by international bodies for any actions they took, short of genocide, towards their citizens. The argument sounds hollow enough these days at the United Nations: what made it irrelevant was that the Privy Council was not an 'international body' but a court, the highest in Jamaica, sitting off-shore but with a duty – not merely a power – to intervene if the law required. And the law of the Constitution plainly did require, once the error of *Riley*'s case had been exposed. On any view of the meaning of words, it is inhuman and degrading to force a man to contemplate his hanging for fifteen years and then to hang him. This did not, however, deter the Jamaican lawyers: they fastened onto another facile comment made by Lord Diplock in Michael X's case – 'Mercy begins where legal rights end' – and argued that condemned prisoners were, in law, the living dead, mercifully permitted to pace their cages in limbo-land for a few more unmerited years before their sentence was implemented.

Courts should have no truck with such metaphysical nonsense: once it had overruled *Riley*, the Privy Council was free to order that cruelty masquerading as mercy should end at once. And that is what it did. 'Any person of normal sensitivity and compassion', the Privy Council decided, would recognise the emotional and psychological suffering caused during a long stay on death row. The plainest statement was best and Lord Griffith (who twenty-two years before had granted bail to the *Oz* defendants), spoke for all seven judges: 'There is an instinctive revulsion against the prospect of hanging a man after he has been held under sentence of death for many years. What gives rise to this revulsion? The answer can only be our humanity.'

Amen to that. But still St Joan's question – 'How long, O Lord, how long?' – had to be answered, first by refuting the fallacy of the Michael X decision, that 'self-induced' delay – i.e. delay caused by the exercise of rights of appeal – could not be the subject of complaint.

> It is part of the human condition that a condemned man will take every opportunity to save his life through the use of the appellate procedure. If the appellate procedure enables the prisoner to prolong the appellate hearings over a period of years, the fault is to be attributed to the appellate system that permits such delay and not to the prisoner who takes advantage of it.

And so the highest court in the Commonwealth proceeded to extirpate the 'death-row phenomenon' from countries as far flung as Belize and Barbados and Brunei and Mauritius. It decided that any delay of more than two years between conviction and execution might arguably infringe constitutional guarantees against inhumane treatment, and this would certainly be so if the delay continued for a further three years. This result had an immediate and dramatic effect: the lives of 105 condemned prisoners who had languished on death row for more than five years in Jamaica, and sixty more in a comparable situation in Trinidad, were instantly reprieved. For the future, it meant that all men who could hold out on death row for more than two years would have an arguable case for having their sentence commuted: if they could last until five years had elapsed from the date of their conviction, they were entitled to commutation as a legal right. Earl Pratt and Ivan Morgan had gambled with their own fate in allowing us to bring this action, but in the event it saved hundreds of lives as well as their own. It is still saving them, as States usually fail to meet the five-year deadline thanks to their own inadequacies and to the alertness of lawyers locally and in London.

*

An external court like the Privy Council, whose judges are not beholden to local politicians, is a priceless safeguard for citizens of small countries if they are to have an independent protection from abuses of power. This is the best – indeed the only – justification for the continuing jurisdiction of the Privy Council over sovereign States. Insulated from the pressures and politics of island societies, this court can offer an objective scrutiny in the same way that the European Court of Human Rights at Strasbourg affords a remedy to European citizens against abuses of power by their governments. The Privy Council would be less open to the criticism of being a white colonial elephant if more judges from the black Commonwealth were invited to sit alongside the British Law Lords. However, the struggle to protect human rights must make use of whatever instruments are available, and the Privy Council is at present the most potent of these for some sixteen Commonwealth countries. Its judgments are accorded considerable respect in all courts which share English common-law traditions, so its decision in *Pratt and Morgan* will influence the development of humanitarian law in nations as far removed in culture and geography as Kenya, Malaysia, India, and New Guinea. Most significantly, that case throws down a legal gauntlet to the United States.

It is one of the great ironies of our time that the nation to which the world looks for a lead on human rights should be so obsessed with inflicting the death penalty. It is hardly a cure for violent crimes – this escalates most strikingly in those states (notably Texas and Florida) which conduct most executions, variously by firing squad, hanging, gas chambers, electrocution, and lethal injection. No procedure is painless: 'execution glitches' occur in the electric chair, as flesh cooks or the wood flames, and in the quasi-hospital surroundings of the lethal injection theatre as 'execution technicians' struggle to find a workable vein in drug-abused bodies. In this open society, where every act of State must be witnessed by public representatives, a semicircle of politicians, journalists, and prison officials clusters around the one-way mirror into the gas chamber or the electric chair. Some states permit the 'executee' to invite guests, much as a theatre allows its star performers to reserve good seats for friends. (The first prisoner to be executed by lethal injection in Missouri was wheeled centre-stage, to mouth 'I love you' to his wife in the front row before writhing and choking on his last breath.) This is, at least, a more romantic ending than is possible in a gas chamber, and there are operatic depths to death by firing squad, since one of the gunmen – they do not know which – has been issued with a dummy bullet, so that each can entertain the comforting thought that maybe he fired the blank. The ingenuity expended on alleviating individuals from responsibility for killing a fellow human being is touching, if morally futile: all who assist are implicated.

The death penalty does not deter murder. On the contrary, I believe that it tends to increase it by socially sanctioning violent revenge. America is an abiding testament to the objective futility of capital punishment: in the year *Pratt and Morgan* was decided, the country sustained 24,000 murders – a colossal level of deadly violence in a nation which believes that executions will have some effect on reducing it. All the executions in the U.S. can have no conceivable impact other than to contribute to a culture in which violence is perceived as a solution, or at least as an exercise which achieves something. What it has achieved is a perversion of the values of lawyers: prosecutors demand the death penalty with more vigour (and hence more publicity for themselves) as their re-election nears; defenders advise their clients, despite their protestations of innocence, to cop pleas of 'guilty' to second-degree murder in order to avoid the risk of a death sentence; judges owe advancement to their record in refusing stays of execution. You cannot blame politicians for taking actions which court popularity – that is their *raison d'être* – but the reason for the existence of courts is to stop those of their actions which infringe fundamental human rights. American judges, by permitting the execution of juveniles and mentally handicapped persons, have betrayed the very purpose of their office, which is to deny that the will of the people is the supreme law whenever that will inclines to barbarism.

The philosophical advance made by British judges through their decision in *Pratt and Morgan* was that murderers condemned to death did not for that reason lose their quality as human beings. In legal terms, that a constitution guaranteeing fundamental rights to all citizens extended to those on death row as much as it did to those anywhere else: that the condemned prisoner no less than the terminally ill hospital patient is entitled to treatment which comports as much with dignity as their different circumstances allow. Is this capable of striking a transatlantic chord? Antonin Scalia, one of the Supreme Court's most hard-line justices, sat with the Privy Council one morning during the Jamaican government's argument. He left early – I would like to think in disgust, although perhaps he had shopping to do at Harrods.

Attitudes to the death penalty are emotional, and tend to be based on personal experience. Ronald Reagan traced his support for capital punishment to a boyhood on the family ranch, watching his father shooting lame horses in the head. He often boasted about being the first state governor of California to introduce execution by lethal injection: he had just started to use this method down on the farm, and found it much cleaner than in his father's day. My first memory – of anything, come to think of it – is seeing Movie-tone newsreels of the funerals of Ethel and Julius Rosenberg in 1952. She left behind a child of six – my own age – who walked behind the dark box covered with white flowers. By then, Caryl Chessman had been on death row for six years – his execution too, in 1960, moved me on the Movietone news. At university, it struck me that the politicians most anxious to inflict the death penalty were those most keen to risk my life by sending me to fight in Vietnam. By this time, criminology provided ample evidence that capital punishment does not reduce crime, and the briefest acquaintance with the American statistics proved that the death penalty is inflicted unequally, arbitrarily and especially on the poor and the black. But statistics can prove anything or nothing; even were it demonstrated that capital punishment has some deterrent effect, the transient and spiritually crippling satisfaction of revenge cannot justify the setting of a grisly example by a justice system which should be committed to promoting the values of humanity.

I am not opposed to summary execution, in cases of necessity: the gunning down of tyrants, and of armed robbers, hostage-takers and terrorists caught in the act. This is poetic justice, in the simple sense that it serves them right. The mistake is to use the legal system in an attempt to dignify killing by the State. This was Winston Churchill's point, in his much misunderstood argument that Nazi leaders should be taken out and shot rather than put through what he thought would be the charade of trial at

Nuremberg. He feared that any aping of legal proceedings would give them more dignity in their deaths than in their lives. It was the mistake the Rumanians made when they gave the Ceauşescus the mockery of a trial before shooting them: it was necessary to kill them, to avoid their secret police rallying to their cause, but that was a practical political decision, not a just or legal one. The court-approved death penalty is wrong. And a system which is committed to the righting of wrongs cannot be used to perpetuate one.

Capital punishment induces vicious behaviour, not only in prisoners on death row, but in the officials charged with their execution. The deviousness of Michael's hanging, with every detail arranged overnight, out of court hours, in breach of custom and procedure, was one example. The killing of Noel Riley and his co-appellants, not in revenge for their unlawful acts but in revenge for their legal actions, is another. So too was the obsessive determination of Jamaica's Governor, His Excellence the Most Honourable Sir Florizel Augustus Glasspole, to 'cat and mouse' Earl Pratt and Ivan Morgan to the gallows in defiance of international law, courts and standards. And so was the deceit practised on the Privy Council in 1994 by the government of Trinidad, which undertook not to hang Glen Ashby but then strung him up while a court was considering his appeal, a few days before his sentence would have had to be commuted. These are examples plucked from my Caribbean case-book: there are countless others. Behind all the truculence and dishonesty of State officials lies a grim determination to kill – not merely as machines performing the dictates of the court, or as honest executors of the will of the people, but as human beings consumed by a positive wish to take other human life. The saddest thing is the sheer waste of energy on all sides. But in the final analysis there is no new argument to be raised against capital punishment. John Bright said it all in 1850: 'If you wish to teach the people to reverence human life, you must first show that you reverence it yourselves.'

Chapter 5

Ferrets or Skunks? The ABC Trial

The trial which in the seventies had the most impact on law and on politics – certainly on lawyer-politicians, and on that amorphous construct, the State – is recalled through its acronym, 'the ABC case'. This stands for the surnames of three defendants, Crispin Aubrey (a *Time Out* reporter), John Berry (an ex-soldier) and Duncan Campbell, a 24-year-old scientific prodigy who had chosen to make headlines as a freelance journalist rather than money as a telecommunications whizz-kid. They were arrested for talking to each other over a bottle of chianti in a London flat on a wet evening in February 1977, and prosecuted on charges laid under the Official Secrets Act which carried (in Campbell's case) a maximum of thirty years' imprisonment. By the time the proceedings ended, with a champagne celebration outside the Old Bailey eighteen months later, Britain was a less secret country. In 1977, the Attorney General's response to Duncan Campbell's ability to uncover State secrets was to try to lock him away. In 1987, when Campbell was about to broadcast details of the Zircon spy satellite, the Attorney General took him to lunch at the Garrick Club instead. This progress, from the stick of prison to the boiled carrots of the Gentleman's Club, showed that a lesson had been learned: in a democracy, the criminal law cannot be deployed as a tool for disposing of those who use their right of free speech to embarrass or inconvenience the authorities.

Termination of Duncan Campbell, if not with extreme prejudice then at least by a long prison sentence, was the object of a prosecution brought by a Labour government. The few who condemned it at the time (most vociferously, a young Scottish MP named Robin Cook) may have learned from history and may not, attaining office twenty years later, be condemned to repeat it. That depends on what they made of their senior colleagues who loudly condemned human rights abuses (like secret trials and the jailing of dissident journalists) in other countries, yet who could approve the prosecution of A, B and C. It was ordered by the law officers, Sam Silkin and Peter Archer, who were leading members of Amnesty and JUSTICE. Foreign Secretary David Owen published pontificating lectures on human rights at the very time officials of the organisations for which he was responsible – GCHQ and MI6 – were pressing for heavy jail sentences on Campbell. Home Secretary Merlyn Rees reneged on his party's promise to reform the Official Secrets Act so as to make the 'mere receipt' by journalists of official information no longer a crime. Civil liberties were not safe in the seventies in the hands of Labour cabinet ministers. Nor were they secured by independent prosecutors or defended by liberal newspaper editors or vindicated by a jury. Most of the credit for their protection belonged to a fierce but fair High Court judge, with help from a fearless QC, an irresponsible television programme, a Marxist historian and a few hundred residents of North London prepared to earn a Special Branch record for standing up against a serious abuse of human rights.

The geo-politics of the ABC proceedings went crudely like this. The cloak-and-dagger spies whom Le Carré and other novelists had convinced the public were crucial to the Cold War had, by 1977, little relevance to it. The top secrets came not through Human Intelligence (HUMINT in security speak) but through ELINT (Electronic Intelligence) and COMINT (Communications Intelligence) as intercepted, cracked and decoded by Signals Intelligence (SIGINT). This is hardly a revelation in 1997, when the wartime work of the Bletchley code-breakers is so widely celebrated, but even that was classified 'top secret' in Britain in 1977. The UK was very much a subservient partner to the United States in Western defence arrangements, but its abiding asset was a spider's web of intercept stations covering the globe, spun from microwave towers located in the outposts of the former British Empire. The spider itself was headquartered in Cheltenham (hence GCHQ – General Communications Head Quarters), its threads criss-crossing the Atlantic to its mate, the National Security Agency (NSA) in Fort Maryland, Virginia.

What the Americans valued most was the signals intelligence scooped up in Cheltenham from a net which ranged from Pine Gap in Australia to Little Sai Wan in Hong Kong to Ayios Nikolaos in Cyprus. Any electronic communication could be caught in the net: an incautious comment by a terrorist in a long-distance phone call; one tank commander talking to another on some benighted border; political leaders chatting on car telephones in Moscow. SIGINT was important to Britain as a guarantee of some continuing influence on American defence strategy. The subject was blanketed by 'D' notices, the curious and very English system whereby the country's newspaper editors – all of them – cravenly complied with directives from a committee dominated by the security services and the armed forces. These notices had no legal force at all, nor any basis in law, but they ensured that SIGINT was unmentionable and unmentioned in the media: the initials 'GCHQ' had never appeared in that order in British print, and any comment on the work of the thousands of technicians and translators in Cheltenham, and on the array of aerials on several dozen US bases in Britain, was forbidden on pain of an Official Secrets Act prosecution. A terror about mentioning the subject had descended on the British media after a case in 1956, when two undergraduates were jailed for wittily recounting some national service experiences at a signals intercept base in Crete.

SIGINT and GCHQ were not so secret to the rest of the world. In America, in the aftermath of Vietnam, a good deal of investigative journalism had focused on NSA and its role in programmes directed against radicals, by both the Johnson and the Nixon administrations. There had been two major inquiries – a Senate committee chaired by Frank Church and the Pike Inquiry by Congress – which had identified the central role of GCHQ in the UK–USA agreement, signed in 1947 by the two countries (and by Australia and Canada) pledging to cooperate in code-breaking and to share all their intercepts. There had been a plethora of published articles – from scientific papers to features in *Penthouse* – about the international eavesdropping alliance, and first-person accounts by American servicemen of work at SIGINT bases. This publicity – much of it critical – had to be suffered in silence under the First Amendment. Thus the consequence of the British security blanket was to keep the British public in ignorance of one major contribution it was making to the defence of the West. The real absurdity was that the Soviets knew all about SIGINT. They had been told, in detail, by defectors: George Blake had given them a fairly accurate global picture during his years in MI6, and in the sixties and early seventies a number of senior SIGINT operatives had defected to Moscow. Moreover, the SIGINT capacity of a base is obvious both to the naked eye and to the Soviet 'spy in the sky' satellite. A microwave transmitter cannot be hidden, let alone the electronic Stonehenge of aerials which announce themselves as intercept stations. There was a cluster of such sites in Britain – most of which Campbell had identified by the time he was arrested – and their existence was no secret to the Warsaw Pact commanders whose communications they monitored.

*

Britain's largest spy network organisation is not MI5 or MI6 but an electronic intelligence network controlled from a country town in the Cotswolds. With the huge US National Security Agency as partner, it intercepts and decodes communications throughout the world. Freelance writer *Duncan Campbell* and *Mark Hosenball* trace the rise to power of the electronic eavesdroppers.

These words – the opening paragraph of a double-page spread in *Time Out* in May 1976 – triggered an immediate response from the State. Hosenball, the 25-year-old son of a Washington lawyer, working as a journalist for the *Evening Standard*, was ordered out of the country by Home Secretary Merlyn Rees on the grounds that he was a danger to national security. Campbell was Scottish and could not be disposed of quite so easily: MI5 watched him and waited. Hosenball went to court, to seek reasons for his deportation but succeeded only in giving Lord Denning, whose love of freedom sometimes stopped short of extending it to foreigners or dissidents, the opportunity to decree that government actions were legally unchallengeable when made on grounds of national security. Hosenball was left to state his case to a tribunal of what were called 'three wise men' (they were more like three blind mice), who heard him out in an oak-panelled room of the Imperial Services Club in Pall Mall. He had no idea why he was being deported until he saw their sudden excitement when he mentioned 'The Eavesdroppers'. His own contribution to the article had been minimal – it was written almost entirely by Campbell, who readily admitted his authorship. Nonetheless, in February 1977, Merlyn Rees confirmed the deportation orders on Hosenball, as well as on the CIA defector, Phillip Agee.

John Berry, a social worker in North London who had, seven years earlier, been a corporal in a SIGINT regiment in Cyprus, was angry enough to write to the 'Agee–Hosenball Defence Committee', care of the National Council for Civil Liberties at Kings Cross. He identified himself as a former member of 'an organisation spending vast amounts of money in total absence of public control' who would 'like to know of any medium through which these concerns could be published'. The Committee knew of only one publication which might be prepared to defy the 'D' notice which had been placed on GCHQ and all its networks, and that is how his letter ended up on the desk of the environmental reporter, Crispin Aubrey, working for *Time Out*, a London listings magazine and the only 'underground paper' to survive police raids with circulation enhanced and politics more or less intact. Since Aubrey knew nothing about electronic surveillance he summoned Duncan Campbell to join him at an interview with this promising source. 'I want you to decide whether he's a bullshitter,' he said as they fixed a time (7 p.m., 18 February 1977) and a place (Berry's flat) for a first meeting. These details were carefully noted by MI5, which was tapping the telephones of Duncan Campbell as well as the telephones of the NCCL, under a warrant which must have been signed by Labour's Home Secretary, Merlyn Rees.

MI5 ordered a Special Branch team to converge on the Muswell Hill basement where A, B and C met as planned. Aubrey had such innocent intent that he brought his new tape-recorder – a Christmas present he had not yet had the chance to use – and ran it for three hours to provide an unassailable transcript of their criminal conversation. At 10 p.m. the tape ran out and the meeting broke up, at which precise point thirteen Special Branch officers descended to arrest them for offences committed under the Official Secrets Act. A, B and C were held in police cells for two days without being allowed to see their families or their solicitors, while Campbell's flat in Brighton was raided and its vast library (including the novels of Hemingway and Graham Greene, and a book listed in the trial exhibits as *The Female Unok*) was transferred to Scotland Yard by police pantechnicon. The three were refused bail, and carted off to Brixton Prison. They were charged under Section 2 of the Official Secrets Act, which made it an offence to give or receive 'official' information, whether secret or not. This was, said the police, a 'holding charge' – i.e. a justification for holding dangerous men in custody until more serious charges were formulated.

I became involved in this case at this point, and by mistake. Hearing a news flash that a journalist named Duncan Campbell had been arrested, I assumed him to be my friend of that name who was then the editor of *Time Out*. I called Bernard Simons, *Time Out*'s solicitor, and offered to stand as his surety. Bernard thanked me but explained that the arrested man was 'the other Duncan Campbell' whom I did not know. Would I like to be his counsel instead, to seek bail from a High Court judge? This application was to be vigorously opposed, so I rustled up John Mortimer to lead me in making it.

The security services in those days believed they could obtain anything they wanted from the courts by incanting the magic words 'danger to national security'. But as Philby and Blunt well understood, there is in England one immunity to the spell: the possession of class. John Mortimer knew this too and carefully eschewed any argument based on freedom of speech. Duncan, he explained, was recently 'down from Oxford' ('Which college?' asked the judge automatically). His lineage, although Scottish, was distinguished. Crispin Aubrey, too, had exemplary middle-class roots (chaps named Crispin do not belong in prison). Ever so delicately, John defused the Crown's allegation that they were out to cause 'exceptionally grave damage to national security' with references to Oxford days and student pranks and young men of good parentage who obviously didn't realise the seriousness of what they were doing. The judge released the two journalists into the custody of their good parents. The ex-soldier, who came from a working-class background, he ordered to remain in prison.

The first Section 1 charges hit all three defendants soon after, and related entirely to the conversation they had taped themselves having with each other. The transcript was made up of long questions by Duncan Campbell – Aubrey said barely a word – and unsensational answers by Berry, who clearly knew much less than his interlocutor. He did describe the boredom of sitting for hours twiddling wireless dials at Ayios Nikolaos, as a member of 9th Signals Regiment, but most of what he said might have been written unexceptionally on postcards home. He did mention how he had tuned into tank traffic on the Iran/Iraq border, and how he had once heard a cry to Allah by an Egyptian soldier as his tank was hit by an Israeli shell during the seven-day war. He described his indoctrinations into secrecy, which could hardly themselves be secret. 'What you see here, what you do here, what you hear here, when you leave here, let it stay here' was not a mantra that would excite readers of *Time Out*. The only piece of information that was rationally classifiable as secret, and then only because it might cause diplomatic embarrassment if published, was Berry's confirmation that his base intercepted communications emanating from NATO partners.

This would not have come as any surprise to the States concerned, but Berry had without doubt breached his service undertakings and had committed the Section 2 offence of communicating official information without authorisation. But his information was seven years out of date and his sentence for imparting it should have been short or suspended. Section 1 of the Official Secrets Act, however, is the most draconian law on the British statute book. It provides up to fourteen years' imprisonment for persons who collect or communicate 'information directly or indirectly useful to a potential enemy' if they did so for 'any purpose prejudicial to the State'. Section 1, uniquely in English law, has oppressive provisions which reverse the burden of proof, and allow guilt by association. It was used against traitors like the atom spies and Gordon Lonsdale and George Blake, agents of a foreign power whose activities put countries, as well as lives, at risk. Section 1 had never been intended for use against journalists – as previous Attorney Generals had assured Parliament in 1921 and 1949. Why was a Labour government breaching those assurances in 1977?

The mystery deepened with the addition, a few months later, of a new Section 1 charge against Campbell alone, relating to the files found in his flat in Brighton. Like any journalist who specialised in military communications and civil defence, Campbell had collected vast quantities of information, all from published sources.

Over nine hundred pages had been culled by MI5 from his files, and were alleged to be of 'direct or indirect' use to a potential enemy. So they were – in the sense that an A–Z of London would be of use. None of it related to debriefing of people in sensitive employment, and there were no documents stolen or obtained without authorisation from official sources.

The real problem, it turned out, was that Duncan Campbell was a prodigy: give him a few published sources (a telephone book, an Ordnance Survey map and a regimental magazine) and he could tell you secrets which not even the cabinet was supposed to know. There was no stopping him, short of either recruiting him into the intelligence services or putting him in jail. MI5 had chosen to do the latter, by charging him with collecting information (from published sources) of direct and indirect use (like most information) to a potential enemy, for a purpose (he might publish it in *Time Out*) prejudicial to the State. Effectively, Campbell was put on trial for being a dangerous maverick, a defence journalist with analytical ability who worked without fear of 'D' notices. What the security services wanted to put in solitary confinement was Duncan Campbell's brain.

It took some time to understand the policy behind this prosecution. I could well see that Campbell was an irritant, one of a new breed of post-Watergate journalists who did not accept the unilateral right of the State to define national security. What made him especially irritating was that, unlike others of this ilk, he had the technical expertise (first-class honours in physics, a Master of Science) to see through official press releases. Defence journalists in this period rarely looked beyond the boundary wire of their 'D' notices and obediently summarised press releases from the Ministry of Defence. There was virtually no informed mainstream coverage of the security services other than by Chapman Pincher, who scavenged leaks from Peter Wright and other irresponsible reactionaries within the service. Campbell, on the other hand, was young and left-wing. He was an altogether more suitable candidate than Pincher for an exercise designed to prove that such critical journalism was as inimical to the safety of the State as the treason of those who collaborated with the enemy. The theory behind the Section 1 charges was that journalists could do as much damage as spies. That is, at least theoretically, true – but the difference, of course, lay in the intention with which they did it. Section 1 did not require the prosecution to prove any intention to help the enemy, or any hostile intention at all.

Since none of the three had any apparent defence to the Section 2 charges – Berry had volunteered official information and Aubrey and Campbell had received it on tape – it should have been possible to negotiate a 'plea bargain' with the prosecution. If the defendants pleaded guilty to Section 2 at the magistrates' court, this would limit their sentence to three months' imprisonment or a measly £50 fine. The benefit to the government of such a course was that it would save large amounts of public money, and more importantly (if its case had any logic) it would save any secret beans being spilled in the course of a lengthy and probably intemperate trial. When I canvassed this possibility with the prosecution, however, I received this chilling response: 'That course might be acceptable for Berry and Aubrey. But the security services want Campbell in prison for a very long time.'

Sam Silkin, the Attorney General, had given his personal consent to the laying of Section 1 charges against these journalists. He was not the only liberal to be spooked by MI5. The government's action went uncondemned and virtually unreported in the national press, which appeared entirely unconcerned by this unprecedented attack on its own freedom. This was thanks to a 'whispering campaign' by MI5 through its editorial contacts on Fleet Street and in the BBC. Duncan Campbell was slandered as a communist, or as a fellow traveller happy to 'put lives at risk'. Editors who should have known better fell for this, and when the *Sunday Times* gave Duncan some freelance employment to tide him over after his arrest, its executives were informed by a cabinet minister that he was a 'dangerous subversive'. Come the committal, however, the State would have to lay its cards on the table: the defendants waived reporting restrictions, so that the media could appreciate how threadbare the case against them really was.

The committal took place in November 1977 at Tottenham Magistrates' Court. The prosecution opened by caricaturing Campbell as a 'thoroughly subversive man who was quite prepared to publish information which was secret'. It went on to claim that his activities could 'even put at risk lives in Northern Ireland' – a wild accusation for which no evidence was ever produced and which was never repeated at the subsequent trials. He was alleged to have collected information of use to a foreign power, although the only foreigners with whom he had corresponded were liberal think-tanks in Washington and a Peace Research Institute in Oslo. At my insistence it was eventually conceded that there was 'no suggestion that he was in the employ of a foreign power'. Duncan's mother, who had worked throughout the war code-breaking at Bletchley, was deeply distressed by the outline of the case against her son. As I comforted her, I realised for the first time just how easily governments and their lawyers can cry 'lives at risk', the formula used eighteen years later on the Public Interest Immunity Certificates in the Matrix Churchill trial.

On the second day of the committal a gigantic horse-box was drawn up at the back entrance to the court, alleged to contain a personage of such secrecy that no mortal could gaze upon him, or learn his name. He was to be known only as 'Lieutenant Colonel A', and his expert evidence would prove that ABC had been engaged on an enterprise severely damaging to national security. The notion that a witness is so significant that the very revelation of his name would imperil the realm is calculated to impress the court. It did not, however, impress the court clerk, a tall, immaculate gentleman of weary manners and surprisingly stern attention to legal detail. Mr Pratt was a Dickensian figure, but a good Dickensian figure, I felt, as he narrowed his eyes at the prosecutor and drawled: 'What's your authority for keeping your expert's identity a secret?' The prosecution was taken aback: its 'authority' was the interests of national security, which would always justify secrecy. But how could I cross-examine Lieut. Colonel A if I did not know his background, his publications, his postings – indeed if I could not even see the man, since it was proposed that he give evidence from behind a screen? The Bench retired, with Mr Pratt to 'advise them on the law', and came back looking as though they had just lost their OBEs. 'Solely on the advice of Mr Pratt and with great regret' they ruled that a court had no power to receive expert evidence from a voice behind a curtain.

After a few days' adjournment, another letter in the army alphabet was produced, Colonel 'not quite so secret' B. His real name might just be disclosable to the defendants and their lawyers, although certainly not to anyone else. The horse-box returned, with its horse of a different colour. There was a portentous silence in court as the clerk was solemnly handed a slip of paper with the witness's real name. It read simply 'H A Johnstone'. I approached the dock and handed the slip to Duncan. 'Hugh Johnstone,' he whispered with a grin. 'I've got masses of information on him.' And so he had, produced in the next few minutes from a bundle of magazines at his feet. It very quickly transpired that the ultra-secret Colonel B was until recently the well-known and popular commander of the 9th Signals Regiment at Ayios Nikolaos. His doings featured constantly in *The Wire*, the regimental magazine available at many public libraries and on subscription to anyone, including the KGB. There were detailed records of his postings to and from Cyprus, cartoons of him playing squash, uncryptic comments like 'Hugh Johnstone, Don of our communications underworld'.

Colonel Johnstone was called as the prosecution expert on secrecy, to prove that the information revealed by Berry was of a kind which fell under Section 1 of the Act. It seemed reasonable, therefore, to test his opinion by reference to his belief in the secrecy of himself. He was a Colonel with the Ministry of Defence – was his Defence Intelligence Department number a secret? No it was not: he actually volunteered it. I asked him whether his own name and rank and number had been widely published whenever he received a fresh posting, and when he hesitated I showed him some material I did not identify – Duncan's copies of *The Wire*. 'Yes, I see my name and rank and number have been published in various publications,' he congenially volunteered. Mr Pratt, who had gone from confounding the State with his legal advice to the unexalted task of taking down the witness's words in longhand to form his 'deposition' or sworn statement, decided at this point to intervene. He could have had no consciousness of the constitutional crisis he was about to ignite, as he leant over towards the witness and asked him in a voice of tired sufferance, '*What* are you looking at?' 'It's *The Wire*,' said Colonel B proudly. 'Our regimental magazine.' Mr Pratt wrote – and spoke what he was writing aloud for the Colonel's benefit – 'I am now aware my posting was published in *The Wire* . . .' Mr Pratt looked up again, with the irritable tone of one who is dotting *i*'s and crossing *t*'s: 'And what edition of *Wire* are you looking at?' Happy to comply, Johnstone looked at the cover and read aloud, 'December 1974–January 1975'. At the end of his deposition, the punctilious Mr Pratt read back this evidence, slowly and in a loud voice.

It is probably a measure of the inward-turning nature of court proceedings that nobody involved – the prosecutor, the clerk, the magistrates, the Colonel or myself – realised that Colonel B, the expert in secrecy, was comprehensively blowing his own cover. Behind our backs, a bearded reporter from *Peace News* was the first to the door, hot-foot to the British Library to look up *The Wire* for December 74–January 75. In no time the Colonel's real name was discovered, as was the fact that he was listed under it, with his actual home address, in the London telephone directory. Soon articles appeared in *Peace News* and *The Leveller* with headlines like 'Who are you trying to kid, Colonel H A Johnstone?' Sam Silkin sent Special Branch officers to interrogate the editors and summons them for contempt of court. A police team even raided the annual conference of the NUJ at the seaside resort of Whitley Bay when they heard that delegates were writing the forbidden name in the sand. The tide washed away the evidence before they arrived.

Then early one afternoon at Parliamentary question-time, when the Speaker was dozing, an obscure backbencher named Robert Kilroy-Silk, followed in turn by three other MPs, rose and asked questions about official secrets and Colonel H A Johnstone. This meant that the press was constitutionally privileged to print the name as part of any report of that afternoon's parliamentary proceedings: it had, after all, gone out live in radio coverage of the House. I am not sure that many newspapers would have bothered, but Silkin and his flummoxed DPP, Tony Hetherington, threatened to prosecute any that did for contempt of court. Foolishly, the DPP sent them an empty but threatening letter which at last provoked the media to show its mettle. In a rare moment of unanimity, the BBC and ITV networks joined with every newspaper to condemn the DPP's unconstitutional threat, and to defy him by revealing Colonel B's real name. For the first time in the 'ABC' affair, the Law Officers backed down: there was at last a limit to the number of liberties they could take at the request of the intelligence services.

I quite warmed to Colonel B at the committal – a serious but pleasant fellow in a grey suit who should not have been testifying in the first place. He was not an 'expert' on secrecy (as he proved by letting himself slip), he was an army commander. What was known about SIGINT, from public sources both in Britain and overseas, was beyond his brief and his belief. His stock answer was that 'any revelation of or about SIGINT must inevitably affect adversely our ability to defend ourselves'. His 'expert' evidence was that no mention should be made of SIGINT – in the press, in Parliament or over private dinner-tables – ever, by anyone who had not been positively vetted. 'Until this case the public has been quite unaware of SIGINT.' So has the national security been damaged by mentioning SIGINT in court? 'Yes, I think it has. I think any reference to SIGINT in the media is damaging.' He flinched when shown detailed articles on SIGINT, published in the *New York Review of Books* and the *New York Times*. He had never seen them before, but at least they weren't *British* media. Local newspapers in Cyprus had published details of his SIGINT installations, and sometimes, political demands for their removal. Colonel B was unfazed. The work of the 9th Signals Regiment might be known in Cyprus, but it must never be disclosed in Britain.

Harry Nicholls, the Special Branch officer in charge of the arrests of A, B and C, said they had only been instructed two hours before they left Scotland Yard. By whom? I politely enquired, but the prosecutor objected to any mention of MI5, the very existence of which was then an official secret. Indeed, these proceedings were the first time that the existence of GCHQ had been admitted, and the prosecution felt it had let enough history slip out for 1977. Major Philp of the Royal Signals Corps was one witness who refused to disguise his admiration for Duncan's technical and journalistic ability. He told of hosting MOD press launches for new pieces of equipment, at which the regular defence correspondents would swill champagne and take away a press hand-out. Duncan, the abstemious journalist then working for *New Scientist*, was the only one capable of discussing the technical – and frequently, surveillance – role of the equipment. 'Get him out of here,' a superior had once told Philp when Campbell was seen at a press launch. 'He asks too many questions.'

The Section 1 'collection' charge Duncan Campbell faced was based on the nine hundred pages culled from his files, all from public or published sources. Major-General Sturge asserted that 'Campbell set about a concerted effort to find out about the communications system of Britain and its relevance to defence. In my opinion this would be of use to an enemy.' So, of course, would a collection of Ordnance Survey maps, or a book like Peter Laurie's *Beneath the City Streets* – a popular paperback about the country's civil defence network for which Campbell had been doing further research, and to which most of his files related. The 'prejudicial purpose' on which the prosecution relied was not helping a foreign power, but research for publication – in books like Laurie's, or in articles for *New Scientist* or *Time Out*. This was not, of course, prejudicial to a democratic State with a rule of law protecting the freedom to publish inferences from available information, although it might well seem so to an authoritarian State which punished journalists who pried into subjects its military did not wish to see discussed in print. The prosecution theory, in a nutshell, was that they could put Campbell behind bars under Section 1 not because of the information he had collected, but because, unlike other journalists who obeyed 'D' notices, he could not be trusted to do what he was told with it.

This was the point I tried to get across to the Tottenham justices:

> The prosecution has mistaken investigative journalism for subversion. Because Campbell is a journalist, he's a ferret not a skunk. Section 1 is aimed at skunks – traitors and spies. In the nine hundred pages of evidence extracted from his library, there's no suggestion that his mind ever entertained a disloyal fantasy or that this information was ever collected other than for his own research. The prosecution describes him as a 'thoroughly subversive man', but the legal definition of a subversive is 'someone who contemplates the overthrow of the government by unlawful means'. There's no evidence that Campbell comes within a mile of that definition. The best synonym the prosecution has been able to come up with is 'anti-establishment'. I thought it was only in Russia that people were put in prison for being anti-establishment . . .

It was a speech delivered with some passion. How could it amount to a serious criminal offence for a journalist to collect information from published sources, or – unless clairvoyant – to question a soldier who had asked to be interviewed and claimed to have something significant to impart? The prosecutor pointed out that under Section 1, they merely had to prove that the information *might* be of use to a potential enemy. Since it was obviously of use, it remained only for them to prove that it was collected for a purpose prejudicial to the State. An obscure sub-section of Section 1 says that a defendant's purpose should be *deemed* prejudicial to the State if he is found in possession of 'any note, sketch, photograph or document' which relates to a *prohibited place*. A place is 'prohibited' if the government declares it to be prohibited, and its declarations over the years covered many well-known places mentioned or photographed in Campbell's files, including the Post Office Tower at Euston, of which Campbell had some postcards. His possession of them meant that he was 'deemed' to have a purpose prejudicial to the State, unless he proved the contrary. The prosecutor made this point with relish: unlike any other crime, Section 1 cuts the golden thread of the criminal law: it presumes that the defendant is guilty until proven innocent.

The lay justices were not lawyers. They sat stony-faced and overawed by the responsibility for protecting national security which had been thrust upon them. They committed A, B and C for trial on all counts. That was the cue for the prosecution to object to bail, especially for Campbell 'now that you have had a full opportunity to assess the seriousness of these charges'. This was MI5 speaking, with the harsh demand that Duncan be confined to prison for the year which would inevitably elapse before the Old Bailey trial. The magistrates retired for a nail-biting half-hour, but returned to set the defendants at liberty as before. Advocacy had not resulted in the removal of a single charge, but at least it appeared to have convinced the Tottenham justices – or the unflappable Mr Pratt who advised them – that the skies would not fall if Duncan Campbell were allowed just a little more time to follow his journalistic career.

The trial would not begin until September 1978; by which time we had to crack the prosecution's Section 1 syllogism:

Whatever is in the interest of SIGINT is in the interests of the State.

Absolute secrecy is in the interests of SIGINT.

Therefore, absolute secrecy on the subject of SIGINT is in the interests of the State.

Absolutely secrecy *had* been necessary during the Second World War, when SIGINT was under British control and was used exclusively for the purpose of defeating the Axis powers. UKUSA was originally a partnership agreement, but by 1978 the four parties to it had ceased to be partners. The UK, Australia and Canada had become clients of the US, which bought control by expending US $15 billion and employing 120,000 personnel world-wide, to give America by far the major stake. The interests of SIGINT had become the interests of a US foreign policy which propped up some of the most tyrannical regimes against democratic challenge. Britain had trained and sent SIGINT operators secretly to be part of the US war effort against North Vietnam; had provided intelligence support for the CIA to destabilise the Allende regime in Chile and to shore up the Shah's rule in Iran; and had taken a soft line on apartheid partly for fear of jeopardising communications facilities in South Africa. SIGINT was also used unlawfully by the Nixon regime to gather information on US residents living abroad (especially in the UK) whom it targeted as 'enemies'. Did British SIGINT give any assistance? Issues like this were regularly raised in the American press: democratic debate over them in Britain had not begun, and would – if this prosecution succeeded – be stifled indefinitely.

We were contacted by Jock Kane, a former GCHQ employee who unveiled for us evidence of widespread corruption and inefficiency. Major electronics suppliers were making fortunes out of SIGINT equipment: the secrecy meant that there was no proper accounting over their profits and no control over spin-off sales to dubious foreign dictatorships. Some of his examples were almost amusing (at Little Sai Wan base in Hong Kong, the Chinese cleaners who were for some years employed to remove the waste baskets of intercepts removed them to the Chinese Embassy). But the scale and detail of Kane's accusations were alarming, and his credibility was unchallengeable (as Mrs Thatcher reluctantly accepted when his allegations were published some years later). What they proved was that beneath a blanket of unaccountable secrecy, insecure and even corrupt practices flourish. The syllogism had been cracked: absolute secrecy was in the interests of SIGINT *officials*, but not always or necessarily in the interests of the State.

I spent much of the summer of 1978 discussing tactics, often on the telephone, with Jeremy Hutchinson – the most fearless and formidable advocate of the day – who was to lead Campbell's defence team. He could not understand why the security services had not been prepared to accept my offer of a plea to Section 2 in return for dropping all the Section 1 charges. Shortly after we discussed whether we might renew it, he found himself invited to a dinner party at which, by the strangest coincidence, there appeared a very senior public servant who took him aside and said that the intelligence services would now be 'very interested' in any agreement which would avoid the need for a trial. So we went to see John Leonard – the sensible and fair-minded silk who had been brought in to lead the prosecution – and we found him more than happy to drop all Section 1 charges, in return for a single plea by all three of guilty to a Section 2 offence. For Campbell this was, on the face of it, a real bargain. Nobody had ever been acquitted of a Section 1 charge, and he was facing two of them. His liability to prison would shrink at a stroke from thirty years to two years. Moreover, the judge who had been allotted to the ABC trial was the fearsome Mr Justice Thesiger, quite capable of putting Campbell inside for many years if the trial resulted in his conviction on Section 1. Although he would probably jail them for a year under Section 2, the pressure on all defendants to accept the plea bargain was intense.

Courageously, they decided to tempt fate. Their bandwagon – the ABC campaign – was rolling towards the Old Bailey and on it by now were several Labour MPs, the NUJ and other trade unions, and some leading writers and academics, as well as Buzby – a large fluffy bird who sat on telephone wires in television ads for the Post Office – and an enormous Chinese dragon which breathed fire and hissed 'silly secrets'. The defendants called a press conference just before the trial to announce that they were going to fight, that they had been offered a plea bargain, and had turned it down. Sam Silkin had been defending himself for consenting to the Section 1 charges on the grounds that they were absolutely necessary in the national interest: the revelation that he was prepared to drop them in return for a plea to a lesser offence suggested that they were not necessary at all. So, on the first day of the trial, A, B and C arrived with the dragon at the head of a colourful procession of supporters waving their 'Military Intelligence is a contradiction in terms' placards and wearing their 'Tell me an official secret' badges, pinned to T-shirts reading 'Buzby says: who's tapping your phone?' (Buzby was given the bird by the Post Office shortly after he became the mascot of the ABC campaign.) What was happening inside the Old Bailey was more dramatic, and of some historic importance.

At our eve-of-trial conference, Duncan had expressed his mistrust of the security services. The publicity given to the plea bargain and its rejection would, he felt, infuriate them and make them want to convict him at all costs. He would not even put it past them to 'vet' the jury. Jeremy Hutchinson had taken a very firm line against this paranoia: jury vetting was, in England in 1978, quite unthinkable. He had never heard any suggestion that such a thing could happen. I mentioned that Viscount Dilhorne had once admitted to removing a communist from a jury trying an official secrets case, back in 1956. Dilhorne was Jeremy's sworn adversary in past courtroom battles, and that night he lay awake, wondering. At 9 a.m. he strolled into the office of the chief clerk at the Old Bailey. 'Has there been any – how shall I put it – *interest* in the jury panel for today's trial?' he enquired innocently. The clerk, honoured to receive a visit from the great advocate, explained that there had been no interest at all over the past six weeks, ever since the prosecution had applied in secret to Mr Justice Thesiger to have the names and addresses of all the jurors on the panel so they could be vetted for the ABC trial.

'They've vetted the jury!' Jeremy was in a fine old state in the robing room, half-enraged at the prosecution's behaviour, half-excited by the mischief he would cause when he stood up in court to reveal it. We both instinctively felt it was an outrage, although we did not, at that moment, know exactly why. The word 'unconstitutional' sprang to my lips, but that is always a tricky notion in the courts of a country which does not have a written constitution. I had a new pupil starting that morning – Andrew Nicol, a lecturer at the London School of Economics – and I sent him urgently back to school to find some authority which might provide a basis for complaining about this unheard-of behaviour. It was a measure of Andy's brilliance that he returned within the hour clutching the first and last word on the subject, Jeremy Bentham's *Elements of the Art of Jury Packing*. This 1821 masterpiece – Bentham's very first book – provided some historical sound-bites to orchestrate Jeremy's impromptu condemnation of a prosecution which had taken a liberty not seen since William Pitt, who had introduced specially vetted juries to convict for sedition defendants who sympathised with the French Revolution. Bentham condemned a vetting system 'which is become regular, quietly established and quietly suffered. Not only is the yoke already about our necks, but our neck is already fashioned for it.'

Just how apt these words were became clear as soon as Jeremy's angry denunciation of it detonated in court. John Leonard explained that the Crown had made a secret application to obtain the names of jurors 'in sufficient time to complete the checks which are normal in cases of this sort'. Ah ha: 'normal' – just what had been going on 'in cases of this sort'? Mr Justice Willis (a last-minute replacement for Thesiger, who had fallen ill) was non-committal – he knew nothing about it, and wanted to know nothing. 'It is not a matter for me,' he said, taken by such surprise that he forgot to ban the ensuing press coverage, which was massive. The public are always, and rightly, anxious at any suggestion of tampering with juries, and Silkin, under fire from all sides, was forced to own up. On taking office in 1974 he and Home Secretary Roy Jenkins had been prevailed upon by the security services to authorise a system of vetting jurors in cases of a class which 'was impossible to define precisely' but 'when, broadly speaking, strong political motives were involved'. Between 1974 and 1978 no fewer than twenty-five cases had involved secret vetting of the jury panel, unbeknown to the defence. The whole system had been deliberately kept quiet, in the hope that lawyers and MPs would never find out. Silkin claimed to have drawn up 'firm safeguards' to ensure that the system was not abused, but these too were of course secret, so no one could ever know whether they were firm, or even whether they had been followed.

The jury-vetting episode provided further evidence for the uncomfortable proposition that civil liberties are less secure in the hands of Labour politicians, nervously striving to prove their responsibility by bowing to pressure from the police and the security services, than of dyed-in-the-wool Conservatives who have no need to prove their law and order credentials. The system, the establishment of which had been deliberately withheld from public debate, involved a secret prosecution application to the trial judge, who would order court officials to hand to Special Branch a list of the names and addresses and occupations of jurors on the panel for a particular trial, so that 'checks' could be made with police and security records to see whether any juror was listed as having strong political views, or any hostility to the State (e.g. by having lodged a complaint against the police). Prosecuting counsel could then challenge the juror, with no reason given. Any information suggesting the juror would be hostile to the *defendant* would never be supplied to the defence, because that would give the secret vetting game away. The system authorised by Jenkins and Silkin was unfair in this quite elemental way, and they should have realised it. The historian E P Thompson, who had joined the defence campaign, responded with a memorable defence of the jury:

> Time and again, when judges and law officers, mounted on high horses, have been riding at breakneck speed towards some convenient despotism, those shadowy figures – not particularly good or especially true – have risen from the bushes beside the highway to fling a gate across their path. They are known to historians as the Gang of Twelve.

Turning to Silkin and his guidelines (hastily made public in an attempt to defuse the criticism), Thompson shredded them both:

> Mr Attorney General, what precision is there in these 'guidelines' you served out secretly to the police? What *is* a guideline? Is it a rule at law or is it a nudge-nudge be-careful-how-you-go? What officers have you appointed to see that these 'guidelines' are observed? What sanctions have you imposed against transgressions? How are we to know if a case be of an 'exceptional type' or not? What rule of law may hang upon the phrase 'it is impossible to define precisely' the cases to which it might refer? If law is now to rest upon such nice terms as 'broadly speaking', who is to speak and how broad may that

speech be? If a person be deprived of his juror's rights (which I had once supposed to be a right and duty inherent in a citizen) because of 'strong political motives' and 'extreme political convictions', who is to determine whether his views be 'strong' or 'extreme'? Yourself? Or Tony the DPP? The prosecution? Or the police? Whichever it may be, you are taking a liberty: the liberty of the people.

Heady as the jury-vetting controversy was, it did not impact directly on the trial. John Leonard opened it by conceding that Section 1 was normally used in 'spying' cases, and that ABC's offence 'came at the lowest end of the Section 1 scale' – a retreat from the more extravagant approach of the prosecutor at Tottenham Magistrates' Court. But an offence was made out if their purpose was prejudicial to the safety or interests of the State, and 'here, the prejudicial purpose is Campbell and Aubrey's purpose of publishing or passing on Berry's information'. The prosecution case against Campbell on the collection charge was that 'when you look at the collection, it goes beyond the ordinary inquisitiveness of a journalist . . . the defendant's conviction is essential to the safety of this country within the NATO alliance . . . if information of this kind is collected, it will affect whether one sleeps well in one's bed at night or not.' Campbell was a 'highly qualified and very able scientist' who had 'taken the pieces of our defence jigsaw puzzle, and put them together'. Since much of his information related to 'prohibited places', the law *deemed* him to have collected it for a prejudicial purpose unless he could prove the contrary. His behaviour, when invited as a journalist to attend the launch of new defence products, was 'to ask questions which he knew perfectly well that the manufacturers were not allowed to answer. He was told these questions could not be asked, yet he went on persistently to ask them!'

It was an extraordinary theory, which proceeded on the basis that there existed an acceptable threshold of journalistic inquisitiveness which Campbell had exceeded by virtue of his ability and expertise. The prosecution could not define the point at which the bulging Campbell files had passed from legitimate research into evidence of the commission of a serious offence, and its case soon came apart under Jeremy Hutchinson's relentless cross-examination. The witnesses were all from the bases which

Campbell had identified in his research as having a defence communications function, and it transpired that all of these 'secret' bases and facilities had been identified in some published source as possessing precisely that function – many of them by large signs (the Regimental Display Board) posted outside their perimeter fences. Their function had often been discussed in local news-papers and in regimental magazines and occasionally in the national press. Their aerials, which gave away that function to any experienced observer (including KGB analysts who saw them on satellite photographs) were also identified on Ordnance Survey maps. There was regular merriment in court when we produced a 'Hazards Map' issued by the Civil Aviation Authority, which showed the location and by inference the function of all the pros-ecution's 'top secret' sites: it was routinely issued to all commercial airlines, including Aeroflot. Each witness was solemnly required to identify his secret base on 'The Aeroflot Map'. When told, at the close of a cross-examination which had featured dozens of public references to the role of his unit, that it was being suggested that this role was a State secret, most were driven to agree that the suggestion was, in Jeremy's words, 'absolutely idiotic'.

But still they came, from places as far afield as Bude and Chicksands and Orfordness and Edzell in Scotland, to identify their units in Campbell's cuttings. Many of these were 'joint facilities', ostensibly operated in partnership with the US, although this was a fiction: they were operated entirely by the US. Their lone UK officers, when called to testify, admitted they had no idea what the Americans were doing, and it was no part of their duty to enquire. 'I am the only British officer on the base. I do not know what it does. I do not know details of its operations. I play no part in them. I am completely isolated. My US colleagues do not speak to me,' said the RAF officer from 'RAF' Edzell. 'I am not involved in the running of the station. That is done by high-ranking American officers. I don't know the details – I'm only the land-lord's representative,' said an RAF group captain whose main job was to raise and lower the British flag outside another 'joint facility'. The officer who came from the RAF establishment at Orfordness was very frank: he said a recent decision to shut down new equipment at the base at a cost of £40 million was 'of the greatest possible public interest'. The secrecy surrounding the base 'can be very annoying. Speaking as a human being, I agree it is absolutely idiotic.'

More amusement was caused when the prosecution called a fifteen-year-old schoolboy who had corresponded with Campbell about the location and function of microwave stations along the East Coast. Phillip Quigley was from Ampleforth College. He had been introduced to Duncan by a schoolmaster, Father Anselm Cramer, who gave lectures on civil defence. This monk was as interested in SIGINT as trainspotters are in trains, and had taken the boy on a 'microwave treasure hunt' by compass near the East Coast as part of a school project. Master and pupil spoke with genuine enthusiasm of their journeys of discovery, of their curiosity about the American bases and the aerials dotting the landscape, and how it never occurred to them that they were breaking the Official Secrets Act by photographing 'prohibited places'. 'Inside every schoolmaster,' Cramer told the jury, 'there is a small boy.' Civil defence had been a compulsive interest, and until the Special Branch had raided Ampleforth: 'I didn't know I was doing anything wrong'.

At the forensic level, the trial was going beautifully for the defence. But I am always mindful of the story about the advocate congratulated by his client on a particularly skilful cross-examination: 'We're doing great.' '*I'm* doing great,' corrected the lawyer, '*you* are going to jail for many years.' Jeremy's cross-examination was delighting everyone in court who was sceptical about official secrecy. Did that include the jury? It was hard to tell: they had listened so attentively as John Leonard told them they would sleep more easily in their beds without Duncan Campbell's curiosity about the signals intelligence system that served the Western alliance. We noticed one juror in particular – a well-built man in his thirties – aiming very hostile glances in the direction of the dock. He had been elected foreman, and our hearts sank one morning as we read the officious note he passed to the judge: 'Only three members of the jury have signed the Official Secrets Act!' We were appalled to learn that *any* member of the jury had signed the Act. The judge made enquiries and it turned out that one of the three was a civil servant, another a former security officer in the army, but the third – the foreman himself – had been a soldier in the SAS, who had done duty in Northern Ireland, the Far East and

Cyprus. Some of the exhibits included articles written by Duncan which were critical of the SAS. All defence counsel applied for the jury to be discharged on the grounds that justice must not only be done but be *seen* to be done, and that A, B and C could not in these circumstances be perceived to have a fair trial. This was a powerful application, but the judge turned it down.

The next morning, a Friday, there came a witness from a top-secret communications station outside Dover. Leonard showed him what he had described in opening as the prosecution's best single piece of evidence: a photograph from Campbell's collection which could only have been taken from a helicopter. The witness agreed it was a very high-quality photograph of a secret site which must have been taken from the air – one juror was heard to gasp at Campbell's audacity, apparently hiring a helicopter and leaning out of it to take the forbidden photograph. Then it was Jeremy's turn to ask whether Marconi had been responsible for the installation (it had been) and whether it had arranged for some aerial photographs to be taken of its handiwork (yes, probably) and whether the photograph had been issued for publicity purposes by the Ministry of Defence (he didn't know). 'It will be the defence case that this high-quality photograph of a top-secret installation was supplied to the defendant and numerous other journalists in a press pack by the MOD,' Jeremy explained serenely. John Leonard, normally the most unflappable of counsel, turned to the MI5 lawyers behind him, who shrugged helplessly.

We broke for the weekend, pleased at the prosecution's disarray but more worried than ever about the jury foreman, who had been overheard in the corridors talking to other jurors about his SAS exploits. Journalists covering the trial found it astonishing that the prosecution could vet a jury for 'loyalty', yet the defence could not object to jurors who had been indoctrinated into the cult of official secrecy. To their frustration, the judge had ruled that none of this could be published. One journalist, Christopher Hitchens, and the television producer Barry Cox decided to take the law into their own hands. Hitchens was the guest that weekend on a late-night satire show produced by Cox and hosted by Russell Harty, called *Saturday Night People*. It was full of 'scripted ad-libs' and when Harty invited Hitchens to tell the audience something they could not read in the papers, he announced that three of the vetted jurors in the ABC trial had signed the Official Secrets Act, that the foreman had been in the SAS and that the judge had refused a defence application to discharge them.

Monday was another dramatic morning: the Special Branch descended on London Weekend Television to seize a video of the offending programme to show in court, after which the judge condemned this 'piece of gratuitous journalistic gossip'. He was now obliged to discharge the jury in fairness to the defendants, since Hitchens had revealed that the defence objected to them. There would have to be a new trial. And there was another surprise in store. John Leonard asked for an adjournment 'in order to take instructions to see whether I can present the prosecution case more economically'. With this most delicate phrasing, he signalled that the Section 1 collection charge would not be pursued. A jury might – who knows – have convicted, but an independent prosecutor, pursuaded of his innocence, was not prepared to take that risk.

A few days later, Mr Justice Willis was rushed to hospital, and doctors declared him too ill to preside over the second trial. The ABC campaign sent him a 'get well soon' card and a large bunch of red roses, which he acknowledged in a note to Jeremy both charming and chilling. 'I am glad I shall not be doing the retrial as I was not looking forward to passing the sentences.' Jeremy fretted about the eventual fate of our clients. 'They will send us the toughest judge they can find,' he predicted. Quite who 'they' were has never been very clear to me: there is no known procedure for appointing a judge for a particular trial. It is all meant to happen by happenstance – the luck of the High Court calendar, a question of who is available on the day. Was it mere coincidence that we first drew the extremely severe Mr Justice Thesiger, followed by Mr Justice Willis who had spent the war in the Royal Signals Regiment? We speculated about which red judge was most likely to put this derailed trial back on its tracks without further damage to the State. 'It's Mars-Jones.' I phoned Jeremy with the news, when the name finally emerged from the Old Bailey list office. 'What did I tell you!' he exclaimed. 'He's the worst possible choice. Juries do exactly what he tells them. He has total contempt for barristers. And his sentences are over the top. Can we object to him?'

I had never encountered Mr Justice Mars-Jones, although I rather liked what I had heard of him: he had conducted the inquiry into Harry Challoner and the bent police officers at West End Central in the sixties and had jailed most of Scotland Yard's Obscene Publications Squad for corruption a few years after the *Oz* trial. He had a son – Adam – who was beginning to make his name as a writer, which seemed a good sign. He had another son, too, who had once gone out with the daughter of Chris Price, a Labour MP who was to be a defence witness in the trial. Clutching this slim reed, we sent the judge a note inviting him to disqualify himself over this family connection, and he sent a message back telling us not to be ridiculous. Jeremy sighed, and prepared himself for the advocate's hardest task – to reach out to a jury which is under the sway of a judicial master. In all the cases I was privileged to work with Jeremy Hutchinson, his instincts were only ever wrong on one occasion. This one.

The second trial began with what was becoming almost a traditional procession to the Old Bailey, led by the 'silly secrets' dragon and the larger-than-life Buzby. Jeremy once again made his attack on the unconstitutionality of jury-vetting, which the judge rebuffed by pointing out that the defence could obtain the names and addresses of jurors and do its own vetting – which would have been fine had we the intelligence services and the Special Branch at our command. That afternoon Duncan bicycled around to the addresses of potential jurors, but the information he obtained was ambivalent. One juror had a beard – was this a sign of unconventionality, or inadequacy? Some of their homes had double locks on the front doors – did that mean they would be too security-conscious? Mars-Jones, gravelled in voice and commanding in presence, seemed determined to live up to Jeremy's fears: with unnecessary ferocity he ordered that nothing should be published about jury-vetting. The media – even *Time Out* – meekly obeyed, but the following week Sam Silkin issued a press statement on the subject. Jeremy, with a show of outrage, demanded that the Attorney General be reported to himself for contempt of court. The Law Officer made a grovelling apology to the judge, and the trial continued.

It was, as John Leonard had promised, a much more modest prosecution. He began it by paying a previously unheard tribute to the role of the press in a democracy. He dropped the 'collection' charge and focused on Section 2, but did not abandon the Section

1 charge relating to the interview with Berry. We noticed, however, that when referring to the contents of the tape, he described them as containing 'matters which *I'm told* are secret'. Early witnesses testified to Berry's indoctrination about the importance of keeping secret the identity of his unit and its location. The prosecution insisted that in open court they be referred to only as 'Unit A' at 'Location 1'. Cross-examination soon showed this secrecy to be bogus: the name and location of Unit A had been mentioned in press and in Parliament, and was well known in Cyprus. Indeed, it was known to any tourist who passed the noticeboard in front of the cluster of aerials outside Ayios Nikolaos, because it read '9th Signals Regiment, British Army'. We asked the judge's permission to identify Unit A and Location 1 in open court, and he readily and sensibly gave it. That was when the DPP personally descended on the court, which went into secret session so the prosecution could beseech the judge not to embarrass Britain by revealing that electronic intelligence was being gathered from Cyprus. The judge grumpily gave in to what he was told was diplomatic necessity, and the upshot was that witnesses were shown the photograph of the sign outside the base, and asked the following:

Q: Is that the name of your unit?
A: I cannot answer that question, that is a secret.
Q: Is that the board which passers-by on the main road see outside your unit's base?
A: Yes.
Q: Read it out to the jury, please.
A: I cannot do that, it is a secret.

And so matters continued for some days, until, on the morning of 24 October 1978, we arrived at court to find it had been cleared on the judge's order. We suspected some new excess by Buzby and the ABC dragon whose out-of-court activities had been a regular subject of complaint, but this time the prosecutors were mystified too. It was towards them the judge turned when he came into court. He had been reviewing their case, and he could not understand why they were proceeding on charges under Section 1 of the Official Secrets Act. This, he declared, was an extremely oppressive piece of legislation, suitable only for dealing with saboteurs or spies in the service of a foreign power. It permitted guilt by association, it reversed the burden of proof – why was it being used against these young journalists? He had read all the evidence, and he was 'extremely unhappy' about this 'oppressive prosecution'. John Leonard replied that the prosecution had been authorised by the Attorney General. 'If the Attorney General can authorise the prosecution, then he can unauthorise it,' snapped Mr Justice Mars-Jones in a voice which at once exemplified and justified the independence of the judiciary.

Everyone in court was stunned. But the judge had not finished. He turned to the defendants. They had no defence to the Section 2 charges that he could think of, and they could save everyone's time by pleading guilty. But whether they did or not, he had formed the very firm view that none of them deserved a custodial sentence. So while the prosecution was taking instructions about dropping Section 1, would they consider whether to plead 'guilty' to Section 2, so we could all go home? The court rose, and the defendants – who had spent the last year reconciling themselves to Christmas in jail – stumbled from the dock into the arms of their equally amazed lawyers. Bill Mars-Jones was an avenging angel, usually, if you were a bank robber or a bent copper. But to these journalists, who had faced for the past eighteen months the prospect of a long prison stretch for talking over a bottle of wine with a peeved ex-soldier, he appeared a red-robed angel of mercy. How MI5 perceived him I do not know, and he plainly did not care.

Much has been said and written, especially from a jejune left-wing perspective, about the unfitness of judges as guardians of civil liberties and as protectors of the citizen against the State. Self-important 'old Labour' politicians and cynical academics have derided the demand for a Bill of Rights, for example, on the grounds that it will be implemented by judges who cannot be trusted with a power which should belong exclusively to Parliament. On 24 October 1978, Mr Justice Mars-Jones proved them wrong. Democracy had done nothing to stop the wrongful prosecution of the '*Time Out* Two': a weak Labour administration, overawed by the intelligence service, had abused human rights by invoking Section 1 and only a handful of its back-benchers had bothered to protest. The press had stayed silent, except for the *New*

Statesman and (up to a point) the *Guardian*. A, B and C were free, not as a result of their own courage (which was a precondition) or of their campaign (which gave them courage, but did not help the courtroom battle): they owed their release to a judge robustly indifferent to the State. Other judges, it is true, might not have recognised the oppressiveness of the indictment, or have called a halt to the case in the same way or at all. But for an era which is remembered for wrongful convictions and the liberties taken by the security services, the action of Mars-Jones is worth remembering, and worth celebrating. It says something for a system when the State, with all its power bent on conviction, cannot intimidate the courts or make prosecutors flinch from their duties of fairness. The Attorney General accepted defeat with good grace, and may privately have been glad to find in the judge's words the power he was lacking as a politician to stand up to the security services. The next day, he instructed the prosecution to withdraw the Section 1 charges.

The defendants, promised their freedom in any event, were not prepared to give up the chance of a sympathy acquittal. So, anti-climactically, the trial limped on for another fortnight under the remaining Section 2 charge. Much of this time was taken in cross-examining Colonel B about the merits of the policy of blanket secrecy over anything related to SIGINT. The Colonel's position was still that SIGINT was an official secret and any mention of GCHQ, no matter how anodyne or how unimportant to the public, was extremely damaging to national security. It did not matter that the 9th Signals Regiment's intercept role in Cyprus had been widely published and was well known on the island. It did not matter that the Soviets had been told by defectors all the details of the base, or that they had spy-satellites taking pictures of it. All that mattered was that HMG had not, for diplomatic reasons, admitted its role, and therefore it did not have one. The secret world has no existence, other than in rumour or as speculation, until it is acknowledged by an official source. 'It only becomes a fact after some official says it is,' Jeremy commented acidly, and Colonel B wholeheartedly agreed.

The trial ended with a whimper, not a bang. Campbell and Aubrey were given conditional discharges, and a helpful judicial reference ('I am sure you are both good journalists with bright futures in front of you'), while Berry received a suspended sentence. They almost escaped conviction: the jury spent three nights in a hotel before reluctantly bringing back the verdict required by the catch-all nature of Section 2. The newspapers, which had been so notably silent about the case, published the front-page stories and editorials they should have written eighteen months before, condemning the prosecution and calling for Sam Silkin to resign, or at least to explain why he had authorised an oppressive prosecution. He did so, in a telling self-defence:

> I personally and critically questioned those who made the damage assessment . . . How could any responsible Attorney General ignore the unanimous views presented to me that evidence of both the material collected by Campbell and the information imparted by Berry could do damage ranging from serious to exceptionally grave to the national security?

Sam Silkin, like other liberal-minded lawyer-politicians, had a psychological need to be perceived as 'responsible' – by the security services, the Americans, the opposition. This is not only a British phenomenon: it was Ramsey Clark, the 'liberal' US attorney, who obeyed J Edgar Hoover's orders to prosecute Dr Spock; it was John Kerr, the 'liberal' QC who became Governor General of Australia and sacked the Whitlam Labour government for reasons associated with CIA concern that it might close down SIGINT bases. Richard Kliendienst, Nixon's crooked Attorney General, claimed on this evidence that civil liberties are safer in the hands of conservatives, who do not need to prove that they are 'responsible', than entrusted to people whose past support for radical causes makes them more vulnerable to police and security service pressure. I once asked Gerald Gardiner why it was that as Lord Chancellor in the first Wilson government he refused to hold sensitive conversations in his office or his house. 'I believed they would be bugged by the security services.' But how could you believe that? 'Because, you see, I'd been a pacifist during the war, I was on the Board of the *New Statesman* . . .' For this reason, Gardiner and Elwyn Jones, the Attorney General, were in the habit of discussing sensitive subjects in a car going round and round Trafalgar Square. ('We trusted the driver.') I do not believe that power tends to corrupt liberals, but it makes them extremely nervous.

The Labour Law Officers were good and conscientious men, much affected by the exigencies of the Cold War. Their failure was in not holding fast to the principle of freedom of expression in a democracy. The quality of 'responsibility' in a law officer includes an ability to distinguish between the national interest and the vested interest of the intelligence community in protecting from criticism their policies and their alliances and especially their budgets. It seems incredible now that the role of GCHQ remained a secret until the 1977 committal proceedings at Tottenham: a few years later it was barely out of the news as the government ban on trade unions and then on homosexuals became running disputes in the courts, and then Geoffrey Prime was jailed for having sold most of its secrets to the Soviets, years before A and C met B. Today SIGINT is known about and budgeted for and expected to play a part in gathering evidence of international crime and terrorism and human-rights abuses. It is pleasing to record that one of the first decisions taken by Robin Cook, when he became Foreign Secretary in 1997, was to direct that intercepts of Bosnian Serb communications gathered by GCHQ from its aerials in Cyprus should be supplied to the War Crimes prosecutors in The Hague. He had read of the existence of this evidence in a newspaper, in the kind of story which would, twenty years before, have provoked a prosecution under Section 1 of the Official Secrets Act.

Chapter 6

Gay News: The Angel's Advocate

To the pure, all things are impure
Oscar Wilde

The Old Bailey had never seen the like of *Mary Whitehouse v Denis Lemon and Gay News*, heard in the summer of 1977. The prosecutrix led prayer meetings in its corridors urging divine intervention in the jury's deliberations (a novel form of contempt of court); the barristers quoted more from their Bibles than from their usual gospel, *Archbold's Criminal Law and Practice*; the judge ingratiated himself with the jury by announcing the cricket score and delivered a summing-up which he later claimed had been inspired by God. The trial has most significance as, in all probability, the last of its kind. In retrospect it appears a miscarriage of justice, and I expect some homosexual Home Secretary will in the future give *Gay News* a posthumous pardon. It stands as a warning – which a later attempt to prosecute Salman Rushdie made indelible – against invoking the blasphemy law to protect one religion against people who adhere to other religions, or none at all.

Both religion and homosexuality have come a long way in Britain in the two decades since the *Gay News* trial. The Church of England now does not concern itself with homosexuals who take communion, so much as with all the gays who give it. *Gay News* was a vital part of the movement which produced this sea change, and Mary Whitehouse was perceptive enough to recognise its potential. She had been a somewhat comic figure until the mid-seventies, when her moral concerns became more widely shared. By 1977 she was riding very high, partly as a result of a moral panic when a Danish pornographer named Thorsen came to London with the idea (or so he said) of making a hard-core film about the sex life of Christ. This stunt played into Mary's hands: her National Viewers and Listeners Association received a letter from the Queen deploring the possibility, and both the Prime Minister and the Archbishop of Canterbury reassured the country that there were laws against such blasphemy. Mary Whitehouse suddenly appeared as the Protector of the Realm. A phrase which briefly entered the language, *circa* 1977, was 'You've got to admit Mrs Whitehouse is right about some things.'

That was when a short poem was published on the literary page of *Gay News*, a serious paper with a tiny circulation of eight thousand which dwelt upon news, arts and happenings of interest to the gay community. It was not a good poem but it was written by a good poet – Professor James Kirkup, who occupied many lines in *Who's Who*. He was then President of the Poets' Society of Japan, and a Professor of English Literature both in that country and at Ohio State University. He had published many books of poetry, and a play called *Upon This Rock*, performed in Peterborough Cathedral. His recreation was 'standing in shafts of sunlight' (when will people ever learn not to make jokes in their entries in *Who's Who*?) and he explained that 'The poem reflects my deeply religious nature. It is about the miracle of the conversion of the Centurion Longinus, and the resurrection of the dead body of Jesus through our human, earthly loves and desires . . . I wanted to present a human, earthly and imperfect Christ symbolising my own outcast state, and that of all outcasts in society.'

Mrs Whitehouse wanted to cast gays out – if not out of society, then certainly out of the Church. She had just published a book which railed against 'the most insidious of all pressure groups – the Gay Liberation Movement'. She claimed that homosexuality was caused by abnormal sexual behaviour by parents 'during pregnancy or just after' and asserted that 'psychiatric literature proves that sixty per cent of homosexuals who go for treatment get completely cured and moved into a heterosexual position'. This book was entitled *Whatever Happened to Sex?* which was a good question, given her revelation that sexual orientation could vanish, like acne, with proper treatment. She famously insisted that 'I am not against homosexuals as people, but believe homosexual practice to be wrong', but as one biography pointed out, 'this was rather like saying that one was anti-Semitic but that one had nothing against individual Jews'.

Nonetheless, I liked Mrs Whitehouse, ever since I had trodden on her toes at the Young Conservatives Ball, but rushed to a law library to blow dust off the ancient law reports when *Gay News* instructed me to resist her application to prosecute them. The last blasphemy case had been in 1922, when a Mr Gott was jailed for distributing *Rib Ticklers for Parsons*, which related that Jesus entered Jerusalem 'like a circus clown on the back of two donkeys'. The old cases in which judges forged the blasphemy law were full of Old Testament cruelties. The leading authority came from 1676, when a madman named John Taylor was heard raving that Christ was a whoremaster and organised religion a cheat. Since a crime against religion was in those days a crime against the State, the court ruled that 'Christianity is a parcel of the laws of England and therefore to reproach the Christian religion is to speak in sub-version of the law'. Taylor was placed in the pillory with a placard around his neck reading 'For blasphemous words tending to the subversion of all Government'.

'You will have to canvass the law at the trial,' said Mr Justice Bristow, giving leave for Mary's prosecution to go ahead. She alleged that the Kirkup poem 'attacked the fundamentals of the Christian faith', and presented an affidavit from an evangelical theologian who claimed that it undermined three fundamental Anglican tenets, that Christ is without sin, that homosexuality is evil and that there cannot be sex in Paradise. As the success of the prosecution would make these propositions a parcel of the laws of England, some doctrinal examination of them seemed in order. Both sides prepared for trial by searching for expert witnesses willing to engage each other in battle over the canons of Christianity.

It was not easy in the climate of 1977 to find many divines to stack up against St Paul. A certain questioning of his letter to the Romans had been sparked by Bishop John Robinson's suggestion in *Honest to God* that Jesus may have been homosexual, and a few liberal theologians had just dared to publish *The Myth of God Incarnate*. But they were nervous of the evangelical wing of the Church and the tactics of Mary Whitehouse. 'That woman!' expostulated Dr Robinson, declining to give evidence. 'I have suffered quite enough at her hands.' A few were prepared to do so – like Donald Craig, and Dr Norman Pittinger of Cambridge's Divinity School. The prosecutrix was having her difficulties too.

She wanted nothing but the best – the Archbishops of Canterbury and of York no less, together with Cardinal Basil Hume. She demanded they enter the witness box to throw the combined weight of the Churches behind her condemnation of *Gay News*. Astutely they declined: the debate over women priests had barely been kindled; that over gay access to Heaven was not to be contemplated.

Gay News was a struggling paper for an oppressed minority, and resisting the resurgence of blasphemy laws seemed a worthy enough cause in which to waive my fees. Curiously its solicitor and co-owner, Richard Creed, wouldn't hear of it. 'You must charge a commercial fee,' he insisted. Then, to my embarrassment, I saw that the newspaper was organising fund-raising activities to meet its 'legal costs' which (given that Denis Lemon was on legal aid) solely comprised the cost of my appearance on behalf of the company. So I renewed my offer. 'No, I've agreed a full fee with your clerk,' said Richard, remarkably happy after this ordeal. Then a gay friend took to telephoning me with accounts of his contribution to the *Gay News* Defence Fund at events around the country. 'Contributed another £5 towards your brief fee, old boy, cost of the disco in Leicester last night. Met the most delightful young man who wants to thank you personally. May I put him on?' The penny began to drop, as did my further offers to waive my fees. The Defence Fund climbed to £30,000, some indication of the number of gay relationships initiated by Mrs Whitehouse.

The most crucial decision was out of our hands. It was the selection of the trial judge. Alan King-Hamilton was appointed, he thinks, because he was a Jew (he was President of the West London Synagogue) apparently on the assumption that this would make him impartial. On the subject of homosexuality, however, he was neither unopinionated or up to date. When trying the publishers of *The Mouth and Oral Sex* in 1970 he had suggested that Gibbon's *Decline and Fall of the Roman Empire* proved that decadence and immorality, exemplified by increasing homosexuality and venereal disease, might herald the end of civilisation as we knew it. (Jeremy Hutchinson, defending, had to point out that Gibbon did not attribute the fall of Rome to a proliferation in sexual practices, but rather to an increase in – among other things – Christianity.) Alan was clever and quick-witted, a good lawyer full of innocent (or rather, guilty) merriment and an excellent judge of fraud trials, but he was not the most temperate judge of morals. On first reading the poem he says he was 'so shocked and horrified and revolted' that 'I wondered if I was right to try the case'. Having considered carefully his own motion to disqualify himself for bias he ruled in his own favour, on the grounds that any other judge would react in the same way. In 1977, this was probably true.

The trial began on the fourth of July. It had been an immensely difficult case to prepare for both sides, since there was no modern law of blasphemy and the old precedents – most of them from the early nineteenth century – had almost all been concerned with disbelief, often that of booksellers who stocked Tom Paine's *The Age of Reason*. The ingredients of the crime had been stated differently at different times, and we could not foretell how it would be defined today or predict whether we would be permitted to call theological or literary evidence. There was some doubt whether blasphemy even existed as a crime: it was said authoritatively to have disappeared in Scotland where there had been no prosecution for one hundred and fifty years, and to be doubtful in Wales as a result of the disestablishment there of the Anglican Church. John Mortimer (who was defending the editor, Denis Lemon) emerged from behind a high pile of centuries-old law books on the first morning:

> Judge: I am just thinking of the jury. How long is all this argument going to last?
> Mortimer: Until lunchtime.
> Judge: Goodness gracious me. I was hoping the case would be over by then.
> Mortimer: I am sorry to disappoint your Lordship, but we should enquire whether this law exists or not.

We lost all the legal arguments. For example, a practice had grown up – it was introduced by Gerald Gardiner at the *Lady Chatterley* trial – of permitting the defence to follow the prosecution's opening with its own address, thus enabling jurors to read the material having heard both sides, rather than fresh from the prosecutor's condemnation of it. This would be obviously fair in the case of a poem open to different interpretations. But the judge required the jury to listen only to the inflammatory prosecution opening – John Smythe, counsel for the prosecution, described the poem as 'so vile it would be hard for the most perverted imagination to conjure up anything worse . . . almost too vile for words, even in the Old Bailey' – and then to sit in their seats, in full public gaze, while reading the work which the prosecution had just interpreted for them. All twelve jurors had, we gloomily noted, taken their oath on the New Testament.

The prosecution applied to call a theologian, Dr J I Packer, author of *Evangelicalism and the Sovereignty of God* which identified as the root cause of error in the Church the mistake of 'subjecting the scriptures to the supposed demands of human logic'. We did not oppose the application. On the contrary, we relished the opportunity to come to grips with a Christian fundamentalism which excluded practising homosexuals from the prospect of salvation, and sought to punish this metaphysical verse-argument as a blasphemy, the very crime for which Jesus was crucified. The prosecution was a simple syllogism: Christ is sinless and homosexuality is sinful, *ergo* imputing homosexuality to Christ is blasphemy. But we found doctors of divinity to dispute both premises. Christ, on Calvary, took upon him the sins of the world. And Paul, when writing to the Romans, had no idea that he would be mistranslated two thousand years later: he was condemning *malakói* (debauched promiscuity) and *arsenokóitai* – catamites who act against their nature, rather than those who follow their nature into same-sex relationships in the late twentieth century. Had these issues been canvassed, as the prosecution suggested, *Gay News* would not have been convicted: there will always be reasonable doubt over the number of angels who can dance on pins.

The judge saw the trap our learned evangelical friends were setting for themselves, and saved them from it. There would be no theological evidence called by either side, he ruled, because the jurors had all taken the oath on the Bible and must be assumed to know what it said. Disappointed, we asked whether they might be told by literary experts about the merits of the poem, or at least how they could try to appreciate them. This was an important application: the chance of acquittal depended upon the jury reading the work figuratively rather than literally. The judge had been bested by experts before, notably by Margaret Drabble in a famous exchange during the trial of Paul Ableman's *The Mouth and Oral Sex*:

> Judge King-Hamilton: We have got on for over two thousand years without any mention of oral sex. Why do we need to read about it now?
> Drabble: (*no response*)
> Judge: Witness, why do you hesitate?
> Drabble: I'm sorry, my Lord, I was just trying to remember the passage in Ovid.

There would be no literary witnesses in this trial, ruled Judge King-Hamilton. And no other witnesses either, because he ruled that the poet's intention was irrelevant, and so was the editor's and the publisher's. There seemed to be no evidence which could be called on behalf of the defence. By this time, legal argument had lasted four days: the jurors had been present in court for barely an hour, to hear the prosecution's opening speech and to read the poem. The judge motioned the usher to bring them in, to hear final speeches. I asked for a short adjournment, and called for Margaret Drabble.

I was faced with an intensely difficult dilemma. The jury had heard no evidence at all in this case: they had had John Smythe's opening sermon, and would now hear his closing one, and John Mortimer and I would speak before the judge's last word would obliterate our efforts. The jury would decide this case on a photocopy of the poem, hearing nothing of *Gay News* or its readership, or of the acceptability in this day and age of publishing a newspaper for homosexuals and speculating about their place in Christianity. Unless . . . I *could* try to circumvent the ban on defence witnesses by calling 'character evidence' for the newspaper. The danger of this course was that the prosecution could cross-examine them on (for example) the personal advertisements featured in a column headed 'Love Knoweth No Law'. This would inflame any jury-room prejudice against homosexuals. We had no distinguished homosexuals for the role of character witness: very few were 'out' in 1977. I figured that of our candidates to speak well of *Gay News*, the two who could most take care of themselves in the witness box were Bernard Levin and Margaret Drabble. So I sowed the wind and waited to reap the whirlwind.

It came as soon as Bernard pronounced *Gay News* a serious and responsible newspaper. The prosecution wheeled into court a trolley piled with back issues – they appeared to have been reading little else, in preparation for this moment – and for several hours bombarded the witnesses with insinuations about the paper's role in propagating homosexuality:

> Smythe: You say *Gay News* is always a responsible newspaper. Look at this review of a book about homosexual love-making. It publishes explicit descriptions and illustrations. Is that responsible?
> Levin: I don't think explicitness is inconsistent with responsibility.
> Judge: Why should homosexuals need help of this kind?
> Levin: Because, like everyone else I suppose, they need to know about sexual techniques.
> Judge: Well, I don't know why heterosexuals should need help to know how to make love.
> Levin: Well, the evidence is overwhelming that many of them do.
> Judge: It's all beyond me, I'm afraid.

Nothing was beyond Alan King-Hamilton. Homosexuality had been decriminalised, but not legitimised: it was a love which still had difficulty owning up. Homosexuals had been refused any protection in the Sex Discrimination Act of 1975, and just a few weeks before the trial Lord Arran's bill to lower the age of consent from twenty-one to eighteen had been overwhelmingly defeated. There were no known gay MPs, other than in the Jeremy Thorpe sense (he was still insisting his relationship with Norman Scott was merely 'affectionate', although he was now publicly suspected of trying to kill him to keep that affection a secret). It was later in 1977 that the first MP was 'outed' by the press, which treated Maureen Colquhoun's lesbianism as a scandal disqualifying her from public office. There were quite a few gay barristers, but none came within a mile of us. I recall lunchtimes in the Old Bailey law library, alone and desperately looking for cases on points of law which had suddenly arisen: there would be a dozen excited counsel from the Bar's Christian wing, all helping the prosecution to research the same point. Twenty years on, the Bar has a flourishing gay and lesbian movement, with annual lectures presided over by High

Court judges, but in 1977 John and I had not one whisper of support, even from the two gay members of our own chambers. *Gay News* was defended entirely by heterosexuals.

Levin and Drabble stood up well, although the 'character evidence' episode ended with the judge repaying an old score:

Judge: (*as if apropos of nothing*) Do you have children?
Drabble: (*Here we go*) Yes, two boys.
Judge: (*crocodile smile*) What are their ages?
Drabble: One is sixteen, the other twelve.
Judge: (*Aha!*) And do you let them read anything they want?
Drabble: (*sees it coming*) Not everything, no. But I would let them read *Gay News*.
Judge: (*pounces*) Have they read the poem?
Drabble: (*thinking quickly*) The elder one has, because I've shown it to him. I'm afraid the younger one can't be persuaded to read anything.

It was the traditional Old Bailey googly, and Margaret was right to play it with a straight bat. But in his summing-up the judge did not let the jury forget the sixteen-year-old Master Drabble: 'We know it is read not only by homosexuals; some probation officers read it, Mr Levin and other dramatic critics, *Miss* Drabble and maybe other literary critics, and *Miss* Drabble's sixteen-year-old son, and *perhaps other sixteen-year-olds.*'

That was all the evidence the jury were allowed to hear, before they were swept into the final speeches. John Smythe, having condemned 'all the filth that is in *Gay News*', denounced the imputation of homosexuality to Christ as an attack on Christianity 'too obvious for words'. How would the jury feel about 'an accusation of homosexuality against a member of the Royal Family? Yet Christ is not just a king, but the King of Kings.' His peroration was tub-thumping: this was a trial of 'vital significance' and 'tremendous importance'. This case was 'about whether anything is to remain sacred. You are being asked to set the standard for the last quarter of the twentieth century . . . a verdict of "not guilty" would open the floodgates. The privilege of raising a banner against the tiny minority who seek to inflict this sort of thing on us and our children belongs exclusively to you.'

It was period rhetoric, this appeal to jurors to set historic standards. It is always attractive, of course, to be part of something historic. But some jurors might baulk at using the criminal law to protect society from one man's imagination. The poem was sixty lines long and I decided that there was nothing for it but to explain, line by line, how it tried to communicate – metaphorically rather than literally, by likening divine love to human love – Christ being the word made flesh. The only way, in other words, to deal with the case for Mrs Whitehouse was to be holier than her. In two of her autobiographies she gives me a kind notice, praising with faint damns:

> I shall never forget the dreadful sense of despair which overwhelmed me after hearing Geoffrey Robertson sum up for the defence. It was a truly remarkable performance. His manner was gentle and persuasive. In the silence that fell upon the court Robertson talked about God's love for sinners and for homosexuals who, like everyone else, must have the hope of salvation and redemption . . . he picked up The Book of Common Prayer and drew the jury's attention to the words of the communion service: 'This is my Body – *eat* this. This is my Blood – *drink* this' . . . God *must* have spoken through Robertson's words, whatever his intent. A wonderful example of the way He can and does use all things to His purpose.

Just call me the Angel's Advocate. But Mary could not resist adding, 'After Geoffrey Robertson's address to the jury, the phrase "the Devil's Advocate" took on a whole new meaning.' In fact, I had made one fatal mistake. I own up to it for the benefit of anyone else called upon to defend a poem on a charge of blasphemy at the Old Bailey. If you must deal with its interpretation, MAKE SURE YOU READ EVERY LINE ALOUD. I funked a few phrases and some six lines that I could not bring myself to repeat. I glossed, I summarised and I read bits of metaphysical poetry. But my failure was leapt upon by the judge, as swiftly as a spider jumps a struggling fly. He told the jury that lines forty-three to forty-eight were 'the ultimate in profanity'. And he reminded them repeatedly that I had not read them out – 'Are you surprised?' And he told them that the test for blasphemy was whether they could read the poem out loud without blushing. The 'truly remarkable performance' was his and not mine.

Reaction to a poem is peculiarly personal. Mine was conditioned, no doubt, by a degree in English literature and the fact that I do not have a gay bone in my body. I could interpret the imagery, but not muster much interest in it. Mary had hooted when she heard I had been seen on a beach in the South of France reading a Bible, and hoped it would do me some good, but she knew nothing of my religious upbringing (there were Plymouth Brethren lurking on one side of the family) or of the fact that I could still weep inwardly at the idea of the crucifixion. I had been shocked on first reading Kirkup's poem, 'The Love that Dares to Speak its Name' – an adaptation of the famous line by Lord Alfred Douglas which Oscar Wilde had been taunted with at his own trial eighty years before. It was a monologue by the centurion mentioned in Matthew as being converted on Gethsemane.

> As they took him from the cross
> I, the centurion, took him in my arms –
> The tough lean body
> of a man no longer young
> beardless, breathless
> but well hung.
>
> I was alone with him.
> For the last time
> I kissed his mouth. My tongue
> found his, better with death.
> I licked his wounds –
> the blood was harsh.

For a poem denounced because 'every stanza was vile', these hardly merited that description. A lonely Roman officer who kept the company of men is left alone with the body, after officiating at an obscene ritual of torture and murder. Little wonder he fantasises, repeating the gossip ('A gluttonous man, a wine-bibber, a friend of publicans and sinners') that had so inflamed the rabble as to demand the man's death. Meant to be understood as the centurion's stream of consciousness, the next six-line metaphysical conceit reflecting a 'love' for all mankind was for the prosecutor the 'worst stanza, too odious for words':

> I knew he'd had it off with other men –
> with Herod's guards, with Pontius Pilate,
> with John the Baptist, with Paul of Tarsus,
> with foxy Judas, a great kisser, with
> the rest of all the twelve, together and apart.
> He loved all men, body, soul and spirit – even me.

For the judges who read the poem, this was the gravest of criminal libels: an allegation of orgies and promiscuous homosexuality. Of course, it had not been intended to be taken literally, but then intention was irrelevant. In court, words are expected to mean what they say. The centurion went on to embrace the body of Christ in words which added little to the indictment, until the passage which the judge suggested was so profane not even I would read it aloud:

> And then the miracle possessed us.
> I felt him enter into me, and fiercely spend
> his spirit's final seed within my hole, my soul,
> pulse upon pulse, unto the ends of the earth –
> he crucified me with him into kingdom come.

Reading this again after two decades, I wonder whether the reason I could not read it was the awfulness of the poetry rather than the grossness of the blasphemy. What I read instead was a sonnet by John Donne ('Batter my heart, three-personed God') which ends:

> Yet dearly I love you and would be lov'd fain,
> But am betroth'd unto your enemy;
> Divorce us, untie, or break that knot again,
> Take me to you, imprison me, for I
> Except y'enthral me never shall be free
> Nor ever chaste except you ravish me.

The ecstasy of the metaphysical poet's union with God has never been more exquisitely put than by the one-time Bishop of London: James Kirkup was not in his class, although parallels between sexual and religious ecstasy have been with us in the imagery of Christian poets since St John of the Cross. Kirkup's fate was to be in the wrong place (*Gay News*) at the wrong time (during a 'moral panic' over the Thorsen film). His poem rallied a bit, I think, in its closing lines:

> And after three long, lonely days, like years,
> in which I roamed the gardens of my grief
> searching for him, my one friend who had gone from me,
> he rose from sleep, at dawn, and showed himself to me before
> all others, and took me to him with
> the love that now forever dares to speak its name.

I did read these lines with more feeling, and reminded the jury of the Eucharist: 'He dwelleth in me, and I in him.' I even read Paul, who wanted to be 'all things to all men' – why not to gay men as well? I also suggested that in small print on page twenty-six (the Arts section) of a paper with a circulation of eight thousand copies, it was not likely to subvert the fabric of society. It was no lavatory limerick, or precursor of a pornographic film, and those who read it through and in context would not find in its tone the vilification and ridicule which is the true gist of blasphemy. It was, in short, a muddled comment about the mystery of the crucifixion and the empty tomb.

John followed me on Friday afternoon, the voice of reason between the two opposing sermons:

> The prosecution in this case appears on behalf of unknown supernatural forces and my learned friend Mr Robertson for a company without any corporeal existence. I alone appear for a human being, who is in the dock in peril on this antique charge which has not been used for more than fifty years. The Sermon on the Mount tells us to love our neighbours, but Mrs Mary Whitehouse has put her neighbour in the dock . . .

He played for time and returned to the crease on Monday morning with a Radio 4 talk on poetry and the role of allegory and parable in Christian teaching. This was a private prosecution which demeaned Christianity by pretending it needed the protection of the criminal law. Jesus had said 'whoever speaketh a word against the Son of Man it shall be forgiven him', and that was how true Christians should react to the prosecution. I should like to have taken a jury vote at this point, because I suspect it would have been split down the middle. An acquittal was never on the cards because the emotional loyalties aroused by the prosecution ran so deep. Although the jury is renowned as a bastion of free speech, this is a demonstrable historical error in blasphemy cases: in the hundreds of prosecutions in British history, with one exception THE JURY HAS ALWAYS CONVICTED. It even convicted Shelley's 'Queen Mab' in 1840 in a private prosecution brought by a free-thinker for a joke.

The trial had in a vague way been unedifying, as both sides used holy scriptures for what I believe was an unworthy purpose: to persuade of an argument rather than to reveal the truth. So the 'result' that I hoped for was, in fact, no result at all. It would be a jury divided on these huge and obsessional questions which could not sensibly be resolved, as could burglary and fraud, down at the Old Bailey. That view was not shared by the judge, as his autobiography later made plain:

> From the time the trial began, I had an extraordinary feeling of unreality: that I was rather watching the trial, instead of presiding over it. I have never experienced a similar sensation before or since. As for the summing-up itself, I can confidently assert that it was the best, by far, I have ever given. I can say this without blushing because, throughout its preparation and also when delivering it, I was half-conscious of being guided by some superhuman inspiration.

The summing-up was a miracle of persuasion, although had it really been devised by the Deity I hope it would have been rather more fair to the defence. It went like this:

First the judge complained that it was necessary to place in perspective Mr Mortimer's attack on this 'antique' law. The laws against murder and theft were just as 'antique'. The fact that there had not been a prosecution for blasphemy for more than half a century showed what a really useful law it was. Mr Mortimer had said that this was a doubtful branch of the law and very complex.

'I have no doubt about the law and do not think it is complex.' It was a question of libel, which is something that damages reputation. To say of a bishop that he committed homosexual acts with a vicar would be the clearest of libels. Was this a libel, therefore, on Christ? Just look at the lines that Mr Robertson did not read! 'Those lines you may think are the ultimate in profanity: but it is for you, members of the jury, not me. Nevertheless, look at it and see what these lines say. Can you imagine anything more profane?' The judge continued:

> There can be no doubt what the poem says. It says Christ was not only homosexual but promiscuous, that he indulged in every kind of homosexual activity with others, singly and in orgies during his lifetime ... It is entirely a matter for you, but I suggest you must ask yourselves whether there could really be anything more profane. If a similar poem were written about a living person, it would obviously defame and vilify and be a clear case of libel, there can be no doubt about that. You may wonder how much more offensive and likely to provoke resentment if the vilification is aimed at Christ ... if the allegation in the poem even *might* have been true, you may think there would not have been any Christian religion at all!

Then the judge told them how utterly irrelevant was the poet's motive and intention.

> Mr Robertson put forward a possible interpretation – give it such consideration as you think that interpretation merits, but the point is, how would an ordinary Christian interpret it? He omitted certain lines. Do you think these lines he omitted in any way express a love of God? ... He said there was no danger to peace because of the poem. I have explained that there does not have to be any danger to peace. He said it was published in a responsible paper and no one was forced to buy it. That is absolutely true but is not relevant anyway. He said Christ was unique and can only be appreciated by comparison, and he said that you are being asked to punish human imagination ... Can a poet not make such a poem without an element of explicit sex and vilification?

This was coming close to a direction to convict, although I suppose the judge's superhuman guide was not bound by the rule in *Stonehouse*. The jury was required to assume that God existed, and to ask themselves: 'Do you think God would like to be recognised in the context of a poem such as this?'

Then the judge reduced the law of blasphemy to some simple questions:

Did it shock you when you first read it?
Could it shock or offend anyone who read it?
Could you read it to an audience of fellow Christians without blushing?

Finally, Judge King-Hamilton (or his superhuman inspiration) used three powerful rhetorical devices. The first was to set up a false dichotomy, suggesting that an acquittal might mean 'anything goes':

There are some [*i.e. Mrs Whitehouse*] who think that permissiveness has gone far enough and that this poem has gone beyond what is permissive. There are others [*hint: the defence*] who think that there should be no limit whatsoever on what may be published. If they are right, one may wonder what scurrilous profanity may appear next. There is a world of difference between opening a window in a stuffy Victorian library and letting in a little fresh air, and on the other hand, leaving both windows and doors open so there is a raging draft, bringing in with it a retinue of attendant dangers with all their consequences.

The next device was the warning couched in terms so attractive that the action warned against becomes a temptation difficult to resist: 'The purpose of the prosecution is not to set any future standard – although it may well be that by your verdict you will in effect be setting a standard, but that is by the way. Do not let it weigh upon you that what you do may be setting a standard for future generations.'

Finally, the punch line: 'If you are sure it is a blasphemy, then it is your duty, to which you are bound by the jurors' oath *which each of you took on the New Testament*, to say guilty.'

Divinely inspired or fiendishly clever? At the defence table, we had little doubt, and moped off to the Bar common room to await the guilty verdict, stumbling on the way over the prosecutrix and her supporters praying for it in the corridor. Surprisingly, it took five hours for these prayers to be answered, and then not in full: two jurors had the fortitude to resist and to record their dissent. Denis Lemon was hauled to his feet: 'Prisoner at the Bar, you stand convicted of crime. Have you anything to say before the court passes judgment upon you according to the law?'

Centuries ago, this served as the cue for blasphemers to make long speeches justifying their crime and increasing their punishment. The ruling that the editor's intention did not matter had prevented Denis from giving evidence at the trial, and there was no point in giving it now. Judge King-Hamilton launched into an attack on the National Council for Civil Liberties for criticising the blasphemy laws, and then turned to praise 'ten of the jurors who had the moral courage to reach the verdict that they did', although given his summing-up, the only 'moral courage' was that displayed by the two dissenters. 'I have no doubt whatsoever,' he continued, 'and apparently ten of the jury agree with me, that this poem was quite appalling and that it contains scurrilous profanity and I hope never to see the like of it again.' It was 'past comprehension' how a university professor could write it and 'touch and go' whether Denis Lemon should not go straight to prison. He was given a suspended prison sentence of nine months, an entirely inappropriate punishment which the Court of Appeal in due course quashed.

The chief interest of the appeal was to see how higher courts would cope with our one overwhelming argument. The ruling that the defendant's intention in publishing the poem was irrelevant flew in the face of most judicial and academic authority, and was contrary to the first principle of criminal law – that the prosecution must prove that the defendant has *mens rea*, a guilty mind. The Court of Appeal solved this difficulty by saying that the law of blasphemy had been invented before *mens rea* became essential. John Taylor in a moment of lucidity had argued that his shout 'Christ is a whoremaster' was not intended literally, but Lord Hale (a judge much given, in his time, to burning witches, but renowned for the legal knowledge with which he did so) had rejected this defence.

Since Lord Hale saw blasphemy as a crime of strict liability in 1676, whatever other judges may have said in subsequent centuries it remained a crime of strict liability in 1977. Between the ravings of a lunatic from Bedlam and the metaphors of a modern Professor of Poetry, the literal-minded law would make no distinction.

The television monitors in the Westminster corridor announced 'Prayers' as the five Law Lords shuffled along the lush carpet to their committee room for our final appeal. Lord Diplock presided, and began by complaining that nobody had supplied them with a copy of the poem. It was handed up, and with the main house at prayer the Law Lords read the blasphemy – except for the devoutly Catholic Lord Russell, who ostentatiously averted his eyes. So much for his vote: could our advocacy persuade three of the other four judges? Louis Blom-Cooper had replaced John Mortimer (who was in Singapore doing battle with the local deity, Lee Kuan Yew) and opened the appeal. Lord Diplock made it clear immediately that he was in our favour. He was given to boast that in his long life as a judge he had only ever changed his mind twice in the course of counsel's argument, and on one of those occasions he had persuaded himself he was wrong. So after five minutes, the score was one-all. It became two–one against a few moments after Diplock's declaration, with a predictable goal by Viscount Dilhorne, the former Conservative Attorney General (Reginald Manningham-Buller) who had opposed all attempts to decriminal-ise homosexuality, and was wholly in favour of imposing strict liability on scribblers.

To win this particular justice game would depend on winning the minds, if not the hearts, of both remaining judges. One was Lord Scarman, who had little criminal law experience but was nonetheless the most towering humane presence in modern British jurisprudence. The other was Lord Edmund-Davies, a devout and conservative man who would loathe the poem to his bones, although they were bones in which the principles of criminal law were embedded more deeply than in any other judge of the time. The betting at Temple Dinners was that we would win over Scarman ('liberal on gays') but lose Edmund-Davies ('Welsh chapel, you know').

The most remarkable thing about a disciplined system of law – its own small miracle in a way – is a judgment that holds fast to principle, even though this produces a result in the particular case which is privately deplored by the judge who gives it. This is what 'fidelity to law' means: it can be observed in appeal courts which set free obviously guilty men because of an error in proceedings which the court refuses on principle to overlook or explain away. The rules of the justice game are supple enough in the hands of judges, especially in the House of Lords (where there is a special rule which allows them to change, up to a point, the existing rules). But Edmund-Davies stuck to them scrupulously, producing a magisterial sweep of authority in favour of quashing a conviction of whose merits he undoubtedly approved. The score was two-all.

This was a hard case. It made bad law because we lost Leslie Scarman. It was an own-goal: he was the only judge who understood the poem (or was prepared to say so), but he had a wider jurisprudential agenda. He recognised, with his law reformer's instinct, that blasphemy should not be a crime at all unless it protected all religions equally. His grand scheme was that Parliament should unchain it from the shackles of history and extend it to cover abusive attacks on all religions, and not merely the tenets of the Anglican Church. On this basis, for the sake of restraining bigots rather than poets, he opted for strict liability for those who 'cause grave offence to religious feeling'. This was his idea of 'the way forward for a successful plural society'. The appeal was rejected, by three votes to two.

The *Gay News* trial lives on in Alan King-Hamilton's memoirs, written on his retirement in 1979. These came after a public uproar over his last trial, in which four anarchists he believed guilty were acquitted. The judge treated the jury like naughty schoolchildren, berating them for being taken in by my final speech and for not understanding 'evidence which would not have confused a child of ten'. He was roundly condemned in the press for this, but replied logically enough that since it is common for judges to express agreement with jury verdicts, he did not see why they should not express disagreement. The reason, I might respectfully suggest, is that they should not express agreement either; as he had so fulsomely with the verdict on *Gay News*. This point of view has gained greater acceptance since, and as a result of, Alan's last innings at the Bailey.

Mary Whitehouse relished her triumph in several autobiographies, although the Church never quite forgave her for embarrassing its Archbishops and promoting the idea that practising homosexuals were excluded from the faith. The Law Commission later noted that a number of practising Christians had become so disgusted with the prosecution of *Gay News* that 'they ceased to be communicant members of the Church of England'. Mary called me after the trial, to ask my religion for a book she was writing about it. 'I'm told you are an atheist. Is that true?' I confessed to sometimes questioning the justice of a God who doles out eternal life not to those who deserve it but to those who pray for it, so she called me a 'Protestant sceptic'. It was as ever a cheery conversation. Mary was a feisty and funny and foxy lady, and I wish I had said, 'We'll meet at Philippi' – the next bisexual Roman soldier she was to engage in courtroom conflict would prove her undoing.

The Sunday after the Court of Appeal judgment in *Gay News* I had found myself, unsceptically, visiting the harvest festival at a church in Dedham, just outside Colchester. Driving back along a narrow country lane, I came very close to killing a woman standing recklessly on the road picking blackberries. The back of her head was dimly recognisable as one I had last seen bowed in prayer in the Old Bailey corridor. Mary (for it was she) was unmoved by her lucky escape – she really did trust in God. The trouble with her faith was that everyone else had to swerve to avoid colliding with her, because she was always in the right. She was genuinely pleased to infer, from the sex of my companion, that I had not undergone any conversion by reading *Gay News*. We took tea together and wondered what a coroner's jury would make of the incident had it ended less happily.

Gay News flourished after and as a result of the trial. It was stocked by W H Smith, its circulation rose to 40,000, and literature for and about homosexuals became commonplace.

The last significant prosecution was in 1985 when the directors of Gay's the Word bookshop were charged with conspiracy to import sixty-eight 'indecent' books. 'Operation Tiger' was an eighteen-month exercise involving a force of thirty-six customs officers who seized any book which bore the word 'gay' in its title – including the works of Gay Talese, a notoriously heterosexual American author. (In the fifties, a similar policy of judging books by their covers had caused customs to impound *Rape Around Our*

Coasts, a story of soil-erosion, and *Fun in Bed*, a book of games for sick children.) The growing confidence of London's gay community was reflected by the defendants: they were articulate, educated and proud of their collective management of Europe's largest homosexual bookshop. They were supported by public figures (from whom we had heard nothing during the *Gay News* battle eight years before) and their defence campaign was led by an able and openly gay MP, Chris Smith. They opted for public committal proceedings, in order to expose the warped priorities of a customs service which devoted more of its resources to impounding literature than to seizing cocaine. The hearing was fixed, appropriately, for 'Gay Pride' week, by which time fund-raising activities familiar from *Gay News* days had already produced £50,000 for 'legal costs'. (I knew better this time than to offer to waive my fees.)

The customs witnesses admitted that they had seized novels by Tennessee Williams and Gore Vidal 'because they had the name of a homosexual author on the cover'. This was a lame excuse for taking liberties: the 'dutymen' had closed down the bookshop for a day and held the defendants in custody, seizing their stock and their personal belongings before going on to raid their homes. We obtained a top-secret blacklist of homosexual publishers, the very existence of which seemed to contradict assurances given to Parliament by a minister whose name was suitably slapstick, Barney Hayhoe. In an atmosphere where everyone was enjoying the prosecution discomfort, I made three mistakes in the course of asking one question in cross-examination. I played to the gallery; I deployed sarcasm, the lowest form of wit; and I asked a question to which I did not know the answer. Pointing an accusing finger at the young customs officer who had code-named the operation, I declaimed, 'You called this operation "Tiger", did you not, because that name was redolent of swaggering machismo?' The officer replied, 'Well, no sir. Actually, I named it after my cat.'

Collapse of stout cross-examiner. The case against Gay's the Word collapsed, more bizarrely, through the agency of a life-size love-doll. I have never been able to conceive of the extremity of sexual desperation which would drive a man to mate with an inflatable rubber woman, but the demand for these companions has been constant and sex-shops imported them in bulk from

Germany. One such consignment, to a firm called Conegate, was declared by magistrates to be an 'indecent' import because 'the dolls when inflated show nearly life-size images of the developed female form with orifices with a vibrator (being some sort of electrical device) and with simulated pubic hair'. I was introduced to one such lady by her prosecutor, a distinguished silk and later a High Court judge, who had hung her up, fully inflated, in the robe closet of his chambers to surprise his clients. No doubt such jollity was the main purpose of these surrogate Fräuleins but the smell of their burning rubber soon reached the European Court of Justice in Luxembourg. The destruction of German love-dolls, it decided, was a breach of the Treaty of Rome: it constituted an unlawful 'quantitative restriction' on imports between member states, and an arbitrary discrimination on trade. The effect of this landmark ruling was that customs had to drop its prosecution of importers of 'indecent' articles: they had to be 'obscene' (in the sense of being likely to deprave and corrupt) and no one could contend that the books stocked by Gay's the Word fell into this class. So gay literature was saved by a rubber doll, and investigating customs officers turned to more important matters – in due course, to the export of weapon-making machine tools to Iraq at the instance of a firm called Matrix Churchill.

So what became of the law of blasphemy, raised from the dead in 1977? To Mary's regret it fell back into a coma when the Law Commission, in 1979 and again in 1985, recommended abolition of the entire offence. The Commissioners considered Lord Scarman's plea to extend it to other religions, but they despaired of drawing any sensible distinction between the religions which would have to be protected, including those of Moonies, Rastas and Scientologists, and they pointed out that some religious doctrines deserve to be attacked. They deplored the crippling uncertainty of an offence which depends on a subjective finding by a particular jury that material is 'scurrilous', 'abusive' or 'offensive' to Christianity, and pointed out that existing public order offences were sufficiently wide to protect *any* religion from disturbance by conduct or pamphlets likely to cause a breach of the peace. So when *The Life of Brian* came out, only a handful of local councils – several without cinemas in their area – bothered to ban it. There matters rested for a decade until the proposed release of *The Last Temptation of Christ* – a Hollywood film in which Christ was pictured making love to Mary Magdalene. Alan King-Hamilton emerged from retirement to write to *The Times,* reminding the nation of his *Gay News* ruling ('I have not of course seen the film in question, but if my information about it is accurate, there can be no doubt there are grounds on which to charge criminal libel'). This intervention caused the distributors to retain me for a second opinion: the film's most scurrilous feature, I thought, was that Christ and his disciples were played by Americans, while Judas and the Devil and all other baddies spoke with English accents.

It was, finally, the Ayatollah Khomeini who gave the crime of blasphemy its *quietus,* on St Valentine's Day 1989, by launching the mother of all prosecutions against Salman Rushdie. Like the Red Queen from *Alice in Wonderland,* his *fatwah* was a case of sentence first and trial later. Salman disappeared from view – for several weeks to my house in Islington which was much favoured by Special Branch because its bedroom windows offered a clear view of any would-be assassins: it overlooked a church. Salman's difficulties had this compensation: they brought many of his North London friends into a closer and warmer contact with officers of the Special Branch than they might ever have thought likely or even healthy. The goodwill flowed both ways: the police enjoyed the literary company rather more than that of the politicians they were normally detailed to protect, while left-wing writers came to see the sense in secret State surveillance of suspected terrorists. Women married to *Guardian*-reading male feminists could not help but notice that on weekends with Salman, it was the police who volunteered to wash up (on the other hand, one or two of them had a somewhat unreconstructed habit of showing a gun in the presence of an attractive nanny).

It was not long before certain Muslims decided to flush Rushdie out from hiding, by using the one device to which he would have no option but to surrender: not a gun, but a summons. Taking a leaf from the book of Mary, they asked a Bow Street magistrate to issue an order against the author of *The Satanic Verses* to attend his private prosecution for blasphemous libel. The magistrate refused, because the crime of blasphemy only related to offences against the Christian religion. The private prosecutor (a Mr

Chaudhury) appealed to the High Court, where I appeared for Salman Rushdie.

Special Branch dutifully informed me that since millions of zealots, and not just Mrs Whitehouse, might soon perceive me as the 'Devil's Advocate', I had been officially classified as 'Potential target – Grade 3'. I was not potential enough to qualify for police protection, but sufficiently at risk to receive some security tips. One which did stick in my mind was that Grade 3-ers should in no circumstances draw attention to the fact that they were potential targets, because then they might become real ones. It might not occur to the *Times*-reading Iranian terrorist that the barrister representing Rushdie would be a satisfactory substitute for his client, unless some further news item put the idea into his head. The same advice was given to the judges: while this case lasts, don't advertise yourselves as potential targets.

We had drawn my favourite presiding judge, Lord Justice Tasker Watkins VC. Most colleagues found my affection for him strange because he was certainly not noted for liberal views. His Victoria Cross had been won (so the story went) when he picked up the machine gun of a wounded comrade and proceeded single-handedly to attack a trench of seventeen startled Germans, killing all of them as their laughter at this hot-headed young Welsh fusilier died on their lips. I always found him full of instinctive passion for justice and liked his sense of humour. That was not the cause of the glint in his eye as he took his seat on the second day of the hearing, to announce dramatically, 'This court is in receipt of a com-munication. Let it be handed to counsel.' It was an ill-written threat of vengeance against us all, should the case go against the Prophet. 'Well,' he snapped with ill-concealed impatience. 'What do counsel suggest we do?' The defence barristers held a whispered conversation at the Bar table, reminding ourselves of the Special Branch advice against saying anything which might turn us – or the judges – into Grade 2 targets. 'Nothing, my Lord,' we murmured quietly. 'We see no need to draw attention to the matter.' 'No need to draw attention to it!' exploded Tasker. 'This is a death threat to Her Majesty's judges and counsel! We shall certainly draw attention to it and say in the strongest terms that it will not be countenanced!' He had, for a moment, the look in his eye probably last seen by seventeen unfortunate German soldiers. The infidel hordes had been warned: let them descend upon the Royal Courts of Justice if they dared.

The prosecution was represented in court by a record number of Muslim barristers, their names in consequence enrolled in the service of the Prophet in this forensic *jihad* (holy war) against Salman the Apostate. The object of their exercise was to ban the book, but their action had this advantage: it forced them to draft an indictment against Rushdie and his publishers specifying with legal precision the way in which *The Satanic Verses* had blasphemed. Might it not conceivably defuse this international flashpoint (already twenty-two lives had been lost in a riot against the book in Bombay, and deadly attacks on its translators were soon to come) by actually fighting the case on its merits and proving once and for all that the allegations against the book were false – that it did not amount to blasphemy against Islam? Salman was dubious but thought it worth a try.

So I turned to the Koran, in the same spirit of professional curiosity as I had studied the Bible during *Gay News*. That modern mortals may meaningfully blaspheme against either of these sacred texts is plainly absurd: the anachronisms that attract our petty criticism pale before their sweep of inspiration. The study convinced me that the author of *The Satanic Verses* did not intend or achieve any blasphemy. The book is the fictional story of two men, infused with Islam but confused by the temptations of the West. The first survives by returning to his roots. The other, Gibreel, pole-axed by his spiritual need to believe in God and his intellectual ability to return to the faith, finally commits suicide. The plot, in short, is not an advertisement for apostasy.

Our thirteen barrister opponents could in the end only allege six blasphemies in the book and each one was based either on misreading it or upon theological error:

– God is described in the book as 'The Destroyer of Man'. *As He is similarly described in the Old Testament and the Book of Revelation, especially of men who are unbelievers or enemies of the Jews.*
– The book contains criticisms of the prophet Abraham for his conduct towards Hagar and Ismael and their son. *Abraham deserves criticism and is not seen as without fault in Islamic, Christian or Jewish traditions.*

- Rushdie refers to Mohammed as 'Mahoud'. He called him variously 'a conjuror', 'a magician' and a 'false prophet'. *Rushdie does nothing of the sort. These descriptions come from the mouth of a drunken apostate, a character with whom neither author nor reader has sympathy. 'Mahoud' is in fact a name that has been used by Christians for the Prophet.*
- The book grossly insults the wives of the Prophet by having whores use their names. *This is the point. The wives are expressly said to be chaste, and the adoption of their names by whores in a brothel symbolises the perversion and decadence into which the city had fallen before it surrendered to Islam.*
- The book vilifies the close companions of the Prophet, calling them 'bums from Persia' and 'clowns', whereas the Koran treats them as men of righteousness. *These phrases are used by a depraved hack poet, hired to pen propaganda against the Prophet. Christ's disciples were derided by his enemies as ignorant fishermen, so it can hardly be blasphemous for an author to imagine the Prophet's followers being subjected to the same kind of criticism.*
- The book criticises the teachings of Islam for containing too many rules and seeking to control every aspect of everyday life. *Characters in the book do make such criticisms, but they cannot amount to blasphemy because they do not vilify God or the Prophet.*

If the law of blasphemy *had* covered Islam, *The Satanic Verses* still would not have infringed it. The High Court did not have to decide as much, since the prosecution was misconceived, although it did set out our submissions sympathetically in its judgment. But even if Salman were to be tried and acquitted by an Old Bailey jury, the verdict would have made not the slightest difference to his dishonest enemies: as one Iranian leader put it, the *fatwah* was not about the book, but 'over the West trying to dictate to Islam'. The case did have one satisfying result: the UK government announced that it would not extend blasphemy to protect other religions, or invoke it for 'divisive and damaging litigation'. The official statement, issued to the Muslim community in November 1989 by the Home Office, declared 'how inappropriate our legal mechanisms are for dealing with matters of faith and individual belief. Indeed, the Christian faith no longer relies on blasphemy prosecutions, preferring to recognise that the strength of their own belief is the best armour against mockers and blasphemers'. Amen to that. There will be no future prosecutions by the State, although Parliament will not abolish the blasphemy law. MPs share that indefinable fear of eternity which makes most of their constituents scribble 'C of E' in the space opposite 'religion' on the hospital admission form. (There are, by such indications, more Anglicans in our hospitals than in our churches.)

The law against blasphemy will remain in the law reports as a blue plaque to the free-thinkers who suffered for their free thoughts in previous times. I have read all their cases and marvel at the unchristian cruelty of the bishops who insisted on having them prosecuted, and of the judges who put them to hard labour in prison. The last was the dying, diabetic Gott, whose jury in 1922 recommended clemency: when a medical report was handed up to the Bench, the Chief Justice sneered 'a sentence of hard labour will cause the authorities to pay greater attention to his health'. There was Thomas Williams, the sickly and penitent bookseller of Lincoln's Inn, with his young children riddled with smallpox: even Erskine, his prosecutor, begged the bishops to forgive him for selling Tom Paine's *The Age of Reason*, but they refused and the judges flung him into the House of Correction. 'I trust it will not be too great an indulgence if I have a bed,' were Williams's last words, to which the Chief Justice retorted, 'I cannot order that: this publication is horrible to the ear of a Christian.' The reports of the old 'State trials' for blasphemy give potted biographies of counsel: the barristers advocating for the angels always flew straight to the Bench, while those devilling for the defence often ended up in the dock themselves at the next Assizes. So it is as much for the ingloriousness of its legal history as for its lack of principle that I should wish the blasphemy law abolished, leaving public order laws to protect, as they amply do, the decent devotions of the faithful of all religions against scurrility or abuse.

II

Lawyers, Guns and Money

Chapter 7

The Romans in Britain

Darkness. Dogs bark in the distance. Silence.
Conlag: Where the fuck are we?

It gets a big laugh, this opening line, although I'm not sure what makes it so amusing. The fact that it's spoken in an Irish accent into the imposing amphitheatre of the Olivier auditorium? A recognition, by an audience in 1981, that it crudely sums up the current state of the peace process in Northern Ireland? A wry acknowledgement that a much better evening could be had at any West End musical, rather than by venturing south of the river to witness an orgy of murder, rape, incest and buggery? John Osborne wrote in a letter to the *Guardian*: 'Why go to the National Theatre when we can get all this at home?'

The Romans in Britain was the first play to be prosecuted in Britain. This was a consequence of the National Theatre giving free opening-night tickets to the leader of the Greater London Council, Sir Horace Cutler. It is hard to think back to the time when London had a GLC, and even harder to remember it not being led by Ken Livingstone. His Tory predecessor is memorable mainly for storming out of Howard Brenton's play at half-time, threatening to cut the National Theatre's grant. His outburst brought much publicity for himself, as he had intended, and for the play, which picked up at the box office. Mrs Mary Whitehouse was informed the next day (so she recorded in her diary) that 'Three Roman soldiers are apparently tearing off all their clothes and raping three young, male Britons in full view of the audience!' She declared herself horrified: 'It has been known for two thousand years how the Romans – some of them – behaved in Britain. We haven't needed to wait all those years for the National Theatre to come and show us.'

The play promised the same ingredients as the *Gay News* poem

– religion, buggery and Roman centurions. Mary demanded that the Attorney General, Sir Michael Havers, prosecute the National for obscenity, but Havers, a play-goer with a renowned thespian son, declined. Mary then divined that a private prosecution was 'what the Lord would have me do'. Rapturously, she confided to the diary she immediately published, 'For a woman of seventy-one, mother and grandmother, to challenge an act of simulated buggery at the National Theatre in the full publicity which would attend the trial – *what* a comment on the days in which we live'. So the Director of Private Prosecutions reassembled her devout legal battalion from the war over *Gay News* and girded her loins for battle against a play she had not seen in a theatre she had never attended. John Mortimer, as a member of the National's board, could not appear for himself, and suggested the counsel Mary had dubbed 'The Devil's Advocate' should be hired to frustrate her new attack on the arts.

First, she had to find a legal loophole, because private prosecutions of the theatre had been banned by the Theatres Act in 1968. This legislation was passed to end the Lord Chamberlain's historic role as censor of the stage and to make producers and directors, like other writers and artists, subject only to the law of obscenity. This meant that they could not be convicted unless the performance 'tended to deprave or corrupt' and additionally had no redeeming dramatic merit. Precisely in order to prevent vexatious or partisan prosecutions, Parliament decreed that no legal action could be brought against stage plays other than by, or with the consent of, the Attorney General. But just as the law did not prevent a prosecution for murder if an actor engaged in a centre-stage assassination, why should it prevent a prosecution for an act of gross indecency? A theatre was, for legal purposes, a public place, and although the actors might be following a script, there was a neat little offence in Section 13 of the Sexual Offences Act 1956 which would convict any male person who directed them. It was defined as 'procuring, by a male, the commission of an act of gross indecency with another male, in a public place'.

The fact that this offence was designed for men who masturbate themselves or others in public toilets did not matter. The National Theatre was no different, for all relevant legal purposes, from a large public toilet (architecturally, it resembled one) and providentially the actors were male and so was the director, Michael Bogdanov. So they charged him in that 'he, being a male person, procured an act of gross indecency between one Peter Sproule, a male, and another male named Greg Hicks'. At the first court hearing, the prosecution demanded that Bogdanov be refused bail unless and until the National Theatre undertook to abandon all further performances of *The Romans in Britain*. This was not a case brought to dowse the lights on a few moments of simulated buggery: as John Smythe QC explained to the magistrate, 'the prosecutrix takes exception to the whole play'.

In this, Mrs Whitehouse had many predecessors. It was Henry VIII who passed the first law providing that 'plays and other fantasies' which criticised his closure of the monasteries should be 'abolished, extinguished and forbidden'. He called it 'An Act for the Advancement of True Religion'. All theatrical events were required to be licensed by the Master of the Revels, an officer of the Lord Chamberlain. Censorship was at first confined to unpalatable political messages rather than to sex and violence, but in 1837 the Lord Chamberlain was formally empowered to refuse a licence 'whenever he shall be of opinion that it is fitting for the preservation of good manners, decorum or of the public peace so to do'. Naked buttocks were not seen on the stage for almost a century, although by 1930 the Lord Chamberlain had relaxed sufficiently to issue formal instructions to the effect that:

Actresses may pose completely nude provided:
>the pose is motionless and expressionless;
>the pose is artistic and something rather more than a mere display
>>of nakedness;
>the lighting must be subdued.

Buggery simulated on a well-lit centre-stage was not what the Lord Chamberlain had in mind, and certainly not in a play attacking government policy in Northern Ireland. Throughout the thirties he banned all plays sympathetic to communism, while suppressing irreverent references to fascist dictators (the line 'Even Hitler had a mother' he excised from a revue in 1938). Any play which conceded the existence of homosexuality (Hellman's *The Children's Hour*, Miller's *A View from the Bridge* and Anderson's *Tea and Sympathy*) was automatically banned until 1958, when another change was announced: a play might have a homosexual as a character provided there was no suggestion that his condition should be lawful. Another formal instruction was issued to all theatres:

'Embraces or practical demonstrations of love between homosexuals will not be allowed.'

The Theatres Act, in 1968, appeared in this context a truly liberating measure. Ken Tynan put motion and expression into nudity on the lit stage in *Oh, Calcutta!* and no prosecution ensued. I had been engaged in 1976 to advise him on a successor entitled *Carte Blanche* which he was staging at the Duchess Theatre. I was the sole member of the audience for an 'undress rehearsal', in the course of which I would occasionally have to ask the actors to 'freeze' so that I could discuss some legal problems with Ken and the director, Clifford Williams. We would mount the stage as the players tensed themselves in position, and I would explain as we bent over their naked bodies just what might provoke a prosecution. Tynan was the most innocent of sophisticates, evincing a genuine wonder at sex and the lawyer's mind, and at what he termed our ability to split pubic hairs. However, it was bottoms that were most likely to cause trouble: 'The law requires a tighter clenching of the buttocks,' I would solemnly advise on close perusal of sagging flesh. 'Really,' he would mutter, wandering around the stage, 'how interesting. The law . . . more clenching of the buttocks? Tighter clefts in the buttocks . . . So, that's what the law requires . . .' *The Romans* was a world removed from Tynan's experiments in the drama of arousal: it was emetic and not erotic. The scene in question was intended to terrify, not titillate.

It came in the middle of the first act of a play which presented, bleakly and bitterly, the atavistic behaviour of men at war and those who get in their way. Nothing much has changed in the psychology of armies of occupation, implied Brenton, from Julius Caesar's invasion of Britain in 54 BC to Brigadier Frank Kitson's low-intensity operations on the Northern Irish borders in the seventies. This was a play about the extremes to which people will go to improve their chances of survival. It did not make for a comfortable night in the theatre, and nor was it very relevant to the world of

1981, frozen in a Cold War in which ethnic hatreds were more or less contained. *The Romans* is contemporary now, after Bosnia and Rwanda: its scenes of violence pale in comparison to the evidence of rape, torture and murder emerging from the war crimes trials at The Hague. Brenton's soldiers are drunk on the same sadistic cocktail of power and patriotism and panic. The play was ahead of its time, but on any view it was a puritanical work, heavy-handed in moral outrage. If the jury could be made to understand it, then acquittal for Michael Bogdanov was certain.

Our most difficult problem was whether the jury would even be allowed to *see* the play in order to understand it. There was a formidable legal issue as to whether any 'reconstruction' was admissible in evidence. The leading case came from the sixties, when the young Paul Raymond was charged with an indecent exhibition at his Soho club, involving the performance of a lady who danced lewdly with a large python. The defence was refused permission to show a filmed reconstruction, on the grounds that the snake might not make the same moves as it had on the night charged in the indictment. On this bizarre precedent, it was unlikely that the judge would permit the jury to see either a special performance or a video of *The Romans in Britain*, or even read the script. They would have to make do with the reheated recollections of Mrs Whitehouse's solicitor, a Mr Graham Ross-Cornes, who had ventured to the National Theatre for the first time in his life to see whatever it was that had outraged Sir Horace Cutler. In his witness statement he swore that he observed from his seat in the Olivier Theatre an actor dressed as a Roman soldier take off his tunic, hold his penis in his hand with the tip protruding, walk across the stage and place the said tip against the buttocks of an actor playing a young druid. If this is what really happened on the night Ross-Cornes had attended *The Romans*, Bogdanov would probably be found guilty of procuring an act of gross indecency. But was it what really happened? For a start, there was more to this play than the few moments mentioned in the witness statement.

Conlag, our comic opening-line Irishman, is a refugee in mainland Britain where warring tribes are more terrified of invading Romans than of each other. Three teenage brothers set the dogs on him but he escapes with a female slave. One of these boys, Marban, is training to be a druid priest: scene three opens with their idle patter after a swim in the river. The boys tease Marban about the priesthood: playing upon their nerves, he responds with a trick of his new trade:

> Do you want to see a ghost? Have you thought why, since we all live beyond the grave, in the sweet fields, the rich woods there, we don't see them more often, the dead?
>> Because of the pain of dying, brother
>> which is like a wall.
>> Solid thick with pain.
>> So the cracks in the wall of death are rare. Tiny.
>> And the life of the dead can only flare through them, for a moment.
>> As they do in the lights over a marsh
>> Like this:
>> (*Marban produces a puff of smoke from powder hidden in a rock which he strikes with a flint stone*)

The scene thus lit by poetic language, the youthful Britons strip and swim, then lie naked in the sun:

> *Brac hands Viridio the wineskin. He raises it to drink.*
>> *Three Roman Soldiers walk out of the woods. The soldiers and the brothers see each other at the same time. There is a considerable distance between them.*
>> *A silence.*
> First Soldier: Three wogs.
> Second Soldier: What are they, d'you know?
> Third Soldier: A wog is a wog. Pretty arses. Give 'em something.
>> *The soldiers laugh.*

First Brac is struck, with a sword in the stomach. Then Viridio, after a defiant curse, has Roman shields slammed against him, and falls dead. Marban, left to defend himself with a knife, manages to cut the First Soldier before he is overcome. The Third Soldier directs the Second to hold the young priest.

> *The Third Soldier holds Marban's thighs and attempts to bugger him.*
> Third Soldier: This isn't no – isn't no – at all –

Second Soldier: In trouble, comrade?

The Third Soldier rolls away.

Marban begins to struggle.

The Second Soldier hits Marban on the top of the head with the butt of his sword. Marban is knocked unconscious. His left leg twitches twice and then is still.

A silence.

Third Soldier: Arseful of piles . . . I mean, what do they do in this island, sit with their bums in puddles of mud all year long?

Brenton allows, finally, a moment of humanity from the Second Soldier, who cradles Marban and, recalling a similar kindness once done to a Roman, brings the boy round, thus saving his life.

That is the scene which the Whitehouse lawyers insisted must be removed from the play before Bogdanov could be granted bail. 'The meaning of the play would be enhanced if it was not there,' Smythe editorialised. I objected that the meaning of *The Romans* would be completely obscure without Scene Three, the dramatic epicentre at which the two worlds collide with the force of the shields which crushed Viridio: the imperial culture of Rome impressing a conquered race with a brutality more calculated than their own. In scene four, Julius Caesar arrives to view the carnage and to reprimand the prefect of the soldiers' legion 'for having lost control of your command, during a minor mopping-up exercise, against a wretched bunch of wog farmers, women and children, in a filthy backwater of humanity, somewhere near the edge of the world'. Caesar speaks the language of military politics, from Thermopylae to Dien Ben Phu. His method of humiliation is more subtle and more devastating than that of his soldiers: around Marban's neck he ties a pendant to a Roman Goddess, and sets him free. Tortured by this spiritual defilement, Marban in the next scene commits suicide: the play is fiercely moral in a way that Mary's courtroom crusaders cannot understand, although perhaps it was the political parable they could not stomach. The fugitive Irish rascal, Conlag, reaches the river Thames with the slave he has by now raped: as he slips, she brains him with a stone. Suddenly the sound of an approaching helicopter wrenches the audience two thousand years forward to the present. By a miracle of stagecraft, it lands and disgorges the Roman soldiers, now dressed in the uniform of the British Army in Ulster tonight. The slave throws her stone at them and is shot. A soldier radios to base as their commanding officer – Julius Caesar in combat fatigues – arrives in an army jeep to justify the killing in the sound-bites of Henry Kissinger:

> Caesar: That everyday life will begin again. That violence will be reduced to an acceptable level. That Civilisation may not sink, its great battle lost.
> *Caesar and the staff turn away.*
> Corporal: Anything on her?
> First Soldier: Just stones.
> *The helicopter roaring.*

This is the interval, so we claw our way to the nearest Olivier bar, the solicitors and counsel who must somehow re-enact this extraordinary play in Court 1 of the Old Bailey. Lenny Bruce always protested at the way policemen did his act in court, reading his allegedly obscene patter from the notes in their pocket books. 'That's not my act,' he objected. Now it was our task to produce some kind of performance which might bring home to the audience (the jury) something of the panoramic power and moral force of Brenton's work. If this prosecution had been brought under the Theatres Act, we could at least ask the jury to read the script. But Section 13 of the Sexual Offences Act makes no provision for the reading of scripts, or for anything else beside eyewitness recall of the actual act alleged to constitute the crime. The prosecution intended the jury to know nothing about this play other than one stage direction: '*The Third Soldier holds Marban's thighs and attempts to bugger him.*'

The best result would be a victory on a point of law which would leave Mrs Whitehouse to pay the costs, thereby deterring other would-be private prosecutors. The cost of defending the play was prohibitive: before long the National had incurred legal fees high enough to fund two new productions. Jeremy – now Lord – Hutchinson was brought in to lead the defence and hit upon a noble solution: we should all defend Michael Bogdanov on legal aid. This would mean less money for lawyers and more for worthier theatrical performers. It would also require the taxpayer to fund the whims of Mary Whitehouse – a potent argument against indulging her urge to prosecute. It was an irrational urge, as National Theatre director Peter Hall pointed out in his evidence at the committal proceedings: 'The scene is meant to horrify in what is a highly moral play; had it been done in half light behind a convenient tree, it would in my view have titillated.'

The magistrate's decision on whether to commit Michael for trial would turn on the strictly legal issue of whether the theatre was immune to prosecution under the Sexual Offences Act. Mr Harrington, who had dealt so fairly with John Stonehouse, was a man of good sense but it was far from clear that the law allowed him any scope to exercise it. At the time the Theatres Act was passed in 1968, Parliament believed that it barred any prosecution of a play for alleged indecency without the consent of the Attorney General. But this intention had not been fully effected by the draftsman, who had specifically excluded prosecutions for most offences of taste and morals but had forgotten all about the crime of 'gross indecency between males'. The loophole was there, so long as the actors were men and not women. After a two-day hearing, Mr Harrington reached this apologetic conclusion: 'It appears illogical, but I must interpret the law as it stands and not as it might have been. I think it absurd that had Mr Bogdanov been a woman director he would have no case to answer, but as it stands that appears to be the law, and I must interpret it as it stands.'

The law was an ass, and that was that. Had *The Romans* been directed by Michelle Bogdanov, or had the druid been a priestess, there would be no case to answer because Section 13, designed to catch sexual behaviour in the gents, applies only to males. Mary Whitehouse would have the opportunity to reapply the Lord Chamberlain's 1958 edict to the British stage: 'Embraces or practical demonstrations of love between homosexuals will not be allowed'. She had produced a situation where a distinguished director was at risk of conviction for a nasty little crime, and the judgment of the National Theatre would be second-guessed by jurors who may never have attended it, or any other theatre.

Shortly after the committal we received a message from the Garrick Club, via a theatrical friend of the Attorney General. Sir Michael Havers wanted us to know that he 'does not lack courage where Mrs Whitehouse is concerned'. If true, this made him unique among Tory politicians. He was certainly taking a long time to display it. But the message persuaded me to write a long letter requesting him to issue a *nolle prosequi*, i.e. to take the prosecution out of Mary's hands and into his own, and then to drop it, under his power as Attorney General to stop any prosecution if that is what he thinks the public interest requires. There were plenty of public interest reasons to stop this particular show. It was a breach of assurances repeatedly given to Parliament in 1968 that no prosecution would be launched against a play except under the Theatres Act, with its special 'public good' defence for drama. Brenton was a dramatist of world standing, and Bogdanov director who had won numerous awards: 'To deny him the opportunity to explain and to justify his work, in proceedings which carry a maximum sentence of two years' imprisonment, would be such a denial of simple justice that it would damage internationally our reputation both for great theatre and for fair trial'.

Sir Michael Havers *did* lack courage where Mary Whitehouse was concerned. He wrote back refusing to enter a *nolle prosequi*. So we had to prepare for trial. It was wonderful to be working again with Jeremy Hutchinson, with his infectious, sardonic humour, endlessly questioning mind, forensic courage and disdain for judges, opposing counsel and Mrs Mary Whitehouse. He knew all about theatre – he had been married, for many years, to Dame Peggy Ashcroft. The regular Old Bailey judges respected him, but we were told that we were being allotted a visiting High Court judge. This news made Jeremy groan. 'Typical. They'll give us some newly elevated tax lawyer who has never been in a criminal court.' Then the name came through: Mr Justice Staughton. 'Never heard of him,' wailed Jeremy, 'and I've been at the criminal Bar for forty years.' I looked him up in *Who's Who* to discover he had enjoyed a practice in shipping law and was the acknowledged expert on a subject of importance to mercantile lawyers, the law of bottomry. Jeremy exploded: 'That's it! The idiots! They've given him this case because he knows about bottomry. They think it's got something to do with buggery!'

The trial was set to commence on 15 March 1982 – nine months after *The Romans* had received its final performance. I had suggested that it be restored to the repertoire to take advantage of the trial publicity, but the National was nervous: it was not sure we would win. Nor, frankly, was I, because Brenton's sprawling canvas about imperialism through the ages would be reduced to a young actor's bare bottom and the alleged tip of another actor's penis, moving stage right and making momentary contact. Having been through it before with *Gay News*, I knew how horrific any depictions of youth and homosexual activities could be made to sound in the Old Bailey, and how powerless considerations of poetry or drama were to defuse the impact. By this stage we had a distinguished chorus of witnesses waiting in the wings: Felicity Kendal, Janet Suzman, Peter Brook, Lord Goodman, Trevor Nunn, John Mortimer. I even planned also to call Lord Olivier himself to give his blessing to what had gone on in his own theatre. But the judge might not allow this evidence: he would want the trial to run like any other public indecency case, depending entirely on whether the eyewitness saw what he said he saw.

There had been a read-through of *The Romans* with the original cast, at the Old Vic Theatre on the Sunday night before the trial opened. It was well attended, although the absence of colour and costume and motion underlined the extent to which Michael Bogdanov's direction had given dramatic life to Brenton's sombre poetry. The Old Vic is in a high-crime area (I am not referring to the artistic crimes committed at the Young Unknowns gallery opposite), and my car was broken into and burgled while I was attending the reading. The thieves extracted the radio and the brief in *Whitehouse v Bogdanov*. I had visions of it being delivered to the *News of the World* but early the next morning it was returned by a smiling policewoman, who had obviously read through it. 'This time, sir, we're on your side.'

The trial took place in Court 1, the Old Bailey's equivalent of the Olivier auditorium. The judge, a tall man with beetling eyebrows, was resplendent in his red robes; his entrance was accompanied by the traditional extras, gowned aldermen carrying the traditional props, of sword and mace. They sat a polite distance from him on the Bench, their wives occupying the best seats, the raised 'stalls circle' behind counsel which offers a direct view across to the jury and the witness box. The public gallery, a 'restricted view' perch in the amphitheatre, was full of 'resting' actors. The director, Michael Bogdanov, was in the well of the dock on centre-stage. We had toyed with the idea of asking permission for him to sit behind counsel, but we could better play on jury sympathy if they saw him in obvious peril of a jail sentence. Mrs Whitehouse was not immediately apparent – no doubt she was praying in the corridor. (In fact, her new QC had advised her to stay and pray at home.) There were a lot of journalists in the stalls – theatre critics in seats less comfortable than those to which they were accustomed, court reporters lured by the promise of druidic buggery, and 'resting' barristers curious to observe a celebrated trial. The audience which mattered – the jury – seemed nondescript. We challenged a few jurors with tabloids under their arms: although as Shakespeare said, there's no art to tell the mind's construction from the face, you do get some idea of the mind if the nose is in *The Sun*.

The trial began with a prologue from the judge, directed at the media. He had read a preview of the case in *The Sunday Times*, and was outraged. 'Welcome to the criminal law,' muttered Jeremy, Rumpole-fashion, under his breath. 'They don't have journalists, down in the Admiralty Division.' Jeremy's *sotto voce* monologues were a great joy, and they continued unabated into the prosecution's opening speech. John Smythe was sick, and had been replaced by Ian Kennedy, whose presentation was less evangelical and more intellectual. His opening speech however, served to shock the judge: Jeremy had to turn on a major piece of advocacy to obtain bail for Bogdanov over the lunchtime adjournment.

The next day the prosecution called its star witness: Mary Whitehouse's solicitor, Mr Graham Ross-Cornes. He took the oath as if he meant it, which he undoubtedly did. He told of booking seats for the performance, and of witnessing an actor with his penis hand-held and erect, its tip protruding, advancing across the stage to place it on or against the naked buttocks of a trembling druid. It all sounded grossly indecent. Mr Ross-Cornes was plainly a truthful witness, and our problem was how to shake his recollection. The obvious first question was to discover where he was sitting, so I had brought from the box office a seating plan of the Olivier auditorium. Jeremy was reluctant to enquire: counsel hate asking questions to which they do not know (or at least strongly suspect) the answer, and it stood to reason that anyone bent on collecting eyewitness evidence against a play would sit in the front row. My argument was that the prosecution must know the answer and since they had not elicited it from Ross-Cornes in his examination-in-chief, it could not be helpful to their case. 'It may be a trap,' countered Jeremy. 'They've left it for us to walk in, have the jury learn that Ross-Cornes was sitting in Row A of the stalls, and ram this home in re-examination.' Maybe, but I did not think our prosecution devious. It was worth the risk. I shoved the box-office plan on top of Jeremy's pride and joy – the collapsible wooden lectern covered with faded green baize on which he had rested his cases for the past forty years – and he nervously beckoned the usher to take the plan over to the witness.

'Now, Mr Ross-Cornes, will you please mark on this seating plan *exactly* where you were sitting when you *think* you saw the tip of the third soldier's erect penis?' The judge, suddenly interested, proffered his pen. 'Mark it with an X,' he said solemnly, as if it might be buried treasure for the prosecution. Ross-Cornes contemplated the plan. He knew exactly where he was sitting. We held our collective breath, as he silently marked the spot and the usher slowly carried this crucial evidence back to Jeremy. He choked back an exclamation of joy. Mrs Whitehouse had sat her solicitor in the gods.

'The back row! *You sat in the back row!* The cheapest seats in the house – Mrs Whitehouse couldn't afford the front stalls? You go to this theatre, knowing your task is to collect evidence for a *very serious prosecution* of my client, a man who has never committed a single offence in his life, on a *very nasty* charge, and you sit *in the back row?*' Jeremy was wonderful, his high-pitched Bloomsbury voice rising in mock horror, detonating little explosions of ridicule. I passed him some ammunition, a note from Peter Hall – the back row of the Olivier is ninety yards from the stage. '*Ninety yards* from the stage! Did you know it was *ninety yards from the stage*? Do you – can you – swear on *oath* to his Lordship and to the jury that you are *certain* you saw the *tip of a penis* from a distance of *ninety yards from the stage?*'

Mr Ross-Cornes was shaken, but not stirred. That was achieved by the most daring and devastating piece of impromptu cross-examination I have ever witnessed.

'Do you go to the theatre *much*, Mr Ross-Cornes?' Jeremy began sweetly. The witness confirmed that he did go to the theatre but not much. 'I go to pantomimes and such like.'

Q: You know that theatre is the *art of illusion*?

A: If you say so, Lord Hutchinson.

Q: And as part of that illusion, actors use physical gestures to *convey impressions* to the audience?

A: Yes, I would accept that.

Q: And from the *back row*, *ninety yards from the stage*, you can be *certain* that what you saw was the tip of the actor's penis?

A: Well, if you put it that way, I can't be absolutely certain. But what else could it have been?

There is a wise adage for witnesses: never ask counsel a question. Jeremy stood to his full height, six foot three inches in his wig, and pushing aside his lectern with his left hand, he held out towards the jury his clenched right fist.

'What you saw, I suggest, was the tip of the actor's *thumb* . . .' (he slowly raised his right thumb, until it stood erect, protruding an inch from his first) 'as he held his fist over his groin – like *this*.' Jeremy flung open his silk gown with his left hand while placing his right fist, thumb erect, over his own groin. It was a *coup de théâtre* more dramatic than any our client had achieved in *The Romans in Britain*. The jurors stared transfixedly at the QC's simulated erection. The witness opened and closed his mouth. At last he rallied: 'I can't see clearly, Lord Hutchinson. Your gown is in the way.' Jeremy swivelled in his direction, holding the pose. The judge was speechless – they certainly do not go on like this in the Admiralty Division. Eventually, the crestfallen Mr Ross-Cornes had to admit that yes, he may have been mistaken. He could not rule out the possibility that it might indeed have been a thumb he had descried from the back row of the gods, and not the glans of the penis of Mr Peter Sproule.

We had turned the corner and the prosecution knew it. Ian Kennedy approached us the next morning, and said he was minded not to pursue the case beyond half-time. He wanted the judge's ruling on some legal submissions, after which he would withdraw the charges, if we had no objection. We discussed this turn of events with our client: did he want to insist on presenting his defence and hope for an acquittal, when we could all go home now? Michael was reluctant to miss the opportunity of jury acquittal but saw no sense in continuing. The judge would be likely to rule most of our witnesses inadmissible, and although we now fully expected to win we could not absolutely guarantee it – a hostile summing-up or the prayers of the prosecutrix might produce a hung jury. It would on balance be better to let the action be withdrawn. And it would have the inestimable advantage of making Mary Whitehouse look extremely silly.

The judge, however, had other ideas. He took the view that once the prosecution had closed its case it had no power to abandon ship, at least without the judge's consent. Ian Kennedy manfully (and correctly, I think) claimed the unilateral right of a prosecutor to withdraw at any time. Jeremy kept out of the cross-fire, after remarking that since we had told our client that the case would be dropped, it would obviously be unfair for it now to proceed. This new tangle displeased the judge even more: the hapless prosecutors were asked to cool their heels in the corridors while we went off to ask the Attorney General to sort it all out. 'He'll have to consider whether to – what do you criminal lawyers say . . . ?'

'Enter a *nolle prosequi*,' Jeremy and I chorused happily.

It was a very twitchy Sir Michael Havers who met us that afternoon. He had an eye problem which caused him to wink at times uncontrollably, and it was difficult to tell whether he was disconcerted or trying to pick you up. It was the first time I had been invited to the Attorney's richly carpeted offices in the High Court, and there is no truth in the rumour spread by one of his mischievous staffers that Jeremy and I re-enacted the scene for Sir Michael's benefit, thumbs and all. Havers saw at once that the prosecution had come apart at the seams, and he recognised the constitutional implications of provoking a confrontation between judge and prosecutors over who has the final say about withdrawing a prosecution. (This is an important matter, of course, but it is the English way to avoid the grasping of constitutional nettles.) Sir Michael ordered his staff to draw up the fabled *nolle prosequi*, taking a grim satisfaction at being forced to do something he had secretly wanted to do all along.

The next morning, the fourth day of the trial, the judge ruled as a matter of law that there was a case for Bogdanov to answer. Then, in bewildering succession:

– The *nolle prosequi* was presented to the court by counsel on behalf of the Attorney General.

– Ian Kennedy described Michael Bogdanov as 'an honourable

man' who had not been 'moved by immoral motives'.

– Jeremy announced that we would have called many witnesses in Michael's defence, and would 'clearly and incontrovertibly have established that the allegation of "gross indecency" was entirely false'.

It was then the judge's turn. He denounced the prosecution's decision to withdraw without seeking his consent as 'misconceived and improper . . . once the prosecution has called its evidence a trial must continue.' Then – all importantly – he awarded us all our legal costs, from public funds, and as a mark of his displeasure he made no order to reimburse Mrs Whitehouse. She sat huddled against the high oak of the judicial bench, in a state described by press reports as 'uncharacteristically vulnerable and on the point of tears'.

Outside court, Michael posed with the winner's champagne, while Mary for once in her life avoided the press. Jeremy could not resist drawing the moral for their benefit: 'You get your knickers twisted if you launch private prosecutions.' Asked the next morning how she would raise the money to pay her legal costs, she supposed that 'God will provide'. The Reverend Eric Mathieson, chaplain to the National Theatre, issued a statement calling on the Deity to do no such thing: 'Mrs Whitehouse's claim to have the moral conscience of the nation in her handbag must be resisted. She is a vain lady; publicity and success influence her not a little. She does not represent thoughtful Christian opinion in this country. She got a good deal of egg on her face today – hallelujah.'

The satirists had a fine time. I particularly enjoyed Miles Kingston's cod legal advice in *The Times*:

I do not understand this stuff about 'nolle prosequi'. Can you explain it?

This is the first case in legal history, so far as I can determine, which deals with a play about Romans speaking English, and is handled by English lawyers speaking Latin. Piquant, n'est-ce pas?

Oui, sans doute. Et *nolle prosequi?*

A plea of *nolle prosequi* is entered when a situation of *reductio ad absurdum* is reached. The defence and prosecution agree to return to the *status ante quo*, everyone goes back to *terra firma* and the lawyers queue up for their *denarii*.

I still don't see what we have learnt from the whole thing.

I think the lesson is very plain. If you are a Celtic peasant in the fields and you see a Roman soldier coming, don't have a go and don't argue back. Run like mad. The same applies if you are a young healthy theatre director and you see a middle-aged woman coming.

Yes, but who has won?

The case cost £400,000. I think we can safely say that the lawyers did not lose.

And so we bade farewell to the courtroom crusades of Mary Whitehouse. She was a chastened figure thereafter, limiting her targets to 'video nasties' and that invader from outer space, satellite pornography. She became less and less relevant, as the Thatcher Government she supported encouraged sexual profiteering – from the groaning porn shelves in every corner newsagent to dirty talk on telephone lines leased from the privatised British Telecom. She had attacked much that was good and innovative in British television, beginning in the sixties with *Cathy Come Home* and *Till Death Us Do Part* and anything penned by Dennis Potter. I recently tried to persuade Channel 4 executives to run a 'Mary Whitehouse memorial season' – a week devoted to the works she has condemned in her lifetime – but there is still a nervousness about standing up to She Who Must Be Dismayed. It is a curious fact that *The Romans in Britain* has never again been performed professionally, in Britain, Rome or anywhere else. It seems a perfect choice for a theatre in Sarajevo or Rwanda or other places which need to know more about the nature of xenophobia. It remains as a footnote in Britain's social history, as the bridge at which a formidable cultural vandal fell – or at least, lost her footing. In her most recent autobiography (she has published three), Mary does not once mention the trial of *The Romans in Britain*. This I take as the greatest tribute she could pay its defenders.

Chapter 8

Invitation to an Inquest: Helen Smith

Helen Smith was a 23-year-old nurse from Leeds, working at the Baksh Private Hospital in Jeddah. On 20 May 1979 the chief hospital surgeon, Richard Arnot, invited her to a party to be held that evening at his fifth-floor apartment in the building next door to the hospital. Richard and his wife, Penny, were giving the party for a New Zealand diver, Tim Hayter, who was leaving the country the next day. Also invited were four German salvage operators who worked with Hayter at the port, Johannes Otten (a Dutch ship's captain) and a French marine biologist named Jacques Texier. Another British doctor named Kirwin put in a brief appearance with a case of whisky. The two young Arnot children went to bed; Helen danced with most of the men but as the night wore on she and Otten became more intimate. The two left the main room at some point through the thick curtains to the balcony, on which was a 'sunlounger' bed. It was ringed by a three-foot-high safety railing, before a seventy-foot drop to the concreted ground below.

Some time after 2.30 a.m. the four Germans decided to call it a night and left to drive back to their quarters at the port. Texier, who lived on a boat fifty miles outside Jeddah, was very tired and decided to bunk down on the couch. He immediately fell into a deep sleep from which he said he was awoken, at about 5 a.m., by a noise from the dining-room. It was a loud orgasm, apparently being enjoyed by Penny Arnot at the instigation of Tim Hayter. These two then went to make coffee in the kitchen where Texier joined them: the three walked out on the balcony to watch the sunrise and Penny looked down and screamed: this time, he said, with horror.

A man, naked, was impaled on the sharp iron arrows set in the concrete wall which ringed the apartment block. The spikes had punctured his stomach and were protruding from his back: his legs made a 'V' sign at the road, while his head hung down on the other side of the wall. His right arm extended to the forecourt, parallel to the long, red streak made by his blood and guts on the white concrete. Passers-by were looking through the gaps in the railings, which had crumpled under the force of the fall. They could see the dead man's erect penis, and began to point and snigger when they noticed the body of the woman.

She lay face down inside the tiled courtyard, her head against the building and her feet towards the red-stained wall. There was no blood on or around her, and no evident bruising: when turned over, she looked as though she might wake. Her right arm was bent as if to stretch and stroke her cheek, which had no imperfection other than a few scratches and a small crater in the middle of her forehead, as if a pen or a ring had been impressed, twisted into the skin. Her simple cotton dress and petticoat had ridden up, her bra was in place but her black knickers were down and on her left leg only.

The passers-by were sniggering because they drew the obvious conclusion: these two toppled over while having sex. The police arrived quickly and ascertained that the couple were last seen late at night on the balcony of an apartment on the fifth floor, seventy feet directly above, during a party at which nine bottles of whisky were consumed by as many guests. The obvious conclusion was taken to be the correct conclusion – that these deaths were accidental. For this was Saudi Arabia, and law enforcement does not have the same priorities, or the same law, as the Western countries from which the party guests had come. In Jeddah, post-mortems are rare, even after violent death, because of Koranic traditions: it would be eighteen months before Helen Smith's body, frozen and filled with sawdust, underwent proper examination in the mortuary at Leeds.

The inquest did not take place until November 1982, two and a half years after Helen's death. Tim Hayter and Penny Arnot refused to attend. Those who did – Richard Arnot, Texier and the four German divers – told stories which were not fully consistent but had one thing in common: if Helen was murdered, they knew nothing about it. The only people who were awake and on the scene at 3.10 a.m., the time Johannes Otten's watch had stopped, were Tim and Penny, and they were the only witnesses from the party who failed to attend the inquest. Penny was living in Langley, Virginia, home of the CIA, with a new husband, the son of the CIA chief in Saudi Arabia.

Snippets like this drove the British press to frenzies of speculation about the cause of Helen's death: it received more newspaper coverage than any other case in which I have been involved. She was raped and murdered by Arab princes. The Arnots were working for MI6, using Helen as a decoy to obtain information from the divers about the top-secret operations at the port. The whisky (worth £250 on the black market) was supplied by British intelligence. Embassy officials were present at the party. The Foreign Office, from Douglas Hurd down to the deputy consul in Jeddah, had conspired to cover up crimes committed in the course of an intelligence operation in which Helen was expendable. All this was nonsense, but the behaviour of the British authorities towards Helen's father, Ron Smith, made it seem plausible. Ron was a rough Yorkshireman – an ex-policeman who ran an electronics business and had a habit of taping everyone who talked to him. Some thought him mad, although many would add that he had been driven mad – by the Foreign Office. It had first withheld from him the details of Helen's death, then told him he could not go out to Jeddah because he could not get a visa (the Saudi authorities issued one within twenty-four hours when he asked them personally); it warned him not to open the coffin because his daughter's face had been smashed to a pulp by falling on it; in Jeddah the embassy even refused him access to a typewriter to make the formal request necessary to obtain a post-mortem.

Some of this official behaviour might be put down to a toffee-nosed reaction to Ron's class (i.e. his lack of it). But the FO's real dilemma deserves to be appreciated. All the party guests had been imprisoned, including two British nationals, Richard and Penny Arnot, and they were additionally responsible for Hayter, the New Zealander. Ron Smith was going round Jeddah alleging that his daughter had been murdered – the opinion of most of the staff at the hospital. The Saudi police, dismissive at first, slowly began to take the possibility seriously. They interrogated Penny so closely that, to give herself an alibi for murder, she said she was having sex with Hayter at the relevant time. (She did not realise that by admitting to adultery she was confessing to a crime punishable more severely than murder, namely by stoning to death.) In the midst of all this, a television programme re-enacting the execution of a Saudi princess for this same crime of adultery (*Death of a Princess*) had been transmitted in the UK, and in revenge the Saudi government was threatening to break off diplomatic relations and to withhold all oil exports and impose sanctions on British companies. Ron Smith's suspicions were, in short, a diplomatic nightmare. The FO was appalled when Penny Arnot received what was in Saudi Arabia a compassionate sentence for 'unlawful intercourse' (eighty strokes of the cane, administered in public) because it knew that her humiliation would be unacceptable to the British public. Finally, through the personal efforts of Lord Carrington, the Arnots were freed without the caning, and returned to England on 8 August 1980 to sell their story for £10,000 to the *Daily Mail*. The newspaper ran it for four days, then described it as 'less than truthful in certain aspects'.

By this time, the canker of cover-up had already been planted in the justice process. Ron had brought Helen's body back to Leeds, within the jurisdiction of the local coroner. A British subject had died violently, and in unexplained circumstances, and the law required coroner Miles Coverdale to hold a proper post-mortem examination. It was conducted by a local pathologist, Dr Michael Green. In July, as the arrangements for restoration of diplomatic relations with Saudi Arabia and the release of the Arnots were being finalised, Mr Coverdale issued a statement to the press. In it, he purported to announce Dr Green's findings: some bone fractures were 'entirely consistent' with the body falling seventy feet and landing on its right side, and some absences (of bleeding, and of skull and long-bone fracturing) were 'not inconsistent' with landing on her right side from a height of seventy feet. There were some 'minor' bruises and scratches, indicating slaps and blows, but these 'did not contribute to death' and so Coverdale concluded 'I do not consider that I would be justified in opening an inquest on the information so far before me.'

This was an improper statement, as Mr Coverdale – a solicitor –

well knew. For Dr Green had in fact found injuries to the thighs and genitals which were indicative of rape, but which Coverdale had directed Green to leave out of his report. Green's true opinion, as he admitted at the inquest, was that if Helen's death had occurred in Britain it would certainly have required an immediate murder inquiry. He said he protested to the coroner, who justified withholding the information because 'he did not wish to cause Mr Smith any further distress'. This could not have been the real reason, for Mr Smith had been publicly canvassing the possibility that his daughter had been raped and murdered for over a year. What distressed Ron Smith were official evasions – like Mr Coverdale's, who continued to suppress this evidence of crime. When Dr Green's conscience impelled him to give hints of his real findings to the press once the Arnots were safely back from Jeddah, the coroner threatened to have him prosecuted for contempt of court. It is precisely when officials behave in this way that the media expect there is more to a story than meets the eye.

Ron Smith was not fooled by Coverdale's censored version of the post-mortem. He sold his business and devoted all his money and time to finding out how his daughter died. The answer was never going to be other than squalid and the 'accident' explanation – toppling over the balcony during drunken sex – was probably the least squalid. But Ron Smith was driven both by the phenomenon that relatives of murder victims can 'make an end' only when someone is punished, and by the condescension he received from diplomats and from the coroner. He managed to interest Holland's leading pathologist, Professor Dalgaard, who offered to conduct another autopsy. Not quite trusting a foreigner, Coverdale insisted that Dr Green and a more senior forensic scientist, Professor Alan Usher, should be present as well. This was fortunate, for these three experts were able to reach a dramatic consensus.

The cause of Helen's death was a blow to the head, which rendered her unconscious and produced bleeding into the brain, causing death a few minutes later. Prior to this fatal blow, she had been punched and scratched on the face about ten times, and possibly held by the neck. (Dr Green had been wrong about the shoulder fracture: there was none, and without it there could not have been a fall from the Arnots' fifth-floor apartment). If the injuries to her body, especially on the right side, had been caused by a fall, it must, said Usher, have been from lower than thirty feet, and Dalgaard concluded she could only have fallen 'a few feet'. He was uncertain whether the genital injuries were the result of forced, as against forceful, sex, although Usher thought they indicated rape and 'suggest that some violent sexual activity had occurred, most probably against the girl's will'. There was one great mystery, to which none of the pathologists could suggest a solution: Helen's sternum (breast-bone) had been broken, but the lack of bruising suggested she must have been dead at the time.

This evidence, made available to Coverdale in December 1980, was so redolent of foul play that an inquest was required immediately. Yet still the coroner temporised, calling for a report from the West Yorkshire Police and then (having received it in March 1981) delaying any decision until re-organisation of the coronial districts in mid-year relieved him of making one. It fell to his replacement, Phillip Gill, to inform Ron Smith in August 1981 that 'as Helen's death occurred outside the jurisdiction of the English courts I am satisfied that this case does not fall within my jurisdiction for the holding of an inquest'. Ron Smith's response to this ruling was delivered the following week. Summoned to his local court for rate arrears, he explained to the clerk (who could not understand why so many journalists were present) that he had run up debts in discovering the truth about his daughter's death, because 'Thatcher, Carrington, Hurd, Whitelaw, and many more people have been involved in the cover-up to protect various people, not the Arnots'.

It is the right of every Englishman to say '*J'accuse*' in a court of law without being sued for defamation – Norman Scott had blurted out his accusation against Jeremy Thorpe in similar circumstances a few years before – and the publicity brought Ron what he had really needed from the outset, namely a good lawyer. Ruth Bundey, a Leeds solicitor who can handle difficult cases and (importantly in this case) difficult clients, obtained legal aid to challenge Gill's interpretation of the law. In July 1982, the Court of Appeal upheld the challenge and directed that an inquest be held immediately.

I was asked to act for Ron Smith at the inquest in November 1982. It would not have taken place at all had this 'cantankerous bastard' (Ron's self-description) believed what officials had told him. The Leeds authorities had earmarked £50,000 to pay for lawyers for any witnesses prepared to come from abroad: most of it went towards Dr Arnot's choice, the ostentatious criminal solicitor Sir David Napley, who reportedly charged a whopping £1,000 a day. There was no money made available for Ron (and there is no legal aid for lawyers at inquests) so I bunked down on Ruthie's couch while my adversary, Sir David, was deposited by his gold Rolls-Royce at a suite at the Queen's Hotel. No sum of money, however, could compensate for the frustration or reward for the privilege of representing Ron Smith. We spent days in his house, listening to the endless tapes he had made over the past three years of people theorising about how Helen met her death, and reading his paper mountain of newsprint. It would have been useful to read all the evidence gathered by the police, but the coroner refused point-blank to let us see it. He would not even tell us which witnesses he was going to call, or in what order.

I had more faith in the forensic pathologists. As readers of Patricia Cornwell will appreciate, their art is to imagine what might have happened once their scientific findings are fed into the known facts. In Britain their role is often underplayed, although they solve more murder mysteries than do police or self-promoting 'psychological profilers' like TV's *Cracker*. Keith Mant, Professor of Forensic Medicine at Guy's Hospital, was their exemplar in 1982, and it was to him I turned for help. The other pathologists – Dalgaard, Usher and Green – had been, in a sense, too close to the body. They had produced evidence for blows about the head and forcible sex, and for patterns of injury which precluded a fall from a height, but they had not been able to interpret all this in the context of the factual mysteries of the case: the broken sun-bed, the fractured sternum, Otten's missing trousers (and the fact his passport had been found a hundred yards down the road) and the scratches on Helen's face and indentation in her forehead.

Professor Mant looked and talked like Leo McKern. He sat in his large laboratory, surrounded by skeletons and skulls and glass containers which held odd bits of human anatomy – a finger here, a bone there, the kind of relics you can see in Catholic churches in Europe, although his came from sinners rather than saints. I sat down next to a glass containing a tough piece of tissue in the shape of a flange, seemingly unscrewed from a corpse (it dawned on me after a while that it was a pickled anus) and played Watson to the Sherlock Holmes of this ebullient professor. How could he explain the break in the sternum? By an accident in the mortuary days after her death? 'No, the pathology showed it had occurred just after the time of death.' Could it have occurred at the moment of the impact from a fall? 'No, she would have had to fall on her face, which would have been flattened and the whole pattern of frontal injuries would have been much more serious.' How then do sternums get fractured? 'In different ways, most commonly in car accidents when the steering wheel shaft impacts on the chest. We do see cases where it occurs in heart-massage – you punch, in a desperate attempt to resuscitate the heart.' Do you? I didn't know that. 'Look at this.' Mant wheezed to his feet and took hold of the nearest skeleton, tapping its ribs. 'The girl had rib fractures – here and here, seventh and ninth ribs closest ribs to the sternum. Probably from the same punching. She's lying, in fact dead, someone with first-aid knowledge, who thinks she might be alive and wants to save her, frantically punches the heart.'

A picture came into frame. Very grainy, of someone desperately trying to revive Helen, just after she died from bleeding into the brain, minutes after the blow to her head. Then someone else, clearing away all traces of Helen and Johannes Otten, spectacles and handbag and the all-important trousers (as someone runs up the street to throw them in a culvert, a passport drops from a pocket). Professor Mant rewound the fuzzy video in my mind's eye with his parting comment: 'You know, this pattern of injuries to the girl. She could not have fallen from the fifth floor. She could – well, she could simply have fallen down the stairs. But I see there was a lift in the apartment.' There was, and the residents complained it was always broken. And so were the lights in the stairwell. I imagine Helen Smith, running downstairs in the dark – from someone? Towards something? Urgently, fearfully, then losing her step and falling, on the right side, and cracking her head.

I soon had reason to be grateful to Keith Mant. The inquest began with the forensic evidence, and the broken sternum was at the forefront of the coroner's mind. He seemed convinced that she had fallen alive from the Arnot's apartment and that her chest must have hit a lamp on the wall as she fell. This was an erroneous theory, which Alan Usher helped to demolish.

Q: If the chest hit the lamp?

A: You would have wounds in the chest.

Q: There was no sign of that sort of chest injury sustained while alive?

A: There was not.

Q: The sternum can fracture with a very heavy punch, sometimes seen in violent heart resuscitation?

A: Very heavy.

Q: The left-side rib fractures are not associated with a right-side fall. But they could be associated with a vigorous attempt to resuscitate Helen Smith, which could have caused the sternum to fracture.

A: Yes, this is a much more convincing explanation for the sternum fracture.

Q: Given by someone with some medical knowledge?

A: Yes.

Q: And the reason there is no blood or bruising is that Helen Smith was already dead at the time?

A: Yes.

One of the books about the Helen Smith case noted that 'Professor Usher looked at Robertson as if he was a very bright student in a tutorial group'. Since he was really looking at Professor Mant, this was hardly surprising. The truth about barristers is that like all players of professional sport, they need a good coach.

The inquest had opened on 18 November 1982 in the council chamber of Leeds Town Hall. Over a hundred reporters had gathered: they were exiled to the public gallery, but permitted to leave a super-sensitive tape-recorder by the witness stand to catch any evidence they might miss – and as it turned out, much more besides. The lawyers sat in a semicircular row, facing the coroner, with the jury watching the proceedings over our shoulders to the right. What these solid Leeds citizens made of it I do not know, although they would not have looked with much favour on Sir David Napley's Rolls, its petrol consumption paid for by their rates. Coroner Gill was pernickety and pin-striped, with an undertaker's pallor. His duty was to examine how, where and when Helen Smith had met with death, and we were all here to help him. Stephen Sedley (for the rest of the Smith family) and myself (for

Ron) would probe for evidence of unlawful killing, while Napley (for Arnot) and the other lawyers (for the FO and the party guests) would suggest it was an accident, but since no one was on trial we should all have the luxury of being seekers after truth. To this end, I began by politely requesting copies of the evidence amassed by the West Yorkshire Police. Gill refused once again: other coroners might be prepared to make such material available, but not him: we would only hear what he chose to make public, from the witnesses he chose to call.

We began with the pathologists, whose evidence cried foul play. Not as loudly as in the tabloid headlines (HELEN: SHE WAS BEATEN! SHE WAS RAPED!), but with sufficient clarity to prove that Helen had been in a fight, that the sex had been violent, that she had died from a blow on the left side of the head and that if she had fallen at all it was from nothing like a fifth-floor balcony. And, as Usher agreed, someone had probably made a desperate attempt to resuscitate her. David Napley confronted them with sound-bites about forensic science being an 'inexact art' and 'requiring speculation'. (This is simplistic: the science part should admit of no mistake, while the art lies in speculation which accounts for the other known facts.) All the pathologists were satisfied that the bruises and lesions they had found on the body were not the phantom marks which can develop in mortuaries and mislead novices (so-called 'post-mortem artefacts'). The local pathologist who did an autopsy on Helen twelve days after her death was an unimpressive witness, who had made many mistakes and had been content to certify death as accidental after having been told by the police that she had fallen flat on her face. Since the undamaged condition of her face made this an impossibility, his conclusion was illogical. He did certify the cause of death correctly, as the haemorrhage in the brain from the blow to the head. The Baksh Hospital's own pathologist testified that from his view of her body, Helen could not have fallen at all and that it was most likely she had been murdered.

The 'witnesses of fact' came next, although very few facts emerged. The divers came from Germany to testify that they had left the apartment some time between 2.30 a.m. and 3.30 a.m. They gave the impression that they had been attending something akin to a vicarage tea-party, and we were not allowed to cross-examine them or any other witness. 'You are here at the invitation of the court,' the coroner would say emphatically. 'Do not indulge in cross-examination. Advocates are allowed only to ascertain information, not to challenge anyone.' No witness could be reminded of a previous inconsistent statement and asked to explain it, or have an answer contradicted or closely examined, although this is one of the best forms of assistance that barristers can offer. The other – a final speech which would make sense of all the evidence – was excluded by inquest rules in any event. The Foreign Office witnesses came and went without challenge: when the FO later issued a statement to the effect that it had not been criticised at the inquest, it knew very well that no one would have been allowed to make the attempt.

At one point, these proceedings to find out how Ron Smith's daughter had died were turned into a trial of Ron Smith. The lawyer acting for the Germans sought to read out a letter Ron had written making accusations against them; I objected, saying that what he might once have written was irrelevant, at which point Ron mumbled, 'I'm not accusing the German divers. I'm accusing Richard Arnot of murder, and Texier.' I spun round, to whisper, 'Ron, please. You are making my task quite impossible.' Ron mumbled back, 'I'm sorry'. The coroner said, 'This is a good time to adjourn. We can perhaps settle this when we return from lunch.' Nothing further was said that day about Ron's 'mumble', because no one appeared to have heard it apart from myself. But the tape recorder picked it up, as the journalists discovered when they replayed it. That evening's television news, and the morrow's papers, were full of Ron's accusations. Sir David Napley was on his feet the next morning, demanding retribution for the 'gross contempt of court' which nobody had noticed at the time. I thought it had been a spontaneous reaction rather than a deliberate provocation, but the coroner was full of righteous anger and imposed a fine to punish Ron for murmuring in court. A day or so later, he announced that the reporting of what he now termed 'Mr Smith's outburst' had caused Texier's elderly mother to suffer a heart attack. This announcement caused everyone in court to look daggers at Ron: he was responsible for risking the life of a dear old French lady. That was how the coroner announced it, but unbeknownst to him his information turned out to be incorrect. It had come from the FO, which had mistranslated an idiomatic French phrase for experiencing a shock (*'coup de coeur'*) as if it literally meant 'heart attack'.

There was in fact no accusation made against either man named in Ron's 'outburst', but at least the publicity given to it caused Texier to change his plans and to come to the inquest. He told of seeing Helen and Otten kissing, in silhouette on the balcony, and of asking Penny Arnot (who could not have welcomed his unexpected request) to sleep on her couch in the main room. At 5 a.m., he said, her cries of orgasm were loud enough to wake him from a deep sleep. He joined Penny and Tim for coffee on the balcony, when Penny looked over the rail and screamed again. There was panic, and Arnot came on the scene: his only thought, said Texier, was to get rid of the alcohol. Texier on this point contradicted Arnot himself, who had already told the inquest he had rushed downstairs first to check Helen for signs of life. Sir David Napley mounted an aggressive cross-examination of the bespectacled Frenchman ('How good are your eyes?' was his first question), and the coroner on this occasion allowed cross-examination – which was fair enough given the direct conflict between the two witnesses, although Sir David's efforts provoked Texier to insist even more firmly that the doctor was more interested in hiding the whisky than in attending to Helen.

Ron Smith disliked Richard Arnot, from the moment they first met in a Jeddah police station and the doctor had said what a 'soopah party' it was and how Helen was a 'soopah girl'. His case against Arnot was on a father-to-father level: he was the senior surgeon who had invited the young nurse, who was the only available woman at a drunken party with a number of men she did not know, and he had gone to bed without seeing her home. But I did not believe for a moment that Richard Arnot was a murderer, or guilty of any kind of crime: he was asleep at the time, because he was on operating duty at 6 a.m. He was himself convinced that the deaths were accidental. He had sat through all the forensic evidence and yet he refused to credit its implications. He told of observing Otten's post-mortem erection, as if it were proof the couple were having sex as they fell. (Keith Mant had chuckled at the notion that a man could hold an erection while falling five stories to certain death. 'Injuries to the spinal column frequently cause an erection after death.') For Richard Arnot the 'one great mystery' was the disappearance of Otten's trousers, which he assumed had been pulled off his legs by a thief.

Tim Hayter we did not meet in the flesh, although he grimaced unpleasantly into the television camera from a hotel suite in Amsterdam, the closest he was prepared to come to the jurisdiction of the English courts. He said he hated Ron Smith and had told the interviewer that at one point in Ron's campaign he wanted to 'put a contract on his head . . . to hurt him, maybe he has a problem walking from then on' but later, he came to recognise the force of the evidence that Helen had been murdered. When first approached by the West Yorkshire Police, in September 1980, Hayter had refused to say a word on the grounds that he might 'incriminate' someone. He was offered every inducement to come to Leeds – fare, expenses, lots of spending money. He temporised and then refused, although he had no difficulty in going to Holland the week before the inquest, to talk to Thames Television and the *News of the World*.

Penelope Arnot, the other crucial absentee, had said she wanted to spend the time with her children in Virginia, and had nothing to add to her statement to the police. In that statement, she claimed to have seen Helen and Otten 'silhouetted on the balcony' about 3 a.m. She denied having sex with Hayter, saying it was the false alibi she used when accused by Saudi police of involvement in Helen's murder. Tim Hayter had no doubt of receiving Mrs Arnot's erotic attentions (he relived them lubriciously for the *News of the World*). At the inquest, Richard Arnot pronounced himself a cuckold, and when Texier told of being awoken by Penny's orgasmic cry, that seemed to put the matter beyond doubt, for everyone but myself. I could not quite credit this well-bred wife and mother letting go so loudly in a room close to the bedrooms of her children and her husband (they might have emerged at any moment), let alone in the somnolent presence of a Frenchman she had not met before that night. If Tim and Penny were bent on having sex, the logical place to have it would be on the sunlounger bed on the balcony, sealed off by closed doors and heavy curtains and the internal noise of the air conditioning, before the dawn's early light. But the balcony may already been occupied by another couple.

One reason why this case gripped the public imagination – it was reported in detail and throughout the world – was its prurient appeal, and not just to tabloid readers. 'Page Three' of *The Sun* is a familiar phenomenon – less so page three of the *Daily Telegraph*, which reproduced the salacious evidence down to the last genital bruise. The serried ranks of lawyers and the procession of witnesses were almost all male; David Napley's constant insinuations about Helen's wild sex life (something which was taken for granted but never proved and would have been of no relevance anyway) added to an atmosphere which bordered on contempt for women generally and the deceased in particular. There was, additionally, 'the class thing': the upper-class consultant and the Oxbridge classicists at the Embassy and the Foreign Office, ranged against the nurse and her Northern working-class father. And how to explain the Arnots' hospitality to drunken, sweaty divers? Other than a literal *nostalgie de la boue*, the media's theory was a British intelligence interest in what lay behind the top security at the port of Jeddah. Ron Smith's battle against the British establishment, from the coroner Coverdale to the Foreign Office gave the case a political edge, taken up by crusading journalists like Paul Foot. But to most people, I suspect its appeal was its real-life conformity to the classic murder mystery. People come and go in a set of rooms at night. By dawn, two of them are dead. There was no butler to serve the whisky, so whodunit?

Coroner Gill was in little doubt that no one had done it. One of the many curiosities of inquests is that although the coroner must in cases of violent death sit with a jury, he is not required to sum up impersonally like a judge at a jury trial. The parties are permitted no final speech: their lawyers cannot even hand up a written theory as to how the death was caused. In this case I felt there was only one verdict to which the jury could, on the evidence, properly come. Although the Smith family believed, on the strength of the forensic science, that Helen had been murdered (verdict: 'unlawful killing') and Dr Arnot thought that she had stumbled over the balcony railing while copulating with Otten (verdict: 'accidental death'), each of these alternatives involved too much speculation. The correct result would be an 'open verdict', on a death in circumstances that were suspicious but required more evidence to resolve.

The coroner announced that he would 'paint a coherent and understandable picture' of Helen's death. This involved, firstly, painting *over* the findings of the experts – Greene, Dalgaard and Usher, who had 'led us all on a wild goose chase'. They had been misled by the phenomenon of the 'post-mortem artefacts' – bruises appearing after death which presented what he described to the jury as a 'mirage of lesions'. Having thus disposed of modern forensic science, Gill fastened onto two matters which emerged from the evidence of the German divers, whose departure to drive to the port had been variously placed at between 2.30 a.m. and 3.30 a.m. They had arranged earlier in the evening to give Otten a lift, but when they decided to leave he was not around (they assumed he was otherwise engaged with Helen). One recalled that when they started their car – parked opposite the apartment – they had trouble with the headlights, which blinked and flashed for a minute before the driver found the switch to steady them. This, the coroner suggested, was at 3.10 a.m. precisely.

> Members of the jury, might not those lights have been seen by someone up on the balcony who realised it was the car in which he was supposed to be departing? And members of the jury, if at that time he was engaged in sexual activity with Helen, possibly with his trousers down round his ankles and pants down, and Helen with her clothing disarranged, would it be a natural reaction for him to try to see what was going on and to see what those flashing lights were and perhaps even attract the attention of his friends across the road? Members of the jury, if that happened, might he not hurry towards the balcony edge? We know there's a sunlounger bed at the side of the balcony . . . Members of the jury, the balcony was dark. Might it be that in his hurry he, with Helen clutching him, came into contact with that sunlounger, pitched forwards over the edge of the balcony, and she, clutching him, went with him? . . . Could it be that his trousers fell off as he landed in the street outside? And someone going to early-morning prayers found those trousers lying in the roadway, helped himself to both trousers and wallet and took care to rid himself of the passport and identity papers?

This was an astonishing theory. Quite apart from the fact that it told the jury to ignore uncontested scientific evidence, it posited:

1) incredible behaviour by Otten on the balcony – rushing to wave at a car in the street while in the middle of intercourse; 2) incredible behaviour on the part of Helen, in clinging to a man going over a balcony to his death; and 3) a fall which she had not, on the bruise patterns, sustained. The coroner's theory offered no explanation at all of the blow on the head which was the direct cause of her death, and it painted a cartoon picture of the German divers, fiddling with the lights of their car without hearing a mighty crash as the plummeting Otten slammed into the spikes, or looking up (every witness said the street was very well lit) to see his legs reverberating. The early-morning prayer-goer, passing this grisly and malodorous sight, who souvenired the trousers and did not report the body, seemed an extra out of *Aladdin*.

As the summing-up finished, Stephen Sedley rose, silently and sinuously, before Gill could stop him. 'I have a duty to point out one or two matters . . .' This was treason to the coroner's faith, that any advocate might contradict him in the presence of his jury. The coroner's rules, Gill interjected, forbade lawyers from raising any questions of fact in the hearing of the jury. Stephen was tough when he had to be, and very fast on the draw: those rules concerned matters of *fact*, and he had a point of *law*. 'I ask you to give a proper direction, to tell the jury not to disregard the uncontested expert evidence merely because you do not like what that expert evidence says.' The coroner began to defend his direction, giving Stephen the cue to point out in front of the jury that the evidence did not indicate that Helen Smith had been carried into mid-air by a man more concerned about his lift home than with finishing either his sexual activity or his life.

The jury was out for seven hours: time enough to wonder about all the evidence that had not been heard or seen. There had in fact been two cameras at the party: Helen's (which was curiously empty of film) and one belonging to a German diver, who had taken pictures which had not come out. The shutter of my own mind's eye clicked again on some grainy images: a brawl on the balcony; slaps and scratches to the face of the nurse; a push, perhaps a shove, intended only to sober a man up or make him go home, but causing him to lose his balance and stumble backwards and over the balcony rail. People running down the stairs to see what can be done. The lift is broken and the lights in the stairwell do not work, the nurse slips and falls head-first, receiving the blow which causes unconsciousness and a haemorrhaging of blood into her brain. In a few minutes she is dead, only a hundred yards from the hospital casualty department where in those minutes her life might have been saved. Someone punches her chest to try to resuscitate her; the heavy blows break her sternum and fracture her seventh and ninth ribs. There is general panic: the dead man's trousers are taken out and hidden in a culvert down the road (the passport drops where it was found, halfway across the street). Then Helen's body is placed near his, as if they had fallen together.

That's when my mental film of this murder mystery runs out. Ironically, what it has *not* shown is that Helen Smith and Johannes Otten were murdered or the identity of those who encountered them before or after their deaths. And their 'unlawful killing' would be manslaughter at most, or a 'lawful killing' by self-defence, or misadventure or even in Helen's case a straightforward accident, if she slipped and fell down stairs in the dark. But the problem with imaginary reconstructions is that they neatly explain all the evidence. Life is never like how you imagine life was like, for in life there *are* no neat explanations. I did not believe the truth ever would be known, although it was most unlikely that Helen's death had happened in the way Coroner Gill had just suggested.

Eventually, the jury came up trumps. The gang of eleven (for some arcane reason, coroners sit with an odd-numbered jury) returned an open verdict. 'It was impossible to decide on the evidence we heard,' said the forewoman. That was understandable, because what had been crucially lacking was any word, report or photograph from the Saudi police who had attended the scene and taken everyone into custody at 7 a.m. It was curious, given the good relations between Britain and Saudi Arabia once *Death of a Princess* had blown over, that the Foreign Office had been unable to obtain the Saudi police records and photographs for use at the inquest.

It was doubly strange that sixteen days after the inquest concluded with its 'open verdict', the Saudis with no apparent reluctance sent to the FO all the police photographs and reports and the original post-mortem on Otten. Three months later, Coroner Gill sent copies to the parties with a press release giving it as his opinion that the documents and photographs 'do not add materially to the evidence given at the inquest'. What they materially added, in my opinion, was further reason to believe that Helen Smith did not die in the way he had suggested to the jury.

There her body was, captured on the police photographs, lying on her stomach – not, as the witness had recalled, on her side. Her head was against the main building – several feet into the alignment of the overhang of the first-floor balcony. She could not, conceivably, have *fallen* in this place. Without any real doubt, the body had been moved to that position from somewhere else. She could not, conceivably, have fallen flat on her stomach: her face was uninjured, apart from a few scratches and that mysterious indentation in her forehead. It had amazed her father when he saw it in the mortuary, and it amazes in this picture: it is so deep and decisive, and can have no relationship to any wound sustained in a fall. It looks as if the tip of a pen or the stone of a ring has been twisted into her forehead: taken with the pathologist's finding of scratch marks and bruises on her face, she must have been involved in some sort of scrimmage before her death.

Even more telling are the pictures of Johannes Otten. He is not 'jack-knifed over the railing' (as several witnesses had claimed) wearing underpants and with his shirt down over his head, as the witnesses had recalled. The photos show that the top of the railings collapsed under the force of his fall, and that he is naked: his head hanging down, his legs pointed upwards in the air. His shirt is not on: it has been placed, curiously unbloodied, underneath his head. Unless he did somersaults, he did not go forwards over the balcony while waving to his German friends in their car – he was knocked or pushed over it backwards, and plummeted down until the spikes intercepted his groin. He was, as the police and the local pathologist confirm, stark naked: there were no trousers to be pulled off (impossible) or picked up by the passing Muslim on the way to the Mosque, because there were no underpants either. The post-mortem report reveals bruises on his lips and chin: the pathologist assumed they were caused by the impact with the wall, and had not considered whether they might have been caused by punches prior to death.

The mistake made by the local police was apparent from their reports: they assumed immediately that both these Westerners had fallen from the balcony of the apartment where the party with all the alcohol had been held. The level of alcohol in both bodies was tested and reckoned as intoxicating, and that is the reason why foul play was not suspected and why Helen's injuries were not properly assessed. There are cultural assumptions rife in these official Saudi documents, a certain unsavviness about decadent Westerners depraved by drink and promiscuity. Whatever level of alcohol Saudi science describes as 'intoxicating', it does not cause a couple who have just met for the first time to have sex on or outside a railing seventy feet from the ground.

The death of Nurse Helen Smith has remained unsolved, and her bruised cadaver remains unburied in Leeds mortuary, a grisly reminder of a father's unending quest for justice and of the limits of human systems to attain it. At least we tried, and the jury at the end of the day did not pretend that there was an answer. Paul Foot, who spent years investigating the case, can only suggest that Helen and Johannes went for sex not to the balcony but to the roof of the apartment block (where Helen sometimes sunbathed) and 'It is possible that she and Otten were interrupted there, perhaps by people whose names we have not yet heard; that a fight broke out, that Otten went over the wall either in or after the fight, that Helen was knocked unconscious, carried down for treatment and dumped after she died.' Anything is possible, and we don't even know for sure the time of this death: Otten's watch stopped at 3.10 a.m. but might have been smashed earlier, or been slow, or since he was a sea captain, might have been set on Greenwich mean time (two hours behind local Jeddah time). The macabre erection Dr Arnot saw at 5.35 a.m. was caused (as in executions) by the breaking of the spinal cord, disrupting communication between brain and genitals. The phenomenon lasts only a short time, rarely more than an hour.

And so the questions multiply, and seeming certainties dissolve with the rise of the Saudi Arabian sun (dawn in Jeddah was 4.19 a.m. on 20 March, with sunrise a half-hour later). Helen had been to the toilet just before she died (bladders replenish quickly, and hers was empty) and the toilet is through the main room where Hayter says (and Penny says twice and retracts twice) that he and Mrs Arnot were having sex. Helen's end came without sudden terror: her faeces were normal and firm, unmoved by the awareness of impending death. So the soothsayers who read the entrails of broken birds would deduce from this strangely unbroken corpse that Helen Smith did not fall and was not pushed. She lost consciousness and died from a blow to the left side of her head, and suffered one injury – from a pen or a pebble – shortly before. There was semen in her body – the Saudis did not think to match it because nobody was very alert to DNA samples in those days, and the police simply assumed the semen was Otten's, in which case the love-making had finished. If the semen came from someone else, then it came from the man who killed her. It may still be stored in a lab in Jeddah – nobody has bothered to enquire. In that case, it may one day accuse her murderer even more loudly, and more accurately, than Ron Smith.

The most important lesson from Leeds Town Hall was that the coroner's inquest is an inadequate procedure for investigating controversial deaths. The arcane procedures and unfair rules surprised all the observers: Why was the coroner not obliged to make the police evidence available to the parties? Why were lawyers not permitted to cross-examine, or make closing speeches, and were sometimes not even informed which witnesses would next be called to testify? Why was the jury not summoned at random, but selected by a policeman who was the 'coroner's officer'? The inquest took place in what was called a 'court', and had all the trappings of one. But the coroner was not a judge: he had the power to summons people who were within the jurisdiction, but no power to require them to answer questions, even if they were witnesses to the death. (This bewildering feature was highlighted many years later by the inquest into the death of black teenager Stephen Lawrence, when those suspected of killing him claimed the right to refuse to answer questions and walked with tight smiles from the 'court'.) Indeed, should evidence pointing towards the guilt of any identifiable person emerge, the coroner has to stop the inquest and send the details to the DPP, who may well decide that it is insufficient for a prosecution – in which case the 'inquest' will have gone nowhere.

Coroner's courts are the weakest part of our justice system, because they are not really part of it at all. Coroners are not appointed like judges and magistrates but are employed by local councils, and tend to be doctors or lawyers (or both) of local worthiness. The coroner's is an ancient office (it was the 'crowner' in *Hamlet* who had to be squared to overlook Ophelia's suicide) and their pronouncements can give comfort to grieving relatives and make useful recommendations about accident blackspots and dangers in toys or swimming pools. But by virtue of the limitations in their procedures, they are not best equipped to discover the truth behind a violent death of great controversy or complexity.

A new mechanism for extracting the truth and drawing lessons from it is clearly required for cases – a few each year – which involve serious factual disputes and raise questions of wide public interest which cannot be answered by a single-sentence verdict. Those whose deaths have been denied full investigation include Blair Peach, Liddle Towers, Jimmy Kelly, Colin Roach, Roberto Calvi, the *Marchioness* victims and most recently, Stephen Lawrence, who has belatedly been accorded a proper inquiry into the insufficiency of previous inquiries. Cases like this should be handed over from the outset to a High Court judge, presiding over a public inquiry at which interested parties can be represented on legal aid and where proper rules are followed. The judge would sit as arbiter, hearing evidence collected and presented by counsel, cross-examined by the parties whose representatives would be entitled to 'sum up' their case, both as to how the death occurred and as to what should be done to prevent such fatalities in the future. The judge would have additional powers – to call for assistance from courts in other countries, to sit overseas or to take evidence by video-link. There would be no right for a witness to decline to answer on the grounds of self-incrimination, although once the judge was satisfied that a *prima facie* case of unlawful killing was made out against any individual, he would be empowered to commit that person for criminal trial.

Unsolved murders are unendurable, a continuing anguish for the victim's family and a reproach to law enforcement. To those who fear such new powers might infringe liberty, I simply say that death is different.

Chapter 9

The Prisoner of Venda

The most courageous man I ever met was guilty of the offence with which he was charged. He was not a political activist but a poet; his fate remains obscure and his name sounds faintly ridiculous. He came from a country of which I had never heard until Amnesty International asked me to go there, and which no longer exists – if indeed it ever really did. His crime was minor, his case was unimportant and his fate was insignificant in the struggle against apartheid, but in a police cell in a city called Thohoyandou I was privileged to observe this man's thought processes as he became a prisoner of conscience, probably at the cost of his life. That was where I met Robert Ratshitanga, the Prisoner of Venda.

Unlike an elephant, you would not know Venda when you saw it. It had no border-posts, and the sign by the roadside on which two elephants say 'Welcome to the Republic of Venda' was battered and dust-covered and overlooked at the speed I drove along the straight and empty bitumen road some hours north of Johannesburg. It was on South Africa's border with Zimbabwe, not far from the Afrikaner outpost of Louis Trichardt, with the Kruger National Park forming its eastern boundary. Its population was put at half a million, mainly subsistence-level mango farmers who lived in kraals run by tribal chiefs, although most of its young men had migrated to satellite townships outside South African cities. In 1979 Venda had declared independence – or rather, had 'independence' declared for it by South Africa – as a 'native homeland'. This was nonsense, since South Africa supplied its public funds and did not permit any political initiative without its approval. Venda's laws were South African laws, its sole judge an Afrikaner and its Attorney General and his staff all prosecutors from Pretoria. No country in the world other than South Africa recognised its 'independence', a fiction which allowed Pretoria to pretend that the murders committed in Vendan police custody and the electric shocks administered to those suspected of supporting the ANC were none of South Africa's business. 'Blame the blacks, who are learning to govern themselves,' was its response to an outcry over the police killing of a Lutheran lay preacher and torture of several of the Church's pastors. It was to observe the pastors' attempt to sue the police, and to monitor some of the treason trials which carried the death sentence, that I first came to the Northern Transvaal in 1984.

The comic opera side of Venda was immediately apparent from the signs which proudly pointed to 'Foreign Embassies' on 'Embassy Row', because the only Embassy in town was not foreign: it was the South African Embassy. The state airline, Venda-Air, was a car-hire service. The largest government department was Foreign Affairs, which lacked any foreign recognition. There was one luxury hotel, where Afrikaner farmers enjoyed vices illegal in South Africa: they came to gamble at the casino, watch hardcore pornography in the hotel cinema, and then have inter-racial sex with black prostitutes (on 'independence' in 1979, the Immorality Act was the only piece of apartheid legislation not applied to Venda). Municipal power reposed in tribal chiefs: there was a Parliament, but the building was locked and my enquiries met with the elliptical response 'Parliament is not in session because it's an election year'. This came from the Director General of the Ministry of Justice, Mr Tshishonga, one of the smart new breed of Vendan civil servants who were put forward to answer questions about the torture of prisoners. 'I am secretary of the committee which is looking into this matter. I cannot tell you what we are doing about it, unfortunately, because our proceedings are confidential.' One of the detainees died of typhoid contracted in prison? 'Yes, that was very unfortunate. But how on earth were we to know the old man was sick? He did not complain.'

Mr Tshishonga was half glad to see me – in an unrecognised country, my visit counted as some confirmation of his existence, if only as an apologist for torture and neglect and murder. He was vexed about Amnesty, however: 'We get all these letters from your members. They say the people we convict are innocent. How on earth do they know?' Amnesty letters never say this: they are carefully worded to complain only of breaches in minimum standards of justice or prison treatment. Mr Tshishonga demurred, and we argued. 'If you like, I will show you the file.' So he clapped his hands to summon his secretary: 'Bring me the file for Amnesty International'. She returned with a drawer pulled from a cabinet, in which there were indeed many letters. Excited now, he emptied all the letters onto the desk. 'There. See for yourself!' I looked at the letters, all addressed to the Minister of Justice, postmarked from Amnesty offices around the world. Not one of them had been opened. I pointed out to Mr Tshishonga that his minister did not seem to read his mail. The Director General's mouth fell open. 'The minister has been on holidays. Since . . . since . . .' he scrambled for some postmarks, 'since last year. He is still on holidays . . .' The members of Amnesty International who conduct 'write in' campaigns on behalf of prisoners of conscience may never expect their letters to be read, or even opened. The fact that they arrive at least brings home to the servants of brutal, isolated States that, somewhere, someone is watching them.

It was to give the prosecution and judges of South Africa the sensation of being watched that I was in Venda, operating under a code which in this period served the cause of human rights rather more effectively than the posturings of Western diplomats and politicians. Apartheid had made South Africa a pariah State, condemned for injustice at Commonwealth conferences by African governments whose own legal systems were far less just. This diplomatic hypocrisy South Africa could ignore – it was more unsettling to have its protestations to fairness taken seriously, by an organisation which expressed no views about the nation's political system, but had a track record of exposing human rights abuses wherever they occurred, even in the US and the UK. For this reason South African judges and politicians and Attorneys General always received Amnesty observers with a nervous politeness, and usually allowed us into their courts and prisons. They wanted us to like them and approve of them, and they knew that Amnesty missions were low-profile exercises in which we would take care to be seen, but not heard giving press conferences. We would not make the snap judgments associated with American trial lawyers, who love to parachute in and make a fuss, and have their names attached to that fuss. Amnesty's measured reports did more in the long term to persuade apartheid's defenders that the system was indefensible.

'I am now the second member of my family to be libelled in *The Times* of London.' Venda's Chief Justice, G P Van Rhyn, angrily flourished a recent press clipping which criticised him for acquitting the policemen who killed the Lutheran lay preacher. 'They attacked my father twenty-four years ago, when he was South African Ambassador to Britain and had to explain why our actions in Sharpeville were necessary.' (In 1960, South African police had massacred sixty-nine peaceful protesters in that township.) 'Now they are saying these things about his son.' Van Rhyn was every inch the Afrikaner lawyer, formerly counsel to that bastion of Boerdom, the Farmers' Union. But the common-law tradition wove its spell: it was precisely because of the upbringing in it we shared that he talked so frankly. 'I am so upset about this because I admire you English lawyers. I once had the great privilege of meeting your Lord Denning. You English lawyers know that rules must be followed.' Lord Denning tended to make up the rules as he went along, but I let that pass. 'You English are very important to South Africa. After all, you are forty per cent of our population!' He paused, to let this sink in: his failure to count seventeen million blacks did impress me. 'Like my father, I too am an ambassador for South Africa.' No he wasn't. He was a judge. 'True, but I am sacrificing some years of my life to help these unfortunate people, before I go back to the South African Supreme Court.' But we were in South Africa, really. 'No, it is a lie by foreign politicians and journalists to say that Venda is not independent. It is completely independent.' South Africa, he told me proudly, was fighting for its life, and he saw himself as a part of its defence force, wearing his wig like a combat helmet. He alone would decide whether to compensate the black Lutheran pastors.

The lawyer for the Lutherans would have an impossible task, and I was anxious to meet him. His name was Ismail Mahomed, and his speciality was driving coaches and horses through apartheid legislation. (In Pretoria, the draftsmen talked about making theirs laws 'Mahomed-proof'.) Ismail was the first black to become a senior counsel after a career in which he suffered every petty humiliation, so he was undaunted at the prospect of appearing before Van Rhyn. The Lutherans were brutally treated in detention (the medical evidence was overwhelming) but they were gentle churchmen with no wish for revenge: their leader gave talks entitled 'Why I forgive my torturers'. So Ismail offered the State a deal: an admission of police guilt and a payment of £10,000 per plaintiff, or else a trial lasting two weeks which would expose the torturers. The State accepted, and afterwards the pastors took me to their mission in Venda's green hills, where they were helping victims of famine. I had thought they made the wrong decision, because it was important to expose to the world evidence of electric-shock torture by South African-controlled police, and this could be done most effectively through a trial. But when I saw the distended bellies of the famine victims I understood why they chose to take the money to spend on food. It was not that they had no stomach for the fight, but that there were too many other stomachs which needed to be filled.

Robert Ratshitanga was offered a bargain as well. He was one of several Vendans charged under the Terrorism Act with 'harbouring' ANC guerrillas. His crime was allegedly committed when three ANC 'boys from the bush' turned up at his back door asking for food. He gave them porridge, in the company of a fellow sympathiser who on arrest had turned informer, agreeing to give evidence against Robert in return for a low sentence. It was hardly a serious offence, but the minimum term of imprisonment had been set by law at five years. This had been much criticised by Amnesty: every law which mandates a fixed sentence produces injustice in cases where the crime does not merit it. But this week (because, I was told by a friendly junior in the prosecutor's office, Amnesty was observing the proceedings) a new deal was on offer. Those charged under the Terrorism Act with minor acts of harbouring may plead instead to the offence of High Treason, where the sentence is at the discretion of the court. The Attorney General would ask only for one year, and Van Rhyn would make a show of being even more merciful, and sentence to eight months. Any time in Venda's typhoid-ridden prisons was dangerous, and the five years mandated by the Terrorism Act was often a death sentence, so this deal was immediately accepted by the first 'harbourer' brought to court. Van Rhyn nodded in my direction as he began his sentencing homily. 'The attitude of the State in this case has been fair, lenient and *almost* compassionate . . . you will find my sentence extremely lenient.' He was talking to Amnesty and to 'The Times of London' as he said this – he had never given a sentence so low for a harbouring offence and would not do so again, I sadly suspected, when Amnesty was no longer watching him. He was, however, prepared to do it in the next case, the least serious of all, involving the plate of porridge provided to the ANC by Robert Ratshitanga.

I was permitted to meet Robert in the cells, while he discussed the deal with his lawyer. He was forty-five, a man of the most extraordinary presence and dignity. For the six months since his arrest he had been held in solitary confinement in a stifling corrugated iron cell in a malaria-ridden bush prison. But Robert had managed to acquire a biro and toilet paper: from the sole of his shoe he produced his prison diary, an Andrex scroll in minute handwriting. He had, in the past, written several books of verse: his poems were pastoral rather than political, but he was still Venda's only published poet. He was not in good health, and believed he would die in prison if he had to serve the full five years under the Terrorism Act. There was only one problem about accepting the alternative: the plea was to High Treason 'with an intention to impair the sovereignty of the State of Venda' and as Robert explained, 'There is no way, absolutely no way that I can bring myself to acknowledge the existence of the State of Venda'. There was no moving him: his lawyer tried and so (stepping out of the role of impartial observer) did I. But this man, for all the pain and privations of five further years of imprisonment, could not acknowledge the existence of Venda as an independent constitutional entity. He was right, of course, as a matter of principle: the State of Venda was a sick joke perpetrated by South Africa as a cover for apartheid. But would it really matter to anyone if he accepted that he had impaired its non-existent sovereignty? It mattered to Robert Ratshitanga. With all the integrity which must have attended Sir Thomas More's refusal to take an oath in full knowledge of the deadly consequences, he unswervingly declined to receive mercy at the hands of a country in which he did not believe. He was truly, thereafter, a prisoner of his own conscience.

So they took him away for his trial under Section 3 of the Terrorism Act. The friend who had been with him when he fed the guerrillas gave an accomplice's evidence against him, shooting nervous glances as he did so at the white South African 'advisers' sitting in the courtroom. Robert Ratshitanga was found guilty, as he undoubtedly was, and jailed for five years as a terrorist, which he undoubtedly was not. He was, rather, the epitome of courage, a man who refused to save himself either by lying to the court or by copping a fraudulent plea.

There were other missions for Amnesty, to watch the justice game being played out as the struggle against apartheid became more intense. Those of the country's true leaders who were not in the bush were often to be found in the vast dock of Pretoria's Number 1 Court on lengthy trial for treason. The stairs from the dock led down to a cavernous room where they were permitted to spend lunchtime with their lawyers. There I met treason trialists like 'Terror' Lautoka and his twenty co-defendants, charged with forming a political movement (the United Democratic Front) to overthrow the State by calling for democracy. The walls of the room were covered in grim graffiti: the names and slogans and counting of days scribbled by political prisoners over the years. If the new South Africa wants a new national monument, it need only exhibit these walls.

South Africa throughout the eighties was a nation at war with itself. Ungainly armoured vehicles called 'hippos' and 'caspirs' patrolled the dusty township streets with conscript soldiers crouched inside, taking nervous aim at any potential demon-strators. Sometimes, there was a massacre – as at Uitenhage on 21 March 1985, when a black funeral procession was mown down by bullets. It was some sort of tribute to the continuing operation of the law that the security forces found it necessary, after killing twenty-nine mourners, to fabricate evidence to excuse their conduct. They had been given orders that petrol bombers 'should be eliminated', so they clumsily manufactured evidence of a 'petrol bomb', using a smashed Fanta bottle and some torn-up news-paper: the surrounding earth was analysed by forensic scientists who found no trace of petrol. The security forces also claimed that the crowd was throwing stones, but there were no stones in or near the position in which their vehicles had stopped. Their evidence was torn to shreds at the Kannemayer Commission, the judicial inquest into the incident which opened in Uitenhage.

While there, I stayed with Molly Blackburn, a doctor's wife who worked relentlessly for the end of apartheid, and was one of the founders of 'Black Sash', a civil rights organisation of like-minded women. I was the guest at a reception thrown by the local law society. 'We particularly wanted to meet you,' said its president, 'to say that we all like to think of Uitenhage as the garden city. We are very upset that its name should be associated with tragedy. We lawyers have nothing to do with these troubles.' Indeed they had not: the local law firms refused to act for the victims, many of whom worked for well-to-do white families in this prosperous city where black servants lived in townships far enough away not to spoil the view from the civic gardens. But some young lawyers from the Legal Resource Centre in Johannesburg had joined with 'Black Sash' to set up an open-air office in the grounds of the local Catholic church, where statements were taken from eyewitnesses to the massacre, and then from relatives of more victims as the violence spread.

There is no textbook which teaches lawyers how to practise under fire, but these young South African lawyers were writing one in Uitenhage. The case of Ndenzile Thembani, for example, began when his body was brought to the church grounds in the back of a pick-up. I thought he was curled up asleep, but because rigor mortis had not set in, he could be uncurled to reveal the bullet holes. Estimating his time of death at about an hour ago, we drove to the scene of the shooting. It had occurred in a township some five miles away, where eyewitnesses said the bullet had come from a caspir, one of a number of shots fired after a group of about eighty youths had been dispersed by tear gas. We noted that there were no stones on the sealed road at the point where Ndenzile had been killed, but we found other rifle bullets in the vicinity. Our white presence attracted attention, and the caspir returned. The officer in charge wanted to know what we were doing collecting evidence against him of culpable homicide. He claimed that eight hundred youths had been stoning his caspir, but he could not explain the absence of stones on the road other than by suggesting that the township residents had gathered them all up and hidden them before we arrived. Why had he not helped the wounded? He was not going to say any more. It was another example of the random shootings of the time, as police and army aimed to kill or cause serious injury, without any credible claim to be acting in self-defence. As Ndenzile's body stiffened, the painstaking legal paper trail began which might one day bring this officer to some sort of justice.

At least the government forces stayed away from the funeral of the massacre victims, held in a sports stadium at Kwanobuhle with Bishop Tutu presiding and the unsinkable Molly Blackburn at his side. Tens of thousands sang ANC songs and listened to church-men giving veiled ANC messages and watched a shock troop of schoolboys perform a military tattoo in front of the coffins. These deaths were not being mourned at a funeral but celebrated in a political rally, led by substitute generals wearing clerical collars. The killings were unforgivable, and this occasion made them un-forgettable. The irony in this country was that a functioning legal system did provide some redress, at inquests and by the possibility of civil action against the police. This was too haphazard a retribution to deter future killings, but it did enable some truth to emerge about the State's responsibility for its arbitrary 'shoot to kill' policy: the one time that these victims received the respect due to them as human beings was when they were beings no longer.

Events like the Uitenhage massacre infused demands for vengeance against black collaborators with apartheid: when mobs formed, someone would suggest 'necklacing' a traitor, or stoning him to death. The police could rarely be certain of the ringleaders – after such incidents they would arrest half a dozen or so members of the mob and impute to them, by a doctrine called 'common purpose', an intention to kill which would result in death sentences for all, unless the judge found that there were extenuating circumstances. In the first five months of 1988 sixty-six men were executed; sixty-five of them black. This was the fate which would have befallen the 'Sharpeville Six' and the 'Upington Fourteen' had they not attracted the attention of Amnesty and other human rights lobbies. I would meet these men in their prisons, then go for drinks with the judges who had sentenced them to hang. A few of the prisoners I thought were guilty but some were innocent, and the same applied to their judges. The inappropriately named Judge

Human, who had convicted the Sharpeville Six, was generally found propping up the bar of the Pretoria Club, which had recently admitted Jews but not blacks or women. He would speak of 'the blacks' and 'the mob' interchangeably, as an entity he endowed hydra-like with an intelligence and a capacity for single-minded action. The 'common purpose' doctrine was not a legal fiction, it was exactly the way he thought. He should, on the evidence, have found extenuating circumstances (and so avoided the death sentence) in five of the Sharpeville Six cases, and was furious when Louis Blom-Cooper (in an article in the *Independent*) attributed his failure to his politics. Judge Human asked my advice: 'Does Blom-Cooper have any money? If I can get libel damages, then at least I can retire.' He did collect damages from a Pretoria paper which republished the Blom-Cooper article: the money helped him drink himself to death.

Judges in South Africa were not all like Van Rhyn and Human: many, especially at appellate level, maintained a fidelity to law unfazed by the pressure of apartheid politics. This in turn sustained an independent Bar and a trial and inquest system which withstood emergency legislation and provided arenas where some truth about State-sponsored killings could emerge through the adversary system. But the scale of human-rights abuse later revealed by Bishop Tutu's 'Truth and Reconciliation Commission' shows how much stayed hidden. South Africa was putting on a show with trials and appeals which suggested that justice, if not in robust health, was at least still breathing. At a submerged level, the enemies who did matter were simply executed without trial or even arrest. Once, in Easter 1988, I strayed within that mine field.

I had flown to war-torn Mozambique on behalf of a young Australian missionary who was facing a firing squad. Ian Gray had been arrested by government soldiers as he distributed Bibles from his combi-van in the bush. Inside one of them were messages he was carrying to the leader of Renamo, a rebel force in bloodthirsty combat with the Marxist government. He was accused of spying – a charge to which he had no defence and the punishment for which was death, unless the Revolutionary Military Tribunal could be persuaded to be merciful. Renamo was not even an anti-Marxist movement, but a group of thugs and desperadoes originally recruited and trained by Rhodesia's white army to destabilise a hostile neighbour. Subsequently it was run by the South African intelligence services, for the same political purpose: Mozambique was the most strident anti-apartheid front-line state and its army had to be kept occupied. Renamo forces raped and murdered tens of thousands of Mozambiquans each year, and its scorched-earth pillages were causing famine in some parts of the country. How had the love of Christ brought an idealistic youth from Toowoomba to serve the most vicious army in Africa?

Ian had fallen in with some American fundamentalists trained at a Bible college in Florida founded and funded by Jimmy Swaggert, a prominent American tele-evangelist. They had been brainwashed into believing that the Lord required a crusade against communism in all its forms, and they convinced Ian of their cause after they recruited him, an innocent abroad, at a pentecostalist meeting in Malawi. Ian was convinced by these new friends that Marxist Mozambique had burned the country's churches and killed its priests and pastors. That is why he agreed to act, under his missionary cover, as the agent of Renamo, smuggling messages which he hid in Bibles to and from its command headquarters in the bush. He was arrested in his Bible-mobile and refused to talk to his army interrogators. He regarded himself as a political prisoner, and was prepared to die in the service of God. What his life depended on was whether he was prepared to confess to his dealings with the enemy, and offer some sort of genuine apology. When I first met him in the police cells, his lips were sealed.

I respected the sincerity of Ian's beliefs, but doubted the facts on which they were based. The government of Mozambique was no worse – in some respects, given the enormity of the problems it faced, it was better – than most other African governments. Its capital, Maputo, was full of churches, and there had been no mass slayings – or any slayings at all – of their pastors. As a lawyer I am bound to help would-be martyrs whatever I think of their cause, but I do have a duty to make sure they know the full facts. In this effort I had an invaluable ally: Ian's father, providentially flown to Maputo the next day by *60 Minutes*, an Australian current-affairs programme, and even more providentially taken, on the night of his arrival, to one of the city's burgeoning pentecostalist churches.

The Gray family belonged to a pentecostalist church whose members spoke in tongues. The tongue in which Mr Gray spoke to his son in the cells the next morning, however, was the broadest Australian. 'You stupid bastard. Do you realise what you have been doing to these good people? You've been helping to kill them. I went to church with them last night, son. There must have been a thousand of them, and do you know what they did? They prayed for you, they got down on the floor with me and they prayed for you, and we spoke in tongues and asked the Lord to forgive you . . .' The two fell weeping into each other's arms, the father's simple faith breaking his son's mental block in a way no legal advice could ever do. He agreed to help us in the effort to save his own life.

I was not willing for Ian to plead 'guilty' to a crime for which he could be executed, or face long years in appalling prisons. Mozambique was a country at war, and its court system was rudimentary: Ian's fate would be decided in secret by a court which frequently handed down death sentences, and it had never allowed legal representation. I needed help, and it was given unstintingly by Albie Sachs, the brilliant South African lawyer exiled in Mozambique as a result of his support for the African National Congress. Albie introduced me to various ministers, translated pleas and submissions, advised on tactics and obtained permission for me to address the Revolutionary Military Tribunal on Ian's behalf. My address to his three uniformed judges, whose own lives were daily threatened by the enemy whom Ian had helped, was the most difficult piece of advocacy I have been called upon to deliver. The upshot was a judgment in which Ian's naivety and contrition saved him from the death sentence, and limited his various treasons to a term of imprisonment from which he was released, through an amnesty, one year later.

Albie had proved a marvellous guide and counsellor and friend, collecting me from the colonial ruins of the Paloma Hotel in his beaten-up red Fiat for trips to lobby ministers and diplomats. He showed me the city sights, which ranged from revolutionary wall murals to the husband of the US Ambassador, an eccentric Anglophile who had imported a London black cab and drove it each day on the main road, stopping to offer free rides to surprised pedestrians. I once asked Albie whether he took any security precautions – his friend Ruth First (wife of ANC military leader Joe Slovo) had been killed by a letter bomb in Maputo, and his account of his own detention, *The Jail Diary of Albie Sachs*, was in print throughout the world, to the discomfort of the South African security service. He gave a self-deprecating shrug: 'I suppose I should check under my car, but that was all so long ago. I really can't believe I'm still significant enough to be on the hit list.' When Ian's trial ended, he invited me to stay with him for a few days' holiday at the beach.

I accepted, but first I had to try to call my chambers. The telephone system at the Paloma was erratic, and I had been incommunicado with London for the past week. Finally, I was put through to Michael, my clerk:

'Thank heavens you've called, Mr Robertson. We've been desperate to contact you, sir.' (Nothing can bring a clerk to use a barrister's Christian name.)

'Michael, what's the matter?'

'You've got silk, sir. You must come back to London immediately, or you'll miss the ceremony.'

'Has it been announced in *The Times*?' I asked disbelievingly.

'Well, no, sir. But your envelope is the right size.'

This is typical of the Bar: clerks tell from the size of the envelope from the Lord Chancellor's Department whether it contains a slim rejection slip or bulky instructions about how to dress in a silk gown, full-bottomed wig, lace ruff, and silver-buckled shoes for investiture as a Queen's Counsel. At this ceremony, if I could make it, I would share the joy of generations of upper-class Englishmen, of being able to wear silk stockings and a suspender belt without embarrassment. I looked out the window, at the sprawling slums of war-torn, famine-ridden Maputo, and I saw the black cab. It seemed like Cinderella's carriage, come to take me back to the pantomime in London.

It was not easy, at this time, to leave Maputo. The road to South Africa had been cut by Renamo, and air transport was sporadic and fully booked. I said farewell to Albie, forgoing with real regret the days with him at the beach, to catch a flight to Swaziland, where I stayed overnight and watched 'The Jimmy Swaggert Bible Hour' on Swazi television. (Swaggert had recently been discredited by his communion with prostitutes in New Orleans motels, but his organisation was paying vast sums to offload his programmes on the cash-strapped television stations of emergent countries.) I then drove to Johannesburg, and took the overnight flight into

Heathrow, where I collected a copy of the *Financial Times* and saw the photograph of Albie on the front page. He was lying beside his crumpled car, one arm in the road a distance from his body, a leg twisted away from his torso. The bomb, said the report, had been activated when he opened the door of his car to drive to the beach.

Albie was put together again miraculously, and is now a judge of South Africa's Constitutional Court where he has joined with Chief Justice Ismail Mahomed in outlawing the death penalty. His own had been passed in secret. I had already mourned, although without anger, the death of Molly Blackburn, whose heroic life had been wasted in the kind of accident so common on South African roads: the brakes of her car failed. That, Bishop Tutu's commission recently discovered, was because they had been tampered with – by men from the secret State. The Bishop now offers an amnesty to killers in return for their confessions, which seems over-charitable. Punishment left to history or to God does not deter the brazen or the Godless, and most State killers are both. For all the difficulties of proving guilt without a confession, some murders are so heinous that a trial is the only proper response. That was certainly my opinion in the case of Dr Hastings Banda.

In the Commonwealth cruelty league of leaders who have kissed the hand of the Queen and received the blessing of Margaret Thatcher, Banda's was the most atavistic presence. By 1983 his control over Malawi was such that when discomfited by some mild criticisms from Parliament's four leading members, he gave orders to his British-trained Chief Inspector of Police to have them killed. The police chief agonised but carried out these orders: a 'special duties' squad (some trained at Hendon police college) arrested the cabinet ministers, took them by night to a lonely stretch of road, and quite literally bashed their brains out. They put the bodies in a car and pushed it over a cliff, and the Cabinet Secretary announced that the four had met with a road accident. There was no inquest, as the law required, because Hastings Banda *was* the law. There was no mourning permitted for Dick Matenje (the Secretary of Banda's Malawi Congress Party and Deputy Prime Minister) or for his three colleagues. There were no coffins, either. Their bodies were delivered to their families in dirty blankets, not only dead but dishonoured. Their names were never mentioned in official records again: they became 'non-persons'. Banda's crime was well known to Britain, but it said nothing. (Malawi was providing important support for Mrs Thatcher's appeasement of apartheid.) It was well known to members of the State's only political organisation, the Malawi Congress Party, because the death squad had stopped at its office in Blantyre and paraded Matenje through it, escorting him obviously to his execution. It was a bestial act, the one which most contributed to the fear which was all-pervasive amongst Malawi's nine million citizens.

I did not meet Dr Banda until 1992, by which time he had been running the country for twenty-eight years, for most of that time personally enshrined in its Constitution as President for Life. His was the familiar colonial story: briefly imprisoned by the British; released to become the leader on independence; quickly dispensing with democracy (or at least with all political parties other than his own, which is pretty much the same thing) and then proceeding to use British law – indeed the emergency legislation under which he himself had been detained – to suppress all dissent, helped by British lawyers. His landlocked country was kept in fear of his secret police and even greater fear of his paramilitary loyalists, the 'Young Pioneers'. The army he kept weak (a lesson well learned from the overthrow of other African leaders), television was banned and developments in the outside world were filtered through the nation's only radio station and newspaper, which he owned. Regular celebrations of himself, Hastings Kamuzu Banda, were held on 'Kamuzu days', in which regiments of women would dance for him and sing his praises. It was a crime to be found in possession of any Simon and Garfunkel album featuring the song 'Cecilia' which might lead to lack of respect for his mistress Cecilia Kadzimira, whom he dubbed the nation's 'official hostess'.

Dr Banda was not by any means senile, although aged over ninety, with a leathery face wizened as a turtle's. 'Ah, you have brought with you a Mbumba!' (a woman, in the Chichewa language) he chortled as he greeted our human rights delegation. 'I am so pleased you have brought Mbumba. I am Nkhoswe (or powerful man, in Chichewa) and I like Mbumba! All Mbumbas in Malawi love their Nkhoswe! They love me and I love them. Wherever I go in Malawi the women sing and dance for me! I am Nkhoswe, you Mbumba!' These 'Me Tarzan, you Jane' remarks were addressed to Jane Deighton, a North London solicitor renowned for bringing cases of sexual harassment, and for a moment I had visions of her reacting in a manner which would give our delegation an unrivalled opportunity to observe Malawi's prison system from the inside.

Banda waved his ornate ebony fly-whisk and ordered his attendant ministers to explain Malawi to us. They told us that it was a State which embodied the rule of law: the Constitution laid down that there shall be only one party, and there was. They were proud of the British laws they had inherited – like the law of sedition, currently being used to jail a trade unionist for saying that Banda was too old to lead the country. They were importing a British QC to prosecute him, to show the world they were fair. British lawyers had helped Dr Banda establish his justice system, in which serious crimes like murders were tried in 'traditional courts' run by tribal chiefs, whose hearings were in secret and where defence counsel were not permitted. Mr John Tembo, the Minister of State, explained that 'President Banda is a highly educated, civilised man, who is very generous in accommodating other people's views. He is loved by his people – you should have seen the crowd singing and dancing for him when he opened a new dam in Lilongwe two days ago. You come from a country which is well known for the Birmingham Six and the Guildford Four and the Maguires. We do not have miscarriages of justice like this in our traditional courts.'

It was clear that Minister Tembo was an avid reader of the *Observer*, then owned by Lonrho, which in partnership with Banda's private company, Press Holdings (managed by Tembo) was exploiting what wealth there was left in Malawi. There was not much left: the World Bank had in 1989 rated Malawi among the six poorest countries in the world, with a per capita GNP of $160, an infant mortality rate of 15.35%, an average life expectancy of merely forty-six years and a literacy rate of barely 25%. Twenty-eight years of Dr Banda's rule had brought few benefits, other than to Lonrho and the Life President and his friends and relations. You would not have thought so, to hear him speak; the minutes give some flavour of our meeting:

Malawi is one of the most prosperous countries in Africa. It is a star performer. The IMF and World Bank are full of praise. This makes me very happy. People are rich in Malawi, not the ministers but the ordinary people in the villages who are growing maize and tobacco and groundnuts. There is no poverty, the villagers are prosperous. They have food, decent clothing, houses with roofs that do not leak when it rains – glob! glob! glob! [the Life President indicates with his hand how the rain water was prone to drip down] – because in Malawi when it rains it pours! My people are happy. They dance for me and they sing for me. You are very welcome here because you have brought a Mbumba with you.

This man had the power of life and death over nine million people. What I remember most vividly from our audience was Banda's Mikado laugh, a kind of hacking, chortling paroxysm which shook him whenever he mentioned the death of an opponent. It wracked him when he mentioned Dick Matenje; it possessed him almost hysterically when he mentioned Aaron Gadama (a Minister for Health who was murdered for daring to suggest that Press Holdings be taking into public ownership). I told him that we had found fear more extensive than food: fear at every level, even among his own ministers, that they would suffer violent reprisals if they spoke or even thought critically of the government. His people were not happy, however much they might be organised to dance and sing for the Life President. Banda replied that his 'one party State was 'just born' because 'the other parties died a natural death' (unlike his opponents). He said goodbye as effusively as he had greeted us.

Those who glibly idealise a life without lawyers should have lived in Dr Banda's Malawi. By 1992, there were only ninety-seven lawyers for nine million people, the lowest ratio in any country in the world. It showed – in the hopelessness the people felt about ever winning a case against the State. I remember most vividly the low voices in which church leaders and judges spoke when whispering to us even the mildest criticisms of the way in which the country was run. Spies were everywhere, and punishment was at the whim of the Life President. After his fall, some secret memoranda were discovered in which his Chief of Police (who had organized the killings of the cabinet ministers) sought his instructions for dealing with citizens:

> Your Excellency, I have the honour to report that police have
> arrested Mr Henderson B Mfipa for subversion. At the time of the
> arrest, police searched his house and found Communist literature –
> *Marxism Today*, *Spy Counter Spy* and *What is to be Done?* by Lenin.
> He graduated BA, joined government service as a teacher and
> became a District Commissioner. May I be directed by your
> Excellency in this matter?

Banda's orders, scrawled in the margin, were 'Have this man
arrested, tried, imprisoned and after whatever sentence he serves,
he must be detained indefinitely'.

Another secret memo from the Chief of Police:

> Your Excellency, I have the honour to report a request to issue a
> passport to Thokozani Manyika Banda to go to the USA for studies.
> The government has approved the trip. Taking into account the fact
> that you are the minister responsible for matters of immigration may
> I have the formal approval of your Excellency before Immigration
> issues the passport? I am, sir, your Excellency's most obedient
> servant.

On it Banda wrote 'Pick the man up right away and lock him away
forever'. His only crime had been to come to Dr Banda's attention,
and to be the son of a man whom the Life President did not like.

The revolution in Malawi had its spark a few months before our
visit, when the country's Catholic bishops issued a pastoral letter
protesting at Banda's repression. Initially, the MCP planned to kill
them, but the country was by now only surviving upon international aid and the donor nations were becoming nervous about
Malawi's appalling human-rights record. Even Douglas Hurd, so
backward in appreciation of human rights, at long last voiced
criticisms. In September, the formation of an opposition party was
announced: our lawyer hosts allowed their names to be published
amongst its founders, hoping that our presence would help them
survive, as at least we would observe their disappearance. A
dangerous moment passed, thanks to the threat that the foreign-aid
tap would be turned off. Banda and Tembo decided instead to play
democracy at its own game and win: immediate multi-party
elections were announced, because they did not think that new

parties could organise in time. They were proved wrong when the people, forced for three decades to dance and sing for Banda, turned out in force to vote him down. At a Commission of Inquiry established by the new government, the police officers who had carried out the conspiracy to kill the four cabinet ministers confessed their guilt. There was only one person in Malawi who could have given the order to his Bramshill-trained Chief of Police to perpetuate a crime of this magnitude, and then order the Whitehall-trained Cabinet Secretary to cover it up.

The new government wanted to prosecute Banda for murder, which carried the death penalty. I advised them that hanging him was not the way to eradicate the memory of a regime which exterminated its opponents. So he was prosecuted for conspiracy to murder (which carried ten years' imprisonment) and permitted to remain at his palatial State home during the trial, after medical evidence that he was too old to sit in court and concentrate for more than an hour at a time. It was Malawi's first murder trial outside the traditional court system, and first jury trial for many years: the judge misunderstood the law of conspiracy and the role of circumstantial evidence, and virtually invited the jury to acquit – which they did. I did not conduct the trial, and although I was later to argue the prosecution's technical appeal against the acquittal, privately I did not think that the verdict was altogether a bad result. True, a man I believed guilty of a crime against humanity had avoided conviction. But the trial had been conducted openly, under rules which were fair to the defence, and the verdict had established what the defendant himself had deprived his people of for so many years: the precious possibility of innocence.

Chapter 10

Show Trials

Kamenev: I, together with Zinoviev and Trotsky, organised and guided this terrorist conspiracy. I had become convinced that Stalin's policy was successful and victorious . . . yet we were motivated by boundless hate and by lust for power.

Vyshinsky: You expressed your loyalty to the party in various articles and statements. Was all this deception on your part?

Kamenev: No, it was worse than deception.

Vyshinsky: Perfidy?

Kamenev: Worse than that!

Vyshinsky: Worse than deception? Worse than perfidy? Then find a word for it. Treason?

Kamenev: You have found the word.

Vyshinsky: Zinoviev, do you confirm this?

Zinoviev: Yes, I do. Treason, perfidy, double-dealing.

Stalin's show trials, 1936–38, are defining events for court-rooms in the twentieth century. The trial process was perverted in order to re-write history, by eliminating those who had made it. Stalin's confidence trick succeeded because it adhered to the *forms* of legality: the trials were conducted before judges, the defendants were entitled to lawyers, and their confessions were repeated under Vyshinsky's dogged questioning. What British left-wing lawyers like D.N. Pritt, who unforgiveably white-washed these mockeries of justice, should have realised was that the confessions had been obtained from men who had spent weeks on 'the conveyor': a disorientation technique in which physical discomfort and lack of food and sleep alternated with interrogation to enhance suggestibility and acquiescence. They fell for prosecutor Vyshinsky's technique for turning their past thoughts into crimes, by constructing a fable about the possible consequences of their opposition to Stalin. In effect, they played out their responsibility for actions to which their thoughts might have led, if they had possessed the courage to act on their convictions. 'The confession of the accused,' explained Nikolai Bukharin, the only defendant to retain any self-control, 'is a medieval principle of justice.' His own had not only been extracted by 'psychological pressure' but because in prison he realised 'you ask yourself, if you must die, what are you dying for? An absolute black vacuity rises before you, with startling vividness.' He confessed because he felt his powerlessness before the almighty State he had helped to construct, the impossibility of beating it at the game it chose to play with his life.

Stalin's show trials still haunt because they prove how legal systems, with their varying procedural rituals for emphasising objectivity and impartiality and apparent ability to extract the truth, can be vulnerable to political manipulation. As Vyshinsky – the most wicked lawyer of the century – explained in his textbook *The Problem of Evaluation of Proof in Criminal Trials*, 'the judge must be a political worker, implacably applying the directives of the Government'. His teaching was taken to heart not only in communist countries, but in certain Commonwealth countries where the colonial courtroom trappings of impartiality – wigs and gowns, the judgments of Lord Denning and the motto *Dieu et mon droit* – were retained for camouflage. When, in the late eighties, I helped dissidents in communist Czechoslovakia and defended them in democratic Singapore, I felt that the outcome was equally predetermined.

A fraud trial has just finished in Prague's shabby central court. The defendant, Karel Srp, has been found guilty of embezzlement, and sentenced to several years in prison. He shrugs and turns to his escorts, who take him down the ill-lit dirty corridors to the van which will carry him back to prison. There is no majesty or drama about these proceedings, no frisson of uncertainty about the verdict. People act like clockwork, as if it's a pre-arranged business best disposed of as quickly as possible. Everyone involved in the non-descript courtroom seems slightly down-at-heel, and slightly ashamed. Outside on the steps, however, and spilling into the adjacent square, there are several hundred youngish people. No bonfires, no banners even: just quiet courage in being there. The sentence is whispered, heads nod and pass the information on. Then, somewhere in the crowd, the singing starts: a ragged, half-crooning chorus of 'We shall overcome'. I turn quizzically to Srp's lawyer, who smiles tightly. 'You can tell which are the secret police. They are the ones who know all the words.'

It is 1986, and this is one of the first threads of the velvet revolution which will unravel a few years hence, when Dr Husak and the political puppets who make up his judiciary and his 'licensed' law society will shrug and leave the stage. Srp is in prison whenever I visit Prague to discuss what can be done to help his defence. The issues – why the case is so important, which lawyers can be trusted to handle it, which families of the men arrested with him most need financial support – are explained in a café beside the Vlatava river, by a man who alternates information about political prisoners with observations on the need to revise the map of Middle Europe so disastrously drawn at Yalta. Vàclav Havel is nervous, because the authorities can return him to prison at any moment. When I find I do not have enough Czech money for our meal, I assume I can pay the rest in US dollars, which are accepted with alacrity everywhere in the city. Havel is horrified and explains (I kick myself for not realising) that he would immediately be arrested by the secret police watching us from the far table as an accomplice in black-marketeering. 'This is the first rule of being a dissident,' he says. 'You must scrupulously obey the law.'

Welcome to communist Prague, home for all lovers of irony. Here only subversives obey the law, secret police sing protest songs to maintain their cover and there is a specific criminal offence of possessing the 1966 edition of the Frank Zappa Songbook. This law is not as funny as it sounds – an eighteen-year-old youth has just been imprisoned under it. 'He was a dissident,' Havel says sorrowfully, 'before he was a man.' Concern about Zappa dates from 1976, when the Plastic People of the Universe, a rock band which took its name from the songbook, were jailed in the government's first major assault on alternative culture. Its latest purge is the arrest of Karel Srp and eight of his fellow executives of the Czech Jazz Society, among whose crimes is numbered the publication of a three-volume *Encyclopaedia of Rock*, a discography which has a large entry on Zappa. Years later, when newly elected President Havel comes to Britain to give a lecture at the Institute of Contemporary Art, he will be asked accusingly by some idiot from *Marxism Today* why he has wasted valuable time by hosting an official visit by the American rock singer. Havel is lost for words, then politeness gets the better of him. 'Because . . . well, because he seemed a very nice man.' It would have taken too long to explain the symbolism, too many imperfect words to conjure up for some pampered English Marxist what it is like to live under constant threat of losing one's liberty for reading another's lyric.

But this really was the case in the eighties. The trial of the 'Jazz Section' (bureaucratically it was a 'section' of the Czech Musicians' Union) had been clumsily dressed up as a case of embezzlement. Communist governments had, by this time, learned to deflect international concern about human rights by pretending that dissidents were imprisoned for real crimes rather than for their thoughts. The case against the Jazz Section executives was that they had handled money unlawfully: 'a crime in your country too', Czech diplomats would say in London and Washington. But when you discovered what the Czech Jazz Society supplied in return for the money willingly given by its members, the reality of the case became clear. It had charged admission fees for punk rock concerts; it had sponsored a tree-planting in honour of John Lennon; it had sold copies of its *Encyclopaedia of Rock* with the entry on Zappa; it had mischievously published banned works by subsequently acceptable authors such as Bohumil Hrabal (*I Served the King of England*) and the Nobel prize-winner, Jaroslav Seifert. Even worse, the Jazz Section had been using funds to forge links with peace movements and 'green' parties in Western Europe; it had affiliated to Britain's Campaign for Nuclear Disarmament and had published material which satirised not only American trident missiles but their Soviet nuclear equivalent, the SS20s.

The Jazz Section, in the eyes of Dr Husak's regime, was worse than subversive, it was successful – attracting over 100,000 young supporters to its 'Rock on the Left Wing' concerts in the mid-eighties. By this time, however, Moscow was bent on reform and the advent of 'Glasnost' was an uncertain time for Prague's old apparatchiks. 'What's the difference between Gorbachev and

Dubchek?' the hardliners would ask themselves, and laugh hopefully at the answer: 'There is none. Except Gorbachev doesn't realise it yet.' They did not realise that Gorbachev's promise to 'return to socialist legality' – any sort of legality, in fact – would prove so potent it would sweep them away. For in Czechoslovakia, legality was a myth of the State's making. Rules had no application, and judges had no independence: the will of the party was the supreme law. The more I came to understand this legal system – and I tried, over numerous visits – the more evident it became that the fate of the Jazz Section would be decided not by the evidence, but by a telephone call to the judge from a party boss.

The trick, which took in fraternal delegations of 'socialist lawyers' from Britain, was played through the ubiquitous system of licensing, under a regime where nothing was permitted which was not officially approved. The Czech Jazz Society had been founded as a lawful communist organisation and trade union branch (department: jazz) of the Musicians' Union. At first it organised concerts and social events, and published regular newsletters, but at these properly constructed occasions amateur performers and youthful minds met and combusted, to produce by the early eighties the art and ideas which the tottering regime could not tolerate. So the Ministry of Culture arranged for Karel Srp to be sacked from his job with a State publishing house, and for his lawyer to have his licence to practise withdrawn. They lived by watering gardens and cleaning toilets while organising more concerts – with such success that in October 1984 the Ministry of the Interior issued an emergency decree abolishing the entire Musicians' Union, and establishing a new one without the jazz department.

The Jazz Section kept playing, proclaiming its entitlement to legal existence through its membership of the International Jazz Federation (a UNESCO organisation) and lodging an appeal with the Supreme Court. This court existed only on paper, although since the paper it existed upon was the Czech Constitution, this manoeuvre caused much political embarrassment. Eventually the government wearied of the cat and mouse game, and arrested Srp and six of his comrades on charges of 'unlicensed trading'. Their prosecution was announced to the world as a fraud case, but this was itself a fraud: the society was strictly non-profit, staffed entirely by unpaid volunteers, and all its income after its licence was withdrawn had been used for publications and concerts for the benefit of its members. It was for the content of these publications, and the talk at the concerts, that the Jazz Section had to be silenced.

Nobody was fooled. Not even the British Foreign Office, so myopic in the face of human rights abuse in friendly countries like Malawi and Kenya and Singapore. At international conferences the UK quoted an aphorism from Norman St John Stevas ('There is no such thing as socialist art. There is only good art and bad art') which entirely missed the point. The art being promulgated by the Jazz Section was often dreadful: leafing through the collections of *Samizdat* proudly produced from beneath the Prague floorboards, I was irresistibly reminded of the colourful effusions from *Oz* and the underground press which had been prosecuted in Britain in the previous decade. As Havel would impress upon me at our meetings, the case of the Jazz Section had to be recognised by the left in the West as a critical test of whether 'socialist legality' could sufficiently respect human rights to allow kindred human spirits to make music and art and even criticism of the State across the doctrinal divide. It was a test which 'socialist legality' critically failed: Srp went to prison, and in due course the system which had betrayed the good in socialism died of shame. Havel went to the Castle in Prague as its first President, welcoming Frank Zappa and appointing the lawyer who had defended Karel Srp to the post of Chief Justice.

I have never much liked jazz – you keep thinking it will turn into a tune, and it doesn't. So I could not at first understand why it was suppressed as 'decadent' by the Nazis and why it was so feared by the geriatrics in power in Czechoslovakia. I would watch them as they hobbled, straitjacketed in dinner suits, to the best seats in Prague's half-empty Opera House to applaud productions of Smetana's work which were as old and dreary as they. The answer became obvious one evening when I was taken to an 'official' jazz concert. Through another exquisite irony, the government attempted to show the West that it was not afraid of music by establishing its own jazz society to replace Srp's disbanded union: in a propaganda frenzy it arranged concerts to which it invited Herbie Hancock and Mike Westbrook, carefully scheduling them after midnight on Sunday. But that was when the youth of Prague turned up, after the sclerotic Russian 'Big Bands' (old men in suits playing Glenn Miller) had left the stage. The place came alive, and I realised why totalitarians distrust jazz – because it's music you can talk under. The talk under the jazz that early morning at the Lucerna Theatre was of the stupidity of the secret police, who had arrested one local band when they realised that its seemingly anodyne title – PPU – was a coded reference to the banned Plastic People of the Universe. It took only three years before the audience dispensed with its musical camouflage and, led by Havel, packed into the same theatre to talk about democracy.

After the velvet revolution, the ironies became over-wrought. Some of us who had supported the dissidents were invited back to help to draft new laws: our hosts delighted in holding conferences in buildings formerly used to train the secret police who had shadowed us, and housing us in the hideously decorated *dachas* built for visiting communist apparatchiks. (It soon became apparent, however, that the new government needed no help with human rights: what it desperately wanted was guidance in drafting laws for commerce and the conveyance of private property.) My own guide from dissident days, Jaroslav Koran, the translator of Kurt Vonnegut, was elected mayor of Prague, whereupon he decorated the Town Hall with abstract art and employed the Jazz Section to organise the city's garbage collection, which in consequence became chaotic. The former communist mayor found a job as editor of the newly launched Czech *Playboy*. At last I had the pleasure of drinking with Karel Srp, who was now running an arts laboratory on the site of a secret police interrogation centre. One of Havel's first acts had been to make him Deputy Minister of Culture, but once a maverick always a maverick: this great provocateur had soon resigned, to find his true freedom in satirising the new regime. The next time he is prosecuted, he will at least have the possibility of being found innocent.

The most fundamental right of all is the right to challenge the State, under a legal system which allows the possibility, occasionally, of winning. To secure that right has been the spur for change in most countries I have visited on human rights missions – countries as diverse as Czechoslovakia and Malawi and Vietnam – because it is the acid test of democracy. It had never been a possibility for the Czech dissidents, who were followed everywhere by the same secret policemen who would dog my steps through Prague's rubbled streets. Once I led them into the city's Jewish cemetery, full of tall tombstones leaning at crazy angles, as if blown by centuries of storms. By the entrance is a small art gallery full of pictures of ordinary life at home; optimistic, childish art about the possibility of innocence. These are the most moving pictures in the world, for they were drawn by the children of the Terezin ghetto, *en route* to Auschwitz. Their art survived the war, unlike the young artists. It was both ironical and logical that the 'unlicensed' publications for which Karel Srp was sent to prison should include studies of art and music of Terezin.

*

Student activists became involved in the labour issues of several factories, presenting themselves as champions of the workers. In 1974, students agitated on the University of Singapore campus. The Communist party of Malaya was attracted to this fertile ground of activism . . . In 1987, a drama society, the Third Stage, was formed by a group of ex-student activists. *No Foul Play* was the first of a series of plays that took a consistently negative view of society and government policy. Articles in Catholic magazines began to deviate from religious subjects and focus instead on political issues . . . there is a Marxist link to them all.

This was the opening of Singapore State television's *Tracing the Conspiracy* – a programme which showed how Stalin's trials would have looked had they taken place on TV in 1987. This city-state was vociferously anti-communist, ruled by English law and a lawyer trained in England. The art of choreographing a show trial had moved on in the half-century since Vyshinsky, but the outline of the script remained the same.

Lee Kuan Yew knew all about communists because he had briefly allied with them, riding the Asian Marxist tiger for just long enough to extirpate first the colonial British and then some short-lived local liberals, before jumping off and shooting the beast between its blood-red eyes. That was in the fifties, and thirty years later, when we crossed words in court, he was haunted by the memory of his escape from the communist cadres he imagined still lurking in the Malaysian jungle. Since he came to power in 1959, his People's Action Party (PAP) had controlled the lives and minds of Singaporeans as closely (and a good deal more cleverly) than any of its counterparts in Eastern Europe. To this end he had kept in place all the British emergency legislation he had reviled in his fellow-travelling days. These laws provided for detention without trial for as long as the government liked: they were operated by a vast and increasingly sophisticated army of secret police, the ISD (Internal Security Department). There were judges in wigs and gowns, who seemed utterly fair and impartial and had never been known to rule against Lee Kuan Yew or the PAP or the ISD or the government, because (no doubt) these entities were always in the right. My appearances in Singapore in the late eighties were to defend an improbable mix of subversives: Catholic lawyers, women playwrights and Dow Jones Inc.

The ISD was adept at securing confessions, but modern Vyshinskys no longer resort to medieval methods. They dressed their victims in cotton pyjamas, and stood them under the full force of an air conditioning unit, facing studio-strength spot lights. Then they applied what the government admitted was 'psychological pressure' to extract confessions – mainly from a group of Catholics whose concern for social justice they had misinterpreted as subversion. The ISD plots were, in their way, as silly as Stalin's: the conspiracy was alleged to revolve around connections with a Trotsky figure named Tan Wah Piow, a Marxist who had fled the country to avoid conscription and was now based in postgraduate digs at Oxford. The conspiracy's clandestine leader in Singapore was a Catholic social worker, Vincent Chang, who had recruited a group of young lawyers, actors, accountants, and merchant-bankers to destabilise the State by writing articles and plays which drew attention to unemployment figures and the low pay of Filipino maids. Under the icy blasts of the air conditioner, these terrified middle-class detainees had 'confessed' to various contacts with Vincent and in some cases to telephonic contacts with Tan. Most importantly for the plot, they admitted to having been encouraged by a number of Catholic priests.

Although only six per cent of the island was Catholic, it was this religion which Kuan Yew had come to fear more than communism. Not, let me make abundantly clear, that he had any concern at all about the Catholic Church: he was as fluent in

Machiavelli as the Vatican, and was rightly proud of his tolerance of all religions as long as they did nothing more than worship. What frightened him was 'liberation theology' – a phenomenon that he credited with toppling Marcos in the Philippines and seemed afraid might topple him. Thus his secret police targeted all Catholics preaching the poison of 'liberation theology' with its subversive concern for human rights. Lee had personally begged the Pope to cut this cancer out of Singapore; his ISD director had warned the Archbishop that there were too many 'truth and justice' columns in Catholic publications. When the Archbishop failed to act, the ISD and the government decided to force his hand. They did not arrest the priests, but they detained in prison twenty-two young Catholic activists for participating in 'a Marxist conspiracy to subvert the existing social and political system in Singapore through communist united-front tactics'.

The Archbishop wavered. His diocese was in a state of terror, and packed the cathedral to pray for God to guide the government. This infuriated Lee Kuan Yew, who regarded himself as Singapore's only God in matters temporal. He summoned the nearest Vatican diplomat and told him to keep the Church out of Singapore politics, or else he would arrest the priests. The Archbishop was paraded at a press conference with Lee in order to say that the detentions had nothing to do with the Church – incautiously he added his hope that the government could prove its allegations against the detainees. 'I have never said that I was going to prove anything in a court of law,' Kuan Yew shot back. 'It is not the practice, nor will I allow subversives to get away by insisting that I produce evidence that will stand up in a court of law.' So the detainees underwent their trial not in a court of law, but in a television programme co-produced by the government-controlled media and the secret police.

The detainees were broken very quickly. Lee was later to sneer about this – how pathetic they were, compared with communists of the past. It did not strike him that this was because they were not communists, but middle-class liberals who wanted to do their bit for the poor. They were shamed by the very fact of their arrests, mortified at the discredit the publicity had brought on their respectable families. They were arrested at 2 a.m. and taken to the Whitely Road Detention Centre, where they were blasted with freezing air and slapped in a way which stung rather than bruised.

Recalcitrance or drowsiness was punished with a basin of cold water. The interrogators indicated what they wanted – long written apologies about how their actions had been influenced by Tan or Vincent. Then they were required to read their confessions in front of television cameras. Various sound-bites were extracted, often out of context, and carefully edited for their television trial.

These twenty-two Catholics were initially detained for six months, but after their release some of them issued a press statement, describing the torture they had undergone: sleep deprivation for up to seventy hours; standing for up to twenty hours' interrogation at a time under the full blast of a freezing air conditioner; dousing with cold water; hard slaps to the face; threats to friends and loved ones; warnings that release would depend on their command performance. (They had been ordered to make statements such as 'I am Marxist-inclined . . .' and 'My ideal society is a classless society' and 'I was made use of by so and so'.) The signatories to this statement were immediately arrested and detained indefinitely 'to get to the bottom of the whole picture', as Deputy Prime Minister Goh Chok Tong explained. That meant extracting more confessions from them. Lee's son and presumed heir, government minister B G Lee (the B G stood for 'Brigadier General' although it was popularly translated as 'Baby God'), was sufficiently arrogant to admit to the BBC World Service: 'The government does not ill-treat detainees. It does however apply psychological pressure to detainees to get to the truth of the matter . . . the truth would not be known unless psychological pressure was used during interrogation.'

Predictably, it was soon announced that the eight detainees had 'withdrawn' their statements, but there seemed no immediate prospect of their release. As the months went by, I was approached to act for most of them in applications for *habeas corpus*, the greatest invention of English law, which requires immediate liberty for a person whose detention the State cannot lawfully justify.

Never have I acted for such good people. There were young Catholic lawyers, like Tang Lay Lee and Kevin de Souza, whose subversiveness had been inferred from 'forsaking a well-paid legal career for a lowly paid job of a helper with the Catholic Students Union'. There were two female dramatists, authors of the mildly satirical *No Foul Play* and *Oh Singapore*, who were charged with 'singing progressive songs and performing plays which exaggerated the plight of the poor and the inadequacies of the existing system'. What was so shocking about these detentions, and ultimately so thuggish, was that the dissidents were (as Lee himself described them, although contemptuously) 'do-gooders' who wanted to help the poor and the dispossessed. Their weak satire and obscure columns in *Catholic News* entirely lacked the mass appeal of the Jazz Section, or even the anarchic ebullience of *Oz* with its reference to sex and drugs which would have utterly horrified these detainees. It was, I think, their simple goodness which rebuked Lee Kuan Yew: for all his materialist might, and his determination to be mentor and role-model to his people, he feared that they were setting the better example.

The struggle to free the detainees was conducted in a country where litigation was a game which Lee Kuan Yew, himself an able lawyer, regularly played and always won. He had abolished jury trial as unreliable, but kept the Privy Council so long as it displayed no interest in upsetting pro-government decisions. Lee used English libel law to bludgeon and bankrupt political opponents for any personal criticism of him made on the hustings. For this task he would import leading QCs from London. John Mortimer would sometimes try to even the odds, by defending Lee's particular *bête noire*, Ben Jeyaretnam. Ben had incurred Lee's enmity by winning a seat in Parliament in 1981 on behalf of the Workers Party – the only seat not held by Lee's PAP. In due course Ben was prosecuted on trumped-up charges of fraud, and jailed for just long enough to be disqualified as an MP. The Privy Council reviewed the whole course of the case and issued a devastating condemnation of the Singapore judges who had handled it. It expressed 'deep disquiet that by a series of misjudgments' Ben and his co-accused had 'suffered a grievous injustice. They have been fined, imprisoned and disgraced for offences of which they were not guilty.'

The robing room of the High Court in Singapore was just like the robing room of the High Court in the Strand, and contained much the same people – English QCs dressing for forensic battles over commercial contracts. The only difference was not apparent: it was bugged by the secret police. This was an apt metaphor for the justice on offer: a surface fairness, with legal submissions dotted with English precedents listened to politely by black-robed judges.

When it came to locking up palpably innocent people without trial, or convicting journalists for mild criticism of the courts, there were plenty of English precedents these judges could rely upon to justify the State's action. Only when you sit in a courtroom in Singapore – or Kuala Lumpur or Nairobi or Venda – and listen to State attorneys endlessly quoting decisions of the House of Lords, do you realise just how poor are parts of the human rights legacy of British law and British Law Lords. With few exceptions, before the Privy Council decision in *Jeyaretnam* in 1988, they showed little conception of the importance of freedom of speech, and always allowed the State's assertion of 'the interests of national security' to block any examination of the rightfulness of detention. In our *habeus corpus* case, the State counsel lingered lovingly over every word of Lord Denning's judgment in *Hosenball*, using it to support his argument that these lawyers and dramatists could be kept in prison without trial for the rest of their lives, were this deemed by the secret police to be 'in the best interests of national security'.

And yet . . . judges throughout the common-law world were becoming conscious of being watched. Their judgments were increasingly published in law reports and commented upon at legal conferences and in law reviews. Some were State lackeys, but they did not like this to be pointed out – especially by the Privy Council. That court's condemnation of the judges in Jeyaretnam's case had deeply embarrassed the Singapore judiciary: since we could still appeal to the Privy Council, they had to watch their step. Especially since I had spotted a fundamental error which had been made by the government when detaining my clients indefinitely. The law required, as clearly as daylight, for the detention to be authorised by a government minister. Instead, it had been authorised by the head of the ISD – a secret policeman. This was such a basic mistake that no decent court could excuse it (although the first-instance judges did) and the Privy Council would, on appeal, be certain to grant *habeas corpus*. So on 8 December 1988 the Chief Justice of Singapore took a deep breath and announced, in a 107-page judgment, that because of what he described as a 'mere technicality' (it was nothing of the sort), the detainees must be released. For five hours on that day, it seemed to them, and to their deliriously happy families and friends, that the rule of law really prevailed in Singapore.

The judgment was delivered at 11 a.m. The release papers were not signed for some hours because the State prosecutor could not be found to agree the order. It was 4 p.m. before the detainees' lawyers arrived at the Whitely Road Detention Centre, where they were greeted by smiling policemen who actually offered them drinks to celebrate our historic victory. These gaolors had been helping the happy detainees to pack up their belongings, even taking care to wrap the pictures they had hung in their tiny cells. They were escorted to police cars which drove them out of the inner gates and down the long sloping road and through the second security gate at the bottom, where their families were waiting. The cars drove past the families and went onto the road to freedom, over a roundabout and back past the families and through the security gate and up the long slope and through the first gate. Now back where they had started, my clients were served with new detention orders, drawn up earlier that day and signed this time by the appropriate government minister. The punishment for their court victory was to be detained again, indefinitely.

In Singapore, the State could not lose, even when it lost. And the prospect of it losing was immediately foreclosed by the Internal Security (Amendment) Act which provided 'There shall be no judicial review in any court of any act done or decision made by the President or the Minister'. That meant no more *habeus corpus*. And for good measure: 'No appeal shall lie to the Judicial Committee of Her Britannic Majesty's Privy Council . . .' That meant no more damaging criticism from independent judges. It was a double whammy, to show the world who was boss in Singapore – the Government of Lee Kuan Yew.

The government next launched a bizarre attack on the Western press for 'meddling in Singapore politics' (i.e. coverage of the opposition parties or criticising the government or reporting the plight of the detainees): *Time*, *Asia Week*, *The Asian Wall Street Journal* and the *Far Eastern Economic Review* suffered what was termed 'gazettal', a punishment which the government insisted did not amount to censorship. Their circulation was cut from up to 10,000 to a mere 400, confined to government libraries and tourist hotels. It was a childish pretence that such a limit on circulation did not amount to an attack on free speech. This was not, however, sufficient for revenge on the *Far Eastern Economic Review*, which had reported on Lee's clash with the Catholic Church. Lee sued the magazine for libel – not in Hong Kong where it was based and where appeal lay to the Privy Council, but in his own courts where such an appeal had just been abolished. Dow Jones, proprietor of the *Review*, believed there was an important principle – freedom of expression – at stake. 'Have fun' was the only instruction I received from its President, Peter Kann, as he sent me off to play the justice game against Singapore's grand master.

'Fun' is not something normally associated with Singapore, and certainly not with cross-examining its Prime Minister. As in Czechoslovakia, my movements were followed, although much more discreetly, except where the purpose of the surveillance was to intimidate. Father Joachim Kang, a priest of enormous courage, was prepared to give evidence to support the *Review*'s story. When I visited him, a police surveillance van was ostentatiously stationed outside his church. A pupil from my chambers, whom I had invited to Singapore to further his legal education, made the mistake of handing me a law book in court: a few hours later he was under interrogation for working without a permit, and had to leave on the next plane. Worse was in store for my junior, Howard Cashin, a highly respected member of the local Bar. To dispel any aura of sanctity about the defence, since we were on the side of the Church, it had been arranged for an ultra-loyal PAP member to allege that his wife had committed adultery with Howard, in a divorce petition filed on the first day of the trial. As the assembled journalists awaited the arrival of the judge, the Prime Minister's press secretary solemnly handed out copies. Greater love for the party hath no man, that he would lay out his wife's infidelity to serve its interests.

The cross-examination of Kuan Yew was lengthy and ill-tempered: we disappointed each other. I expected the historical figure I admired, and some residual evidence of his Cambridge double-first: instead, I found an evasive and truculent witness whose mind was set in the communist-infested fifties and whose main concern was to stop the publication of informed criticism (ill-informed criticism, curiously, he did not mind at all). He complained bitterly to the judge about my style of cross-examination:

I see counsel, Queen's Counsel at that, groping madly, wildly looking for nooks and corners to get me on some hook to turn me upside down. My Lord, I am not a child and he is not an inexperienced counsel. And we have wasted hours, he repeating the same question and getting the same answer from me. I am amazed, truly amazed, my Lord. I had prepared myself for this cross-examination. I had identified the main points. Those points which, if I met a cross-examiner like John Mortimer, he would have gone straight for, and I would be prepared for it. But here, I am vexed.

Poor Lee Kuan Yew – he had even scripted his own trial. The problem was that when he did not get the questions he wanted he nonetheless gave the answers he had prepared, so we did not get on and neither did the proceedings. The *Review*'s case involved an assertion that the Roman Catholic Church had a traditional mission to relieve poverty and social injustice, even in Singapore where such things did not officially exist. It also involved an exploration of how this doughty fighter against British colonialism and then the menace of communism could come to despise human rights as forcefully as he did. The trite answer, I was forced to conclude, was that he despised everything that might interfere with his right to run Singapore as he thought best.

Lee admitted that he had been frightened by what he saw in the Philippines before the fall of Marcos: 'Catholic priests in clerical robes spouting forth . . . it was a united-front conglomeration with trade unions – they were in it; human rights – they were in it; professional associations – they were in it; lawyers – they were in it'. After the detainees were arrested, what he could not abide was how their families had been permitted to speak in the cathedral after mass. 'Emotions were let loose. That is my concern. I am not interested in whether they spoke truth or untruth.' The fact that more prayers had been said for the government than for the detainees cut no ice at all, because they were 'prayers for truth and justice', and that was 'tendentious agit-prop'. That the Catholic Church – or any Church for that matter – should conceive itself to have a social justice mission was 'totally unacceptable':

Q: You suggested to the Apostolic Nuncio that the Vatican should clip the wings of these four priests, and find out their source of inspiration?

A: Yes. I mean by that, keep them out of the political arena and find out who in the Philippines or who else was giving them these ideas of justice, freedom, democracy and so on . . .

Q: But you accept that it's a matter for the Church to decide whether –

A: I did not accept that. I accept that it is a matter for the Government to decide whether churchmen are in politics or out of politics but I leave it to the Church to decide what they do to ensure that their priests stay out of politics.

Q: It is a matter for the Church to decide whether its mission and tradition requires priests to speak out on social policy issues, isn't it?

A: This is the first time any church, or anybody else, has put that proposition to me.

Judge: Listen, Mr Lee. Look, Mr Robertson. I don't think we need to go into that.

So we didn't, although it was the real issue in the case. This libel action was about what happened at a meeting between the Prime Minister and the Vatican diplomat. The *Review* had quoted a priest as suggesting that Lee had attacked the Church. Lee claimed that this was a false and defamatory suggestion, because he had merely asked for a change of archbishop:

A: All I told the Vatican representative was, please can I have an archbishop who can keep his priests out of politics.

Q: 'Send me an archbishop who will keep his priests out of politics.' Was that what you were saying?

A: No. Yes. (*Laughter*)

Judge: Look, would the people up in the gallery please contain yourselves. It's not a theatre, it's a court. These are serious proceedings.

They were for the *Far Eastern Economic Review*. But the only safe place to laugh at Lee Kuan Yew in Singapore is in a courtroom when he's suing for libel. If you write satirical plays, you can be locked up without trial indefinitely, and (so Lee told me) 'no amount of human rights agitation will get the government to back off'. On the contrary, he boasted, human rights agitation and

238

habeas corpus applications would be counter-productive, because his government believed that the more aggressively it responded to such 'pressure', the more cowed its opposition would become. It was, by this logic, keeping the detainees in prison not because of anything they might have done, but because people were still pressing for their release.

The *Review*'s report of Lee's dealings with the Church was true enough and fair enough to pass muster in any country which honoured the principles of free speech. In Singapore, however, it became expensive speech, published at the cost of S$230,000, the amount of damages awarded to the plaintiff. (There was some slight satisfaction in this, since Lee's QC had told me before the trial that he would settle only for a grovelling apology and S$350,000). The judge had decided that the damages should be increased because of my cross-examination, which was 'calculated to be offensive and to increase the hurt to the Prime Minister's feelings'. The Malaysian Bar Association immediately commented that this was the first evidence that Lee Kuan Yew actually had any feelings.

Kuan Yew now affects the role of an elder statesman promoting 'Asian values' against the Western fashion for human rights. To do him justice (and one would not wish to do him anything less), his chosen weapon has been the libel writ rather than the hammer to the head, and the interrogation techniques of his secret police may have left victims shaking with cold and flu but have always left them alive. Familiar criticisms of Singapore are misplaced: they focus on the laws against jaywalking in the streets and urinating in the lifts and dropping chewing-gum wrappers on the pavements, which only make me wish we had similar laws in Britain. This superficially clean image of the State serves to disguise the fact that Singapore functions as a base for dealing and running arms. Should that great secret begin to be exposed by local journalists and lawyers, I suspect that the air conditioners of the Whitely Road Detention Centre will be reactivated for a threat to the State of much greater moment than any that the 'do-gooders' from the Catholic student centre were ever capable of offering.

Lee Kuan Yew finally stepped down from the Prime Minister-ship, bequeathing his second-generation leaders a country without *habeas corpus*. He laughed under cross-examination at the English language press 'telling us benighted natives how to conduct our affairs', but the real joke was that he had to use English law and English lawyers to muzzle his opposition. I do not blame him for cashing in – there are plenty of politicians in Britain who happily exploit its libel laws. But Lee's strategy is catching: from Malaysia to Mauritius, from Ghana to Grenada, the common law of libel and contempt and official secrecy have all been employed to suppress dissent. It is instructive to observe how China, on regaining Hong Kong, announced that it would re-introduce a number of colonial ordinances providing for contempt and sedition and criminal libel prosecutions: by these devices, acceptable because they remain the law in the UK, any necessary suppression of speech will be effected. Britain no longer rules the waves, but throughout the Commonwealth it is the British rule book that tends to be waved to declare freedom of speech off-side.

Hope for change comes, ironically, from the involvement in international human rights courts of judges recently liberated from communism. A few years ago I represented a young journalist named Bill Goodwin who refused to obey a court order to name the source for a news story. We lost unanimously in every court in England, by nine Law Lords to love, but won by eleven votes to nine in the European Court of Human Rights. Our majority was largely secured by the verdict of judges from newly liberated Eastern Europe – the Czech Republic and Poland and Latvia and Estonia and Slovenia. They knew the importance of free speech, because they had lived without it for so long.

Chapter 11

Fantasy Island

A large and lively crowd gathers at nightfall in the public square in a Bogotá suburb, to cheer the man whom all opinion polls predict will soon be President of Colombia. Dr Luis Carlos Galan walks to the front of the makeshift rostrum to acknowledge the applause, which is suddenly punctuated by the dull repetitive thuds from rifles firing. The candidate crumples, while through the frenzied, screaming citizens, his assassins make their escape, dropping a Galil assault rifle as they run.

I have watched this news clip many times. The assassination happened on 18 August 1989 and I spent much of the following year studying the arms and money trail which made it possible and which also facilitated the murders of dozens of judges and journalists. It was an unusual job for an Old Bailey barrister, and it took me to the beaches of Antigua and the banks of Bermuda, to the cattle and cocaine valleys of Colombia and to the gun factories of Israel, ending in Washington with testimony to a Senate committee. I served as counsel to an inquiry set up by the Governor General of Antigua, after the discovery that Galan's killers – the Medellin cartel – had been supplied with lethal weapons by the Antiguan defence force. The story is about sleazy adventurers and politicians with blind eyes, but it is told as a tribute to courageous lawyers – those judges in Colombia who did justice, although they knew they would lose their lives for doing it.

These men and women, who refused to become party to the corruption that cocaine spawned, were assassinated by a small army commanded by Rodriguez Gacha, the militant partner of Pablo Escobar. Gacha's force was remarkable for the efficiency of its killings and its kidnappings, its bombings (especially of newspapers opposed to the cartel) and its major barbarities, such as the destruction of a commercial airliner with the loss of III lives. The secret of Gacha's success was two-fold. Firstly, his force had been taught by mercenaries from Israeli anti-terrorist units and the British SAS, at training camps on Colombia's *La Isle de la Fantasia*. Secondly, they had somehow managed to acquire the most modern and most effective weapons. That much was clear from examination of the gun which killed Dr Galan – a state-of-the-art Galil assault rifle, recently manufactured by Israeli Military Industries (IMI), a section of the Israeli defence ministry. The production number on its barrel identified it as having been shipped from Israel as recently as March 1989, in a large consignment of arms ordered on behalf of the Antiguan Government and delivered to the Quartermaster-General of the island's defence force.

Antigua is a different kind of fantasy island. Only fifty-four miles square in the eastern Caribbean, it has 365 palm-fringed beaches ('one for every day of the year') and cricket and calypsos. It echoes with English gentility, from Peter de Savery's yachtclub near Nelson's dockyard to the bewigged barristers in its courts and the unarmed policemen patrolling streets where rusty coronation arches still stand in memory of Queen Elizabeth's last visit. Thrice-weekly, BA jumbos disgorge middle-class tourists from the shires, who take their tea and cake promptly at 4 p.m. in the shade of its luxury hotels. It is that place in the world where author Ken Follet, paragon of political correctness, tells readers of the *Guardian* he would most like to live. When I remind Ken of the reality – that his fantasy island is the most corrupt country in the Commonwealth Caribbean – he is genuinely surprised. 'But I thought Antigua was a parliamentary democracy.'

That is the problem. Antigua is a nation of fewer than seventy thousand people, with a vote at the United Nations and an overdraft at the World Bank. It has been dominated for thirty years by one family, the Birds, whose supporters, retainers, hangers-on, beneficiaries, dependants, and political cronies, together with those too frightened or too depressed to vote against it, have ensured its electoral hegemony. Papa Bird, now in his eighties, was the trade union leader who emerged before independence to become the first Prime Minister, a post he still occupied in 1989 with the assistance of his two sons, Lester, the Foreign Minister, and Vere C Bird Jnr, the Minister for National Security, Public Works, and anything else which his father thought appropriate. According to the Israeli government, in its explanation to Colombia, it was as Minister for National Security that Vere Jnr ordered 400 Galil assault rifles, 1,000 Uzi sub-machine-guns and 200,000 rounds of ammunition, at a cost of US$350,000, for delivery to the Quartermaster-General of the Antiguan defence force. This force has no 'Quartermaster-General': it comprises ninety-four soldiers, whose weapons and ammunition are supplied free by the United States. The guns, including the one dropped by Galan's killers, were destined for the Medellin cartel.

On receipt of the Israeli explanation, the Colombian government issued a formal but ferocious protest note to the government of Antigua. It was received by the Foreign Minister, Lester Bird, who immediately called his brother's office, demanding to speak to Vere 'on a matter of life or death'. Vere ambled outside, to take this private call in his ministerial limousine, without bothering to remove one of his 'special advisers' dozing in the back seat. The layabout was woken by the Foreign Minister's voice booming through the car-phone speaker: 'We's in deep shit now'.

The traditional way for a government to emerge from the state known in Antigua as 'deep shit' and in Britain as 'presentational difficulties' is by setting up a judicial inquiry, which takes so long to get under way that those responsible have time to cover their tracks and so long to report that public fury will have abated when it does. So Papa Bird asked his Governor General to appoint a Royal Commissioner to find out why arms purchased in the name of his government had ended up in the arsenal of a Colombian drugs cartel. To placate Colombia and Israel, and allay US concern, the British Foreign Office was asked to recommend a suitable Commissioner, and suggested Louis Blom-Cooper QC, whose appointment was announced by the Governor General before Papa Bird realised that a Blom-Cooper inquiry had led to the dismissal of a corrupt government in the Turks and Caicos Islands. Bird Snr immediately asked the Governor General to revoke the appointment, but he refused. Cyclone Louis was about to hit Antigua, and the Birds could only try to limit the damage. To do so, they hired at enormous expense Lord Michael Havers, the former Lord Chancellor, and two more Queen's Counsel. Vere

Bird Jnr, the minister who had apparently ordered the weapons, was separately represented by no fewer than six counsel, three of them QCs. Louis Blom-Cooper asked me to act as counsel for the Commission, which had to piece together a jigsaw of contemporary international villainy. The story that follows is found in the Commission's Report.

It began on the luxury ranches of the Middle Magdelena Valley in Colombia, with their white fences and private airstrips and advanced communication systems in contact with the light aircraft which transported heavy bags of cocaine across the Caribbean to the United States. In 1988 Rodriguez Gacha was the king of the Medellin cartel, his fabulous wealth attracting mercenaries from Britain and Israel to train his troops on intensive ten-day courses held on *La Isle de la Fantasia*. There were twelve soldiers of fortune imported from England – a motley collection of old Angola hands and recent dishonourable discharges from the army and the SAS – but the team from Israel was altogether more professional. It was led by Colonel Yair Klein, a retired parachute regiment commander, now the director of Spearhead Ltd, a company offering what its brochures euphemistically described as 'survival schools' and 'VIP and executive protection training' by instructors culled from elite commando units. Gacha's son Freddy was among the first graduates of Klein's 'survival school'; he made a video showing untrained killers from the streets of Medellin being turned into trained killers by the latest Israeli army methods. All they needed were modern Israeli weapons and here, too, Klein was useful – through his contacts with a network of ex-army officers based in Miami, which dealt arms to most of the dictatorships of Central and South America as agents for Israel Military Industries. One was a retired brigadier-general named Pinchas Schahar, who lived in Miami's exclusive Turnberry Island, where he was the friend and neighbour of a man named Maurice Sarfati.

Sarfati had first visited Antigua in 1983, a penniless adventurer until he nestled with the Birds. They made him a director of Antigua and Barbuda Airways, and formally appointed him as a 'special envoy' of the Antiguan government. Thus armed with free air tickets and government backing, he embarked upon a project to siphon millions of dollars in American aid money into and out of his own pocket. Taking advantage of Antigua's status as a third-world country, and of the fashion for funding 'sustainable development', he persuaded a Washington bank to provide millions of dollars in interest-free loans to finance a melon farm on the island. Much of this aid money he used to acquire his Miami condominium, replete with Mercedes and swimming pool, and to put his two sons through finishing school in Switzerland. To keep the Antiguan government sweet he opened a credit arrangement at the farm, whereby certain VIPs might draw $1,000 in cash at any time. Vere Jnr had a more flexible credit limit, according to Sarfati's secretary, who was to claim that she was directed to make $5,000 payments to the minister's wife, who lived in New York. The aid millions were quickly dissipated and by 1988 the farm had amassed debts of about US$7 million. But Sarfati had not finished making monkeys out of the Antiguans. He provided $9,000 to one minister, who subsequently issued him with promissory notes backed by the government to the tune of $4 million. Sarfati immediately discounted them, through 'junk bond' dealers Drexel Burnham, in return for cash to maintain his lavish lifestyle. The notes were counter-signed by an official who was building a new home. Maurice Sarfati helped him import, duty-free, some fixtures from Miami: a jacuzzi, five ivory toilet seats, and six pairs of gold taps.

At the Turnberry Island Yacht Club, Maurice Sarfati was nicknamed 'The King of Antigua'. But by the middle of 1988, he had run his kingdom into so much debt that he dared not return. He stayed in Miami, fending off bankruptcy petitions and awaiting another big scam. Gacha needed arms, and at this point Yair Klein came, as his emissary to the Israeli military merchants. In this diaspora of arms dealers and mercenaries and conmen, plans were hatched which would never be proved by direct evidence, but which left their computerised traces in telephone bills, hotel records and airline tickets. These told the Commission that telephone traffic between Sarfati and Vere Jnr was intense throughout August and September 1988. Vere was Antigua's Minister for National Security, and hence was the boss of Colonel Clyde Walker, commander of the country's tiny army, equipped fully and for free by the Pentagon. At 3.07 p.m. on 4 October, Walker telephoned the arms dealer Schahar. The next day, he flew from Antigua to Miami. He said he had gone to do some shopping, although the Commission found that he had gone to Schahar's office, where he placed the order for Galil assault rifles, Uzi sub-machine-guns and 200,000 rounds of ammunition. The weapons were to be shipped from IMI in Israel, ostensibly for the Antiguan army, once payment of $350,000 was received. In due course, the money arrived in Israel, not from Antigua but from Klein's bank in Panama via Schahar's account in America.

The next step for Gacha was to work out how to transfer the weapons from Antigua to Colombia. According to the Commission's report a breathtaking scheme was envisaged, conceivable only because of Sarfati's hold over the Antiguan government. Klein's training school in Colombia had become difficult to conduct in secret, and he desired to move to a more permanent location. Sarfati suggested Antigua, where facilities could be rented from the defence force and the local Minister of National Security could be its patron. So a prospectus was sent to the Antiguan Cabinet for a 'Security Training School'. It explained that each pupil would be issued with a pistol, rifle and sub-machine-gun, and a daily supply of 110 rounds of ammunition, and would be taught how to 'forestall the growing wave of corporate exposure to terrorist and criminal activity' by shooting at mobile targets. The centrepiece of the school would be a 'speciality shop' selling guns and ammunition to pupils at the end of their course. The Commission likened this to a pro-shop in a golf club, where the well-trained terrorist would be able to pack his kit full of ammunition for his Galil and Uzi before departing. What the brochure did not explain was that the school would be supported by the Medellin cartel, because it would be training its troops. Klein and Schahar visited the Birds in November 1988 to explain how the project would be good for Antigua. It would of course be good for Gacha, and for any paramilitary organisation which wanted to take advantage of these unique facilities.

This whole plot may belong in a James Bond movie, or in a drug baron's wishful hallucination. But Gacha did not take drugs, and he executed any of his followers who did. On 16 November, Schahar, Klein and another Israeli mercenary named Dror flew to Antigua. They were met by Eva, Sarfati's personal assistant, and driven around the island by Colonel Walker to inspect the army's land and select an appropriate spot for the school: they were joined by Vere Bird Jnr, and were taken to meet the Prime Minister. Were the Antiguans aware that they were being asked to host a training school which might be used by terrorists? The Commission thought that this should have crossed the military mind of Colonel Walker, and even the mind of Vere Bird Jnr, who was smart enough to have passed his law exams at Gray's Inn, although both men firmly denied it. It was from Colonel Walker's office, on 19 November, that their Israeli guests made what was to prove a highly significant four-minute telephone call, which was followed by Rodriguez Gacha sending the money for the weapons to Klein's account in a Panama bank. It was then transferred to Schahar's account at the Bank Hapoalim in Miami, and was sent from there to IMI in two tranches: a down-payment in December and a final payment in February 1989, after IMI had informed Sarfati that all the weapons were ready for shipment – to the 'Quartermaster-General' of the Antiguan defence force, a name someone had noticed on an old sign in front of the derelict British garrison house at the main town, St John's.

The IMI agents in Miami had been selling so much military hardware to South American governments that a large cargo vessel, the *Else TH*, had to be chartered to deliver it to their armies. It was aboard this vessel that the container was loaded for Antigua, a convenient first stop for a voyage that would take it through the Panama Canal to disgorge more containers of lethal weapons at Bogotá for Colombian government troops. (It is an ironic tribute to the amoral Israeli arms dealers that their customers – the forces of law and the forces of lawlessness – would soon be aiming guns from the same shipment at each other.) The *Else TH* began its ominous voyage to St John's harbour on 28 March 1989. The day after it sailed from Haifa, the government of Colombia delivered a diplomatic note to the government of Israel, complaining that some of its nationals – Klein was mentioned by name – were running 'training schools' for the Medellin cartel.

The Colombians had just made an intelligence breakthrough, as the result of the defection to the security services of Gacha's personal physician, Dr Diego Viafara Salinas. He had served as medical adviser at the training camps, and had a copy of Freddy Gacha's video of Klein instructing his father's men in jungle warfare. Nothing stayed secret for long in Colombia, and on 10

April – while the MV *Else TH* was on the high seas, just two weeks' sailing time from Antigua – the story of Klein and his terrorist training camps in Colombia was published in *El Espectado*, the much-bombed Bogotá newspaper hostile to the cartels. There was no time to be lost, and on the same day Klein rushed back to Antigua to meet Vere Bird Jnr. All plans to use the 'VIP training school' to launder guns for Gacha now had to be abandoned: Yair Klein's cover had been blown.

But the weapons and ammunition were already paid for and on their way. The conspirators worked frantically to salvage the situation, with faxes flying between Sarfati (in Miami) and Klein (in Minister Vere Bird Jnr's office in Antigua). A boat owned by the Medellin cartel – MV *Seapoint* – happened to be pottering about Haiti. It was diverted post-haste to St John's, where Sarfati ordered his shipping agent to transfer to it the container for the 'Quartermaster-General' which would be unloaded from the *Else TH*. By a marvel of synchronised shipping, these two sinister boats – the *Else TH* and *Seapoint* – anchored within hours of each other outside St John's harbour. The Israeli vessel unloaded the container of arms and ammunition. It was left unguarded on the dockside, sitting in the sun for seven hours, in full view of customs and port officials, until the *Seapoint* sidled in, collected it, and then sailed for a deserted beach in north-west Colombia. There the container was put ashore at nightfall, and another cargo – two and a half tons of cocaine – was taken on board. By May Day 1989, Gacha had his new guns, courtesy of IMI and the government of Antigua. He fired them as follows:

– 4 July 1989, Medellin. Assassination of Dr Antonio Rolan Betancourt, Governor of Antioquia, and five members of his family.
– 28 July 1989, Medellin. Assassination of Judge Maria Helena Diaz Perez.
– 16 August 1989, Bogotá. Assassination of Magistrate Dr Carlos Valencia Garcia.
– 18 August 1989, Medellin. Assassination of Police Colonel Valdemar Franklin Quintero.
– 18 August 1989, Bogotá. Assassination of Liberal Party Presidential Candidate, Dr Luis Carlos Galan.
– 2 September 1989, Bogotá. Attack on *El Espectado* newspaper,

sixty people injured.

– 11 September 1989, Medellin. Assassination of Dr Pablo Pelaez Gonzalez, former Mayor of Medellin.

– 16 October 1989, Bucaramanga. Attack on newspaper *Vanguardia Liberal*. Two dead and seven injured.

– 17 October 1989, Medellin. Assassination of Magistrate Dr Jose Hector Jimenez Rodriguez.

– 1 November 1989, Medellin. Assassination of Magistrate Ms Mariela Espinosa Arango.

– 6 December 1989, Bogotá. Terrorist attack on the building of the Security Administration Department (DAS), seventy killed, several hundred wounded.

On 16 December, ten days after this mass-murder of their colleagues, the security forces finally located Rodriguez Gacha. His ranch was surrounded and he was blown away with ammunition delivered to the army from the *Else TH*. In an armoury underneath the ranch they found several dozen of the Uzi sub-machine-guns and 200 of the Galil assault rifles which had been carried as far as Antigua on the same ship. The rest of the weaponry, and what remained of the 200,000 rounds of ammunition, was deployed against the citizens of Colombia over the following years by forces directed by Gacha's surviving partner, Pablo Escobar.

It took some months for the Colombian authorities to obtain an explanation from Israel, which alleged that the weapons consign-ment had been ordered by army commander Clyde Walker and verified by an 'End User Certificate' apparently signed by the Minister for National Security, Vere Bird Jnr. This was the allegation which had put them, as the Foreign Minister said on the car-phone, in 'deep shit'. As far as the government of Antigua was concerned, Bird shit would not stick to the Birds. They soon had a scapegoat – a nineteen-year-old customs clerk, Sean Leitch, who was arrested for signing some shipping documents presented by Sarfati's agent. On his slim shoulders the nation of Antigua laid its guilt for aiding and abetting the murders of the Colombian judges and journalists, policemen and politicians.

The above story emerged in the course of the Blom-Cooper Commission. The only facts it had to begin with were those elicited by Colombia and admitted by Israel, namely that the weapons found on Gacha's ranch had been supplied to Antigua by IMI, in the belief that they were destined for its armed forces, but had been transhipped aboard the *Seapoint* on the instructions of Maurice Sarfati. He was blamed by everyone else for masterminding the whole affair, and for dragging their names into it without their knowledge. Vere Bird Jnr and Colonel Walker swore they knew absolutely nothing about the arms order: they recalled meeting Yair Klein and receiving the prospectus for his 'training school', but said they were opposed to the project and did not in any event know who it was intended to train. Klein himself maintained that he had only been helping cattle ranchers in the Middle Magdelena Valley to protect their herds from rustlers, and that the arms shipment was destined for Panamanian exiles wishing to overthrow General Noriega.

International law enforcement arrangements are rudimentary when it comes to investigating trans-border criminal conspiracies. This was, after all, an enterprise to put lethal weapons in the hands of criminal assassins, working for a drugs cartel hell-bent on undermining the police and the judiciary of a democratic country. The clues to the people who profited from it could be found in a trail of bank transfers, telephone communications and hotel records, yet there is no developed system for getting at the truth of plots without frontiers, let alone for punishing their progenitors. I quickly discovered that the fabled 'Interpol' is useless – a police databank full of outdated data. As for the DEA, the spearhead of America's 'war on drugs', this billion-dollar bureau knew nothing about the arms shipment to Gacha. From America, at least, I had the help of Larry Barcella, an experienced fraud prosecutor, and my Antiguan assistant was Inspector Truehart-Smith – a policeman whose integrity lived up to his name, which is why he had not been promoted. But in Antigua, the trails mostly ran into the sand. The over-arching design had been developed by telephone and fax from five countries simultaneously. They were Colombia, Panama, the United States, Israel, and Antigua, with some meetings and communications taking place in Paris, London, Bermuda, Amsterdam and even in South Korea (where Vere Bird Jnr had been staying at one vital stage, as 'manager' of the national team at the Seoul Olympics). The Commission had no legal power to compel testimony by anyone beyond Antigua's shores. The only power I possessed was not legal at all. It was the power of pity, for the victims of Gacha's gunmen.

It was that power alone which broke open what the Commission eventually found was a conspiracy, because it worked on the consciences of two women: Sarfati's Girl Friday, Eva Van der Wall, and Vere Bird Jnr's secretary, Ethlyn Thomas. It was their sense – of humanity, I suppose – which caused them to speak out when they might more safely have remained silent, and to testify to the conduct of their former employers. Eva had been recruited by Sarfati while holidaying in the Caribbean, and had enjoyed helping him to help himself to the aid money and the government loans meant to sustain the development of the melon farm. Her task, she said, had been to organise the bribes and favours: such was her importance that she was given a set of keys to the cabinet office. But Eva was genuinely appalled to learn the arms had gone to Gacha, so much so that she volunteered details of the relationship between Sarfati and Bird Jnr. She told of meeting the delegation which arrived to promote the 'training school'. One of the Israelis had left her his calling card, which she had kept on her return to a new job in Amsterdam. On it was the name of IMI's agent in Miami, Brigadier-General Pinchas 'Pini' Schahar.

Once that connection was made, the jigsaw slowly fell into place. It was reassuring, at one level, to discover how international arrangements of this kind leave interlocking pieces on hotel records and on telephone company dialling print-outs. For example, Klein's visits to Antigua did not show up on immigration records, because he had been ushered into 'the VIP room' at the airport, and then out through a door which led to the pavement rather than to immigration control. But once Eva had recalled his hotel, it was a simple matter to check the register and to find the dates of his visits, and then to recall the computer entries which proved that his bill had been paid through Schahar's American Express account. An important investigative bonanza came from telephone records. The Royal Commission had subpoena powers over companies in Antigua, and Cable and Wireless (West Indies) Limited had print-outs for every call made on every telephone and fax machine on the island. It scrupulously logged the date, time, duration and cost of each international call made, and listed the number and the country in which that call had been received. I spent weeks foraging through thousands of printed-out pages of calls made over the last few years on the home and office telephones of Vere Bird Jnr, whose explanations did not square with the dates and times and duration of the calls made from his telephone to Sarfati in Miami, or to Klein and his lawyer in Israel. For example, at the very time Sarfati was arranging for the *Seapoint* to collect the arms container, he was receiving calls and faxes from Bird's private office at the Ministry. It was not, of course, known what was said, but Bird had denied all contact with Sarfati at this period. Most memorable of all was the four-minute telephone call made by the Israelis from the office of Colonel Clyde Walker, after the army commander had shown them around the island to select sites for their 'training school'. It was to a clandestine number in Medellin, which the Colombian government confirmed had been used at the time by Rodriguez Gacha for his cartel business.

The Royal Commission held public hearings in a mission hall rented from the Moravian Church. Its proceedings were broadcast live throughout the day by Antigua radio, and for five hours each evening by the local cable television service. The more it exposed the corruption and incompetence over which he had presided for so long, the angrier Papa Bird became about the behaviour of the tribunal which international pressure had forced him to establish. 'I'm sick and tired of this Blom-Cooper inquiry,' he told a British television team – so sick, in fact, that Lord Havers said he was too ill to appear before it. I went to see the Prime Minister and formed the opinion that what must have made him sick was the prospect that Maurice Sarfati would give evidence, to unravel the spider's web he had managed to weave around the Bird administration. I had managed to make contact with Sarfati, who was hiding in Paris and said he would be willing to testify in London. I was also anxious to take evidence in Israel, where Schahar was now living. There seemed no legal difficulty in the Commission taking evidence abroad: its mandate from the Governor General directed expressly that 'if the Commission considers it necessary, the Inquiry may take evidence outside the jurisdiction of Antigua'.

Nothing could have been plainer. This Commission had, under the law of Antigua by which it was established, the power to take evidence abroad, and no judge could, or at least should, stop it so long as the Commissioner believed, as he did, that this was a necessary step to get at the truth of a public scandal. A local judge named Mitchell did stop it, however, after Vere Jnr swore an affidavit that 'none of my counsel is prepared to travel to Israel, given the politically explosive situation in that country. The atmosphere of political violence also pervades the city of London.'

Mitchell's judgment has to be read in full by anyone who wishes to consider my opinion that it was as fundamentally wrong in law as in common sense. It decided that:

> The Commission of Inquiry Act . . . does not, by its words, in clear and unambiguous language, attach significance for Commissions within the jurisdiction to facts and events occurring outside the jurisdiction, as this Blom-Cooper Commission is purporting to do, moreover, it does not empower or authorise this or any other Commission as a matter of law to do so . . . our legislature is under no obligation to protect the interests of persons overseas in Israel or England . . .

This judge went on in this vein, overlooking the simple legal fact that the Commission of Inquiry, pursuant to the Statute under which it was established by the Governor General, had a duty to take relevant evidence wherever in the world it was available.

Vere Jnr turned up for the last stage of the inquiry looking smug: thanks to Mitchell's ruling, witnesses had to be found within the island of Antigua, or not at all. He took the stand to explain away the telephone records which implicated him in the conspiracy. Under cross-examination he denied everything and relied on an exceptionally bad memory. He could not recall receiving cash from Eva, or requesting the cheques which had been paid by Sarfati into his wife's bank account in New York. What about helping Gacha to obtain lethal weapons? The telephone and fax traffic looked suspicious: the lines from Vere's office hummed Sarfati's telephone and fax numbers at each moment that the conspiracy advanced or retreated. Asked about suspicious call after suspicious call, Vere Bird Jnr would pull himself up to his full height (six foot, eight inches), scowl, and repeat his denials of having made them. I asked him who had, and that is when he made what the Commissioner found was his fatal mistake.

He blamed his secretary. He said it was she who must have given permission to Eva and Klein and Schahar to use his Ministry's official telephone and fax machine to do business with Sarfati. His allegation was transmitted live on radio and later on television, throughout the island, and it struck me that Mrs Ethlyn Thomas, who had been Bird's private secretary at the time, might have something to say about it. Truehart-Smith went to her home that night to ask her whether she could assist the Commission. Courageously, and more in sorrow than anger, she attended the hearing the next day. She was a witness from within Antigua, and Vere's ingenious lawyers could think of no way to bar her testimony. Besides, they did not know what she was going to say.

Nor did I. There had been no time to examine her privately, to extract her story and rehearse it before she was called. This turned out to be an advantage, in that nobody could accuse us of collusion: she had come of her own accord, because it had suddenly seemed right that she should speak out. Ethlyn Thomas had been under heavy pressure to stay silent. As a public servant, she was expected to remain loyal to her minister. As an Antiguan, she was all too well aware of the prominence of the Bird family. As a woman in male-dominated West Indian society, she was expected to follow orders and find whatever consolation she required in church. She was not expected to do what the Commissioner found she in fact did that morning: testify, with utter clarity and credibility, to her minister's deep involvement with Sarfati, and in the conspiracy to supply arms to Gacha.

Ethlyn Thomas was the inquiry's last witness, and after I had taken her though her testimony I waited to see what mud Vere Jnr's purse of silks would throw at her. They asked, and were given, time to consult their client, after which they announced that they would not cross-examine her. This, the Commissioner concluded, was a coded acknowledgement that her evidence was true. It was also a sign that Vere Jnr had some decency, or at least a sensible appreciation that an attack on Mrs Thomas would be counter-productive. Vere Jnr was broken: his leading counsel depicted him, in a final speech, as the ignorant and foolish dupe of the evil Maurice Sarfati. This was true, to the extent that Sarfati had forged his signature on the End User certificate, but the Commissioner ultimately found Vere Jnr to be a willing and witting accomplice.

I had spent many months prevailing on reluctant people to tell me what they knew or to show me what they possessed, not because I had legal powers of subpoena but because I had a power of persuasion based on the enormity of the crimes against humanity that Gacha had committed with the guns from Antigua. Mitchell's judgment rankled because I thought it was wrong in law and because its consequence of hindering the discovery of the truth was upsetting to those who, at some risk to themselves, had told what they knew of it. Its consequence seemed an insult to the memory of those judges and magistrates in Colombia – Maria Perez, Dr Carlos Garcia, Dr Jose Rodriguez, Mariela Arango and others – who had been shot by criminals for doing their duty. Mitchell's ruling stopped the Commission from formally sitting to take evidence abroad about the arming of their assassins, but it could not stop me from travelling abroad with a tape-recorder.

The Israeli Foreign Ministry had been reluctant to co-operate with the Antiguan inquiry, because, it believed it would be biased toward that government. Mitchell's ruling *against* the Commission, ironically, convinced the Israelis that we were independent. So the Foreign Ministry required Brigadier-General 'Pini' Schahar to face my questioning, and its officials listened with some interest to his answers. Schahar was a small, slightly shabby man, his narrow face given some character by a pencil moustache. He was voluble, and aware that he had been the original agent for a deal which had brought his country much criticism. He explained that he was merely a businessman earning an honest living in Miami in the all-embracing work of 'import–export'; Klein had approached him with a project to sell to credulous Miami Catholics some quantities of 'holy water' from the River Jordan, in crucifix-shaped bottles. (So far, so credible: Klein would do anything to make a buck, and his business did extend from guns and mercenary services to traffic in religious reliquaries.) Schahar said that he was one of many Israeli ex-servicemen who were used as 'agents' by IMI in relation to weapons' sales, and that his neighbour Maurice Sarfati had arranged for Colonel Walker to visit him and place an order on behalf of the Antiguan defence force for sub-machine-guns and assault rifles, which he had duly communicated to IMI. (Walker denied this, claiming that his trip to Miami on the date of the meeting had been for shopping, although on this issue, the

Commissioner believed Schahar.)

But Schahar's claim that he had acted only as an introductory agent was difficult to square with evidence that he had stayed at the Trade Winds Hotel with Klein, as a member of the delegation which came to promote the 'training school'. He said that he did not know that Klein was staying in the same hotel at the same time, so I showed him his own American Express card stub, found at the hotel, confirming that it was he who had paid Klein's bill. More importantly, the US$368,000 paid to IMI for the weapons had been transferred through his account with Bank Hapoalim. How had he come to do this, if he was so uninvolved in the deal? He was merely helping out the Antiguan government, he replied, who had sent the money to him rather than to Israel. (Alas for Schahar, when an American Senate investigation later opened his bank account, they found that the money had come from Yair Klein's account at a bank in Panama, where it had doubtless been deposited on behalf of Gacha.) When the interview had concluded and the tape was turned off, Schahar took me aside. 'Look,' he said, 'we all make mistakes in our lives. I have a family, please do not publish my name . . .'

They all have families and their mistake is not to think of other families, bereaved by the killers who were trained and armed through the actions from which they profited. Israel eventually prosecuted Yair Klein, but merely for exporting military techniques without a licence: his punishment was a suspended sentence and a fine of about £20,000. In Antigua, Vere Bird Jnr showed no remorse. He remained in Parliament and won his seat in the 1994 elections which brought his brother Lester to power, Papa having retired at last. He may one day achieve his ambition of becoming Prime Minister, if a local judge quashes Blom-Cooper's recommendation that he be barred forever from ministerial office. Colonel Walker was relieved from his post, as a result of a Blom-Cooper recommendation, although four years later a local judge was prepared to quash this without even hearing argument in its support. (The Lester Bird government, disgracefully, did not bother to defend the Commission or even to notify the Commissioner.) But at least there was one result of the Commission's work which can never be undone: it was able to clear the name of Sean Leitch, the nineteen-year-old customs clerk whom the authorities had attempted to make the scapegoat for the entire affair.

Antigua is a place where it is difficult to stay angry. We were quartered in beach-front rooms at Galley Bay Surf Club, a secluded resort on palm-fringed sands. I would wake to the lap of waves on the deserted beach outside, before entering the armed convoy which processed us to the hearing. We were guarded round the clock by four armed Special Branch officers who feared for our safety, not only from cartel hit-men but from goons in the Antiguan Labour Party who had publicly urged that we should be run off the island by force. They were detailed to look after my wife, the Australian author Kathy Lette, who was heavy with our first child. I would return in the afternoon to find their guns abandoned in a hammock, while they were flat out on the sand doing pregnancy exercises with her. Our entertainment was to slip out to calypso competitions, an art form which at its best provides a lethal fusion of catchy music and political satire. The calypso tent is a libel-free environment, in which the most defamatory allegations are made, enjoyed by the audience, and then vanish on the soft breeze. Clues to corruption on the island were contained in the songs. They were enjoyed by the public precisely because they told truths which everybody suspected but none could publish. I sat stiffly, trying not to smile at the attacks on politicians, while police and public alike roared with laughter. This was the Caribbean equivalent of jazz in Prague, the funny, bitter journalism of shanty-town, the real calypsos which Harry Belafonte dared not sing.

The anger which does remain is the memory of the wrenching poverty in the slums on the outskirts of St John's. This is an island of fewer than seventy thousand people, and its tourist income, if well-managed, is sufficient to provide a reasonable standard of living for all. It was managed by a political elite running government as a private business, leaving schools and hospitals and social services starved of State funds and people dependent upon (and grateful for) hand-outs from the Birds. The Antiguan writer Jamaica Kincaid explains, in her book *A Small Place*, how powerful family networks have operated since independence to monopolise government, business, and public service on the island: little of the tourism wealth or the foreign investment ever percolates down to the people. At a time when 'sustainable development' has become a buzzword for aid programmes, the melon farm of Maurice Sarfati stands as an abject object lesson in how *not* to sustain development. He went to well-intentioned Washington lenders with a plausible project, and inveigled massive loans, most of which he creamed off or used for political pay-offs. Sarfati's bankruptcy lost the government millions through its partnership in his project, and foreign aid institutions, having burned their fingers so badly, were reluctant to lend to other Antiguan ventures. Their place is increasingly being taken by disreputable foreign companies, buying slices of national heritage sold for short-term gain.

The Royal Commission published its report in November 1990. A further report, detailing political corruption, was later completed by Larry Barcella: it was never published by the government, nor were the prosecutions Barcella recommended ever pursued. What is really required, to crack international conspiracies of this scale, is nothing less than an international commission, empowered by agreement between all the countries whose nationals are suspected of involvement. This point was made in 1991 by the US Senate sub-committee on Investigations, which conducted a parallel inquiry into the Antiguan arms transhipment. Under its formidable protective powers, Dr Diego Salinas Viafara described the training camps run by Klein and the British mercenaries on Fantasy Island. I had no muscle to follow the money trail through American banks which insisted on client confidentiality. The Senate investigators, with their statutory subpoenas, were able to open the relevant accounts and trace the money paid to IMI for the guns back through Schahar's account to Yair Klein's account in Banco Aleman-Panameno. But their subpoena powers did not extend to Panama, so there the money trail which would have wound back to Gacha went dead. Unlawful arms trafficking will never be capable of proper investigation and exposure unless nations are prepared to subscribe to a treaty under which they permit an international authority to take evidence from their nationals, or at least from all their banks, under legal compulsion.

There has been some movement in this direction in respect of nuclear proliferation, but the lesson of the Antiguan arms transhipment was drawn by Senator Sam Nunn: 'The international community as a whole needs to do more to control conventional weapons, which so easily find their way into the hands of the world's narco-traffickers and terrorists'. Much larger arms shipments have been delivered – by nondescript, Panamanian registered black freighters – to guerrilla armies along the coasts of South America and Africa. The UN's concern with nuclear weaponry overlooks the way most innocent victims of organised crime die: from clinically accurate assault rifles fired at a distance or from mini-machine-guns hidden beneath coats. The glossy IMI brochure advertises 'the legendary Uzi' in a version which whets the appetite of all would-be assassins: 'permitting easy concealment under ordinary clothing and carriage in minimal space in vehicles, its perfect balance makes it easy to control during automatic fire, permitting sustained accuracy . . . the Mini Uzi is today's weapon'.

How are today's weapons to be kept from tomorrow's criminals when their manufacturers will do business with whoever is at the other end of a fax machine? IMI was more than happy to accept a forged End User Certificate by fax from Maurice Sarfati, promising on filched government notepaper that the weapons would not leave Antigua. IMI did not bother to ask the obvious questions: Why was the order for fifteen times as many guns as there were soldiers in Antigua's army? Why purchase Israeli weapons when it was equipped free of charge by the US? Why would a friendly government pay commission to intermediaries like Sarfati and Schahar, when it could order direct? Once the money was paid, the weapons container was shipped with as much care as a consignment of fluffy toys. It was just dumped on the dock. While it is too much to expect of arms dealers that they will make scrupulous enquiry into the use to which their product is put, the deadly nature of that product imposes a duty on governments which deal in arms to take some care to ensure that they do not fall into the hands of criminals and terrorists. The Israeli government defence department, which runs IMI, took no care at all. Blom-Cooper recommended that there should be established, through the United Nations, an international register of End User Certificates, which would provide some check on their authenticity and some sanction in the event that the arms are later found to have been diverted. The idea was at first taken up enthusiastically at the UN but has yet to be implemented, because governments which sell arms claim that End User Certificates are confidential and the government officials who sign them – often for large bribes – are not disposed to disagree.

International law also failed the people of Colombia through the absence of any effective rules against the recruitment and use of mercenaries. The training camps at Fantasy Island turned un-trained killers into trained killers, by teaching them techniques of anti-terrorism which are, when reversed, the techniques of terrorism. This permitted organised crime to organise itself as a military force. The British 'soldiers of fortune' hired by Gacha were a disreputable lot who had made their plans and preparations in London, yet Scotland Yard declined to prosecute. This was following the lead of John Major, who when Foreign Minister made a hypocritical speech at the United Nations exuding com-passion for Colombia, but pretending that nothing could be done to stop British ex-soldiers from helping its terrorists. In fact, the conduct of the mercenaries breached at least three English criminal statutes but the authorities simply were not interested: there is a long and inglorious tradition of allowing men trained by the British army to sell their services to murderous regimes (e.g. Amin's Uganda) and to terrorist armies (as in Angola). In 1989 the United Nations passed a resolution condemning the use of mercenaries, but the opposition of the US, UK, France, Belgium and Germany has prevented any further developments by the international community to restrain the whores of war. The sooner nations agree to withdraw mercenaries' passports, and to prosecute their recruiters, the fewer lives will be lost around the globe.

That, at least, we owe to Colombia, for the reason given by Gabriel García Márquez in 'The Future of Colombia':

The drug-traffickers' reprisals were violent and scientifically planned, with paramilitary squads from training schools run by mercenaries bought for gold in London and Tel Aviv. The schools recruited adolescent criminals from the poorest shanty towns of our cities, who would then grow up to spread terror and death throughout Colombia . . . Judges and magistrates, whose miserable salaries were barely enough to provide for the education of their children, were faced with an impossible choice: either to sell out to the traffickers or be killed by them. The most admirable and heart-rending thing is that over 40 of them, and many journalists and officials as well, chose to die.

Practising law in Britain is among the safest jobs in the world. No real courage is called for: 'fearless advocacy' is little more than polite disagreement with a grumpy judge. The experience of being protected from cartel vengeance for a few months made me appreciate just how 'admirable and heart-rending' was the behaviour of those magistrates who did their duty, when signing a warrant for the arrest of a suspected drug-trafficker was tantamount to signing their own death warrant. This level of courage is astounding, and calls for the continuing pursuit of all those who make it necessary.

Chapter 12

Come Up and See My Boggs

Have you ever thought of money in quite the same way before this case? That pound note, Harold Wilson's pound in your pocket, crumpled and grubby and going all too quickly at the supermarket, has a kind of beauty, which is brought out by my client because he is an artist and not a forger. Take the portrait of the Queen on a banknote. In the Boggs drawing, Her Majesty takes on a much more human quality. No longer is she a mass-produced image. An artist has actually laboured to give her life, adding lipstick and a touch of eye-shadow and a look that lends a radiance which is lacking in the ordinary banknote. His work is saying that the Bank of England is fortunate that it has a fragrant Head of State, above political controversy, to lend dignity and credibility to its currency. Not some failed political leader or furry animal. The Bank of Denmark puts squirrels and ducks on its banknotes. France features composers of second-rate music, Germany eagles and sailing ships, Australia sheep and kangaroos. The Central African Republic has a picture of Emperor Bokassa, known to eat small children, while America has Ulysses Grant – an incompetent and corrupt president – on its fifty dollars, and on its most valuable $1,000 banknote it features Grover Cleveland, who infamously ordered troops to fire on striking railway workers. We feel more comfortable, do we not, members of the jury, with the Queen rather than with an engraving of Mrs Thatcher?

I have realised every law student's dream. It is November 1987 and I am addressing a jury in Court No. 1 of the Old Bailey, a vast and imposing forum lined with sombre wooden benches sweeping up to a high platform on which sits, centre-stage, a 'red judge', ushered in by attendants holding swords and maces. Behind and above me is the packed public gallery. Beyond the oak table before me sits the jury, perched above the press bench crammed with journalists. To my left, in mid-court, is the nation's largest dock, built to hold gangs of traitors or bank robbers. Its high panelling almost obscures the defendant and the armed prison officers who flank him as he sits on that chair once occupied by traitors like Roger Casement and William 'Lord Haw Haw' Joyce. The young American with a thin face and long matted hair is on trial for a kind of treason: he has defied the Bank of England and dared to paint pictures of the currency of the realm.

The work of J S G (Stephen) Boggs is propped against the table in the well of this historic criminal courtroom, where people in his position were once regularly taken out and hanged – on a gallows rather than in an art gallery. Pictures of British banknotes – some five-feet high, some life-size and framed under glass – range from the now-defunct one pound to fivers and tenners and fifties. At first blush, they look to be closely copied, although they are generally signed 'J S G Boggs' rather than 'Robin Leigh Pemberton' and have other differences which the evidence in the case will exhaustively explore. Since they are obviously artworks rather than legal tender, none of the law's familiar constructs – from the man on the Clapham Omnibus to the moron in a hurry – would accept them at face value. So why is Boggs occupying the country's most important courtroom?

The answer lies, as a matter of language, in Section 18 of the 1981 Forgery and Counterfeiting Act, which makes it a crime to 'reproduce on any substance whatsoever, and whether or not on the correct scale, any British currency note or any part of a British currency note'.

On one view (the prosecution's) this is exactly what Boggs has done. He has 'reproduced' banknotes in the sense laid down by the Oxford English Dictionary, which defines 'reproduction' as 'a representation in some form or by some means of the essential features of the thing'. He has most certainly reproduced parts of

British currency notes – their serial numbers, for example, as the judge will emphasise repeatedly to the jury. The judge thinks that this is the most open-and-shut case he has ever tried, and cannot understand why the defendant has not been told by his counsel to plead guilty. One reason is that plain English words have nuances and can be open to different interpretations, and I have found a sense in which a reproduction is not a 'reproduction', an argument for saying, of a picture of a pipe, '*Ceci n'est pas un pipe*'. So I plough on:

> When Andy Warhol depicts tins of Campbell's soup, more precisely than Boggs depicts banknotes, he does not 'reproduce' the label on Campbell's soup. He is presenting an image which makes people think about mass-production and common experiences and advertising messages, about being left on the shelf in a supermarket society; in short, about their life, rather than about the nutritional ingredients of Campbell's soup. When Van Gogh, that anguished and tormented artist, painted a picture of irises, he could have had no idea that in 1987 his picture would be sold for £25 million to Alan Bond. A life-size photograph, a true 'reproduction', can be bought for a few pounds. So can real irises. For £25 million you could have thousands of real irises delivered every day for the rest of your life. The Bank of England would say, 'Oh, that Van Gogh original is a reproduction of the irises growing in a field in the South of France in the spring of 1876'. The art critic might say the picture is not about irises at all, it's about human anguish, about rage against the squalor and shortness of our life compared with the eternal beauty and refulgence of nature. We don't know what Mr Bond thinks. It may be no more than a good investment, or a reminder that he has more money than other people. And money brings us back to Boggs. What is he saying, when he talks like Van Gogh of 'bleeding into his pictures'?

Van Gogh had not said this while being interviewed by police officers under caution. Boggs had been arrested by a flying squad of senior detectives who burst into the gallery, seized his work from the walls and deposited it in the back of the car in which they drove the artist to the nearest police station. This was an event you would expect in Dr Husak's Czechoslovakia. The artist who provoked it was not a political dissident or a pornographer but a mild-mannered humorist who occupied a bed-sit studio in Hampstead, and was holding his first exhibition at the 'Young Unknowns' Gallery. He became a 'Young Known' as a result of the raid, but notoriety was not at first his objective. His was a talent to footnote, before Scotland Yard gave it international recognition.

Boggs had been born in New Jersey and had studied art in London, but his inspiration came on a visit to Chicago's Art Expo, as he waited for the bill in a coffee shop, idly doodling a copy of a one-dollar bill on his table napkin. 'Wow, that's great,' said his waitress – a muse in uniform – as she presented him with a 90¢-bill for his cup of coffee. 'Can I buy it?' 'It's not for sale,' snapped Boggs – then, softening at her disappointment, he agreed she could have the drawing of the dollar in payment for his coffee. As he was leaving, she called out, 'Wait, you're forgetting your change' and handed him a ten-cent piece. This dime he kept, under glass, much as billionaires frame the first dollar they ever earned. For this transaction in the Chicago coffee shop inspired a form of performance art which was to bring Boggs to the attention of the art world, of intellectual journals, and of the police of three continents. As the *New Yorker* put it after the trial, in the first of a series of articles on his life and work: 'What is art? What is money? What is the one worth and what the other?'

Boggs became fascinated by paper money, travelling through Europe to gather banknotes which he used as models in his garret in Hampstead, painstakingly transferring their images to canvases large and small. Having completed a 'Boggs', he would then go out and 'spend' it, offering it at its face value to pay for what he purchased at pubs and restaurants and shops. This performance was an essential part of giving 'value' to the work, once he happened upon a shopkeeper or barman with the imagination of the Chicago waitress who appreciated the banknote as 'art' of sufficient merit to accept it at face value and give him the change. The final act was to call an art dealer – in London or Basle or New York, who had clients who 'valued' his work – to announce that a drawing had been 'spent'. Days later, the barman or shopkeeper whose faith in the artist had caused them to exchange real money for the drawing would be rewarded by a call from a connoisseur offering to buy the picture for hundreds of real pounds. If they sold

– and a few, remarkably, did not – the entire transaction would be 'mounted' in a gold frame: the drawing, together with the evidence of its value which the connoisseur would purchase from Boggs: namely the shop bill and the change (which he kept for this eventuality). Boggs the wealth-creator remained poor, and this was part of the joke. It was on him when his completed 'works' sold for several thousand pounds. And now the joke was on me, since I was representing him on legal aid, rather than accepting the notes he offered to draw to cover my fees.

The art of Boggs was amusing and original, and self-evidently harmless. You could interpret it as satire on the over-pricing and over-prizing of modern art, the *reductio ad absurdum* of which was to paint and exhibit the very thing which pretentious people collect modern art in order to flaunt, namely their possession of large amounts of money. Or you could interpret it as homage to that human quality upon which both art and money depend, namely the faith and trust reposed in them by their consumers. Boggs was not lacking in respect for the currency, and his notes were always sold for more than they were notionally worth. His was not the hubristic art of Picasso, who boasted that the cheques he signed had never been cashed because his signature alone was worth more than the amount. Nor was it as exquisite as the work of Marcel Duchamp, from which to some extent it derived: Duchamp had settled his dentist's bill by 'drawing' a large cheque and signing it, and having it accepted by the overjoyed orthodontist. Duchamp had not asked for change, but Boggs was working in the more mercenary era of Mrs Thatcher. To suggest that what he was doing was a serious crime called for accusers entirely lacking in humour, imagination and common sense. It called, in other words, for the principals of the Bank of England.

These bureaucrats had read about Boggs and they did not like what they read, especially since they read it in their house journal, the *Daily Telegraph*. It was not just that he was reproducing the currency: he had compounded his crime by failing to obtain their permission. When respectable advertisers broke the law against reproducing the currency, as Saatchi and Saatchi once did in a massive way with photographs of banknotes used in nationwide publicity for Silk Cut cigarettes, the Bank accepted their apologies and never dreamt of launching a prosecution. But the artist was different. The artist was unreliable, subversive and American – definitely not 'one of us'. That is why the Bank of England decided that Scotland Yard should seize Boggs and destroy his works of art.

The case seems, on reflection, an object lesson in how foolishly people in authority can react if teased. In August 1986 the *Daily Telegraph* reported from New York the success of a British resident, J S G Boggs, who had interested galleries in that city in his work. 'I don't think there's anything wrong in an artist making money,' quipped Boggs. 'Everybody else makes money.' To this good-humoured piece was appended a footnote – '*our legal correspondent writes*' – referring to Section 18 of the Forgery and Counterfeiting Act and pointing out delicately that since he did not have written permission from the Bank, 'Mr Boggs may have been inadvertently committing a criminal offence by drawing his sterling banknotes'. When Boggs read this, he wrote a grovelling letter to the Governor of the Bank of England apologising for overlooking Section 18, explaining the nature of his work and requesting permission to continue. He received an immediate refusal. For future reference, however, he was sent the Bank of England's rules on reproduction, which are themselves an absurdist classic:

> The Bank think it proper to draw to the attention of those wishing to seek their approval to make reproductions that they have been advised by Leading Counsel that the preparation and reproduction of artwork for the purpose of seeking the Bank's consent is itself an offence under Section 18(1) insofar as they reproduce a Bank of England note.

This was positively Gilbertian: an artist could not draw the currency without the Bank's consent, and he could not obtain that consent without submitting a drawing; since drawing the currency without the Bank's consent was an offence, however, he could not draw the currency in order to obtain the Bank's consent. What he could do if he really insisted upon trying the Bank's patience was to submit in triplicate a sketch of his proposed artwork, leaving the proposed area of the banknote blank. The Bank might, if the spirit moved it, then authorise the artist to complete the sketch, but only for the purpose of obtaining the Bank's approval to paint a picture based on the sketch (which would then have to be destroyed). On one overriding consideration, the Bank was very clear: 'Decisions which might be seen by the public as lowering the dignity or prestige of the currency will not be permitted'.

In the Bank's opinion, the public would not perceive the use of notes in Silk Cut advertisements as lowering their dignity: perhaps it respected drugs as a source of wealth. Art was another matter, a trade in which the value of the money depicted depended upon an appreciation of the worth of the depiction: and the more money is contemplated, the more it might be seen as, for example, the root of all evil. No artist could possibly comply with the Bank's conditions for obtaining approval, which explains the absence of money – coins and banknotes – as a subject in modern British art, or even as a peripheral detail. So it has come about that our art omits almost all reference to the main preoccupation of our people, and to the standard by which its own value is measured. There had been healthy satire of the Bank and its pretensions in the early nineteenth century – James Gillray's *Old Lady of Threadneedle Street*, for example – but very little since, after the law now enshrined in Section 18 was passed.

Boggs pleaded with the Bank after its refusal, urging that 'the nature of my work is entirely optimistic about the value and function of money'. He sent them slides of his paintings: they replied, contemptuously, that the slides were also 'reproductions' which contravened Section 18. They destroyed the slides and called Scotland Yard: three meetings followed in quick succession between 'principals' (i.e. senior executives) of the Bank and senior policemen, summoned to do something about the threat from Boggs. A very English compromise was agreed and formally minuted: 'The meeting decided to take no action against Boggs unless he drew attention to himself again.' The very next day, a front-page article in the *Independent* announced that Boggs was about to exhibit in the 'Young Unknowns' Gallery. It was, *horribile dictu*, illustrated by a Boggs drawing. The bankers were livid: they wanted Boggs's head on a plate if he raised it again. No fewer than three inspectors from the Forgery and Counterfeiting Squad were detailed to lead the raid on the gallery.

The word 'gallery' conjures up the spacious art showrooms of Mayfair: the 'Young Unknowns' inhabits a small shop (formerly a butcher's) in The Cut, between the Old Vic and the Young Vic.

The detectives realised that there was no time to lose if the public were to be spared its display of unlawful art: they set off in three police cars and arrived just as Boggs was holding forth to a TV news team, which providentially filmed his arrest and the ransacking of the tiny gallery. Boggs and his artworks were marched past the Old Vic and placed in a police car – the art in the boot – while another police team raided his flat. At Southwark Police Station, the Detective Chief Inspector cautioned the suspect and interrogated him thus:

Chief Inspector: This afternoon from the Young Unknown's gallery, I took possession of a number of drawn items which resembled Bank of England currency. Did you paint or draw these items?

Boggs: The works of art are original works from my own hand and are not reproductions, nor are they currency.

Chief Inspector: But you agree that some of the items contain many if not all of the detail of Bank of England currencies?

Boggs: A painting of a horse may contain depictions of details created by God, yet you would not place a saddle on that painting.

Chief Inspector: This appears to me to be a painting of a £10 note. It appears to my mind to be an attempt to reproduce an item similar to genuine British currency. Did you draw or paint that article?

Boggs: It is my job to allow my thoughts and feelings to be expressed and communicated through the visual work of my hands. For art to be true and just and honest, I must allow my inner self out.

Chief Inspector: Did you draw or paint it?

Boggs: Inspector, I truly don't mean to be difficult. The work originates in a hidden and subconscious part of my being. I've gone into my mind to the place where art originates and it is a very expansive place: I am only just beginning to explore it.

Chief Inspector: Did you, with your hand, with a pen, pencil or paintbrush, irrespective of the reasons, paint, draw or colour this item?

Boggs: If you are asleep and you have a dream, are you then responsible for the creation of that dream? I have bled onto this piece of work.

Chief Inspector: It appears to me that certain criminal offences have been committed, in particular, producing reproductions of

Bank of England notes, without authority. I must again caution you that you are not obliged to say anything but what you do say will be taken down in writing and given in evidence.

Boggs: I am an artist, not a criminal. If I have committed an offence it is the crime of being born which was not my choice.

The police had stopped his television interview, seized most of his artwork, searched his home and car and even visited his local Midland bank manager in Hampstead, who had been hoping to mount the exhibition – 'Art is wealth' – after it finished at the 'Young Unknowns'. I had the distinct feeling, when I came to examine these sensible policemen a year later, that they felt the Bank had over-reacted. The penny must have dropped when they took a closer look at one of the exhibits they seized from the gallery – a 'Coat of Money', made of apparently forged Bank of England notes, each in the sum of six pounds. When it was realised that this denomination has never existed, common-sense reasserted itself and Scotland Yard declined to prosecute. The Bank of England disagreed. Boggs had defied them and had to be punished, so they used the police evidence to mount a private prosecution.

Boggs was represented by the solicitor for the 'Young Unknowns' Gallery, Mark Stephens, a legal 'young unknown' himself at this time. In his early thirties, like Boggs, he had formed a small firm which specialised in representing impecunious artists. Stephen Boggs, with his sense of humour, would have hired Mark for his name alone: the firm is called Stephens Innocent. Ten years on, Stephens is one of London's best (and certainly best-known) litigators, and he demonstrated his skill as we combed the art world in search of expert witnesses. The British art establishment is surprisingly conservative, but Michael Compton, who had just retired as keeper of exhibitions at the Tate, did not share its inhibitions about giving evidence against the Bank of England, nor did Sandy Nairn, the brilliant young curator at the Whitechapel Gallery or René Gimpels, a Boggs aficionado who had galleries in London and Switzerland. I prevailed on Robert Hughes, art critic of *Time* magazine and author of *The Shock of the New*, to provide a witness statement. It was as lofty in its own way as the attitude of the Bank, but had the saving virtue of being right – or at least as right as it is ever possible to be about matters of art. Having placed

Boggs somewhat diffidently in the tradition of Warhol ('the only remarkable fact about Boggs's work is that it has become the object of prosecution'), he made the helpful distinction between 'reproduction' (mechanical and exact copying, to produce a facsimile of the original) and 'representation' (making a picture of a subject):

> If I sit down with my watercolours and draw a tree, I am representing it. Nobody is expected to compare my drawing with a real tree, although (if I am lucky) there may be people who admire the fidelity and truth with which I have represented the tree – the way its branches go, the colour of the leaves and so forth. This simple distinction will, I hope, clarify the nature of what Boggs has been doing in these works. The Bank of England is putting itself in the position of the silly bird which, in Pliny's story, flew down and pecked at a bunch of grapes painted by Zeuxis, believing them to be the real thing.

We are in Court 1 of the Old Bailey on the opening day of *Regina v Boggs*. Unfortunately but inevitably, Mr Justice MacNeill does not think like an art critic. He is a sound lawyer and thinks like one. It is a crime to reproduce any part of a British banknote, and Boggs – accepting the OED definition of 'reproduce' – has done that beyond any reasonable doubt. Why, he has even copied some serial numbers – evidence which the judge shall in due course tell the jury is devastating to the defence, although, of course (thanks to the rule in *Stonehouse*) 'it's all a matter for you'.

I am on one level relieved that we have drawn (so to speak) David MacNeill – he is one of the younger, gentler generation of High Court judges. Some of his older brethren would be apoplectic that this case was even being defended. On the other hand, judicial apoplexy might be a great help to Boggs: there is nothing so prone to provoke a 'sympathy acquittal' as a judge who exudes bias against the defence. MacNeill, however, will nudge the jury towards conviction with his charm and moderation, impose a small fine and order the pictures to be surrendered to the Bank (the Forgery Act gives the Bank special power to destroy them). I can imagine the Governor and his principals sipping sherry as Boggs's larger pictures burn in their boardroom grate: his smaller drawings will go to Scotland Yard's 'Black Museum' as mementos of its successful struggle against crime.

Much will turn upon whether we are allowed to call expert evidence. It doesn't much matter what our experts say: their very appearance will impress upon a jury that Boggs is not a pavement artist or a graffiti provocateur, but a creator of something they should hesitate to destroy. The prosecutor understands this and opposes my application to call the experts. So does the judge, and his is the final decision. But it is a decision which must be governed by law. This is where defence lawyers do matter, in their ability to ransack their dusty case-books to find precedents for requiring a judge to do what he does not want to do. The argument is taken at the outset of the trial. What we really want is to call experts to say Boggs is a good, even important, young artist, but as the judge rightly points out, that is precisely what the law disallows. 'This is not an obscenity trial,' Mr Justice MacNeill chides, 'there is no artistic merit defence to a forgery charge.' Expert evidence, he rules, is inadmissible on the subject of Boggs's talent: it would only serve to confuse the jury. Boggs might be Vincent Van Gogh, but that would not save him from conviction were he proved to have reproduced a British banknote.

We are not going to give up so easily. This is an attempt to use the law against forgery and counterfeiting to destroy works of art, and we should not pretend otherwise: somehow the jury must be told about the extra dimension, the limits of language in the definition of crime. It is like the problem which is used to test law students: imagine a regulation which makes it an offence to bring 'vehicles' into the municipal park. This rule is aimed at cars, but can it also cover golf-buggies or skateboards or motor-bikes, or aeroplanes making forced landings? These hypothetical cases are solved in real time by judges who juggle the literal meaning of the words with the purpose of the statute and the mischief against which it was passed, and purport to discover whether Parliament intended to cover the particular example. This is usually a fictitious exercise, since MPs pass such laws in a stupor late at night without thinking about their potential consequences. So it must be decided by judges, applying not their prejudices but the principles of their trade.

We came up with an argument which runs like this. The cases say that expert evidence may be called to explain any technical or cultural background to an issue which jurors could not be expected to understand from their own life experiences. Jurors may be expected to know something about art and to have visited a gallery occasionally. But they cannot be expected to know about the surrealist movement, or about the *trompe-l'œil* school where some of Boggs's ideas originate or about the concept of performance art in which the artist does not merely paint the picture but plays a part in its appreciation. The prosecution, predictably, says that this is irrelevant: the judge agrees, but is troubled by the weight of the case law which permits jurors to be given some expert insight. Reluctantly, he rules that I can call evidence as to the *genre* of Boggs's art, but not its merit. 'I shall keep you on a very tight rein, Mr Robertson.' That's fine, Judge. They'll be passing around Magritte's pipe in the jury room by the end of the trial.

The jury is selected. We still have seven challenges per defendant, a right soon abolished by Tory MPs who claimed that defence lawyers were abusing it to empanel stupid or anarchic jurors. On the contrary, I had always used these challenges to try to obtain intelligent-looking jurors (my favourites carried the *Financial Times*), who may be less likely to follow the judge's dictation and more capable of comprehending 'reasonable doubts'. The jury which is selected to try Boggs looks intelligent, certainly looks interested and has a lower proportion of *Sun* readers than the population as a whole.

The trial begins with the prosecutor, the charming and vastly experienced Robert Harman QC, presenting the jury with an open-and-shut case. He is a bit condescending to Boggs, a young American who clearly does not fully understand our British ways, and defensive about artists. 'A man cannot call himself an artist and expect to be above the law.' This is received wisdom at the Old Bailey in all cases involving literature or art: acts which are criminal if done out of greed or malice are equally criminal if done for some higher good. The only possible issue, the QC tells the jury, is whether the Boggs banknotes are sufficiently similar to original banknotes as 'to suggest that original to the mind of every person seeing the picture'. They obviously are, but the jury looks unsatisfied – like a comedian's audience awaiting a punchline. Is there to be evidence that Boggs had passed off his drawings as the real thing in a dimly lit pub? Or that he had inspired a school of artists busily churning out exact copies of the currency? No, admitted the prosecutor, there is not. The reason why Boggs deserves punishment is that he has disobeyed the wishes of the Bank of England.

The Bank's witnesses strike pinstripe poses and insist that they had been right to stop Boggs pursuing his artistic endeavours. Not that they had been consistent in their refusals: they are forced to disclose the fact that in the past few years they have granted hundreds of permissions to reproduce British currency, to building societies and estate agencies and merchant banks and mortgage companies – organisations apparently deserving of the right to reproduce money because they make huge amounts of it. The bank had once even given a sex-shop the right to reproduce a fifty-pound note on the crotch of erotic lingerie. But the application by my struggling artist had been rejected with contempt – they had not even bothered to contact an art gallery to discover whether his work might be worth encouraging. The Bank officials claimed that since some of the pictures were the same size as real banknotes, there was always the danger that they might be taken out of their frames and passed off as genuine. So cross-examination became a 'spot the difference' competition, in which members of the jury were supplied with real banknotes to compare and contrast with the drawings arrayed around the courtroom. It took a day of valuable court time for the defence to establish beyond reasonable doubt that, *inter alia*:

1. The banknote is a three-dimensional physical object used to make purchases. The Boggs is a picture to be looked at on a wall.
2. The banknote has a constant value, assigned by the government. The Boggs has value only in the eye of its beholder.
3. The perspective is different – you can see through a banknote, but not through a Boggs.
4. A banknote has two sides. A Boggs has only one side.
5. A banknote crinkles and has a distinctive smell when fresh. A Boggs is odourless.
6. Banknotes are unsigned by their designers. A Boggs is signed by Boggs in the place reserved in the banknote for the signature of the Governor of the Bank of England.
7. Banknote language is not exactly replicated on a Boggs. 'Pay

Bearer on Demand' becomes 'Pay Bear on Demand': the language of officials becomes mock-officialese.

8. The banknote is legal tender, the Boggs only acceptable to those who like it.

9. The banknote originated in Pitt's decision to replace gold and silver coinage during the Napoleonic Wars. The Boggs originated historically in a Chicago coffee shop in 1980.

10. Banknotes were originally an artless promise to pay. Art was introduced to make forgery more difficult and then as a means of inducing loyalty and pride in national achievement. A Boggs has no national symbolic purpose, and no attempts have been made at this stage in the artist's career to forge his work.

I had not engaged in an exercise like this since I studied metaphysics at university. 'Banknotes and Boggs notes bear no comparison. They are as different as chalk and cheese – or perhaps I should say, members of the jury, different as a piece of chalk and a piece of chalk-shaped cheese. The one is not the reproduction of the other. If we look at the *Mona Lisa*, we don't say that is a reproduction of a sixteenth-century Italian woman with a slight smile, do we?'

No doubt I thought this point profound, although the lines now read as if they might more appropriately have been delivered by John Cleese. Cross-examination of the senior bank officials was designed to ridicule the Bank of England's rules on reproduction:

Let me see if I have this right. If Mr da Vinci was proposing to include some pound notes in his upcoming painting of *Christ Driving the Money-lenders from the Temple* you are suggesting that, in keeping with the guidelines, he'd have to send the bank a detailed sketch, in triplicate, taking care to leave the space intended for the notes blank pending your approval of the whole scheme? And, in keeping with your guidelines, were you to grant permission, he'd still be required upon completion of his project to destroy all materials associated with the image's manufacture. What does that include? The brushes? The palette? The easel? The painting itself?

Most witnesses adopt avoidance techniques to deal with hypothetical questions to which the answer 'yes' makes them look ridiculous: the principals of the Bank of England, however, actually agreed with these propositions, and did so with relish, having first made the serious point that money-lenders in Christ's time would not have been counting out *British* banknotes. They had no difficulty at all in envisaging the destruction of great art, were it to 'lower the dignity or prestige of the currency'. Messrs Freshfields, their expensive commercial solicitors, were not often seen in the well of a criminal court, but they had a client determined to waste money by defending it.

Our experts located the accused's *genre* in the mainstream of three artistic traditions. There was *trompe-l'œil*, 'deceiving the eye' by the ambiguities of depicting flat objects (like documents and dollar bills) on a flat surface. There was *collage*, exploiting the contradiction between the flat surface of the canvas and the three-dimensional objects represented. And there was *performance art*, deriving from Marcel Duchamp. 'Boggs's work belongs to the tradition which raises the question of the relationship of the picture to the thing represented,' averred Michael Compton, instancing Magritte's *The Use of Words* and Jasper John's 'Flags'. 'The meaning, as with all true works of art, must be supplied by the viewer, but they inescapably raise questions of the relation of art to money and money to power. The banknote is intended to exude anonymity and authority. Boggs's drawings instantly and overwhelmingly exude individuality.' The judge intervened – the expert was telling the jury too much – but the jury did not seem to mind.

Behind the high wall of the maximum-security dock, the artist in question had been busily breaking the law by sketching more banknotes, at the request of the prison officers meant to be guarding him. He was entitled to his right of silence, but no true artist can resist the platform provided by the witness box at the Old Bailey. Boggs was loquacious, but polite and sincere as he told of his struggles as an artist (for several years he had worked part-time in a blood bank) and of the epiphany in the coffee house and of the long hours he lovingly invested in painting the currencies of many nations. He was the walking embodiment of Adam Smith's dictum 'labour creates value'. He told the jury how, as part of the concept, he acted as advocate for his own art, persuading shopkeepers to accept it at face value (giving the appropriate change), and then notifying the collectors who would contact the purchaser, offering to buy it for a much higher price.

This evidence was so obviously true that there was not much to ask him in cross-examination: the prosecutor's tactic was to raise a little heat by accusing him of 'defying the Bank of England', as if that were a crime, and trying to trap him into the assertion that he was above the law because he was an artist. Whether this was damaging would depend on the way it was phrased, and Boggs was delicate:

> Harman: Are you suggesting that because your drawings are works of art, they are incapable of being reproductions?
> Boggs: I suppose so, because once you crossed over the line into reproduction, it would no longer be a work of art.

Robert Harman's final speech was short and to the point: Boggs was a reproduction artist. Given the similarities between his notes and the real thing, any defence was preposterous.

My speech was long and not so much to the point. Barristers are artists, in a way: the exhibits we make are of ourselves:

> By drawing a picture for exhibition, the artist makes an effort and invites his viewers to make an effort to appreciate it. This was the point Boggs made to the police when he said that a picture of a horse may have all the features of a horse but you don't saddle it. This was a point made by Magritte, when he drew a picture of a pipe made for smoking tobacco against a plain background. Underneath he wrote 'This is not a pipe' and signed the drawing. A picture like that is not what it represents, and is not a reproduction of what it represents. The pipe and the banknote do not exist: what does exist, and has reality as we look at it, is a drawing which provokes thought and triggers memory.
>
> I don't know what associations a Boggs banknote might trigger in your mind, if you viewed it in a gallery. You might be mildly amused at a penniless artist who can only make money by drawing it. You may think, despite the expert evidence, that Boggs is an artist of little merit. That you wouldn't have a Boggs in any room of your house if he paid you. That a Boggs isn't worth the paper it is drawn on. 'Come up and see my Boggs' may not be an invitation you

would wish to extend to anyone under any circumstances. That should not affect your answer to the question 'Is he guilty of reproducing banknotes?' Because however you respond, Stephen Boggs has created something so completely different, that it cannot be described by any stretch of language as a reproduction.'

The judge began his summing-up by telling the jury that this 'pretty straightforward' case had nothing to do with art – which must have come as a surprise. Lawrence Weschler's report in the *New Yorker* gives the flavour of the judge's directions:

His tone was friendly, congenial, but finally no-nonsense. He was particularly succinct in his summary of the case for the defence, enumerating each defence argument in turn and affably declaring each, in turn, to be utterly without merit. After reviewing the basic provisions of Section 18, he said, for example, 'The fact that a drawing might not resemble a currency note in every particular cannot provide a defense against this charge. The fact that the maker did not intend it to be passed would not provide a defence, either. Nor would the assertion that the copy in question were a work of art constitute any sort of defence whatsoever.' He paused to smile warmly at the jury, and resumed, 'This case is not about artistic freedom or freedom of expression or anything of the sort . . .' Even veteran British trial reporters, who had seen a lot of biased summations by judges, were taken aback. 'This is the world's most friendly hanging judge,' one reporter scrawled in a note he passed to another.

'It provides no defence whatsoever that the drawings in question may be worth more than the originals,' the judge continued. 'You would be untrue to your oath if you took mitigating circumstances into account in finding the defendant not guilty.' The judge seemed to be directing his jury the way Captain Hook directed his prisoners down the plank.

'Really, ladies and gentlemen of the jury, we have a pretty straightforward question here. The word "reproduction" is a perfectly common one used in everyday discourse, we all know what it means. And we can recognize that Section 18 forbids not just the reproduction of entire bills, but even a "reproduction in part". If there is no more than just the reproduction of an actual serial number, you may find it difficult not to find that "reproduction in part" has taken place.'

I seem to remember Mr Justice MacNeill rolling up his red sleeve to deliver this last knock-out punch, but that may just be my imagination. Only the rule in *Stonehouse* stood between Boggs and his conviction, preventing the judge from ordering the jury to find him guilty for reproducing the serial numbers. It was a devastating summing-up, delivered so persuasively that I feared the jury would convict immediately. My first thought as they retired was how to dissuade the judge from ordering the forfeiture of the offending pictures. The Bank of England officials had, in their evidence, spoken of their determination to destroy them, but Nicolas Serota had volunteered to give them sanctuary in the basement of the Tate Gallery for however many years it took for the Bank's anger to abate. I would do my best to save Boggs for the nation, I assured the artist as we trooped miserably out of court towards the canteen. Before we even reached it the Old Bailey tannoy suddenly crackled, 'Will all parties in the case of *Boggs* return to Court 1.' So it was a guilty verdict – the jury was going to do what the judge had indicated they should do, in this 'pretty straightforward' case.

Dejectedly, we returned to court. The jury were brought in – it was less than ten minutes since they had been sent out. The foreman (we had picked him as a merchant banker) stood sternly for the clerk's question. 'How do you find the defendant, guilty or not guilty?' He uttered an emphatic 'NOT guilty!' and only then broke into a smile. Several jurors had difficulty suppressing giggles, and the judge whispered from the corner of his mouth, 'Well, Mr Harman, you learn something new every day'. We bowed and packed up the canvases. Outside, Boggs did the victor's walk down Old Bailey for the benefit of the photographers, clutching the largest of his paintings.

I like to think that this case was won by my knowledge of modern art and the law of evidence, by my cross-examination and my rhetoric. Barristers kid themselves that they 'win' cases and that their opponents 'lose' them. But deep down I knew exactly how this case was won, and where. It was won every lunchtime, in the jury canteen, and the dialogue would have gone something like this:

'What you doing then?'

'Murder. Disgusting photos – woman fainted and got discharged.'

'I've got a rape. Really vicious, evil bastard in the dock.'

'What about you?'

'IRA bombers. We're in the top-security court, have to be frisked, get a police escort going home. Have they ever knee-capped a juror?'

'Nah. What you doing then? In Court 1 – must be a big case.'

'Well, there's this artist. He's been drawing pictures of banknotes.'

'And?'

'Well, that's it really. They get sold to art collectors.'

'What? Come off it! You must be joking. No seriously, what case *are* you doing? What's the *crime*?'

That, I suspect, is where *Regina v Boggs* was decided. Our jurors could now go back to the canteen with the boast that although they may not have been trying a real crime, they reached this verdict in record time. And juries must never be underestimated. A week after the case I received a note from the foreman – who *was* a merchant banker – saying how much everyone on the jury had enjoyed it. They were meeting for a reunion party at his flat in the Barbican, and would I like to join them for wine and cheese and further discussion of art?

The trial altered the face of British currency. The Bank, *post Boggs ergo propter Boggs*, was humiliated into printing an ordinary copyright notice on the bottom left-hand corner of both sides of every banknote: © THE GOVERNOR AND COMPANY OF THE BANK OF ENGLAND. Governor and co. had finally realised they could not overawe an Old Bailey jury: if they wanted to protect their designs, then like everybody else they would have to sue for breach of copyright.

Boggs himself went onward and upward. Having beaten the Bank of England, he felt invincible in a courtroom. He also, after a time, began to crave more publicity. So he took a TV team to Australia, where his efforts to draw and spend the local dollar soon resulted in his arrest, Australia having inherited the colonial equivalent of Section 18. These authorities were smarter than their

English counterparts, however, and dropped all the charges. Back in America, Boggs had many appreciative purchasers, and was in due course appointed Research Fellow in Art and Ethics at the Carnegie Mellor Centre for the Advancement of Applied Ethics. He has occasional run-ins with the Federal Reserve and the Secret Service. Imitation being the sincerest form of flattery, his success has attracted forgers and counterfeiters. In a determined effort to stop the traffic in reproductions of Boggs, he now 'signs' the back of each original with a thumbprint.

III

Hard Cases, Real Time

Chapter 13

Ali Daghir and the Forty Nuclear Triggers

The discovery at Heathrow in March 1990 of forty 'nuclear triggers' bound for Iraq was a fairy-tale more frightening than any to have come out of Baghdad. It made front-page headlines in every country as newspapers reported that this joint US/UK customs action had stopped Saddam Hussein developing an Islamic bomb. President Bush and Prime Minister Thatcher publicly congratulated the customs team, presuming the guilt of the exporter, Ali Daghir, who was later convicted at the Old Bailey and sent to prison for imperilling the safety of the world. His forty 'nuclear triggers' were not, however, destroyed after the case: they were issued to senior customs officials for prominent display on their desks whenever they posed for press photographs, which they sometimes did before the collapse of the Matrix Churchill trial.

It was during that trial that I first met Ali Daghir. I had been thumping the lectern to insist on fuller security service disclosure. 'Don't you know' whispered a prosecution lawyer 'that there's an Iraqi spy in the public gallery?' He indicated the thin, bespectacled gentleman who had sat jack-knifed over the front row, exhibiting such a close interest in the defence that I had previously assumed he was from MI5. Daghir had just been released on bail after fifteen months in prison, and asked me to handle his appeal. He was a friendly, over-talkative Iraqi businessman, who had an obsessive love for Britain and a family which had excelled at its universities – his wife as a lecturer, his children as students. How had he come to betray this country, by trying to arm its enemy with nuclear weapons?

Back in 1988, the notion of Iraq as an 'enemy' was not entertained by the British government. Despite Saddam's use of poison gas against the Kurds, the Iraqi state enterprises (which had monopolies of both civil and military manufacturing) offered lucrative trading prospects, so Government ministers officially visited Iraq to drum up business, allowing the country trade credits of £750 million. The DTI even issued a booklet – 'Hints for Exporters' – helpfully listing those state enterprises which were in the market for British goods. One was an establishment outside Baghdad called Al-qaqaa, whose representatives were welcomed to Britain and encouraged to place their orders. Daghir's company, Euromac, won a small contract to supply capacitors, manufactured by a company in San Diego called CSI. Neither Daghir nor anyone else at Euromac had handled military orders before, or had any inkling at this stage that the capacitors were wanted for military purposes.

This was understandable, since capacitors have thousands of harmless uses. They are found in kitchen toasters and refrigerators, and in radios and lasers and air-conditioning units. They are also used in nuclear bombs. They are a necessary building-block of any circuitry where the discharge of pulses of electricity is required. Rather like a battery, a capacitor is a simple device which accumulates and stores electrical energy passed to it along a circuit: on the triggering of a switch it releases a burst of that energy at split-second speed. In a nuclear bomb, energy passes almost instantaneously through the capacitor to wires which lead into the explosives packed around the fissionable material at the core. When the electricity hits, the explosion occurs, compressing the fissionable material, which in turn causes the chain reaction and nuclear explosion. The capacitor is not in fact the 'nuclear trigger' – if anything it is the flint, the 'trigger' being the krytron switch which is thrown to set the electricity on its deadly split-second journey. When CSI's President, Jerry Kowalski, received this order from Euromac for Al-qaqaa, he suspected from the specifications (which had been supplied by the Iraqi delegation) that these particular capacitors could be used in the ignition process of a nuclear bomb. So he telephoned the CIA, and was placed under the control of Dan Supnik, a US customs agent, instructed to find out as much as possible about the Iraqi nuclear programme.

Normally, CSI would simply have notified Euromac that since the capacitor was suspected to have a military application, an export licence would not be granted for sale to Iraq. Instead, at Supnik's direction, CSI told Euromac that it could fulfil the order without the slightest difficulty: 'We do not anticipate a problem with obtaining an export licence for Iraq.' It proceeded to deluge Euromac with faxes expressing the company's willingness to fulfil the order. Kowalski visited England twice to meet Daghir, reporting back to the CIA the surprising fact that he was 'not technically literate'. When Daghir actually asked, on one of these visits, what the capacitor might be used for, Kowalski told him 'it might be used for a laser'. Daghir, without his knowledge, was being used by the Americans as their middle-man in eliciting information from Al-qaqaa which might provide valuable clues as to the progress of its nuclear programme. For this purpose, their duplicity was entirely justified. It did put Daghir to a lot of time and expense, and began to lock him into a relationship with Al-qaqaa which he would not otherwise have had – he had not done business with it before or since the original order, the value of which was only U.S. $10,000. But anyone seeking to do even legitimate business with a dangerous dictatorship takes the risk of attracting the attention of intelligence-gatherers, and of being exploited in the wider interests of world security. Morally, I think their motto should have been 'Use him, but don't abuse him.'

The Americans were concerned when Daghir suddenly faxed CSI to say he was no longer interested – 'the project has been terminated'. Over the following weeks, on Supnik's direction, CSI bombarded him with faxes and telephone calls urging him to reconsider. Daghir's response was important: he urged CSI to deal direct with Al-qaqaa. On four separate occasions Daghir and his assistant, Jeanine Speckman, made written requests asking CSI to bother them no longer. Neither had shown any awareness of the potential nuclear use, and Euromac did not deal with arms-related exports. In August 1989 – twelve months after the intelligence operations had commenced – it must have been clear to US and UK authorities that Daghir and Speckman were no longer interested in procuring the order for Al-qaqaa on behalf of their company.

So far, so good. The secret agents had acted commendably, using Daghir as an unwitting agent to gather intelligence. The next stage would be to cut Daghir out altogether, as he in fact wished, and for the Americans to develop their own relationship with the scientists of Al-qaqaa. In mid-July, the Iraqis had issued an invitation to Kowalski to visit their secret factory, and later they extended this invitation to Supnik and even sent him a visa. Taking up this offer would have provided an intelligence bonanza. Al-qaqaa was the site of Saddam's nuclear project, and here were the Iraqis wishing to discuss with CSI a joint project to manufacture capacitors and krytron switches. It would have been the perfect opportunity to observe their nuclear progress. Supnik and Kowalski were courageous men committed to US interests, and they asked permission to go. Incredibly, Washington ordered Supnik to refuse, thereby depriving the West of direct and early access to Saddam's most secret factory, and also jeopardising Supnik's cover as 'sales director' of CSI, since he could give the Iraqis no good reason for his refusal. Why this astonishing decision to abandon the opportunity to gather intelligence on Saddam's bomb, and instead to set Daghir up for one of the world's most publicised arrests?

A US Customs Service memorandum dated 4 August 1989 reads:

> The British authorities have also added their total support to the *proposed operation* and the British Prime Minister was advised of the status of the investigation and is very much interested in its progress and successful outcome.

The British Prime Minister was Mrs Thatcher, and the operation now being proposed was to trap and jail Daghir and Speckman for involvement in the export to Iraq of goods which, at this juncture, they had on four occasions refused to have anything to do with. Yet here was the Prime Minister apparently expressing her interest in a 'successful outcome', a factor which persuaded the US Treasury to fund what soon came to be called 'Operation Quarry'.

Ali Daghir rather than Saddam Hussein became the 'quarry'. When Al-qaqaa engineers came to London on an official trade delegation, Supnik and Kowalski were rushed from San Diego to meet them and discuss Al-qaqaa's capacitor requirements. The Iraqis never actually explained why they wanted capacitors of this specification, but Supnik (posing as CSI's sales director) promised Daghir he would arrange the export 'and will do it safe so that you are happy'. Daghir blew hot and cold – in telephone calls to Supnik he asked him again to deal direct with Al-qaqaa, and faxed him on 14 November and again on 6 December to say that Euromac did not want the capacitors shipped 'through us or to us'. But US Customs prosecutors were not interested in evidence of innocence: in November, they had Daghir and Speckman indicted by a grand jury sitting in a secret session in San Diego. Supnik tried to lure Daghir to California to inspect the capacitors so he could be arrested on the spot, but his pressing requests were declined. On 29 December 1989, when Supnik called to say that CSI insisted on exporting the capacitors to Euromac in London, Daghir declined to accept them. 'I don't want to get into any trouble,' he said as he asked CSI to call the whole deal off: 'Just say sorry.'

Suddenly, there arose a political motive for Daghir's arrest. Farzad Bazoft, the *Observer* freelance arrested for snooping around Al-qaqaa, had made a televised 'confession' in January 1990 to working for British and Israeli intelligence. His trial was imminent, and a death sentence on the cards. The British Government was extraordinarily concerned about his fate, according to a top-secret US memorandum:

> UK Customs asked US Customs if it were possible to speed up the Euromac sting. The reason for the request was that the British were grasping for any leverage they could get on Iraq so they could avoid the execution of the unfortunate UK journalist Farzad Bazoft.

The idea of 'speeding up the sting' for this purpose – presumably, so Daghir could be used in a projected spy swap – was bizarre, not least because Daghir was of no importance to Iraq and any offer to 'trade' him for Bazoft would have been otiose. In any event, however humane the objective, it would have been wrong to use the legal process to serve diplomatic expedience. But the Americans were receptive, and the 'sting' did move swiftly to its conclusion. Supnik told Daghir that CSI insisted on sending the capacitors to him in London, rather than direct to Iraq. He also told Daghir for the first time that in his opinion they were designed for nuclear warheads, at which the man laughed disbelievingly. After much persuasion he agreed to accept them, then later changed his mind and again refused delivery. What finally persuaded him was not pressure from the Americans but from Al-qaqaa, furious with Euromac over its delays. The company was warned that it would be blacklisted by all Iraqi state establishments unless it delivered the capacitors. As most of his business was with Iraqi state enterprises, Daghir was threatened with commercial ruin. On 13 March he succumbed, wrongly, to ensure his business's survival. He agreed to accept delivery of the capacitors in the UK. Three days before, Bazoft had unexpectedly been brought before a military court, and sentenced to death.

If Daghir's arrest was to be used as a bargaining counter for Bazoft's life, then there was no time to lose. But six days were lost. The capacitors were booked to arrive at Heathrow aboard TWA flight 760 which did not depart until 19 March – the US Customs needed time to arrange some self-serving television network publicity. The British must have assumed that international appeals and diplomatic interventions would delay Bazoft's execution – another fateful misreading of Saddam. On 15 March, without warning, Bazoft was hanged.

There was no point now in using arrests of Iraqis in London as 'leverage' to save Bazoft. But the final phase of the sting operation was well under way: by now a 'world exclusive' deal had been done with NBC, which was given the scoop of filming the capacitors (henceforth invariably described as 'nuclear triggers') as they were loaded aboard TWA flight 760 in San Diego. This cargo was seized on arrival at Heathrow, and 'dummy' capacitors substituted and duly delivered to Euromac. Daghir handed them to Omar Latif, manager of Iraqi Airways, for special onward transit to Baghdad, at which point everyone was arrested. US Customs exulted at a boastful press conference which put the story of the 'nuclear triggers' on front pages throughout the world. British newspapers ignored the law against prejudicing trials and assumed the guilt of Daghir (they described him as an evil Iraqi whose acts threatened world peace) and of Speckman (whom they depicted as a cruel and callous Frenchwoman). Daghir was not permitted bail. 'Operation Quarry' and the UK Customs investigators who played a part in it basked in the adulation of a hundred editorials and were soon celebrated by a television series, *The Quarrymen*. After that massive prejudice, the result of their trial at the Old Bailey must have seemed a forgone conclusion: they were convicted in June 1991, a few months after the triumph of 'Operation Desert Storm'.

By the time the appeal was heard – in May 1994 – Daghir had done fifteen months in prison before obtaining bail pending appeal against his conviction and five year sentence. Jeanine Speckman had served her eighteen-month sentence in full, having been advised by her trial counsel that she had no grounds for an appeal. The appeal focused on the decision taken in August 1989 to transform the intelligence-gathering exercise into 'Operation Quarry', designed to entrap Daghir and Speckman. It must have been a joint decision by US and UK agencies, so we asked for all the intelligence documents on 'Operation Quarry' at that time. I was told (although I could scarcely believe it) that all such documents were routinely destroyed after six months, so there was by now no evidence of how the most celebrated co-operation between UK and US agencies on the subject of the 'Islamic bomb' had come into existence. I turned to American sources, and called the Washington counsel assisting Harry Gonzalez, Chairman of the US Congressional Committee which had investigated 'Iraq-gate'. He sent me the explanation given to the US Treasury to obtain funding approval for 'Operation Quarry'.

It was a six-page memorandum, prepared by US Customs and dated 4 August 1989 at a time when Daghir and Speckman were never alleged to be involved in any criminal offences and indeed had no idea that the capacitors had any nuclear or even military use. This document revealed that British military intelligence had given its 'stamp of approval' to what was plainly envisaged as a long-term entrapment operation. The memo predicted how, when Supnik and Kowalski were finally able to arrange a meeting with Daghir and the Iraqi engineers, Supnik would 'elicit the conversation and develop the evidence' necessary to bring about an agreement to provide the capacitors, and would thereafter 'develop and obtain the evidence' necessary for a prosecution. To this end an Assistant District Attorney in San Diego 'has offered his support in guiding the operation towards a successful conclusion'. 'Operation Quarry' had one overwhelming purpose: 'of developing and obtaining that evidence necessary to prosecute the subject of this investigation – Ali Daghir and Jeanine Speckman'. There could scarcely be a clearer example of 'the State' – in this case, the United States – deciding to manipulate two citizens in a way which, nine months later, was to end in their arrest and imprisonment. Had the trial judge possessed this information, he may well have ruled the prosecution evidence generated by 'Operation Quarry' inadmissible on the grounds that it had been obtained by an *agent provocateur*. It was designed from the outset to 'develop' (i.e. to create) evidence of crime, under the guidance of an obscure prosecutor in San Diego, apparently spurred on to a 'successful conclusion' by the wishes of the British Prime Minister.

International law enforcement should not operate like this. Ali Daghir became a pawn in an intelligence game that turned stupid. His alleged crime would never have been contemplated had he not been drawn into an endlessly frustrating, expensive and time-consuming relationship as intermediary between CSI and Al-qaqaa. By the time Daghir arranged the unlicensed export in March 1990, he was at the end of his tether: the eighteen-month deception had created expectations in Iraq which he was now under some business compulsion to fulfil. He should not have surrendered to that pressure, but he should not have had it applied so relentlessly: there were fifty-two recorded telephone calls between Supnik and Euromac in the closing months of the sting: the vast majority of them were initiated by Supnik. The tragedy of 'Operation Quarry' was that Supnik's superiors dumbed a clever piece of intelligence-gathering down into a plan to catch two very small fry, in order to propagate a false story about how western intelligence had caught Saddam with his finger on the nuclear trigger.

By the time of the appeal, evidence had emerged to cast grave doubt on the basis of this story, that these particular capacitors were for use in nuclear bombs. After the end of the Gulf War, the UN sent teams of scientists into Iraq to inspect its nuclear programme, which was frightening enough, but they found no evidence that the CSI capacitors were designed to play any part in it. The prosecution case, which pivoted upon their nuclear use, appeared with hindsight to have been misconceived. Of course, it is a fair bet that they were not being sought for the benign purpose of air-conditioning laboratories against the desert heat or providing pop-up toast for engineers' on-site breakfasts. Al-qaqaa was the place of a mysterious explosion which had killed a number of Egyptian scientists in 1988, and Bazoft's execution for snooping on its perimeter suggests that those who ran it were up to no good. It is impossible, even now, to hazard a confident guess as to what use the Iraqi engineers had in mind for those particular capacitors, which were certainly not 'triggers' and were not 'nuclear'. They would have suited research lasers and high-speed flash photography units of a kind used at Al-qaqaa. They could also have been deployed in the separation stage of a Scud missile and this was a possible use had they ever reached Iraq. It was not an attractive use – indeed, it was a deplorable one – but it was not a use known to, or which the prosecution had charged against, Ali Daghir.

The appellants had another, and unanswerable, argument. Their trial judge had made a fatal error in summing the case up for the jury. Its task was to decide whether the capacitors were designed for use in *nuclear* detonation, but he had mistakenly told them to convict if they were satisfied that they had *any* military use, whether nuclear or not. This ground of appeal was short, simple and overwhelming: their conviction had to be quashed. I believed it should be quashed for other reasons as well: because the evidence was obtained by entrapment, and because of the fresh evidence from the UN nuclear inspectorate. But the shortest point came first, and after just two hours of argument the Court of Appeal judges pronounced themselves convinced that the convictions could not stand.

Outside the Gothic façade of the High Court it was Ali and Jeanine's turn to pose with the regulation bottle of champagne, and mumble a few forgiving words about British justice finally being done, five years after the secret organs of two great nations had decided to interfere with their hitherto insignificant lives. They had been scapegoats in the West's love–hate relationship with Saddam Hussein, which took the form of secret government approvals to arm him to the teeth while at the same time permitting occasional law enforcement forays to reassure the public that they still regarded him as a threat to world peace. This Janus-faced policy was aptly described by Congressmen Gonzalez as 'stupidity on a grand scale', and criticism must be moderate in the light of the confusion this policy produced at every law enforcement level. The lesson for the quarrymen, and for those in military intelligence, is not to spoil an information-gathering exercise by turning it into a public relations exercise. Supnik and Kowalski were clever and courageous men who might have become the unsung heroes who penetrated Al-qaqaa: instead, they were directed to entrap Ali Daghir. There is always an argument which seeks to justify the imprisonment of those who have been gulled by *agents provocateurs*, by reference to its deterrent effect on those who might be minded to act likewise. On the contrary, it teaches them to mind how they go. There was no reduction in arms sales to Iraq in the months after the sting: the published details of how it was accomplished merely served to alert the arms procurement network and its willing suppliers about the danger of being 'Supnikked'. Otherwise, it was business as usual: discreet and deadly.

The story of Ali Daghir and the forty nuclear triggers demonstrates, perhaps more pointedly than any other in this book, how the adversary system allows the most disadvantaged of defendants a chance, clutching at David's slingshot, to defend themselves against the Goliath of the State. Ali Daghir was an underdog and an outsider. He was an Iraqi whom the intelligence services of America and Britain had decided – for reasons which seemed helpful to the West – to trick and trap into committing a serious crime. He was rash enough, in the end, to attempt to export goods without a licence, an act which was sensationally portrayed as a kind of treason to world peace. Millions of pounds were spent, first to ensnare him and then to convict him: he was jailed after a six week trial as an enemy of the people – of all people, in that he had supplied 'nuclear triggers' for Saddam's bomb. People would not care that he had been incited, or that the capacitors were not intended for nuclear use. The very fact that he was prepared to contemplate assisting Saddam would be warrant enough for leaving him to rot in prison. But entities independent of the State took up his appeal: legal aid paid for his lawyers; an independent judge gave him bail; an appeal court quashed his conviction because of a basic mistake in the summing-up, after this had been effectively conceded by an independent prosecutor. The court did not flinch from finding his trial unfair, for all the embarrassment that caused to government agencies in the US and UK.

In previous decades the courts might have fudged – if Daghir had been accused of assisting the Soviets or the IRA – but by now we were in the nineties, and in this decade the justice game has lifted at appellate level precisely because there were so many wrongful convictions in politically charged trials of the past. Daghir's appeal court was presided over by a great Chief Justice, the late Peter Taylor: if convinced there had been a fundamental mistake, he would simply shrug his shoulders and quash the conviction. (He was not standing for re-election like Distict Attorneys in America, so keen for that reason to guide the big cases to a 'successful conclusion'.)

Ali Daghir was overjoyed by the appeal results – curiously, less by the fact it meant he would not return to prison than by having his simple faith in British justice restored. Jeanine Speckman was more detached, and understandably: she should not have been convicted in the first place, and she had served out her sentence with a wintry fortitude.

These last two paragraphs read complacently, as if written by a self-satisfied lawyer congratulating the system on doing justice by the final whistle. Certainly, I was impressed by the lengths to which the Court and the prosecution went in 1994 – under the impetus, it must be said, of the continuing Scott enquiry into Matrix Churchill – to harry the UN Nuclear Inspectorate to provide evidence helpful to the appellants. But I have, even now, an uneasy feeling about this case. Books on the Gulf War still recount, as if a matter of historical fact, that Saddam's 'nuclear triggers' were intercepted at Heathrow in the hands of Ali Daghir. He was blasted by the media as the leader of a 'nuke bomb gang'. *Newsweek* uncritically carried the false claims of U.S. prosecutors, identifying him as 'an Iraqi intelligence officer' who 'had done billions of dollars of business on behalf of Iraq's war effort'. It was so easy to use NBC to promote the story in return for a scoop, and for the San Diego prosecutors to release their 'sealed indictment' to the world's press – i.e. to reporters who were 'not technically literate' and were too excited to check the facts. In the result, Ali Daghir and Jeanine Speckman became the only persons ever to be jailed in Britain in respect of arms to Iraq, although leading British companies, with secret government approval, supplied vast quantities of weapons-related goods to Saddam in the years before his invasion of Kuwait. It is difficult to forget the 'warm congratulations' so publicly bestowed by Mrs Thatcher, four days after Daghir's arrest, on all involved in Operation Quarry: 'The whole nation has reason to be grateful to you.' Politicians should postpone such plaudits, with their presumption of the defendant's guilt, until after the final appeal. The guilt of 'outsiders' – foreigners, Irish republicans, blacks, ex-prisoners, mental patients – can too readily be assumed, especially in sensational cases: when it unravels, finally, in the Court of Appeal, after their lives have been scarred, we cannot feel over-much pride that 'justice' has been done at last.

What remains unsatisfactory about the Daghir appeal is that it succeeded too well, or at least too quickly, relieving the court from considering the important argument about entrapment, fuelled by the fresh evidence we had obtained from America about the political direction of 'Operation Quarry'. The use of '*agents provocateur*' by State agencies is an issue that has concerned me ever since I began to practise at the Old Bailey in the early seventies. That was when corrupt drugs squad officers would use informers to set up 'busts' for which the informer would be rewarded with part of the cannabis, which he was expected to sell, returning a share of the profits to the police. Such problematic tactics have exercised every criminal justice system since Adam was arraigned in the Garden of Eden: whether to punish a person who has been talked and tempted into committing an offence. Dr Samuel Johnson, whose chambers I occupied for many years, had a pretty good grasp of human nature. 'There is,' he asserted to Boswell, 'a proof to which you have no right to put a man. You know, humanly speaking, there is a certain degree of temptation, which will overcome any virtue.'

In the US, if defendants admit that they committed the crime but satisfy the court that they would not have done so without the 'creative activity' of the police or their agents, they are entitled to acquittal. The purpose of law enforcement is to detect crime, not to test virtue by tempting citizens selected as scapegoats by the State. In the words of American Supreme Court Justice Felix Frankfurter,

> The power of government is abused and directed to an end for which it was not constituted when employed to promote rather than to detect crime and to bring about the downfall of those who, left to

themselves, might well have obeyed the law. Human nature is weak enough and sufficiently beset by temptations without government adding to them and generating crime.

'Entrapment', as it is called, is not an easy defence to run, because the court will draw a line between 'the trap for the unwary innocent and the trap for the unwary criminal', and will readily infer that far from being a lamb led to the slaughter the defendant is a wolf snared on the prowl. Nonetheless, an entrapement defence should have succeeded for Daghir. He had been caught red-handed trying to export the capacitors without a licence. But he would never have been placed in this position without the most remarkable methods of persuasion and cajolement, employed for eighteen months by US undercover agents with the approval of British Intelligence and the CIA. There is no 'entrapment' defence in English law, but there is a line of legal authority to the effect that every trial judge has an inherent power to exclude evidence 'obtained by conduct of which the Crown ought not to take advantage, even though tendered for the suppression of crime'. The moral imperative – 'ought' – opens the window, at least a crack, to the full blast of an argument about the immortality of the State itself creating the crimes it was meant to be prohibiting. It was that argument which I wanted to make for Ali Daghir, because if it succeeded for him it would have to succeed for others suckered by the State into crimes they would otherwise not have contemplated.

There are many who think that people who eventually succumb to temptation from State agents deserve to be punished nonetheless. The better view is that officials charged with maintaining law should not arrange for it to be broken. Secret policing is essential, but no State which puts a value on the liberty of its citizens can allow it to operate without rules for ensuring that unwary innocents do not stumble into traps laid for unwary criminals. Daghir gave in to pressure, but the rules of the justice game provided for his eventual acquittal, notwithstanding his technical guilt or the extent of the State power ranged against him. These rules – the disclosure obligations on the prosecution and the power to exclude unfairly obtained evidence – are under constant attack for 'protecting the guilty'. In fact, they serve to protect people who turn out to be not so guilty after all.

Chapter 14

Friendly (*sic*) Fire

The scene of the crime was featureless Iraqi desert, over the border from Saudi Arabia and on the way to Kuwait, a route taken on 26 February 1991 by a convoy of British tanks and armoured cars which encountered little resistance from the enemy. At 3 p.m. they were resting, a short breathing space before the next push for Operation Desert Storm. On the armoured vehicle known as 'Call-sign 22' nineteen-year-old Fusilier Ferguson sat reading a letter from his girlfriend; his comrades smoked and joked, watched by Private Halliwell, driver of 'Call-sign 23' parked a short distance away. At 3.02, Halliwell saw the vehicle explode in flashes of fire and steel, and heard the screams of men with fire in their hair and shrapnel in their legs. It was a mine, evidently, and there were likely to be more. Halliwell grabbed a first-aid kit and ran over to help, fearless of flying shrapnel from the exploding ammunition, risking his life and, ironically, saving it by the same action. For behind him as he ran came another searing explosion: he turned to see that his own tank had been turned into an incinerator in which none of the crew could survive.

There were American planes in the clear blue sky – an A-10 was seen by some soldiers to bank away with a waggle of its wings which later they would interpret as a 'victory roll'. For the present there were frantic mine-detection operations, then the wounded had to be helicoptered back to base hospitals and pieces of the dead collected for the body bags. They stuck a simple cross in the sand, ringed with nine helmets bearing the red and white hackles of the Royal Regiment of Fusiliers. The chaplain came, to offer up a prayer for that 'safe lodging, holy rest and peace at the last' which is to come after 'the fever of life is over and our work is done'. These teenage lives had barely encountered fever or started work: they had been blown away by American airmen.

'Stop! Stop! Stop!' As the second maverick missile hit Call-sign 23, Squadron Leader Pearce was screaming across frequency Tad 209 at two A-10 pilots who had shot first and then condescended to tell him – their ground control – where they happened to be. As the American pilot lazily read the grid reference off his Inertial Navigation System (INS), Pearce and McSkimming and Evans – the British air controllers sitting in a horse-box sixty miles behind the lines – became alarmed. 'Grid references' were six-figure readings which pinpointed the plane's exact location, and this plane was directly above an advancing British battalion. The enemy these two pilots had been ordered to engage was twenty kilometres further on. They had unloosed two missiles and scored direct hits. Either the retreating enemy had turned and sped back to engage the British, or . . .

It could not be. The two pilots had been given the correct grid reference ten minutes ago and had read it back to ground control for confirmation. The A-10s had been 'made available' to the British controllers to mop up a few Iraqi tanks lying abandoned in their ditches. A flight of four F-16s had already shot them up: it was leaving as the A-10s approached. To make doubly sure that there was no confusion, the British controllers requested the F-16 leader to describe to the A-10 pilots the target area, which he did in some detail. ('You fly over three road intersections, then there's a police station, next you see the smoke from burning hulks and there are the targets: a few immobilised Iraqi tanks.') The A-10 pilots went quiet for a few minutes until controller McSkimming radioed to ask whether these targets were worth another mission. The lead pilot replied that they had just destroyed part of a moving line of fifty Iraqi T-55 tanks.

That was when the penny dropped: the grid reference was urgently requested, and the awful truth began to dawn. The A-10 pilots were twenty kilometres off course, over terrain which looked nothing like the F-16's description. They had attacked, without obtaining clearance to fire, a target utterly different from a few tanks immobilised in ditches. Besides, British tanks had a different configuration to the T-55, and had painted 'V' signs on top and orange fluorescent panels on their sides, visible from the air as a warning against 'friendly' fire. Something – many things – had gone wrong.

Just how wrong may be appreciated by comparing the conduct of the A-10 pilots with that of the F-16 pilots who had preceded them to the target. The lead, Kenneth Schow (Call-sign Benji) was a pilot who flew by the book. He made contact with the British controllers and received the target grid coordinates and the information that 'friendlies' were as close as ten kilometres away. That meant, as every pilot should know, that this was a 'close air support' (CAS) operation, which has special rules to prevent attacks on allied forces. The first rule is to obtain clearance before firing. Schow asked for a target description: 'a few tanks in ditches'. He observed a column of smoke and some moving tanks (the British force and the Iraqi gun emplacement they had destroyed) and immediately checked his INS which gave him a grid reference telling him he was still twenty kilometres from the target. So he flew on that distance to another column of smoke and descended to eight thousand feet to establish visual contact with the ground so that any 'friendly' markings on the target would be seen before it was too late. (There were no Iraqi planes, and no anti-aircraft fire in these last few days of the war.) He read back his new grid reference to Squadron Leader Pearce, obtaining his clearance to attack the few tanks configured like T-55s which he could see lying in man-made ditches. The F-16s 'worked the target' for fifteen minutes, until 'Bingo for fuel': as Schow pulled away the British controllers asked him to talk the incoming A-10s onto the target, which he did, stating very clearly that the target was at the second column of smoke. At this point it must have seemed inconceivable to the listening air controllers that the A-10s could go wrong. Their INS grid reference would take them precisely to the spot. A totally new target – a column of moving tanks – would require careful visual inspection and checks with control before permission to attack. These protocols were fundamental in CAS missions. Why were they ignored?

The two A-10 pilots were having a bad air day. They had taken off at noon from King Khalid military city in Saudi Arabia, and spent an hour in heavy cloud. They had missed their first refuelling rendezvous with an air tanker. Then, tasked onto a target, they swooped only to find it covered by a sandstorm. At command control, when it passed them on to the British ground controllers, their voices sounded irritable and frustrated and their responses tense. When they finally found a target – an Iraqi supply truck in a bulldozed trench – they attempted several times to strafe but missed this 'sitting duck' on each run. By now their frustration was intense and their fuel was low: they had only a few minutes left before they would have to return to base. As the lead pilot put it in a statement written later that day:

> Both of us made two passes and missed on every attempt, so I shifted targets trying to not 'be stupid'. There was no observed threat in the area and that jived with what Benji had briefed us. As I came off my last strafe pass it was then, about one mile south of the trench we had tried to strafe, that I saw about fifty vehicles on the move northbound. I did a binoculars pass at eight thousand feet . . . no friendly markings were observed. By all appearances I thought they were T-55 tanks and associated support vehicles. I launched a maverick missile . . .

In a CAS operation the rules are crystal clear. Before launching any lethal attack, these pilots had a duty to obtain and check the target coordinates from their British controllers. The target they identified was so startlingly different from the target described by the controllers and by Benji that it was essential to follow the fundamental rule, because terrain descriptions are notoriously confusing. In any event a binocular pass from eight thousand feet would clearly have shown the distinctive outline of the British tanks and their orange fluorescent panels. They were attacking near the first column of smoke, which did not 'jive' with Benji's warning to fly to the second column. All this was done in 'turkey shoot' conditions: under a clear sky with no enemy threat from the air or from the ground. Yet in radio silence these pilots took the law into their own hands, killing nine British soldiers and leaving twelve others seriously wounded.

The cover-up began as soon as the deaths were recognised as resulting from 'friendly fire'. Neither the British nor American leaders wanted this incident to spoil their triumph. General Schwartzkopf (whose care of his own men was legendary) said,

'There's no excuse for it, I'm not going to apologise for it'. But he went on to refer to bad weather, and 'the extreme differences in the language of the forces' (English and American English in this case) and 'very, very close combat' in the area. The little white lies to the parents started in the official condolences letter a few days later. The first came from HRH the Duke of Kent, Colonel in Chief of the Fusiliers, who said each soldier 'was killed by an Allied airborne attack in very bad weather and visibility'. When the families heard from survivors that the weather was good and visibility perfect, they were angered by the Duke's dismissive palliative 'you have the consolation of knowing that he died on active service for his Queen and country'. This 'Colonel in Chief' was safe in St James's at the time of the incident, but these incorrect excuses were echoed by others. The commanding officer of the 4th Armoured Brigade wrote that 'the incident occurred during particularly confused fighting when it was difficult to define exactly where we and the enemy actually were' (not with grid references it wasn't), while the battalion commander wrote 'we were in the midst of battle at the time . . . there was much confusion . . . there is no bitterness here over what happened to us'. There was, of course, aching bitterness and real fury, amongst the men of the 4th Brigade and the middle-ranking officers who cared for them. They could not forget the victory roll.

But why mislead grieving parents? In letters that were genuinely meant and otherwise considerate, but which gave them every reason, once they had spoken to their sons' comrades, to suspect a cover-up? It struck me as the 'Ron Smith syndrome' all over again – the attitude that you can make soothing noises to the working classes about their children's death, and they won't have the clout to find out the awkward truth. What once again was lacking was any sense of what 'justice' requires so that the grief of a bereaved parent may run its course. When a tragedy of this kind inexplicably occurs, there must be a full inquiry – for the sake of future combatants as well as for the sake of families who want reassurance that their sons did not die in vain.

A Board of Inquiry must by statute be held into deaths on active service. Its report was claimed by the government to be a top secret. The families were sent a summary of its conclusions, under cover of a letter which Tom King – the Secretary of State for

Defence – did not even bother to sign. 'He very much regrets,' said an official letter signed by a secretary in his office, 'that, in spite of all our efforts, the Board could not resolve the conflict of evidence over why the aircraft were in the wrong place and why two Warrior vehicles were misidentified. It is clear that all UK and USAF personnel were striving to achieve their individual tasks. Given the understandable pressure of events on all those involved, it is inevitable that, at some stage, difficulties may arise.' This became part of the official summary of the Board's findings presented to Parliament by Tom King, who added that there had been a *conflict of evidence presented* by the A-10 pilots and by their British controllers, and the whole tragedy must be put down to the *difficulties which may arise* when individuals are under pressure in a *fast-moving battle*. The full report was secret because 'it has been the practice of successive governments not to publish reports of this kind'. (King did not disclose that the full report had been sent to the Americans weeks before.)

The simple truth was that this so-called 'inquiry' sat briefly on 15 May at an air base near High Wycombe, and only heard three British witnesses. There had been no 'evidence presented' by the A-10 pilots. All the Board was shown were the short statements they wrote on landing. And it was not clear at all that the A-10 pilots were 'striving to achieve their individual tasks' – the attack on the Warriors was nothing like the task they had been given. There was no 'fast-moving battle' at the time, and no 'pressure of events' or other 'difficulties'. The summary misled Parliament both about the incident and the inquiry into it.

The Prime Minister, a few months later, was shamed by some media coverage into writing another letter to the parents, which he took care to sign personally. John Major's letter excused the delay 'because it was very important for the Board to pursue all lines of investigation so that the clearest possible account could be established . . . Like us, the Americans wanted to make sure that there was no information that had been overlooked and that everything had been made available to the Board of Inquiry.' This was nonsense. The Americans had withheld the most crucial evidence – the testimony of the pilots themselves – by refusing to allow them to attend the Board of Inquiry, which had been so cavalier in its investigation that it failed to insist upon their presence. Major continued: 'I do appreciate that your grief may have been lessened if the Board had been able to allocate responsibility for the accident, but the information available simply does not enable this to be done.' That, of course, was because the pilots were never seen or questioned. Major nonetheless went on to defend them, on the basis that since 'they believed that they had positively identified enemy targets on the ground, in the circumstances they would have seen no need to make further contact with the [British controller] before attacking'. What is quite breathtaking about this passage is that it ignores the first rule of close air support operations, namely that no lethal attack should be launched without receiving a target coordinate. Here was the British Prime Minister, making a bogus excuse for the negligent conduct that had killed nine young Britons.

I was approached to act for all the parents at the forthcoming inquest – their final opportunity to establish the truth. I was reluctant: my father had been a wartime fighter pilot and I had no wish to accuse the A-10 airmen of an 'unlawful killing'. But Denis McShane, an MP who had taken up the parents' cause, asked me to meet them – and that changed everything. They have been described and have described themselves as 'just ordinary people', some from families who had given generations to the army. I do not find anyone 'ordinary' and what was so moving about these parents was their continuing torment, not only from the loss of their sons, but from being treated as though that sacrifice did not matter. They had been palmed off with false information and an inadequate investigation, then patted on the head by the Prime Minister and told to put up, shut up and cheer up. Against the all-important political purpose of not upsetting the Americans, they were nothings. There is no legal aid for inquests, and barristers are entitled to refuse to work for nothing. I would not be working for nothings but for men and women who had sacrificed their children and were asking only for justice in return.

The body bits and pieces had been landed at Brize Norton, an airbase within the jurisdiction of the Oxford coroner. He announced that he would sit without a jury and hear the inquest in one day. Mark Stephens, by now a leading litigation solicitor, was persuaded to bring his firm into the fray, with Keir Starmer as my junior: they threatened High Court action and as a result the coroner changed his mind. He summoned a jury, and conceded that the case might last for six days. He was a good deal more accommodating than some other coroners: he sent us a list of witnesses, and the MOD at the last moment supplied us with their statements. The MOD was represented by the Treasury solicitors, and fielded a large team of seven lawyers. They were keen to establish that no blame could be attached to the British ground forces or to the air controllers but they baulked at the logical conclusion, which was that the A-10 pilots had been responsible for the killings. They wanted a verdict of accidental death. That had been the verdict of the Air Force Board, and of the British government, confirmed by the Prime Minister himself. As for the United States, its verdict had been delivered in Haig-speak by its deputy Commander-in-Chief:

> No dispersions [*sic*] can be cast on either side [*i.e. on US pilots or UK controllers*]. Both were operating at a hectic combat pace on a rapidly changing battlefield where the fog of war is inevitable at some point. Many factors and misunderstandings led them down the primrose path, but the bottom line is that they were not on the same sheet of music and that led them to disaster . . . we believe there is little to be gained by further investigating this incident.

What was to be gained by further investigation was apparent from the first day of the inquest at Oxford Town Hall. The public seats were packed with the families of the deceased, listening with fierce intensity as their sons' comrades and officers testified to the moments when the missiles hit. During breaks in the hearing, witnesses and parents fell into each other's arms, pooling emotions: the survivors as much as the relatives needing to articulate, simply and directly, the horror and the heroism obfuscated until now by the official reports. Fusilier Halliwell, who had risked his own life in an effort to save their sons, was the first witness. But the real question for everyone in court was: where were the American pilots? I made a public request for them to come and explain the 'staggering discrepancies' between their initial debriefings and the evidence of the British controllers. I pointed out that 'it is vital to hear from the A-10 pilots to find out what information they received and why they fired. Nothing can happen to them: one would think it better for them to do the decent and humane thing, rather than face accusations of cowardice.'

It was a gauntlet intentionally flung at the outset, when I still had an open mind about whether the British controllers could have been partly responsible (Pearce had handed over the tasking of the A-10s to McSkimming at a vital time). I thought the pilots could and should be defended. The MOD knew their names, but refused to tell me or the coroner. The United States had not even instructed lawyers to appear on the pilots' behalf – a calculated snub to the coroner's inquiry. It had sent a USAF lawyer, Colonel Robert Bridge, merely to observe: he sat in court flanked by two armed officers from the Police Special Protection Squad. This was a stupid insult to the parents, who were the last people in the world to offer violence to anyone. The Colonel was confronted outside the court, in the glare of television cameras. 'My son is dead,' pleaded Peter Atkinson. 'Why won't the pilots come over? Let them come. Nothing is going to happen to them.' The cringing Colonel could only mutter 'I'm sorry' and add that it was a matter for the pilots' personal choice. President Bush, a few months before, had received Peter and other parents at the White House and publicly promised there would be 'no hiding place from the truth'. For the American government, in the light of that false promise, this was a deeply unattractive scene. For all the carefully contained expressions of sorrow and regret, the reality was expressed in an unguarded moment by USAF Commander 'Chuck' Horner: inquiries into 'friendly fire' deaths, he said, were like 'picking at scabs'.

The authorities desperately wanted the inquest to end quietly, and with a verdict of 'accidental death'. The coroner appeared to share that wish: he had been in contact with the Pentagon, which had 'taken the view that it was inappropriate for them to interfere in a British inquest, or send anyone to answer questions'. I despaired of him at first as a mouse who would not roar at the Americans – but would anything more than a squeak come from Malcolm Rifkind QC, our Minister of Defence, fortuitously in Washington at the time of the inquest? There were some who thought that he might ask, in the interests of justice, that the pilots be sent to explain themselves at Oxford, where the evidence against them was beginning to mount.

The evidence quickly destroyed the official claim that anyone was 'under pressure in a fast-moving battle'. There had been no battle, and no confusion at all, said army officers who had been on the ground, until the maverick hit. Then came the air controllers – Pearce and McSkimming and Evans – the men the Pentagon insinuated were really to blame. I had instructions to find out the truth so I cross-examined them critically, but their accounts gelled and had support from notes they made at the time. These men had demonstrably followed CAS procedures for all flights to this particular target: for some reason, the A-10 pilots alone had completely ignored the instructions. If McSkimming had not asked what they were up to – and then where they were up to it – they might have gone on shooting missiles at the British column, as if knocking down a row of coconuts at a fair. It was impossible to ignore the evidence of the senior British Air Liaison Officer in the Gulf, who confirmed that the pilots had 'flouted CAS procedures' and had acted 'neither adequately nor correctly'. They seemed to have treated the verbal description of the target given to them by Benji as clearance to fire on a totally different target. He said that by no stretching of the rules of aerial combat could this be countenanced. 'The A-10s had no authority to select their own target, except at a grid reference.'

The evidence was pointing to gross negligence. It was vital for the pilots to make some sort of appearance, if only by radio, to answer for their conduct. The coroner, initially reluctant to offend the Americans, had changed his mind, and criticism of their non-appearance had erupted in the media. All we heard from the pilots came second-hand, from another British officer who had been stationed in the USAF command centre. He had there made the fatal request for another mission to follow up Benji and his F-16s. The US controllers said they had two A-10s which had been stooging around for two and a half hours without success, so this officer wrote down the grid references of the target and listened while a US controller read them to the pilots. (So they had grid references twice – once from the American command, and then later from McSkimming.) The officer described hearing the lead pilot's voice. 'This was a pilot who wanted something to happen quickly. It was a voice that was not relaxed. It was irritable. They wanted to get on with things.'

The important thing was that they had acknowledged, tersely, the correct grid reference and they had an INS which would take them precisely to that target – a few Iraqi tanks in their ditches. How did they end up twenty kilometres away, shooting up a column of fifty British armoured vehicles? The next witness, an air liaison officer, volunteered an explanation: 'Maybe they thought kill zone conditions were still operating.' The 'kill zone conditions' had operated in the early weeks of Desert Storm, when pilots were permitted to select and destroy their own targets in Iraqi areas hundreds of miles from allied troops. The 'kill zone' rules had been suspended once the invasion of Iraq began. I put to him: 'They had been briefed that there were friendly forces no more than ten kilometres away. It would be staggeringly negligent to use "kill zone" procedure in an area where there are friendly forces?' That question hung in the heavy air: this witness was the airman who had ordered up the transport for the dead and the wounded. He just looked at the jury with a face haunted by the memory, and slowly nodded his head.

At the end of his evidence at Oxford it was midday in Washington. Malcolm Rifkind was shortly to lunch with his opposite number, Dick Cheney. He had a letter from the parents which his office had promised the press he would discuss with the US Defence Secretary. The MOD had presumably briefed him on the day's damning evidence: as a QC, Rifkind should have known the importance to justice in this country of having the Pentagon arrange for one of the A-10 pilots to answer questions. I have no idea what happened: Cheney snorted afterwards that there was no way he was going to make the pilots available for a 'media circus' (this from an American) while Rifkind was reported as saying 'The Americans are handling the affair sensitively'.

It should be recorded that the MOD knew the identity of these pilots, and in breach of the coroner's rules it withheld the names from the inquest. This was at the request of the Pentagon, which feared it would subject them to 'unwarranted public scrutiny'. (Since they had killed nine men, some public scrutiny might have been warranted.) It would also deter 'uninhibited testimony' about other deadly mishaps – an admission, in effect, that the pilots would be in danger of incriminating themselves if they testified. It is interesting to note the Pentagon's *volte face* shortly after the inquest, when it identified and court-martialled pilots of an AWACS plane whose negligence led to the shooting down of two helicopters over Northern Iraq and the loss of twenty-six lives. The principal difference was that the lives lost were those of American officers, not British squaddies.

The evidence concluded on a Wednesday afternoon. The inquest was adjourned for several days, and the coroner called the Pentagon with a last request that a pilot be made available by video or radio link. The request was declined in an arrogant response which falsely stated that their 'additional evidence would be of no relevance to your inquest'. The sadness and stupidity of the Pentagon's approach was that the families were as forgiving a group as I have ever met. I have no doubt that had an A-10 pilot turned up to apologise for making an appalling mistake, they would actually have embraced him. These pilots did not even have to attend in person or identifiably: they could have given evidence by video or radio from their base to the coroner's court, remaining unnamed and unseen. There could be only one reason why they and their commanders declined even this minimum option.

On the last day, we asked the coroner to leave open to the jury the possibility of returning a verdict of 'unlawful killing' – not murder, but manslaughter by gross negligence. The CAS rules for aerial warfare were as well known as the Highway Code – do not attack without using target coordination and 'if in doubt, don't shoot':

> The A-10 pilots, told friendly forces were in the target vicinity as close as ten kilometres, launched a lethal attack without heeding, let alone checking, the target coordinates given them. The pilots must have known that they were contravening a fundamental rule by making a CAS attack without target coordinates and must as a consequence have known of the risk involved to friendly forces, but nevertheless attacked without checking with the British controller, who was but a flick of the radio switch away. It follows that a verdict of 'unlawful killing' must be left to the jury. To withdraw it would be a boon to every hit-and-run motorist, who might be led to think that by staying away from an inquest he could obtain a verdict of 'accidental death'.

The coroner – and for this the families were grateful – allowed the jury to listen to my submission before summing up. His directions favoured 'accident' or an open verdict, but at least left 'unlawful killing' as a possibility, if the jury were satisfied 'beyond reasonable doubt' (he stressed) 'that the pilots acted in a way that would have created an obvious and serious risk to friendly forces, and either they gave no thought to the possibility of that risk or if they did, chose to ignore it'.

Spending all the adjournments with the parents, in a smoke-filled back room, I had sensed how the case for unlawful killing, at first unanswered and then unanswerable, had become a psychological necessity: they needed that verdict in order to bury with dignity the memory of their sons. Relatives of murder victims have a similar psychological need to attend the trial, despite the gruesomeness of the evidence, in order that they may cease mourning once a defendant is convicted and jailed. Where there has been no trial the inquest must offer a substitute, becoming a place of catharsis where the dead may be put to rest with the dignity that comes from a determined search for the truth. The families needed to purge their bitterness after the deaths of their sons had been trivialised by being wrongfully excused by the 'fog of war'.

The jury did not let them down: it delivered the verdict of 'unlawful killing': aerial manslaughter, by gross negligence. It was a true verdict, and the parents' battle to obtain it was heroic because it was fought against two governments determined that it should not come out.

The families hugged one another, their tears the most joyful they had shed since the knocks on their doors by army messengers in the early morning of 27 February 1991, fifteen months before. They heard the coroner say he was satisfied that they had not been 'properly or sympathetically informed' of the facts surrounding the deaths and he promised to pass on their recommendation that no joint military action should again be taken with the Americans unless they first agreed to cooperate with inquests held in Britain. The families had one final formality which they had thought to do whatever the verdict: they presented a red rose to each juror.

Counsel must not get tangled up in their clients' emotions – that is for solicitors, for campaigners and for support groups. But privately I was elated by this verdict because I knew how much it would mean to the families. I had held no brief for the American pilots: had I done so, with clients who condescended to come to Oxford, I might have thought differently and so might the jury. So, certainly, would the families. They wanted only the truth, and had it been offered by the pilots, in person and apologetically, that would have been the end of their quest. There was much talk about whether civil actions and financial compensation and even criminal prosecutions should follow from the inquest verdict, but the families did not want anything further. They had made their point, and if not the Pentagon made it for them, by the statement it issued immediately after the verdict: 'It is obvious that a terrible accident occurred in the fog of war on the battlefield.'

The American military publicly pretended not to understand, but the inquest verdict sent a message which shocked the political and military establishments of both nations, because it contravened their certainty that *these things happen in the fog of war.* It rejected the fatalism of Sir Peter de la Billière, British commander of 'Desert Storm', in his condolence letter to the parents: 'Careful arrangements were made to prevent just this sort of tragedy, but I am afraid the risk is always present in the confusion of war.' General Sir Peter Inge, the Commander-in-Chief of the British Army of the Rhine, wrote to them in the same vein: 'sadly such mistakes are bound to happen'. But they are not. The fog of war does not excuse negligence: it lessens the standard of liability, but never removes it completely. The question always depends on what standard of care is appropriate in the circumstances. An army surgeon operating under bombardment in a makeshift hospital is not expected to display the calm professional judgment required of a consultant undertaking the same operation at Guy's, but he must not act with gross negligence. A general with the lives of men in his hands, and a pilot with the lives of men at his fingertips, must not use that power recklessly. There are rules for driving in fog, and there are rules for driving in the fog of war. It was the achievement of the 'friendly fire' parents to vindicate the simple idea that the rules for the conduct of war, devised to prevent accidents, should not be recklessly disobeyed – otherwise, mistakes *are* bound to occur.

In the *Observer*, Michael Ignatieff wrote of this inquest perceptively:

The fog of war argument is a form of the highest cynicism. It says it doesn't really matter how someone dies once they are dead. It says the truth is never to be found on a battlefield. It says justice is for lawyers, not for soldiers. Small wonder the women believed they were pitting the logic of their grief against the logic of an officer class which, in ceaselessly repeating that accidents will happen, was saying in effect that their sons were no more than cannon fodder.

Even in war, the legal rules which nail human responsibility to a standard of care should never be forgotten. To invoke them may be unseemly, raining the tears of parents on the victory parades of generals. That was how it seemed at the beginning of the inquest, but by the end few who had heard the evidence could disagree with the verdict. The 'fog of war' argument had lifted in the court, and the verdict may have done something to dissolve it forever.

Chapter 15

UK Ltd: The Matrix Churchill Trial

> Truth is a difficult concept.
> *Ian McDonald, MOD*
>
> Half the picture can be true.
> *Sir Robin Butler, Cabinet Secretary*
>
> I quite simply misled myself on what I thought the situation was.
> *Eric Beston, DTI*
>
> Something I was not aware had happened turned out not to have happened.
> *John Major, Prime Minister*

Paul Henderson, the managing director of Matrix Churchill, a manufacturing company in Coventry, had been committed for trial with two of his executives, on charges of being knowingly concerned in the exportation to Iraq of machine tools programmed to make bombs and rockets, with intent to evade the legal prohibition on such exports. Their destination, over the three years before Iraq invaded Kuwait in August 1990, was the Nassr armaments factory outside Baghdad on the road to old Babylon's 'Hanging Gardens'. The offences carried a maximum sentence of seven years' imprisonment and after reading the thousands of pages of prosecution evidence, I thought it likely that Mr Henderson would receive three to five years inside.

Usually, I manage to suspend disbelief until meeting the defendant, but something about these papers carried conviction. Government policy prohibited the export of machine tools 'specially designed' to make weapons, but the Department of Trade and Industry (DTI) said it had been fooled by the company's licence application which described them as destined 'for general engineering purposes'. Henderson knew this was not the full truth, since they were going to munitions factories to make munitions. It was alleged he had given the incriminating order which customs officers had found written in a Matrix Churchill file: 'Nothing military to be stated'. The DTI Minister, Alan Clark, had apparently been fooled as well, at a meeting with Henderson in January 1988. In a witness statement about that meeting, he said: 'The advice I gave to the machine tool manufacturers was based upon the assumption that the exports were intended for civil application.' So *R v Henderson* seemed an open and shut case, and an important one. Customs described it as a 'flagship case' and I could only envy their counsel, Alan Moses QC, bringing to justice a businessman clever enough to deceive ministers and DTI officials while flying back and forth to Baghdad to superintend the installation of his machine tools in the arms factories. There was extremely prejudicial evidence that bombs made by Matrix Churchill had been found on battlefields where British soldiers had fallen: once the jury heard that it would be the end of any chance of acquittal. I did not think I would like Mr Paul Henderson. He seemed, from these voluminous prosecution papers, to be the very model of a modern merchant of death.

Two assumptions made me presume Paul's guilt. The first was that although customs occasionally became confused (like everybody else) about pornography, I credited them with the ability to know an unlawful export when they saw it. More importantly, I did not actually believe that the British government lied. Not like that, straight out, to Parliament and the public, and over a period of years. On 29 October 1985, the Foreign Secretary, Sir Geoffrey Howe, had promulgated 'guidelines' which seemed pellucidly clear. Britain would not supply, either to Iraq or Iran, defence-related equipment which would 'significantly enhance the capability of either side'. After the Iran/Iraq war fizzled to an uneasy truce in August 1988, Parliament was still routinely assured that the Howe guidelines remained in force. Yet British machine tools – worth hundreds of millions of pounds – had over this period been exported to establish an indigenous rocket- and bomb-making industry in Iraq. On any view, this was a very significant enhancement of Iraq's military capability, and it was going to be difficult to mount a defence which pivoted upon the proposition that the British government had connived at such a massive breach of rules they had regularly promised Parliament they were strenuously enforcing.

But Paul Henderson claimed that HMG must have known what he was up to, for the simple reason that he had told them. He had been working for MI6, spying on the arms factories he visited in Iraq and revealing the information at debriefing sessions with his MI6 controller, a man who had used the pseudonym 'John Balsom'. He was not the first client to have instructed me of a connection with MI6 – several have believed the intelligence services to be sending lasers into their brain, and have wanted to obtain an injunction against them. But he produced the only trail that MI6 had left, to back up his story: records of the security guards at the Matrix Churchill gate, showing that a 'Mr Balsom from the DTI' had regularly come to visit him. Clutching this thin reed, I suspended disbelief. There was one other reason: the whole-hearted devotion of Kevin Robinson, a respected Sheffield solicitor, to the innocence of Paul Henderson. 'He's not what you might expect from reading the prosecution papers,' explained Kevin, anxious to arrange an early meeting. 'I think you'll like him.'

I did like Paul Henderson, from the start, for much the same reasons as it later emerged that MI6 liked him. He was open about all he had done, and humble to the point of dismissiveness about his bravery in Iraq. He had made the moral accommodation necessary to keep one thousand Coventry workers in skilled work, based on an intimate knowledge of the machine tools in question. He had been apprenticed to work these lathes and grinders and milling devices from the age of sixteen, and he spoke almost with affection of how he would harness their power to cut raw metal and turn it into screws and flanges and axles and engine blocks. The machine tool, he would say with real passion, was the building block of industry. The Matrix Churchill machines which went to Iraq were standard, off-the-shelf models which could be used to make anything – bombs today and buses tomorrow. They were not 'dual-use' so much as of infinitely variable use, although many of them went in the first instance to munitions factories. Like other Iraq-watchers, he believed that after the 1988 truce with Iran much of this dual-use technology would be transferred to civilian production, and he highlighted this prospect in his correspondence with officials. But whenever pushed – as he was by the *Financial Times* as early as September 1989 – he frankly conceded their military use in the past and their potential for military use in the future.

On this score, Paul Henderson was unapologetic – as a law-abiding managing director, he would sell them and send them wherever government policy permitted. And since the government knew full well that his orders came from Iraqi munitions factories, he saw no reason to reproach himself for fulfilling them and securing jobs for his workforce. He had acted as the law requires of every director – lawfully and in the best interests of his company. It was for the government to make the political and moral judgment on whether a British company should be permitted to provision bomb factories in Iraq, and that judgment had been unequivocally in the affirmative. His problem was caused by the fact that the government was just not prepared to make it out loud.

When I looked up the law I expected to find a clear rule which banned arms-related trade with Iraq. What I discovered instead was a law requiring exports of machine tools to be licensed by the DTI, which had a special department which would grant or withhold licences according to ministerial policy at the time. That policy, as published, was the Howe Guidelines. But since policy is discretionary, it could change secretly, with a change of minister or a minister's change of mind. The law was what the government did, not what it said. So if there *was* a secret policy operating to allow weapons-related trade with Iraq, we might have a defence. But how could this be proved, when two ministers and two very senior civil servants would be called by the prosecution to deny it? Such a massive boost to Iraq's capacity to wage war would never have been permissible under the Howe Guidelines: this they maintained, with what seemed from their witness statements to be a straight face. Against the word of people of such probity, the case looked hopeless.

I cannot claim much credit for the action which burst a vast dam of mendacity, releasing a torrent which eventually drowned the prosecution and almost capsized the government. The tactic was obvious as we sat at our first meeting around the large table in my chambers in Doughty Street. What I said to Paul Henderson was 'the truth will set you free'. That is a trite sentiment but rare as professional advice: for someone facing jail it had a consequence that needed to be spelled out. 'If your story is true, there will be a paper mountain in Whitehall to prove it. Every meeting you had with MI6 would be written up, analysed and circulated. That will establish whether you really did tell them what Matrix Churchill was doing. You say you were encouraged by Alan Clark, who knew the tools were to make bombs – there will be official minutes of that meeting, briefing papers to the minister – that's the way Whitehall works. The truth will be trimmed and twisted a bit, but it will be there. If it's not there, then the jury will be sure you are lying and convict. If we don't ask for the documents, then maybe – just maybe – they will believe your word. Do you really want us to demand disclosure?'

Henderson answered in a way which demonstrated genuine surprise that I had found it necessary to ask. I had given carefully phrased warnings about how damaging it might be if he was *not* telling the truth, for in that case we would be excavating evidence *against* him – the downside for any defendant who demands disclosure. Paul's reaction was that of a man utterly and honestly convinced that the truth *would* set him free. So on 15 June 1991 we sent a formal four-page letter to the prosecution, demanding disclosure of all the documents which had to exist if Paul Henderson was innocent.

We were under no illusions about the difficulty of extracting this material – most of it would be embargoed from release for thirty years under the Public Records Act, while all MI5 and MI6 records of dealings with Henderson were suppressed by that Act for a century. But the law under which Paul was charged pivoted upon government policy, so we must be entitled to the documents which revealed what government policy really was. Further, Paul's defence was that 'HMG knew' because he had told it, as part of the information he was providing to MI6, and so it was essential to see records of what he had told his MI6 controller. Our application came just at the time when the Court of Appeal, overturning the wrongful conviction of Judith Ward for an IRA bombing, had warned prosecutors most emphatically of their duty to disclose all relevant documents to the defence.

I had no idea at the time of the fury that our discovery application caused in Whitehall departments, or that Alan Moses was climbing up the wall in anger at their reluctance to comply.

The heads of these departments decided to bring in their biggest guns – four senior government ministers, no less – to certify that the documents we needed for Paul's defence could not, in the national interest, be entrusted to us. These documents fell into two separate categories. There were policy documents – comprising some five hundred pages of minutes and memoranda to and from ministers which we hoped would demonstrate that no fewer than three departments – the DTI, the MOD and the Foreign and Commonwealth Office (FO) – knew that the Matrix Churchill machine tools were going to Iraq to make bombs and rockets; and intelligence documents – a swathe of several hundred pages from MI5 and MI6 recording some forty meetings with Henderson and his colleague, Matrix Churchill's sales director, Mark Gutteridge.

Release of the policy documents was essential if justice was to be done. Their release would cause no damage, in the sense that they gave away no secrets and revealed nothing which, eighteen months after the recapture of Kuwait, could further harm British relations with Iraq. Nevertheless Malcolm Rifkind (a QC) and Tristan Garel-Jones (a barrister) formally certified to the court that it was 'against the public interest to reveal the process of providing for ministers honest and candid advice on matters of high level policy'. Hence the production of the policy documents 'would be injurious to the public interest and it is necessary for the proper functioning of the public service that the documents should be withheld'.

These ministers were solemnly stating that secrecy was *essential* to the functioning of the public service. Their argument that future civil servants would be inhibited from giving 'frank and honest' advice to ministers because of the possibility it might be revealed in a court was insulting and irrational: on the contrary, the prospect of disclosure is a spur to candour and honesty. Indeed, the documents were to show that what civil servants had been giving ministers was not candid and honest advice at all: it was advice on how to be uncandid and dishonest, how to mislead Parliament and keep policy changes from the public. It was astonishing that anyone could think that such behaviour represented a public service functioning 'properly'. Michael Heseltine (ironically, the only non-barrister to sign a PII certificate) privately recognised the danger of injustice, but the Attorney General (Sir Nicholas Lyell QC) brushed aside his concerns and did not even bother to read the documents before directing that these certificates should be presented to the court, in an attempt to persuade the judge to withhold the documents from the defence. (The inability of all these barrister-ministers to comprehend where the interests of justice lay shows how important it is to remove politicians from having any role in criminal trials.)

Alan Moses was scrupulous to invite the judge to read the documents and make the final decision. The PII certificates were designed to stack the odds heavily against us, however, because they were government declarations that revelation would damage the national interest. The judge would weigh against that their importance to what he imagined the defence case would be, and here Alan made and repeated the claim that the documents would provide no assistance at all to the defence. This argument was (as Lord Justice Scott later found) 'quite unreal': I would have given my 'eye teeth' for them because their value for cross-examination was 'so obvious as to be hardly worth stating'. How could Alan Moses say otherwise? The fact that he was the fairest of prosecutors led one co-defending counsel to urge me to abandon the application.

The answer is important because it illustrates a limitation of the adversarial system. However competent and fair an advocate may be, he or she is nonetheless a player in the justice game. We become so psychologically committed to our own side that objective judgment becomes impossible. Alan had very little time to digest seven hundred photocopied pages, and he had no idea of our defence. He thought it would pivot on a technical quibble about whether the machine tools were 'specially designed' for arms, and to this the documents *were* irrelevant. He did not turn a blind eye, because his eyes were only focused on the case he had prepared according to his instructions. This astigmatism affects all counsel, and the fact that in the Matrix Churchill trial it affected the fairest serves forcefully to make the point that no prosecutor can be expected to decide what is truly relevant to the defence.

Are judges any better as determiners of what information the defence should have? Only marginally, I think, despite Judge Smedley's celebrated decision that we should have the policy documents. He had been placed under considerable pressure by ministerial claims that 'unquantifiable damage' would be caused by disclosure (under examination by Scott, Garel-Jones gave the risible reply that by this he intended to mean 'unquantifiably small' as well as 'unquantifiably large'). Smedley was a careful and cautious judge who agonised over his decision and came up with the Solomonic solution that the interests of the public service might be damaged in defending Mr Henderson, but not the interest of national security – so he denied us the intelligence documents. Faced with the ministerial certificates, I suspect many circuit judges would have buckled and denied the policy documents as well.

In respect of the intelligence documents – the MI5 and MI6 records of meetings with Henderson and Gutteridge – Home Secretary Kenneth Clarke certified:

'their disclosure is likely to prejudice national security by revealing matters knowledge of which would assist those whose purpose is to injure the security of the UK, and whose actions in the past have shown that they are willing to kill innocent civilians both inside and outside the UK in pursuance of this purpose'.

You can't argue against that. 'Innocent lives at stake' is the ultimate argument, one that when made by the Home Secretary of the day no court can ignore. The judge upheld it, as any judge was bound to do. Yet all I was asking for was the evidence of what *my client* had said to his controller, the best evidence to establish his defence that HMG knew about his arms-related contracts because he had told MI6 all about them. This was vital to prove his innocence and could not conceivably have put lives at risk. I did not even need the actual records of his meetings – a retyped transcript, without the MI6 layout, would have served. After the trial collapsed, the government would claim that PII certificates were formalities which judges could easily brush aside, and were in no sense 'gagging orders'. Ken Clarke's certificate was exactly that, because it played the one card – 'lives at stake' – which in litigation trumps all others.

Clark's PII certificate won the day: Judge Smedley upheld it and refused to let me see the intelligence documents. But wait a minute – on reading the *policy* documents overnight, it became apparent from them that Whitehall knew very well that the Matrix Churchill machine tools were going to make bombs. Where would they have obtained this knowledge, but from the Security and Intelligence Services? And where would SIS have obtained it, other than from its Matrix Churchill agents, Gutteridge and Henderson? So I decided to have another crack. The judge had ruled against me with the usual put-down that the defence was 'on a fishing expedition'. This has never seemed a good reason for refusing disclosure – probably because I am a keen fisherman and the object of all my fishing expeditions is to catch fish. What I needed for this exercise was a sufficiently strong line to reel in the MI6 catch. Barristers dislike revealing their defence until the last moment, but the logic of Paul's defence was that the truth would set him free, and the sooner the prosecution came to grips with it the better. It would mean blowing his cover by revealing in open court his spying role and that of his friend Mark Gutteridge. But Clarke's PII certificate left me no choice: it was ironical that the Home Secretary's hysterical claim that lives were at stake was itself an action which put these two innocent lives at some risk. It was with mixed feelings that I rose to renew my application for the intelligence documents.

> The case against Henderson is that he deceived the government. We will show that the government was not for one moment deceived. We intend to support that proposition by evidence that the Security and Intelligence Services, the agents of the government in this matter, were supplied by Paul Henderson himself, and to Paul Henderson's knowledge by Mark Gutteridge, a colleague and fellow employee of Matrix Churchill, with information about all the Matrix Churchill dealings with Iraq . . . There is no doubt that records exist of the meetings between them and their respective SIS controllers . . . we contend that the Home Secretary is under a legal and moral duty to disclose these records. It arises from the fact that Mr Henderson was prevailed upon, despite a risk to his life and to his job, to provide detailed information about the activities of senior Iraqi intelligence officers . . . he cannot now be denied the evidence which arises from his loyal work for the Crown and which is necessary for his defence to a serious criminal charge.

The argument went on – legal arguments always do – but in its course Alan Moses interrupted, first to agree with its legal basis (that disclosure to MI6 was disclosure to HMG) and then actually to concede. He asked for a short adjournment to consult SIS, and returned to promise the intelligence documents that very afternoon. In a matter of minutes, documents the revelation of which the Home Secretary had sworn would endanger innocent lives were to be handed over – without even bothering to tell him that his PII certificate had just been torn up and binned. I doubt whether the judge would otherwise have decided the point in our favour, since he had decided against us on the previous day. But now, suddenly relieved by the prosecution of any need to weigh justice to the defendants against possible loss of life, he ordered the release. After the trial the media fêted him as a liberal hero, although this accolade more accurately belongs to Alan Moses, who took the decision that justice came first, ahead of the Home Secretary's wild claims about national security. He demonstrated the virtue of a system which entrusts control of prosecutions to barristers independent of the State.

Put together with the policy material, in a vast chronology, spanning ninety-two pages and the decade from the beginning of the Iran/Iraq War to the invasion of Kuwait, these documents transformed the trial. The story they told was that the defendants had not deceived HMG: on the contrary, HMG knew and HMG approved.

It was a story of a government which wanted it both ways. It wanted to strut the world stage wringing clean hands about the horror of the long war between Iran and Iraq which cost one million lives, while at the same time encouraging British business to profit by helping the warring parties to kill each other. To cash in and to condemn while cashing in, that was the object. It was accomplished because the sermons were publicly delivered through one great department of State (the FO) and the arms were delivered by secret permission of another (the DTI), while a third (the MOD) looked on apprehensively. It was a classic exercise in diplomatic hypocrisy, but if the cake was to be both had and eaten, the British people and their irritating representatives in Parliament (who were always asking questions in the hope of getting their names in the newspapers) had to be kept in the dark. Ministers answered their questions by obfuscating, then by equivocating and then quite simply by lying. The only people who knew they were lying were the civil servants who drafted the mendacious answers, sometimes for ministers so naive that they did not realise they were lying. Vast amounts of defence-related exports were licensed for Iraq (or for Jordan, in the knowledge that it was a 'front' for Iraq). On 1 August 1990, Saddam spoilt it all by invading Kuwait.

Until this point both faces of the British State had smiled on Paul Henderson. He had been permitted by the DTI to export to munitions factories, on which he spied for the FO. He had been run by MI6 (which works under FO cover) and had risked his life gathering information about Iraq's armaments on his visits to its closely guarded weapons factories. The reason he had such unique access was simple: he was exporting arms-making equipment to these factories. Indeed, the Coventry company of which he was managing director was actually owned by the Iraqi government and chaired by the head of its arms-procurement effort, the high-ranking intelligence officer Dr Saffa Al-Habobi. Anyone who knew these facts could deduce that Matrix Churchill was in the business of supplying arms-related equipment to Saddam. So were many other bigger and better-known British companies, like Racal and Plessy. As a result, Britain gained money, jobs and friendly diplomatic relations. To enjoy these benefits, it was necessary to overlook the brutal nature of Iraq's Ba'athist regime, and the fact that on 17 March 1988 its army loosed off hydrogen cyanide at Helebja killing 5,000 Kurds and maiming 7,000 for life. Saddam would use his British machine-tool-made arms to kill Kurds and Iranians (until the truce in August 1988), and thereafter would use them to kill other peoples he hated, most especially Jews and Saudis, although it was the Kuwaitis he turned on first – calculating that countries happy to sell him military technology would not object too strenuously if he used it.

The cost-benefit analysis of weapons-related trade with Iraq would, one might think (if one were not William Waldegrave), be worth debating in any democracy – in Parliament, on television and in pubs and clubs throughout the land. But it could *not* be debated or even mentioned, for then our diplomats would be unable to affect a high moral tone at conferences in Geneva and New York. And any debate might upset the highly strung Saddam and cause him to take his trade elsewhere. So the government decided that democratic debate there should not be. The Howe Guidelines were altered without any publicity. The changes, permitting substantial defence exports to Iraq, were made in secret and communicated in secret to exporters, who were told to ship their goods quietly. This truth could be gleaned from the documents, in hand-written comments by departmental heads: 'We must keep as quiet as possible about this politically sensitive issue. We do not wish to face the FO with presentational difficulties,' said one mandarin from the DTI. 'If it becomes public knowledge that the tools are to be used to make munitions, deliveries would have to stop at once. The companies should be urged to produce and ship as fast as they can,' said a very senior diplomat at the FO, secretly conniving at a massive breach of the Howe Guidelines.

This suited Paul Henderson. He had been given the message by Trade Minister Alan Clark in person at their meeting in January 1988 – export bomb-making equipment, but don't mention anything military. So on the licence applications his firm sent to the DTI the purpose was described as 'general engineering'. The forms made plain, however, that his machine tools were going to Nassr, well known as Saddam's biggest bomb factory. Logically, there can only be one use for general engineering tools in a factory dedicated to making bombs. The DTI already knew it because MI6 had told them repeatedly. Everybody within Whitehall cleared to receive intelligence information knew: it was no secret, except from the public. Paul Henderson happily signed contracts for machine tools capable of making bomb and rocket fuses. He kept visiting Iraq and meeting MI6 afterwards (some twenty times in 1989 and 1990) for debriefings. The documents showed he was a good manager, a good engineer and a good spy.

The invasion of Kuwait had brought the cosy accommodation with Saddam Hussein to a sticky end, and ministers and diplomats affected moral fervour against a man they now likened to Hitler. How could they then face the awful possibility that the bombs made by the technology they had permitted him to import from Britain would be used to kill British soldiers? As Operation Desert Storm gathered in early 1991, with an election only a year ahead, it became a political impossibility for the Conservative government to admit its role in arming Saddam. So the equivocation in Parliament became blatant dishonesty (the Howe Guidelines had been 'scrupulously and carefully followed' said a DTI minister in January 1991). But would anyone sniff out the truth? Paul Henderson's arrest and charge (a week after the Iraqi surrender) had the consequence of shutting up the media, which could not thereafter comment without committing contempt of court. It also stymied a parliamentary committee investigation into the 'Super-gun', since all the evidence was now *sub judice*: senior DTI officials could and did refuse to testify on the pretext that this might prejudice Henderson's trial. The only downside was that government documents revealing the truth might be required by Henderson's defence. So officials decided to resist disclosure by the device of the PII certificate. The case was committed for trial in November 1991 with two PIIs (from Kenneth Baker and Peter Lilley) up the government sleeve which would stop the truth about Britain's 'Iraqgate' emerging in the magistrate's court. It had not emerged by April 1992, when the Conservatives won the general election. Had the extent of their involvement become public before then, together with their misleading of Parliament, the result of that election might have been different.

That, matter of factly, is what happened – at least on my reading of the documents. Scott was correct to conclude that there was no conspiracy, in the sense that there was no grand design, or grand designer. When under threat, the State (its mandarins as much as its ministers) protects itself instinctively, like an octopus disturbed by a stick. The coils swirl in different directions, the overall pattern is unplanned, but the motive is always self-protection: damage to others is incidental. There was no masterplan or master-planner, no shadowy Whitehall manipulator who decided to make Paul Henderson a scapegoat so that the government could keep the lid on the scandal until after the election. The prosecution of Matrix Churchill was not a conspiracy, but nor was it a cock-up in the sense of a series of accidents or a coincidence of incompetencies. It was a lot of people, each with some small amount of power, jerking their knees in protection of the State.

A senior civil servant at the DTI exemplified the prevailing mindset, shortly before the invasion of Kuwait, when on hearing of a Customs Investigation of Matrix Churchill he asked his ministers in a memo, 'Do you really want the DTI's dirty washing aired in court?' Of course they did not: ministers and civil servants alike were convinced of the need to cover up the stains. So pressure was put on Customs to drop the investigation. After the invasion, however, it became much more convenient for the government to have Henderson charged and tried. PII certificates were relied on to keep the dirty washing under wraps, and other measures were taken, such as trimming witness statements, in an attempt to keep the dirt from festering in the evidence. I think this is what Scott meant when, having found so many people responsible for trimming the truth, he exonerated all of them from having acted in bad faith. They were not acting maliciously, but reacting like men who had taken instinctive decisions to protect the State from embarrassment, in the genuine belief that this was for the public good. Scott exculpated the makers of these decisions because they sincerely believed it was for the best. But their sincerity stemmed from the improper assumption that protection of the State is more important than justice to the individual or honesty to Parliament.

These decisions were all directed to making it more difficult to establish Paul Henderson's innocence. Many of them concerned items of relevant information they did not want me to know (hence they were edited out of the witness statements) or relevant documents they did not want me to see (hence the PII certificates). The witness statements supplied by the Crown showed a regular, properly brought and fully evidenced prosecution. The full story, once the secret documents were fed into the master chronology, was sensationally different. The truth *would* set Paul Henderson free. The problem was to get the trial to tell it.

If this trial were to proceed, the nature and extent of Henderson's contacts with MI6 would have to be publicly revealed in his defence. The prosecution had served an unsigned statement from 'John Balsom', his MI6 controller, carefully crafted to play down his importance. It made no mention of the fact that before Henderson's visits to Iraq he was warned solemnly and scarily about the risks he was taking. To drive the warnings home, Balsom had given him a book entitled *Republic of Fear* written by a dissident Iraqi. Paul had kept the book, which described Saddam Hussein as a megalomaniac whose secret police and court system were deployed to torture and execute 'spies, saboteurs and foreign agents'. If this was MI6's warning to its agent, then he was not merely a businessman who passed on trifling information: he was a spy tasked to risk his life. The book made very clear that any exposure of his spying role would make him, as long as he lived, a target for Iraqi vengeance. He might be safe for the moment, while Iraq was licking its war-wounds, but in years to come he would be one of the Saddamned, a traitor marked out for vengeance.

This was the most worrying thing about the prosecution of Paul Henderson. He had done the State much service, at the risk of his life. That did not of itself mean that he was innocent, but it did mean that he would be punished irrespective of his guilt or innocence merely by being put on public trial and having to raise his intelligence work as a defence. This was a painful inducement for him to plea-bargain rather than to reveal his role as a spy. He would make, in this way, the perfect scapegoat: a man who would have to carry his knowledge of secret government approvals with him to jail, because the alternative – an Iraqi assassination – was less pleasant than a short prison sentence in return for a plea of guilty. This was exactly what had happened earlier in the year when Paul Grecian (the 'Ordtech' director who had first told the intelligence services about the 'Supergun') pleaded guilty in order to keep his own spying role secret from the Iraqis – although in return he had been offered a suspended prison sentence. I later represented him at his appeal, which succeeded after we obtained documents which had been wrongfully withheld. They included this chilling MI6 memo:

> If Ordtech ends up in court Grecian may be persuaded to keep quiet about his connection, but there is the obvious risk he would try the 'working for British intelligence' ploy . . . However, his personal future might be in some doubt if ever publicly identified as the man who blew the gaff on the Iraqi Babylon [Supergun] project. If we were not too squeamish we might use this point to ensure silence.

Paul Henderson had no intention of keeping quiet to protect his personal future. His dilemma was agonising, although I knew the intelligence services were in a double bind as well. They routinely debrief businessmen who travel to countries which pose potential threats to world peace or to British interests, and confirmation of this fact in court would increase the danger to British citizens – whether involved with MI6 or not – whose jobs took them within the jurisdiction of paranoid regimes. They would be most unhappy to learn that if prosecuted by an independent agency like Customs, MI6 might abandon them or even give evidence against them. On the other hand, it might be no bad thing to emphasize that they cannot obtain immunity from English law by doing intelligence work on the side. Only one person could, constitutionally, resolve the dilemma: the Attorney General. As guardian of the public interest, it was his duty to make the most careful investigation of this case, weighing the public interests at stake and permitting the trial to go ahead only if the evidence of Henderson's guilt was overwhelming. This never happened, and his failure to take a grip on the case was the basis upon which Scott found him 'personally at fault'. But it was by now the second week of October, and all government ministers were preoccupied: it was the 1992 Tory Party conference. The trial would go ahead.

'I know you think this trial will be important. I do too, and I've told my editor. But . . .', – Britain's best investigative reporter, working for the trenchant *World in Action*, lowered his eyes to study the blue carpet on the floor of the Old Bailey courtroom – 'but my producer has heard some silly rumour about John Major having an affair with a cook and has ordered me to look into that instead of covering the Matrix Churchill trial.'

It was the opening day of the trial. I looked from the shamefaced David Leigh across to the press box, which would remain largely empty for the next few weeks until the prosecution was on the point of collapse. For all the ministers and civil servants and government lawyers these proceedings would ultimately draw into the lashing coils of its post-mortem, the media would go scot-free. It neither covered nor comprehended the case, after its combined investigative talents had failed to discover how 'UK Ltd' had been arming Iraq in contravention of stated government policy ever since that policy was first stated by Geoffrey Howe back in 1985. The Old Bailey press gang had been and gone, doing their usual thing of reporting the prosecution opening, then disappearing to cover rape and murder trials until returning, vulture-like, for the verdict. The BBC did not attend at all until the very last day. (One of their most experienced reporters had asked to be assigned to what he described as 'the political trial of the century': they sent him on a course instead.)

By contrast, the *New York Times* had made itself aware that information of some importance might emerge at the Old Bailey concerning allied policy towards arming Saddam in the years before his invasion of Kuwait, a scandal they had dubbed 'Iraqgate'. They assigned Dean Bacquet to the case, who turned up one morning to meet me at court, but was refused entry: he was black and he lacked the pass issued to 'approved' court reporters by the Metropolitan Police. I went down to the front desk to greet him through the security gates: 'Don't worry, I'll arrange for you to come into court so you can sit in the press box'. He smiled and shook his head, and said what no British reporter would ever contemplate: 'That's OK, I'd prefer to sit in the public gallery'. And he did, overlooking and overlooked by the prosecution on one day when the press box was empty, and it revealed how allied intelligence learned about the Iraqi procurement network in 1987 – three years before the arms it procured were used in the invasion of Kuwait. Mr Bacquet's week of anonymity in the public gallery produced three stories for the front page of the *New York Times*, yet still the BBC and the British press did not bother to attend. The most regular exception was Richard Norton-Taylor of the *Guardian*: he was one journalist who, when the trial collapsed, had any real idea why.

We made a bad start with the jury. When asked whether there were any classes of juror we wanted to exclude, my fear was of Jews: Matrix Churchill machine tools had made rockets, and the memory of Scuds hitting Tel Aviv was all too fresh. But I phrased my objection ineptly and the judge would have none of it. The jury was sworn, and Alan Moses delivered the first two hours of his carefully prepared address before the lunch break. That is when the Jewish juror declared: 'I'm sorry, I've got relations in Tel Aviv; thinking of them makes me emotional. I wouldn't have an open mind.' He need not have apologised – others might have sat silently and put their prejudices into play in the jury room. He was replaced, and Alan had to recite his opening all over again for the newcomer's benefit. The incident brought home just how difficult it was going to be to scale the mountain of animosity against anyone who had – government permission or no – done deals with Saddam Hussein.

Over the next fortnight, I lived a double life. By day in court I would examine engineers about the technical capacities of lathes and milling machines. By night I would take a magic carpet ride on the documents covering my desk at Doughty Street, from the secret corridors of Whitehall to the arms factories of Baghdad. This was the big political picture of how Iraq established a procurement network for its vast munitions factories, making weapons described as 'conventional' – a comfortable adjective that eased the conscience of those who approved the export of raw materials and machine tools which could turn them into unconventional weapons: rockets and missiles capable of delivering chemical gas and nuclear bombs. It is tritely said, by arms dealers and their apologists, that weapons are neither good nor bad – moral judgment can only be made on people who use them. What the documents revealed, however, was precisely the opposite: the Thatcher government's moral judgments *were* being made on the weapons and not their wielders. 'Conventional rockets good, nuclear and ballistic missiles bad' was their simplistic thinking, without realising the overlap and without reading the MI6 runes about Saddam and his regime. Why were copies of *Republic of Fear* not placed in the red boxes of Clark and Trefgarne and Waldegrave?

For the numerous Tory ministers who visited and courted Iraq in this period, the country was simply a marvellous trading opportunity. That it was a tyranny with an agenda which extended to the destruction of its neighbours gave them no pause at all. Alan Clark could at least justify his position on the crude basis that it was no bad thing if unpleasant Arabs kill each other, and it was even better if Britain made money out of it. William Waldegrave, the Fellow of All Souls, shrank from such uncouth honesty. His officials were becoming alarmed: by February 1989 their internal memos recorded their understanding that Iraq was developing a nuclear capacity and their belief that the machine tools were 'essential for the production of nuclear weapons'. Senior F.O. mandarin David Gore-Booth sent Waldegrave a memo stating that he was 'distinctly uncomfortable' at the prospect of British machine tools contributing to Iraq's nuclear programme. The minister wrote in the margin, in spidery hand, this pearl of moral absolution: 'Screwdrivers can be required to make hydrogen bombs!' This personal 'Eureka' echoed around the doors of the Foreign and Commonwealth Office. It was repeated like a mantra in their internal memos: 'Please note the minister's comment that screwdrivers can also make nuclear bombs'.

What really did for William Waldegrave was not the poverty of his thinking but his terror of sharing it with Parliament or the public. It was he, not Alan Clark, who insisted that the changes to the Guidelines must be kept secret – because, Scott suggests, he was too afraid to defend them. He personally devised 'a form of words to use if we are now pressed in Parliament over the Guidelines'. They were to say: 'The Guidelines on the export of defence equipment to Iran and Iraq are kept under constant review, and are applied in the light of the prevailing circumstances, including the cease-fire and the developments in the peace negotiations'.

This was a masterpiece of paltering equivocation. It was not so much economical with the truth as positively parsimonious with it. How, under this formula, could MPs ever divine that the guidelines for defence sales had tilted to Iraq so drastically as to allow a vast range of military equipment which was being withheld from Iran? Scott concluded there was a 'deliberate failure' to tell Parliament the truth about arms sales policy, and that 'the overriding and determinative reason was fear of strong public opposition'.

It was serious enough for a government to hide the tilt to Iraq from Parliament, but even more serious to attempt to hide it from a criminal court where it was relevant to the defence of men facing serious charges. In this respect, the DTI evidence was brazen. A licensing official was put up as a prosecution witness to say on oath: 'if we approved a licence to Iraq it would not be for military or military-related goods. If it were for straightforward general engineering, no military involvement, then there was a possibility a licence would be approved, but if there was any military element to it then a licence would be refused.'

The truth, to the DTI's knowledge, was quite the contrary: massive exports to Iraq with a military element had been regularly approved. The DTI had actually sold £987 million worth of high-tech military equipment to Iraq's defence ministry and its army and airforce in the years prior to 1990, throughout the period when the Howe Guidelines were ostensibly in operation. Even during its war with Iran we sold a £4 million battlefield communication system for five hundred stations; we sold millions of pounds' worth of jet engines and navigation equipment for Iraq's jet fighters; night-vision equipment, a 'quick-fire artillery control system' and 'hostile fire indicators' for the army; while Racal and Plessy won multi-million pound contracts to supply 'battlefield encryption units' to encode messages during the fighting. The list went on and on, ranging from a computer command control for the airforce to diagnostic testing kits to check whether soldiers had AIDS. (This was said to be a 'humanitarian exception', although Iraq's punishment for its soldiers who tested positive would not have been humane.)

One DTI witness pretended that nothing would have been licensed for export to Nassr had they known it might have a military use – time and again the documents confounded him:

Q: Now, rifles and shotguns are lethal equipment, are they not?
A: Yes.
Q: Just look will you please at page ten. Here you approve a licence to export some £88,000 worth of rifles and shotguns to the Nassr State enterprise.
A: Yes.
Q: And we find the entry 'sporting use'?
A: Yes.
Q: What sport was being played at Nassr that required these shotguns?
A: I don't know.
Q: Nassr was not a game park. They were going to kill humans, not animals?
A: I don't know.
Q: Do you really want to confirm your earlier answer that 'if there was any military element to it a licence would be refused . . .'?
A: Well, as you say they are lethal weapons and . . .
Q: They were, and they were going to Nassr?
A: Yes.

Q: Are you really telling us that throughout your time as DTI representative on the Inter-Departmental Licensing Committee you had no idea what Nassr was?

A: Yes, I am saying that.

Q: Here you were approving a licence for shotguns to go to a place and you had no idea what it was?

A: Well I do not recall that particular case, I'm afraid.

The government knew that Matrix Churchill machine tools were going to make munitions at Nassr, and secretly approved their export for this purpose. All that was required to stop this trial was to find a witness who was prepared to say so without equivocation. Frankness was not forthcoming from the DTI. Its most senior official was Eric Beston, nicknamed 'Sir Humphrey' at the Bar table on account of his slip-sliding answers. He would not accept that he knew the machine tools would make munitions. Yes, he knew that they were going to Nassr, and yes he knew that the factory made munitions, but he did not 'necessarily' know that the machine tools would be used there to make munitions. (He had written to superiors some time before the trial: 'Cross-examination could prove tricky. Departments were aware that machines were destined for munitions manufacture.') Beston cut a sorry figure at the Scott Inquiry when confronted with his misleading answers. 'I got myself into quite a tangle . . . I simply misled myself . . . I got myself into a state of confusion.' At the time, I felt he was trying to get *me* into a state of confusion. Scott's conclusion was that 'Mr Beston's evidence given at trial . . . was not frank evidence but was overly conditioned by a desire to avoid answers that might prove embarrassing to senior officials and ministers of his department'.

The intelligence documents Kenneth Clarke alleged would put lives at risk were eventually delivered to my chambers by commercial motor-bike. Much of the information on them was blacked out, or 'redacted' – an awful Americanism our civil servants have borrowed from the CIA because it sounds better than 'censored'. The censorship was not consistent: sometimes the well known and widely published postal addresses of MI5 ('Box 500') and MI6 ('Box 850') would be blacked out – truly a redaction *ad absurdum*. The judge, unaware how frequently they had been published over the last twenty years, seemed to think that they were a top-secret code, and could not understand why they were mentioned in court. He had, like the prosecutors, been 'positively vetted', and his attitude to anything alleged to involve national security made cross-examination akin to talking on eggshells.

The Crown had no option but to call the two secret servicemen who had been Gutteridge and Henderson's controllers, to try to block Paul's defence that 'HMG knew'. They came to court with all the aura of the secret State to enhance their testimony: the jury would want to believe them, because they had the imprimatur of organisations we all trusted with the fight against the IRA and the KGB. Moreover, their credibility would be enhanced by the security precautions the judge was determined to take: a specially built witness box, curtained off from the press and the public gallery, with entrance through a special passageway. Their real names would not be known, their background and expertise would be taken for granted. All these precautions would cry out to the jury, 'Believe these men. They are testifying to you at the risk of their lives.' The normal arrangements which conduce to truth-telling by witnesses – the simple fact that they are seen for what they are, and can be prosecuted for perjury if they lie – would be missing. That fate can hardly befall a pseudonym.

Balsom, the man from MI6, was tricked up in an ill-fitting wig and spectacles of clear glass. Did he, I wondered, feel any real friendship for Paul Henderson, or was he regarded merely as an agent to be milked of information and then professionally disconnected when he became an embarrassment? The latter, I suspected, and it coloured my initial approach to this witness whose statement had been so niggardly with the truth. No serving MI6 officer had ever given evidence in court before, and Paul certainly had the sense – it was deeply and hurtfully felt – that the agency had abandoned him. We feared Balsom would be well rehearsed for his public debut, trained to play the cross-examiner's nightmare – a skilled witness adept at turning your every question to your client's disadvantage. So I had prepared a different style of examination, one which would try to disconcert him before taking him to task over the gaps in his witness statement.

I started my prepared line of questioning, hoping that it would disrupt his prepared line of answering. Then, somewhat to my surprise, in explaining his concern that Saddam was developing nuclear weapons, he added 'And thank God he didn't'. For the first time in this trial – which had now lasted four weeks – you could sense a jolt of passion. All the previous witnesses had spoken of Saddam Hussein as if he were as morally neutral as their milkman. This witness had just given away, by invoking the deity, the fact that he really cared about the potential victims. So I changed mental gear, closed my notebook and opened instead the book he had given to Paul – *Republic of Fear*:

Q: You remember giving him this book?
A: Yes.
Q: And inviting him to read it to understand just how dangerous the characters and personalities he was dealing with were?
A: Yes. And also because I think that it is a superb description of the appalling regime in Iraq.
Q: Its message is that there has been a ruthless and relentless build-up in Iraq of terror; and that Iraq was a dictatorship based on terror?
A: Yes, I agree.
Q: And it describes Saddam Hussein himself as the only genuinely free man in Iraq, as a megalomaniac whose secret police and court system have been devised to torture and execute those who were disloyal to the State?
A: Yes.
Q: And it particularly stresses that disloyalty was regarded as acts of spying, or hostility to the State?
A: Yes.

This was MI6 speaking. If the regime was so terrifying, what did they think of the man whom they were encouraging to spy on it? Balsom did not even draw breath – he blurted out the character reference before I had finished the question:

Balsom: Mr Henderson was a very brave man. Together with all the pressures on his business, to take this extra risk he was extremely brave. There are very few people who would take such risks and take them so much in their stride, with all the pressures on him.
Q: You accept that in Iraq he was running personal risks?

A: Absolutely. Our relationship was voluntary, but as I say he was a very, very brave man.

This was the most electric, transforming moment of the trial. For four weeks the jury had heard about Paul Henderson the deceiver of ministers and the merchant of death. They had been bored stiff by my questions to engineers about 'special design', a possible technical defence, and they had fidgeted while I fenced with fork-tongued civil-servants. Suddenly, the full horror of Iraq had broken through the verbiage, and the man in the dock had been turned into someone more deserving of a medal than a prison sentence. I was simply thrilled – I could feel my neck hairs tingle under the horse-hair of the wig. Paul Henderson's courage had been a burden for months, and now, for whatever reason, it had been lifted. Was this MI6's answer to Customs, its punishment of the prosecution for putting its agent's life in peril? Or was it what it really seemed: a spontaneous and heartfelt answer? That was how the jury took it, and they began to narrow their eyes in the direction of the prosecutors.

That afternoon, Alan Moses became so concerned about the propriety of prosecuting a man who had rendered such service to his country that he doubted whether he should continue with the case. His anxiety was relayed to the head of Customs, Sir Brian Unwin, who fired off a highly improper letter of complaint to Sir Colin McColl, the head of MI6. 'We were extremely surprised – to say the least – at the nature of the testimonial your officer gave to Henderson in response to questions from Henderson's counsel . . .' It received a robust response from Sir Colin: 'Whilst I can quite see why this was less than welcome to prosecuting counsel, I myself see no cause for criticism where a witness speaks sincerely and impartially on such a matter'. Lord Justice Scott, asked later to referee this extraordinary spat, fully agreed with MI6: 'That Mr Henderson had been at great personal risk should have been blindingly obvious to Customs and to anyone else who considered the matter. Mr Barzoft's fate demonstrated the fact.'

I was not privy to the prosecution's disarray: I was too busy preparing for the big event of the morrow, the confrontation with Alan Clark. His reputation preceded him into the witness box. He was an intelligent and witty historian. (Where did you read history? he was asked. 'In an armchair,' he replied.) He had a classy lifestyle and a sweep of mind that made journalists fawn (his sex life had yet to hit the headlines). In the familiar bestiary of the British class nursery, I suppose Alan Clark is Mr Toad: an animal of somewhat reckless vanity who nonetheless inspires great affection from kind and decent colleagues, but provokes the constituted authorities – policemen, judges, permanent secretaries – to humourless rages. His obsessions are as fervent as Toad's, his home (Saltwood Castle) even more stately and his collection of vintage cars just as impressive. He stood out from the stoats and the weasels of the Thatcher regime, partly because he was more honest and partly because he was completely untouched by the petty corruption and petty cowardice in which many of them were mired. Like Toad, he escapes. The government tried to make him the sole scapegoat for the collapse of the Matrix Churchill trial, but he persuaded Lord Justice Scott that he was not to blame. I do not myself approve of all that he says or does, but I approve of him, for a fairly simple reason: Alan Clark genuinely cared about the possibility of Paul Henderson's innocence.

I did not know this, of course. I had never met the man. I had his witness statement which was implacably hostile, and a recent press cutting from which he seemed more friendly. My approach to our day together at the Old Bailey was to try to get inside a head that might turn too easily. There was no point in trying to bully or cajole: he was a politician, experienced in playing with words, and a wit adept at playing on words. He could be hostile if put on his mettle by criticism, or derisive if stung by sarcasm. I really had no idea what would happen, just an inkling that the key to it all might be history. The documents were the raw material of history, and Clark was by training and predilection a historian. So cross-examination would work, if at all, as a history seminar, in which Clark the popular historian would interpret, with some prompting, an episode laid bare in contemporary documents. That was, I think, how and why we got on.

The seminar was to last only three hours, but by its end Alan Clark had demolished the prosecution. Our history book was the 'defence bundle' of five hundred indexed pages extracted over the Government's objection from the secret policy and intelligence documents: without it, the cross-examination would simply not have been possible. Clark relaxed, after a time, and gave us his interpretation of the events in which he featured at the centre, almost as a fly on his own ministerial wall. He explained how the 'tiresome and intrusive' guidelines had been secretly changed to 'tilt to Iraq' in the supply of conventional weapons. He was invited to decode the official minutes of his meeting with Henderson and other machine tool manufacturers on 20 January 1988. It had been called because the DTI had learned – from information supplied by Gutteridge to the Intelligence Services – that Iraq had ordered machine tools to equip its munitions factories. With this knowledge, the government had to decide whether to license their export, and if so, whether to encourage Matrix Churchill to fulfil future orders from the same Iraqi factories.

Choosing his words carefully and noting that the Iraqis would be using the current orders for general engineering purposes Mr Clark stressed that it was important for the UK companies to agree a specification with the customer in advance which highlighted the peaceful, i.e. non-military, use to which the machine tools would be put.

On the true meaning of this sentence in the official minutes, the trial was about to turn.

Q: The writer of this minute is attributing to you a statement: 'The Iraqis will be using the current order for general engineering purposes' – *which cannot be correct to your knowledge*.
A: Well, it's our old friend 'being economical', isn't it?
Q: With the truth?
A: With the *actualité*. There was nothing misleading to make a formal or introductory comment that the Iraqis would be using the current orders for 'general engineering purposes'.
Q: You go on to say, in the same breath, at least in the minute-taker's breath, 'Mr Clark stressed that it was important for the UK companies to agree a specification in advance which highlighted that peaceful, i.e. non-military, use to which the machine tools would be put'. In saying that, of course you knew that the machine tools were currently being put to a munitions use. And that the

follow-on orders, so long as the Iran/Iraq war lasted, would also be likely to be put to a munitions use?

A: Could be put, yes.

Q: Yes. In this context, knowing that, you invited the companies to agree a specification, i.e. get something in writing 'to highlight the peaceful use to which the machine tools would be put.' Even though to your knowledge, it was, at least so long as the war lasted, very unlikely they *would* be put to a peaceful use.

A: Yes, I would agree with that.

Q: And so, you want to receive at the DTI in future some sort of written specification or indication that these future consignments, these 'follow-on orders', are going to a peaceful use – a 'general engineering' use?

A: Yes.

Q: A specification which highlights a peaceful use?

A: I doubt I used 'highlighted'; I think I would have said 'emphasise'.

Q: Emphasising or stressing, the peaceful use that they would have?

A: Yes.

Q: You didn't want to let anyone know that, at this stage, these machines and their follow-up orders were going to munitions factories to make munitions?

A: No.

Q: And the emphasis on 'peaceful purposes' and 'general engineering' and so on would help keep the matter confidential?

A: I do not think it was principally a matter for public awareness. I think it was probably a matter for Whitehall cosmetics.

Q: A matter for Whitehall cosmetics, to keep the records ambiguous?

A: Yes, yes.

Q: So the signal you are sending to these people is 'I am the minister. I will help you get these orders, and the follow-up orders, through the rather loose guidelines and the rather Byzantine ways of Whitehall. Help me by keeping your mouth firmly shut about military use.'

A: I think that is too imaginative an interpretation. I think it was more at arm's length than that.

Q: But in any event it was how they would help you, by not making the Whitehall cosmetics run, but rather by keeping quiet, stating 'nothing military'?

A: Yes. I do not think they needed that advice from me but,—

Q: But they got it?

A: Not in so many words, I do not think I said 'nothing military'.

Q: They got it by implication?

A: Yes, by implication is different. By implication they got it.

This was an admission that the crime for which the defendant's liberty had been endangered – deceiving the government by not stating a military use on export application forms – had been instigated by the government itself. It was an admission by an historian that itself made history, because after it the trial could not continue. Alan Moses so advised the Attorney General, who had no alternative but to withdraw the prosecution. Confused and panic-stricken briefings issued from Downing Street, seeming to blame Alan Clark for telling the truth.

All the media did attend at last, on the day the trial collapsed, to photograph the defendants with their victory champagne and to begin to work out how 'UK Ltd' had armed Saddam. The withdrawal of the prosecution meant that the policy documents ministers had tried to suppress could be provided to Robin Cook, who used them to great effect in forcing the Prime Minister to establish the Scott inquiry. On becoming Foreign Secretary several years later, Cook's first announcement was that henceforth human rights would be a central consideration in policy-making. This lesson he may have learned from reading the five hundred pages of documents about the making of British policy towards Iraq, and discovering that human rights were not once mentioned.

That it should take a criminal trial to expose Iraqgate rather than an investigation by Parliament or the media is in one sense an outrage, but in another a reassurance: try as it might, the State cannot confidently use legal proceedings as a tool for suppression. That was the lesson of the ABC trial, where there was nothing of embarrassment to cover up, and it was the more painful lesson of Matrix Churchill, where there was. No doubt the State can and has succeeded from time to time: it did with Ordtech, where a judge refused to direct the prosecution to produce vital documents. It did not work here because Paul Henderson was not prepared to accept the role of scapegoat. And once he had taken that position, the State became bound by the rules of the justice game, where the penalties for cheating are severe and the prospects of being found out by the other side should never be discounted.

The Matrix Churchill trial collapsed on 9 November 1992, and a few days later Lord Justice Richard Scott was appointed to conduct an inquiry. His meticulous, non-judgmental approach produced precision analysis of what had gone wrong: 'constitutional impropriety' beginning with a criminal law permitted to pivot upon secretly changeable government policy and ending with an approach to public interest immunity which was wrong in principle and absurd in practice. Scott's severest strictures were reserved for the witnesses who had misled us and for the 'in-house' lawyers who had approved the trimming of their evidence. Nicholas Lyell, the Attorney General, was found 'personally at fault' for his failure to take seriously his own public interest duty to supervise the prosecution. William Waldegrave was firmly identified as the architect of the policy to 'designedly mislead' Parliament by pretending there had been no change in the Howe Guidelines: although he had been acting honestly, he was held to have breached repeatedly the convention of ministerial responsibility to Parliament. This gave rise to a not very good joke: 'There are three different ways of breaching the principle of ministerial accountability. They are, in ascending order of seriousness, the grave, the very grave, and the Waldegrave.'

Publication of Scott's inquiry findings in February 1996 was a defining moment for the government. It came replete with a massive disinformation exercise presented by Ian Lang, President of the Board of Trade, involving a propagandistic distortion of an 1,800-page report which opposition spokesmen had been given only three hours to read. The puerility of this behaviour, and the shameful failure of any member of the government to apologise to the defendants for a trial which everyone agreed should never have taken place, made for one of the most unedifying episodes in recent British politics. At 10.45 p.m. on 26 February 1996, I watched from the *Newsnight* studio as MPs trooped through the lobbies on the censure motion over the Scott Report: the government's winning margin was by one single vote. 'The end of the Matrix Churchill affair?' Peter Snow taunted. 'Just the beginning,' I replied, for want of anything better to say.

On election night, over a year later, the BBC cameras recorded a different story: the whey-faced William Waldegrave, the trembling Malcolm Rifkind, the traumatised Ian Lang, lined up like aristocrats off the tumbrel to be guillotined by the returning officer. The blade of people's justice cut deep: the heads of most other ministers and MPs who played minor roles in the affair rolled into the basket of oblivion. Future historians may well attribute the beginning of the Labour landslide in 1997 to the rumblings of Matrix Churchill after the trial collapsed: first Scott's much reported hearings, the leaks from his report and finally the report itself, showing how Parliament was misled. Some Tory seats might have been saved had just one minister accepted responsibility and resigned, or even offered an apology to the defendants, but *hubris* dictated otherwise. The mistake the government made was to brazen out the affair in the belief that arcane points of PII law and sophisticated arguments about ministerial accountability would leave the ordinary voter unmoved. The 'ordinary voter' understands what is wrong about secretly selling arms to a dictator, and what is wrong about making it hard for innocent men to establish their innocence. They understood – and if they didn't, *The Sun* spelled it out for them in its own erudite summary of Scott's 1,800-page report: 'Politicians are just slippery, power-hungry opportunists who will use any legitimate device to save their necks'. That was not the whole truth: Scott's point was that in this case, their devices had been constitutionally illegitimate.

Chapter 16

Diana in the Dock: Does Privacy Matter?

On St Valentine's Day 1995 I was scheduled to meet HRH the Princess of Wales, across a crowded courtroom. I would be representing the manager of a health club where she had worked out for several years, until the *Sunday Mirror* published a 'world exclusive': *DI SPY SENSATION – The most amazing pictures you'll ever see*. They were spread over seven pages and were photographs of her exercising on a contraption called a leg-press, taken by a camera hidden in the gym ceiling. The pictures were certainly striking, not least because they were unposed: they showed Diana, calm and confident, pitted against a fitness machine. But the sight of her image in a gloating tabloid caused such a deep humiliation and sense of violation that she determined to do something that had no direct precedent in British law: to obtain damages for the invasion of her privacy. She asked the court to shape the common law so as to shelter her from the very world of tabloid editors and paparazzi which had become an essential feature of her life and, in due course, of her death.

These sneak pictures had been published in November 1993, and everyone deplored both Bryce Taylor, the gym manager who had taken them, and the *Mirror* which had paid him £125,000 and increased its circulation accordingly. Diana had been the victim of a dirty trick which provided windfall profits to undeserving people. But could she, and if so should she, sue? The two questions must be separated: whether the law can be made to provide recompense for infringement of privacy came first, but the second – whether it was sensible for someone like Diana to exercise the assumed right – depended on a very different calculation. Could the justice game be won convincingly and without damage to herself? At first, she carried all before her, obtaining injunctions and orders of every kind against Taylor, freezing his assets and effectively ruining him. He offered to give Diana all his rights and profits in the photographs if only she would call off the lawyers. She refused, presumably because she wanted a legal example made of him, as the precedent for a privacy law. At this point the very fair judge who was to try the case became concerned: justice would hardly be seen to be done if she changed the law by prevailing over an unrepresented defendant. So legal aid was extended to the impoverished Mr Taylor and the task of defending him fell to me.

Practice at the Bar involves no moral quandary, in the sense that our ethics are those of the cab-rank on which we ply for trade. I might have preferred to act for the Princess: ironically, I was the author of a textbook that analysed and deplored the absence of any privacy law in Britain, pointing out the hollowness of the boast that 'an Englishman's home is his castle' at a time when photographers encounter no legal difficulty in crossing the drawbridge and proceeding directly to the bedchamber. But these photographs were not a clear-cut case. They had been taken at what *Time Out* described as 'the least private gym in London' which had a motto for shirkers: 'you have no hiding place'. LA Fitness comprised one giant room, criss-crossed by catwalks, so that everybody could see everybody else. The leg-press machine that Diana used was in front of a vast glass wall looking onto a public thoroughfare: it was like working out in a shop window. She had not objected when children pressed their noses to the glass and exclaimed, 'Look at the Princess of Wales!'

But did this matter? *The Mirror* bought the pictures not from street photographers or fellow gym members but from its manager, who owed Diana some measure of consideration. She had been turned on to LA Fitness by an article about one of its personal trainers which appeared in the *Daily Mail* in September 1990. It announced 'All you need to achieve the body beautiful is to get down and cardio-funk'. My first question in cross-examination would be 'What, Ms Windsor, is cardio-funk?' and the reply would be 'an exercise which combines funky dance steps with aerobic moves set to hip-hop music'. The judge would interpose 'What is hip-hop music?' and we would be off into the nether world of choreographed colonics and the art of toning buttock muscles on the lifecycle, the rotary torso, the lateral pull-down machine and the concept II Rowing Ergometer (to prepare for this case I had gone where sedentary lawyers fear to tread, and briefly joined a gym).

When Diana first visited his health club, Bryce was every inch the forelock-tugging manager, offering her honorary membership and giving her – literally – free reign. She made the mistake of accepting this freebie: by saving £500 per year she weakened her claim that he owed her confidentiality, because she had not paid for any. It was not a 'club' in any real or exclusive sense, but a suburban business which would take anyone if they paid, be they criminals or Irish republicans or tabloid journalists. On her first visit she was assured by Taylor that her visits would be treated confidentially, and it was on this undertaking that her lawyers relied to argue that there was a 'fiduciary relationship' between her and the gym manager which he had breached by taking the surreptitious photographs. What he had done, by rigging up the secret camera, snapping her unawares and selling the pictures to the tabloids, was certainly sneaky and many would think 'there ought to be a law against it'. But was there?

The alternative analysis was that although she was welcomed as a guest whenever she chose to grace the premises with her presence, she acquired no enforceable rights against covert photography. Attending a gym is like going to a disco or eating in a restaurant, an ordinary transaction which establishes no special fiduciary or 'trust' relationship between customer and management. The gymnasium, from ancient Greece onwards, has been a public arena, and this modern version with its throbbing funk music and MTV system was a place people came to work out together and to socialise. That was the very reason Diana would leave Kensington Palace and drive for up to an hour, two or three times a week, to this everyday place full of nondescript people, to chat them up and light them up. She could much more conveniently have used the gym at Buckingham Palace, which had the very same leg-press machine for footmen who wanted to keep one step ahead. *The Mirror* had depicted what dozens of members had seen with their own eyes, and what children had seen when they gawked through the window. 'It was not as if you had rigged up your secret camera in the changing room or the toilets,' I said to

Bryce Taylor. 'Funny thing – she never used the changing room or the toilets,' he replied, and I wondered how much the tabloids would have offered if she had.

The facts of this case were nicely balanced, and the law was not entirely clear. Bryce Taylor's motive was mercenary and he made no pretence that it was not. But before taking the photographs he had gone to see a leading city solicitor who told him that since there was no protection for privacy his actions were not illegal, and on that assurance he had gone ahead. The *Mirror*, however, which was his co-defendant, had to find a 'public interest' justification. It said it had only published these 'amazing pictures' (*World Exclusive: turn to pages 2 and 3, 12 and 13 and centre pages*) because they revealed the inadequacy of her police protection. If Bryce Taylor could shoot her with a secret camera, the IRA could shoot her too. This argument would justify the press violating every important person's privacy in order to check on their security arrangements. The *Mirror* tried to compensate by oozing compliments about how good she was looking and carrying on as if it were starting a health education campaign to get Britain back into shape, but none of this made up for the original violation, the shock and sense of powerlessness that the plaintiff had suffered. The newspaper's humbuggery made her more determined on revenge.

But Diana wanted privacy only when it suited her. There was confusion left in the wake of *Diana – Her True Story* by Andrew Morton. Outraged at his revelation of the tawdry secrets of the Royal marriage, and after assurances from Diana that she had absolutely nothing to do with him, the Palace complained so vociferously that Harrods and some other stores refused to stock the book and the Press Council roundly condemned the newspaper which serialised it. On further investigation the Council came to the belief that the book's intrusions 'had been contrived by the Princess and her entourage'. This is a matter which I might have had to explore with Diana in the witness box, and no doubt she would have revealed, as Andrew Morton did after her death, that she had collaborated so closely with him that she even corrected the proofs of his book. The Princess of Wales had, in effect, invaded her own privacy, and had certainly conspired with Morton to violate her husband's. She had, after all, married into a British constitutional arrangement which by tradition extracted a certain price for placing her on a pedestal. She was not prepared to pay that price, but nor was she prepared to relinquish the pedestal. No one could criticise her for the breakdown of her marriage, but afterwards silence was always an option. Instead, she had chosen to revel in the role of Queen of Hearts, a high-profile and unique life, in which the paparazzi were an occupational hazard.

It is hard to remember, after the world's grief over her death, how equivocally this woman was viewed when her case came to trial in February 1995. Her reputation picked up subsequently, with the *Panorama* interview and her landmines campaign, but before then her conduct – which can now be diagnosed more kindly as manifestations of a stress disorder – seemed calculated to promote a self-indulgent culture of victimisation and complaint. She had begun making her fleeting visits to AIDS clinics and hospitals, but these appeared to be quests for photo opportunities – it was said she was taking a leaf out of the Benetton advertising book, using the diseased and the dying as visual props to make herself look better than she was. Against this background, one answer to her sudden assertion that she had a legal right to restrain the publication of photographs taken without her consent was that although she had not been asked, she had nonetheless been inviting it to happen.

At any event, the time came to prepare for trial. The Princess, we heard, had constructed a miniature courtroom at Kensington Palace to rehearse for her cross-examination, and had hired a private detective (ex-MI5) to check on the defence. She went to New York a few weeks before the trial to be presented with a prize for her humanitarian work by Dr Kissinger (whose decision to bomb Cambodia counts for many as a crime against humanity). At her request, she was pictured hugging dying black AIDS babies. By this time, 940 journalists had applied for the seventy-five seats available in Court 36 of the Royal Courts of Justice. Their coverage would have little to do with the rights and wrongs of the case, or its fine legal points: the stories would be written to boost circulation. 'This will be the end of your reputation,' said Alan Clark cheerily when we met at a book launch. 'No matter how your cross-examination goes, it will be reported as an absolute triumph for Diana – that's the story that will sell.' The television news 'courtroom artists' had already painted their impressions: I was depicted, all jowls and splutter, rebuked by Her Radiance as she stood serenely in the witness box.

Still, I tried to keep an open mind: I was in favour of privacy law but opposed to monarchy, believing with Tom Paine that an hereditary Head of State is as sensible as an hereditary poet. My only recent Royal connection had been in the previous year, when James Hewitt sought my advice. He was being hunted down by the media after the publication of *Princess in Love,* and called me from his hideout – a pigsty in Languedoc – just as a battalion of *Sun* journalists reached a neighbouring village. In true Bulldog Drummond fashion he had an army pal lift him in a helicopter to High Wycombe, and another drove him to Islington where, following Salman Rushdie, he bunked down in my attic – the last place the tabloid lynch mob would expect to find him. Their real grudge was, I suspect, that he had turned down their offers of half a million pounds in order to tell his story for comparatively little to Anna Pasternak. James did not deserve the obloquy heaped upon him: his affair with Diana was bound to come out, and he made sure it was told as a fairy-tale, with malice towards nobody, in romantic (but excruciating) prose. The episode brought home a point that Tom Paine never took into account, namely the contribution made by Royalty and all its associates to public entertainment.

To that end, the defence was now given a taste of what the plaintiff had endured. My solicitor's mobile telephone conversations with a potential witness were intercepted and sold to a newspaper. The strangest stories began to appear: it was alleged that James Hewitt was still in my attic, to be produced as a surprise witness. *The Times* described me as 'anti-establishment, republican and Australian', presumably in ascending order of horror. My elderly parents were 'doorstepped' by reporters late at night, 10,000 miles from London, and asked what advice they would give Diana. 'I would settle out of court,' said my father, always eager to help.

I have related these facts about the case in order to make a subjective attempt to square the circle – more accurately, to locate points on a penumbra – spanning the two values of press freedom and privacy. Professors of law and journalism solemnly locate the point at which the line should be drawn between free speech and privacy by distinguishing what is in the public interest from what is of interest to the public. But to what purpose? That which interests the public is *ipso facto* in the public interest, because this determines what makes the news. So in every country press freedom boils down to a bargain, a three-way deal between State power, popular instinct and the media's muscle. Everywhere, the press is only relatively free. In some countries the definition may be nothing more than the one offered by Tom Stoppard's African dictator in *Night and Day*: 'We have a relatively free press, by which I mean a press run by my relatives.' In the West, a free press is more complicated.

The 'free press' in Britain is distinguished by the most oppressive libel laws, which prevent reportage of great importance about crime and malfeasance. For example, no journalist could properly write about the life and crimes of Robert Maxwell until he was dead. Yet there is no law at all to protect personal privacy: 'Kiss and sell' stories by bedroom sneaks are staple reading. In contrast, across the Channel, France offers the most stringent protection for privacy. French people first became aware of President Mitterrand's illegitimate daughter when she was nineteen (and then only with Mitterrand's implicit consent). The paparazzo who telephotoed the sucking of the Duchess of York's toes was fined £70,000.

The deal struck for a country's press invariably expresses its national preferences and values. In America, for instance, the deal is often brokered by the courts, against the background of a constitutional presumption in favour of the media. It is only liable for defamations of public figures if they are published recklessly, heedless of the truth. But even celebrities are protected against gross invasions of their privacy – in publishing their health records, for example, or photographs of them lying injured in car crashes. And it was the US Court of Appeals that defined 'paparazzo' as 'a kind of annoying insect, perhaps roughly equivalent to the English "gadfly"', when in 1973 it refereed the clash between Jacqueline Onassis and the gadfly in question, the photographer Ronald Galella. Galella had exceeded the reasonable boundaries for news-gathering by intentionally assaulting Mrs Onassis and by entering her son's school, disrupting her children's riding and water-skiing lessons and endangering their safety in car chases. The result of this case was an acceptable compromise between free speech and privacy: Galella was prohibited from approaching closer than twenty-five feet to Mrs Onassis and thirty feet to her children, or blocking their movements, or doing anything that might jeopardise their safety or cause them genuine alarm. Otherwise, his taking and selling of pictures was not restrained. This is the very least that public figures should expect from the law, anywhere in the world.

The laws governing the British press also reflect the country's values and preferences. Libel is a rich man's sport, a class act which serves to unblot escutcheons and cover up awkward truths about important plaintiffs. Newspapers bear the burden of proving truth in court and have no 'public good' defence. But this, after all, is a society that's known for prurience and prudishness. The newspapers most despised for invading private lives are also the most popular: they mirror rather than create the national character. This is a society in which tens of thousands of people report their neighbours for not paying their annual television licence fee; in which the security services have still not been brought under democratic control; in which telephone tapping and other forms of covert surveillance are permitted by the Home Secretary without police first having to apply to a court; and in which eavesdropping is a popular pastime. Today's true Brit is perhaps Cyril Reenan, the retired bank manager whose hobby was snooping on others' conversations with the assistance of a £1,000 radio scanner linked to an antenna in his garden. When he intercepted Diana's 'Squidgygate' conversation with an old boyfriend, James Gilbey, he insisted he did not want to hurt the Royal Family; that, evidently, is why he delivered the tapes to the *Sun* for safekeeping.

The deal that has been done allows Britain to snigger over what people are like in bed rather than worry about what they are like in their bank accounts or business dealings. The apogee of this state of hypocrisy is a body called the Press Complaints Commission (formerly the Press Council), funded by newspaper proprietors as an insurance policy against the advent of privacy laws. Every time there is an outrageous invasion and it is said that the press is 'drinking in the last-chance saloon' the Commission is there to find an excuse for the saloon never closing. It will promote endless amendments to its 'code of conduct' which everyone knows will be ignored by editors in the interests of circulation, because breaches involve no fines or payments of compensation to victims. After Diana's death it was the same story: amendments to the code, pious promises not to pay six-figure sums for pictures of celebrities caught in some sort of *flagrante* (until someone else publishes them somewhere first) and business as usual. A 'code of conduct' without any sanction, which does not even offer to pay the psychiatric bills of victims injured by its breach, is simply a confidence trick.

The question that all editors who affect concern for human rights should ponder, before they engage in further attempts to stave off the advent of a privacy law, is this: why is privacy a value which calls for protection under every human rights treaty ever devised? There is, I am convinced, a psychological need to preserve an intrusion-free zone of personality and family, and there is always anguish and stress when that zone is violated. Hence the European Convention and other charters speak of a 'right' to respect for private and family life, home and correspondence. But in the same breath, these declarations also speak of the 'right' of freedom of expression. In real life, the two rights are rarely seen to co-exist. Influenced, perhaps unduly, by the media's self-interest, we have become much more concerned about free-speech violations than privacy violations: the former attract the undivided attention of human rights organisations (some formed solely for this purpose) while the latter are rarely condemned. We are inclined to perceive loss of privacy merely as a *quid pro quo* for being rich and famous, forgetting (as Orwell never did) that this was how communism deprived *all* citizens of any right to privacy from the State. The concern is not merely, or even mainly, for princes or film stars or potentates: instant international exposure is liable to alight upon anyone caught up in a major disaster or unperfected moment of heroism or horror. The same protection should be offered to all, implemented by law rather than left to our better nature.

It is a mistake to see privacy only in terms of the excesses of the tabloids. A whole range of intrusions – from unlicensed private detectives to bailiffs and credit agencies and secret intelligence services – take liberties in this area as well. What matters is that the law should enforce respect for a few fundamental decencies, so that privacy and freedom of expression are recognised as values which are universal and complementary. Public figures, whether crowned or elected or created by happenstance, might then enjoy the reputation they deserve. Reputations, in other words, which must withstand revelations about all aspects of their lives *except* that part lived behind a door marked 'do not disturb'. This part will be located by laws which will generally deny entry to the cradle, the school and the toilet, to the bedroom, to the hospital and the grave.

This is because a 'right' is empty rhetoric unless it can be enforced. 'Voluntary self-regulation' is a fraud. The media must be obliged to recognise a lowest common denominator of decency which says about certain photographs (of Diana in the changing room, for example) 'up with the publication of this we will not put'. In her lifetime, considerations of decency and respect for privacy were treated with contempt. When Diana was surreptitiously photographed by the *Sun*, pregnant on a Caribbean beach, the newspaper was immediately condemned by the Press Council – a ruling which it used as an excuse for republishing the photographs under the banner headline 'THIS IS WHAT THE ROW'S ALL ABOUT, FOLKS!' After her death, however, there seems to be a new awareness of two limits: dimly, one imposed by conscience, and more keenly, a fear that readers content to be treated as voyeurs will revolt if regarded as ghouls.

I had hoped Diana's case about the gym photos would be decided by distinguishing between subject matter that is truly private and that which is fair game. It was, and it remains, important to edge British law forward from its current position, seen in its paradigm failure to protect the privacy of the intensive-care hospital room of TV star Gordon Kaye, photographed and recorded by intruding journalists as he was struggling to regain consciousness after a brain operation. The Court of Appeal ruled in this case 1991 that there was no satisfactory legal remedy for what the judges admitted was a 'monstrous invasion of privacy'. A court in New Zealand was prepared to create such a remedy, when asked by children to stop the showing of scenes in a pornographic 'splatter' movie which had been shot, identifiably, on their parents' grave. These are examples of a privacy which requires protection not because of any contract or confidentiality or fiduciary relationship, but by reason of our humanity. Diana's claim would have been unanswerable on that score had the secret camera captured her in the sauna or in the showers or in the lavatory (all places she was smart enough to avoid at LA Fitness). But enthroned on the leg-press, in a communal atmosphere which cannot historically or culturally be located within the sphere of 'the private'? I think – tentatively – not, although I was looking forward to reading the judgment. Win or lose, this case would change the law for the better. It would focus it on the quality of the privacy invaded, rather than the relationship between the parties or the reprehensibility of the means by which the photos were obtained.

But it was not to be. A few days before 'the case of the century' was due to be tried, there was a deal done between the parties to avoid any embarrassment my cross-examination might cause to the Princess of Wales. This was disappointing, if only because I would probably have caused more embarrassment to the newspaper. It is always deflating for a counsel when a 'big case' settles at the door of the court (a condition which my wife calls *courtus interruptus*), and this was a lost opportunity to make some good law. I imagine the Princess was disappointed too: she had been led to believe that she would win a great victory, and even the Duke of Edinburgh had publicly congratulated her when she issued the writ. But victory was not assured, and perhaps she lost heart at the prospect of reliving the violation all over again, in a witness box. This is the great irony about all the fuss the media makes about a privacy law: it will in practice be rarely used, because very few wish to go through an ordeal in the courtroom which invades their privacy all over again.

As for Bryce Taylor, it was claimed by some newspapers that he returned to New Zealand a very much richer man, as the real beneficiary of the out-of-court settlement. They said that a syndicate of Royal admirers had clubbed together to pay his legal costs and to reward him for going away quietly. The size of his reward was put as high as half a million pounds. In this event, he would deserve to go down in legal history as the first defendant to be paid for the privilege of being sued, and paid even more than the damages claimed by the plaintiff.

In 1997 Diana was killed fleeing the flashbulbs she so often positioned herself to attract, a terrible end to the Faustian bargain she had made with the media. Her death has, however, provided some wider understanding of the universal need for a right to be let alone. The law she failed to create in court will, I hope, come about under the impetus of the privacy guarantee of the European Convention on Human Rights, once it is incorporated into British law.

Chapter 17

Cash for Questions?

Editor: Can we legally publish the evidence against all these Conservative MPs? The public interest is overwhelming, on the brink of an election when some of them are candidates.

Lawyer: That's not a defence to the crime of contempt of Parliament, which you will be committing if you publish these confidential transcripts.

Editor: What's the punishment?

Lawyer: That's up to your judges, who are all MPs. They keep a special cell for contemners, just beneath Big Ben. The chimes will drive you mad. Black Rod hasn't put anyone there since Charles Bradlaugh, back in 1880, but if the Tories get back, you never know.

Editor: If I publish this evidence, they won't get back.

There was some nervousness in the editor's office six weeks before the 1997 election, on the day the Prime Minister prorogued Parliament. John Major's action meant that Sir Gordon Downey's report into the *Guardian*'s allegations against Neil Hamilton and other MPs could not be published until after the election. The newspaper, however, had been sent transcripts of his secret hearings, embargoed from publication. They revealed that half a dozen Tories had variously confessed to breaches of parliamentary standards, acceptance of money and favours, avoiding tax and a range of conduct unbecoming an MP or anyone else in a position of public trust. I advised that publication of the confessions would be in breach of confidence and would constitute the crime of contempt of Parliament, but would be the public duty of any editor who took democracy seriously. Some of these MPs were standing again, for very safe seats – and this was something their electors had a right to know.

The electors should, of course, have known about this evidence when it was given. The *Guardian* had persistently urged Downey to hold open hearings but his advisers had insisted upon secrecy. Downey's report should certainly have been published before the election, as John Major had promised when he called for this inquiry into 'cash for questions'. But now it could not be published, for he had prorogued Parliament. So Alan Rusbridger decided to overlook the legal dangers, and to publish important extracts from the Downey secret hearings. There was some concern at the paper that night about whether Conservative Central Office might get wind of the scoop and prevail on a sleepy judge to grant an injunction. So the editor took another unprecedented decision. 'No newspapers to *Newsnight*.' It was the *Guardian*'s publicity manager's ritual responsibility to have a front page at Television Centre by 11.15 p.m., for Paxman or Snow to wave the headlines: the Downey memorial edition was kept under wraps for fear of alerting the Tories that the game was up. I felt able to advise that Black Rod would be unlikely to put Alan over Mrs Betty Boothroyd's knee for the crime of contempt of Parliament, since the one person more guilty of contempt for Parliament was the Prime Minister, who had dissolved it a few days before Downey was due to report.

It was this publication by the *Guardian* of extracts from Sir Gordon's secret hearings which set the sleaze ball rolling through the Tory campaign. MPs' misconduct became the biggest single issue at an election which swept away not only the accused Tory MPs but many more who might have held their seats, had Neil Hamilton not made a fateful decision to play the justice game against the *Guardian*. He started the firmest of favourites, and only a month before the libel trial was reckoned by his lawyers at 9–1 on, a racing certainty. That he is now something of a seaside entertainment, a latter-day Rector of Stiffkey, may be due on one level to his vainglory, but on a more important constitutional level, to the absurdities of a system of Parliamentary self-regulation which puts MPs beyond the law of the land.

If John Major had acted sensibly when it all began, he might still be Prime Minister, or (more probably) have led a healthy opposition. On 20 October 1994, the *Guardian*'s front-page story was 'TORY MPs WERE PAID TO PLANT QUESTIONS SAYS HARRODS CHIEF'. It alleged that Tim Smith, the Northern Ireland minister, and Neil Hamilton, minister at the DTI, had accepted sums of money in return for putting their powers and privileges as MPs at the service of Mohammed Al Fayed. The proprietor of Harrods claimed he had been told by the lobbyist Ian Greer that 'You need to rent an MP just like you rent a London taxi.' The *Guardian* had some evidence to support Al Fayed's allegations against Hamilton – a few fawning letters, and the £5,000 bill (at today's prices) for a free week's stay at the Paris Ritz. It had none against Smith, apart from the fact that he, like Hamilton, had asked parliamentary questions and tabled parliamentary motions on Al Fayed's behalf. But the morning this story was published it was Smith who admitted receiving 'commissions' from Al Fayed, and resigned from the government. Hamilton clung to office ferociously by issuing a libel writ and by assuring Michael Heseltine, his boss at the DTI, that he had not had any financial relationship with Ian Greer. It was principally public disgust at the size of his bill at the Ritz that persuaded the Prime Minister a few days later that Neil Hamilton should resign as a minister in order to spend more time with his libel lawyers.

Among advanced democracies, only in Britain could allegations of this seriousness against government ministers receive no law-enforcement response. The Prime Minister should immediately have instigated a full-scale police inquiry. Al Fayed should have been interviewed, and so should the three witnesses who later came forward to support his story. On this evidence, Smith and Hamilton should have been arrested and sent for trial, with an Old Bailey jury deciding whether or not they had acted corruptly. Neil Hamilton would then have been conclusively condemned or vindicated, long before the 1997 election. In the United States, equivalent allegations would immediately have been sent to a 'special prosecutor' with powers to bring politicians, and even presidents, before a court. In Australia they would have been investigated forthwith by a judge heading an 'Independent Commission Against Corruption' – a body established to root sleaze out of the democratic process. But this was Britain, where in the time-honoured tradition of the Gentlemen's Club a committee of fellow MPs occasionally met to decide whether a chap had gone too far. 'We can exploit our healthy majority on the Privileges Committee,' gloated the government whip David Willetts, and that is precisely what they did, finding Neil Hamilton merely 'imprudent' in taking on the Ritz. The Privileges Committee did nothing at all about Tim Smith. He slipped from ministerial office to the Deputy Chairmanship of the Public Accounts Committee, and prepared to present himself as a fit and proper candidate for the safe seat of Beaconsfield. Hamilton, together with Ian Greer, proceeded with his libel action against the *Guardian*.

London is the libel capital of the world because English law heavily favours the plaintiffs. 'Defamation' is in law no more than criticism – a statement of fact or opinion which lowers the plaintiff in the estimation of right-thinking people. All that the plaintiff has to prove is that the defendant published a defamatory imputation about him: the burden then shifts to the defence to prove that it is true. When corruption is alleged – as it was in effect by the *Guardian* – that burden is very heavy indeed, almost to the criminal standard of proof 'beyond reasonable doubt'. So there have been celebrated cases where newspapers have published the truth, yet lost: John Profumo collected damages for the suggestion he had been sleeping with Christine Keeler; Richard Crossman and other politicians perjured themselves in the witness box to succeed against the *Spectator*; Liberace won massive damages against the *Daily Mirror* for implying he was homosexual. In the US, and in most European countries, newspapers which act responsibly have public interest defences for publishing credible allegations about politicians when they cannot be proved, and even when they turn out to be unfounded, but there is no such defence in British law. So it was a great relief to the *Guardian* when Neil Hamilton's libel action first came unstuck. A judge ruled that a court did not have the power to try allegations which turned on motives for asking questions in the House of Commons, because of a clause in the 1688 Bill of Rights which forbids courts from questioning an MP's performance in Parliament.

This was actually fair enough. It was a rough *quid pro quo* for the absolute privilege MPs enjoy from legal action over anything they say in the House. They can, and sometimes do, make the most false and scurrilous accusations – against people who are afforded no right of reply – and it is not therefore unreasonable that they should themselves suffer suggestions that when they shoot their mouths off, someone else is pulling the trigger. Neil Hamilton and his wife Christine did not see it that way: they went to see John Major and his Attorney General, Nicholas Lyell, to demand that something be done to enable them to pursue the *Guardian* for libel. The Attorney came up with the answer: an amendment to the Bill of Rights (for the first time in its three-hundred-year history), designed to enable MPs in Hamilton's position to bring libel actions if they waived their parliamentary privilege. By an incredible lobbying effort (expertly stage-managed by Ian Greer) and furtive government support, the necessary changes were rushed through Parliament. Many MPs were motivated by self-interest: they would retain the right to hide behind the coward's cloak of parliamentary privilege in order to defame others, while enjoying a new power to sue any newspaper critical of their own conduct in the House. But they also believed in Hamilton: if he was so obsessively determined to proceed with his libel action, it stood to reason he must be innocent.

The 'Hamilton amendment' received Royal Assent in July 1996. Suddenly, an action put to sleep more than a year before sprang to life. In the normal course it would take many months to come to trial, but in August the plaintiffs pulled off another coup: a slot for a long trial to start on 1 October suddenly became available, and they persuaded a judge that their case should fill it. It was the only slot available before the elections, and Hamilton demanded that the court allow him to vindicate his reputation before he stood again for the constituency of Tatton. The *Guardian* was horrified: it needed six months to prepare, but instead was given only six weeks. The newspaper did not even have a QC, and the Bar was away, *en bloc*, on summer vacation. The call from the newspaper's solicitor came while I was staying at John Mortimer's villa in Tuscany. I mentioned, over dinner, that I had been asked to defend the *Guardian*. 'You poor chap,' joked a guest, Tony Blair, 'if the story is anything like their usual level of accuracy.'

Win or lose, I hoped the case would provide an opportunity to teach politicians a lesson about the dangers of tampering with our few ancient liberties. Now that they could sue for libel over stories about what they did in Parliament, their behaviour in the House would for the first time be open to examination in a court. They might come to rue the day they cavalierly tore up a small piece of the constitution in order to win money from the press. Now that lawyers could investigate MPs' conduct – with implements for opening cans of worms, like subpoenas and orders for discovery – their whole hopeless system of self-regulation might be called into question. If counsel were to examine MPs' in-House conduct before a libel jury in the High Court, there could be no objection to examining it before a jury down the road at the Old Bailey. It would be far better for MPs to be prosecuted and jailed if they really were corrupt, or acquitted by a jury if they were not, rather than politely ticked off by their colleagues on the Privileges Committee. This would have the great advantage of making MPs subject to the laws they have laid down for everybody else.

To do justice to this challenge would require lengthy and detailed preparation but the sting in the tail of this brief was that it had to be mastered in a few weeks. The timetable was well-nigh impossible, but I had at least the consolation of knowing that my slog would not be wasted, because this was the case that could never settle. The *Guardian* could not back down: it had staked its credibility on this story. There was no possible compromise, because Neil Hamilton and Ian Greer would not bottle out at the last moment – their political and business future depended on winning a resounding victory. They claimed the *Guardian* article meant that they were corrupt – a libel worth a large sum at going rates, and together with a bill for the legal costs, this case could easily cost the newspaper a million pounds. Not content with this prospect, the plaintiffs demanded more: Hamilton claimed that the *Guardian* story had forced his resignation, and so demanded 'special damages' for loss of his ministerial salary. Greer went much further, alleging that the *Guardian* article had lost him clients and projects worth £10 million. If his damages claim for that amount succeeded, there would not be much to read in the slim-line *Guardian* when the time came to pay out. And succeed all these claims would, unless the newspaper could prove that Mohammed Al Fayed, a man condemned by an official DTI inquiry some years before as a liar, was telling the truth.

*

I rushed back to London to take stock of the evidence. It showed that the Hamiltons had a week-long pig-out at the Paris Ritz at Fayed's expense, where every night they ran up a bill of £400 (at today's prices) in its restaurant, sometimes followed by a champagne breakfast the next morning. Still, much as he might be a glutton whom you would never invite home for dinner, was there proof that the MP had received thousands of pounds in brown envelopes? The defence case, at this stage, rested largely on the word of Mohammed Al Fayed. It was the same with Greer, and if the case against him were lost, his unprecedented 'special damages' claim for £10 million would then succeed, at least in part. The *Guardian*, unlike most publishers, was not insured against libel, a fact which freed it to fight this action (libel insurers would long ago have cut their losses by insisting on apologies to both plaintiffs) but made it a fight unto the death.

Neil Hamilton insisted that nothing he had ever done in his political life needed any apology. It was his belief in laissez-faire competition which provided the reason why he had taken up Al Fayed's cause so vigorously. He had acted, not for reward but out of deep fellow-feeling for this poor Egyptian, attacked by a virulent media just as Hamilton had been when the BBC's *Panorama* mistook his high-spirited Thatcherism for fascism. (He had sued, and won £20,000 when the BBC withdrew – a victory which may have convinced him that it would be easy to win another.) Christine Hamilton had worked for ten years as secretary to Sir Michael Grylls MP, marrying Neil and then becoming his secretary when he was elected an MP for the safe seat of Tatton in Cheshire. They made a career choice to have no children, but had aged parents who were distraught when they read allegations about the MP's cash-and-carry arrangements at Harrods. The country was to see Christine in Tatton a few months later not so much standing by her man as standing over him, but in court she would seem a delicate bloom callously and cruelly scythed by the *Guardian*.

To add to these woes, there had been a devastating ruling from the judge who had ordered the case to be tried so precipitously. The *Guardian* had always clung to one common-sense support for Al Fayed. He alleged he had paid 'cash for questions' not only to Hamilton, but to the dour accountant Tim Smith, who had admitted to receiving 'fees' from Al Fayed which he had not disclosed on the Register of Members' Interests. He had resigned from the government, and the Prime Minister had described his conduct as 'seriously wrong'. Now if Al Fayed was telling the truth about Smith, why was he not telling the truth about Hamilton? As a jury point this was impressive (Downey later found it compelling), but a legal catch would prevent it from being made on behalf of the *Guardian*. When Parliament gave MPs the right to waive their privilege and sue for libel, it limited the waiver to the MP who was the plaintiff. Tim Smith had not waived *his* privilege: indeed, he was taking legal steps to prevent his name from even being mentioned at the trial. The judge had indicated that nothing could be said to the jury which might 'question' Smith's conduct. The Prime Minister might describe it as 'seriously wrong' but the paper's counsel could not. The judge agreed that this would be unfair to the *Guardian*, but it was an unfairness decreed by Parliament through the botched way it had amended the Bill of Rights.

A month before the trial, Ian Greer says, both plaintiffs were assured by their lawyers that their prospects of victory were ninety per cent. This was the stage at which my solicitor, Geraldine Proudler, asked me to meet the *Guardian* executives because 'they are becoming very nervous'. There was no tranquilliser I could prescribe: I estimated their chances as reasonable on Hamilton (because most jurors would take a dim view of his behaviour at the Ritz) but shaky on Greer. Even if the jury awarded him the libel raspberry (the lowest coin in the realm) that would mean not only paying his costs but enduring a second trial over his £10 million damages claim. The only way to improve the odds was to go on the offensive, spending much more money in the hope it might save millions later. We needed a team of journalists and accountants, and approval to issue expensive subpoenas to obtain government documents and to summons to the witness box an array of government figures including John Major, Michael Heseltine, and the Cabinet Secretary Sir Robin Butler. These requests were granted, not so much as a vote of confidence as a throe of desperation.

'I think it would be a good idea if you met Mohammed Al Fayed,' said Geraldine, with her usual engaging understatement. There had been no contact with him for over a year, and although he had supplied a short witness statement, it was in his solicitor's words, not his own (which were said to be littered with four letters). So much was being staked on him, despite the DTI report – which claimed he had lied about his background, his assets and his life when he obtained consent to take over the House of Fraser (which owned Harrods). He had even lied, it said, about his year of birth. 'Mr Fayed, when exactly were you born?' would make a good opening question for any cross-examiner. So we ascended to his fifth-floor offices, via the Harrods escalators. It was like a magic carpet ride through Aladdin's cave, with tempting treasures offering, as the Harrods motto has it, 'something for everyone everywhere'. By the time you reached the top, anyone would crave a brown envelope. I wondered how I might introduce myself to this vital witness, to win his confidence, and decided to mention that I sat occasionally as a judge of Knightsbridge Crown Court, in the large building just behind Harrods. The court had moved to Southwark while its premises were, we understood, being refurbished.

The fact that I was a judge of Knightsbridge Crown Court did not have the expected effect. Al Fayed threw back his head and roared with laughter. 'I have just bought it.' I begged his pardon. 'I have bought it from the Lord Chancellor's Department,' he guffawed, 'I will use it for office space.' This turned out to be true: Mohammed *had* bought the court. (You could now buy anything at Harrods, they would say, including justice.) At least he would be entertaining for the jury: a dumpy man, with a hook nose above a mouth that grinned or looked grim by a fractional change of the same muscle: it was a face uncannily resembling that of Mr Punch, whose magazine he was relaunching that very day. It cheered him when I begged a free copy, to cushion his pained look when I refused the Harrods silk ties he was about to propel across the table in my direction. I had steeled myself to refuse all gifts because I did not want to hear the laughter in court when my opponent cross-examined Al Fayed about his legendary generosity. 'Now tell us, what did you give my learned friend?'

We chatted pleasantly for half an hour. His cross-examination by my opponent, Richard Ferguson, would be a bewildering cultural duel for the jury to referee. Dick's portentous Northern Irish Protestant vowels would beat the courtroom air, above the frank and fractured English of this effusive Egyptian. When he looked accusingly across the crowded courtroom at Greer and Hamilton, would they shiver and shrivel under his gaze? This was the man they had fawned upon for four years: the more their counsel accused him of being corrupt, the more their own grovelling letters to him in that period would return to haunt them. In view of the DTI report, I would have to say something about his credibility, like: 'Mr Fayed, members of the jury, may not have a head for detail. He may not know when he bought a house or a limousine. But he *knows when he has bought a man*.' Would the jury buy the argument? That would depend on his – and Hamilton's – performance in the witness box.

My view of Mohammed Al Fayed was at first that of prosecuting counsel, grateful he agreed to turn Queen's evidence but not excusing him for paying any bribes to which he was prepared to confess. As we talked, a kinder characterisation suggested itself. He had grown up in Alexandria at a time when Egypt was still British. He had been taught to believe in Britain and its institutions, by comparison to the decay and corruption all around him. When he discovered, after settling here, that much of this was a confidence trick, he became disillusioned, and then angry and then almost Messianic. He was determined to make Parliament – like Harrods, like the Ritz, like *Punch* – the exemplar he had in his youth imagined it to be. (Ex-colonial reformers of my own circle – Peter Hain, Bryan Gould, Patricia Hewitt – have I suspect been similarly motivated, to make Britain live up to the expectations their school lessons aroused.) 'Ah, you have understood my idealism,' Al Fayed beamed as I ventured this tentative fellow feeling. 'I am indeed working on a new democracy, a new political advance for Britain. It is being prepared by Lord Anthony Lester and Alex Carlile. Perhaps you would like to join them?' I explained that if I had wanted a peerage I would have joined the Liberal Democrats long ago. Mohammed would be buying the Garrick Club next, and almost certainly the *Observer* – if its sister paper the *Guardian* lost this case.

To prevent that, we were going on the offensive, with a salvo of subpoenas. John Major and Michael Heseltine could give evidence which was relevant to rebut Hamilton's claim for special damages, so they could not refuse to take the stand. A summons to attend the High Court on 1 October was served on the Prime Minister by a process server, together with a cheque for 90p. This is what the law terms 'conduct money': the cost of public transport to the court. In this case it was the price of a bus fare from Downing Street to the Strand. 'MAJOR SUMMONSED FOR SLEAZE CASE' screamed the *Sun*, 'WORLD-EXCLUSIVE'. It had, clearly, the most alert mole in Downing Street. The Prime Minister was so rattled that his wife Norma was immediately required to withdraw from a book-signing session arranged for her – at Harrods.

Hamilton issued a press statement predicting that he would smash the *Guardian*. Rusbridger responded valiantly that we had all the evidence we needed to win. We hadn't, although we were working on it. And how hard everyone *was* working: Geraldine and her team, the *Guardian* journalists, my junior Heather Rogers, extradicted from her summer holiday in Canada, the forensic accountants (who were being paid more than any of us). In a kind of pious panic, I read every word Neil Hamilton had ever uttered in the House of Commons since he had entered it in 1983. I read every edition of the Register of Members' Interests and every report on the subject of declaration of MPs' interests, every book and press cutting that existed on lobbying, Lonrho, the House of Fraser and the political interests of major Greer clients. I read Neil Hamilton's book on taxation, and decided to subpoena his tax returns. Most significantly, as it turned out, I read *The Right to be Heard*, Ian Greer's book on the art of lobbying. It drew attention to the importance of back-bench Conservative committees as a means of putting pressure on ministers, and highlighted the potential of one in particular – the Trade and Industry Committee. Its chairman at the relevant time was Michael Grylls, and its vice-chairmen were Tim Smith and Neil Hamilton.

The contemporary genre of courtroom fiction, popularised in the novels of John Grisham and Scott Turow, is peopled by proactive trial lawyers who take depositions and harangue judges and meet crucial witnesses in hotel rooms in mid-trial and find, by the last chapter, the smoking gun. It's not like that in Britain. Here, you just read and read and read. (I had bought an office carousel for my forty-eight red lever-arch files which began sprouting tabs of adhesive yellow paper like fields of daffodils in spring.) Then you bend double over your desk for a week, summarising everything of conceivable relevance in chronological order: every meeting, every letter, every telephone message, every government decision. Only then, when the master chronology is printed out, can you see clearly what had happened, years ago. It's not a process which offers much to the descriptive novelist, punctuated as it is in real life only by cups of strong black coffee, Mars bars and travels to and from the toilet. The drama – and it is dramatic – is all in the mind, as the jigsaw takes shape. This is the process that worked in Antigua, as the telephone calls enmeshed the conspirators at vital times and on vital days; it worked in Matrix Churchill, where the chronology proved that HMG must have known. A fortnight before this trial, the third draft of the master chronology was fifty pages long, and the picture of parliamentary democracy in the 1980s was coming nicely into focus.

I watched it take shape with the emotion of a medical scientist diagnosing a fatal disease from a stool sample. It showed Ian Greer at the centre of a spider's web of influence – peddling in Westminster. When hired by Al Fayed, he immediately called on Hamilton, who tabled in Parliament some questions critical of Al Fayed's enemy, Tiny Rowland. These were reported, under privilege, in the press, in stories that were pro-Fayed and anti-Lonrho. The proprietor of Harrods was mightily impressed: Greer was the wizard in the Parliamentary court, who could conjure up questions and (subsequently) early-day motions and adjournment debates and meetings with powerful DTI ministers. Greer organised his MPs like an army. The snipers – Tim Smith, then Sir Andrew Bowden and Neil Hamilton – at the front, firing questions. The captain – Sir Michael Grylls – encouraging them from behind the lines. The general – Sir Peter Hordern – parading these troops as a show of force to the DTI and its ministers. These moves were masterminded by Greer, under the regimental colours of the Tory back-bench Trade and Industry Committee.

These mercenaries did not disclose the fact that they were being rewarded. (As Tim Smith later admitted to Downey, 'his representations might be more effective if they were thought to come from the Conservative Party back-bench Tory Trade and Industry Committee rather than from a paid lobbyist for Mr Al Fayed'.) The exception was Hordern, whose role was to be the upfront man, always scrupulously declaring his own retainers with the House of Fraser as he introduced the others as officers of the Trade and Industry Committee. (He did not tell anyone how much he was being paid by Harrods: a whacking £24,000 a year.) Hordern represented the old-fashioned, genteel form of lobbying, taking money for services rendered by standing order and declaring it on the record. The new breed of Thatcherites wanted their 'commissions' in ways which need not be declared on the Register of Members' Interests.

It was an unattractive game even when played by gentlemen – the knights from the shires like Grylls and Hordern and Bowden, honoured for 'services to politics' which were sometimes difficult to distinguish from services to themselves. In their pinstripe suits with dandruffed collars, they had swarmed over the fabulous Egyptian like flies on a pile of ordure. These honourable members, whose constituencies were hundreds of miles from Knightsbridge, became the Members for Harrods: they worked to stave off the DTI inquiry into Al Fayed's honesty for a year or so; they had one of its inspectors removed; they persuaded the minister not to refer the House of Fraser take-over to the Monopolies and Mergers Commission; and they managed to delay the evil day of publication of the damaging DTI Report for about two years. All this by purporting to represent back-bench interests in Britain's trade and industry, to which Al Fayed contributed rather insignificantly. It was Greer's genius to make Al Fayed matter to ministers and MPs who should not have cared less about him. His enemy, Tiny Rowland, paid the Tory MP Edward du Cann £400,000 each year to run the Lonrho counter-attacks. Rowland was aptly described by Edward Heath as 'the unacceptable face of capitalism' while Al Fayed had been denounced by the DTI inspectors. These MPs involved themselves in a billionaires' grudge match, of no conceivable interest to their constituents or to the public weal. The arteries to the heart of the body politic were clogged with grease and it was time for open-court surgery.

In the last week before the trial was due to commence, the case somehow became too much for the plaintiffs to bear. Telephone records from Harrods purported to show that Hamilton had called up to request an 'envelope' – should it be couriered to him in Cheshire? There were several intriguing messages from Greer:

'remind Mohammed that he still owes £5,000 for the last three months'. What could this mean? Greer's retainer was paid by standing order, and these messages made no sense unless they referred to some undisclosed arrangement with Al Fayed. The secretaries who had taken the messages, Alison and Iris, could not have been ignorant of what was going on, but our problem was that Al Fayed had always sought to protect them from publicity and harassment. In the final week he was prevailed upon to allow them to be interviewed.

Meanwhile, the law had levers that could be pulled in the interests of justice. The civil courts have a process called 'discovery' by which each party is obliged to disclose all documents in their possession which are relevant to an issue in the case. Hamilton had disclosed virtually nothing; he had lost all his Al Fayed files and his relevant diaries when he had moved ministerial offices in 1993. Greer had disclosed most of the letters written in the course of the Harrods campaign, but we knew there must be important documents about his financial arrangements with Hamilton and other MPs. We applied to a High Court judge, ten days before the trial was due to start, to require him to disgorge this material, and to obtain an order that Hamilton should disclose his tax returns. Both plaintiffs undertook to comply.

The information in Greer's accounts was sensational. It transpired that he had been paying Hamilton in ways which the MP had never disclosed to Parliament. Christine went shopping for garden furniture on Greer's account at Peter Jones. Greer paid for summer travels in 1988 to New Orleans and Aspen, Colorado. The MP purchased a picture at a gallery in Cornwall and sent the bill to the lobbyist. These benefits were part of £10,000 worth of 'commissions' paid by Greer in return for Hamilton introducing him to new clients. But one of these clients – the National Nuclear Corporation – was his constituent. Hamilton was paid from the public purse to advise constituents, and his action in pocketing a secret profit from this activity was in my opinion a breach of his public trust. The generous payment of £12,000 for introducing another client – US Tobacco – he shared with his old Monday Club buddy Michael Brown MP. Neither disclosed it, as Parliamentary rules required, on the Register of Members' Interests, nor to the taxman nor to the ministers they lobbied in the cause of allowing children to buy 'Skoal Bandits', a nicotine chewing gum which causes cancer of the mouth. They were not the only MPs in receipt of payments from the lobbyist: tens of thousands of pounds went to Sir Michael Grylls, under the all-purpose rubric of 'commissions'. The amount of £5,319 was paid into the 'Andrew Bowden Fighting Fund', shortly after Bowden had put down four questions on Al Fayed's behalf, drafted for him by Greer. The plaintiffs were claiming that the 'sting' of the *Guardian*'s libel was this quotation from Al Fayed: 'Mr Greer said you need to rent an MP like you need to rent a London taxi'. If that defamed anyone it defamed London taxi-drivers, who at least work for a fixed fare and do not stop for a free week at the Ritz.

We were compiling a jury album – *Hamilton's Travels*. It started with photographs of Room 356 at the Paris Ritz; then Ballnagown, Fayed's Scottish castle where he had holidayed; then the sumptuous hotels where he stayed in New York and even London at the expense of US Tobacco. We would ask for the jury to be taken on what lawyers term 'a view' in order to appreciate the evidence – a Eurostar trip to Paris, to see with their own eyes the opulence of the Ritz and L'Espadon restaurant. The judge would probably demur – 'surely your photographs are enough to make the point' – but other evidence could be admitted at the trial. In the witness box, Al Fayed would produce £2,500 in crisp banknotes, and demonstrate how he would place them in a brown envelope. The envelope would then be handed to the judge, made an exhibit and passed around from juror to juror, to give them a feel for the sensation Fayed alleged that Tory MPs craved.

It would, under the onerous libel rules, be for the *Guardian* to satisfy the jury that Al Fayed was telling the truth. They would hear the cross-examination of Hamilton, and his counsel's challenges to Al Fayed. The defence case would no longer hinge on his word alone. A few days before the trial three witnesses came forward to support Al Fayed. There was Alison Bozak, now a trainee solicitor with a city firm, who said she had stuffed cash in envelopes for Hamilton and Greer. There was Iris Bond, who recalled couriering the cash and preparing envelopes for collection. Then there was a security man at Al Fayed's block of flats in Park Lane, who said he had handed the plaintiffs 'brown envelopes' on several occasions. Were these new witnesses all prepared to lie under oath, or would their evidence be compelling? Hamilton had brought this case so that a jury would decide, one way or the other.

There was another surprise in store. On the Thursday before the trial a judge ordered the government to hand over documents relevant to Hamilton's resignation. Memories of Matrix Churchill flooded back, as I saw the familiar DTI letterhead, with 'secret' stamped on the top and hand-written notes about 'presentational difficulties' in the margins. I pored over these documents, reading beneath the redactions and decoding the Whitehall euphemisms. The documents showed the government to be more concerned to avoid embarrassment than to conduct a proper investigation into Al Fayed's allegations. The whips had manipulated the Tory majority on the Privileges Committee, and self-regulation had taken its gentlemanly course. The only minister who emerged with credit was (as in Matrix Churchill) Michael Heseltine. He had demanded Hamilton's assurance that he had never had any financial relationship with Greer. Hamilton gave it, and Sir Robin Butler minuted that 'Mr Hamilton has given him (Heseltine) an absolute assurance that he had no financial relationship with Mr Greer.' What stood out from this minute – assuming it was accurate – was one unforgettable fact: Neil Hamilton had misled Michael Heseltine, and through him the Prime Minister and the Cabinet Secretary. Might it not seem possible to a jury, if it accepted that he deliberately misled the President of the Board of Trade, that he was prepared to mislead them?

The *Guardian*'s legal team had little sleep that night: the next day, Friday, we ran on adrenalin. We had to put all the last-minute evidence into fresh pleadings, and prepare a bundle of documents for the trial the following Tuesday. By lunchtime we were ready to call our opposite numbers: curiously, they were unavailable to take our calls. What was happening? I felt a personal concern for Dick Ferguson, the plaintiff's QC, who would need to see the fresh evidence as soon as possible, so I called him at his home at 5.30 p.m. Before I could utter more than a pleasantry he asked whether my clients would agree to 'walk away' from the case. That meant settlement: if the plaintiffs withdrew, would the *Guardian* refrain from demanding any legal costs?

This was the action that could never settle: the parties had been baying at each other for two years. Only a fortnight ago Hamilton had issued a press release promising to prove the *Guardian* guilty of telling 'sensationalist lies'. But when the word 'settlement' is spoken at this point in libel cases it almost always follows. In that part of a barrister's brain which tingles at the prospect of a *cause célèbre* I felt the beginnings of a dull ache, the onset of '*courtus interruptus*'. But my duty was to obtain victory without firing a shot, so I told Dick I would consult with my client and return him an answer the following afternoon. The *Guardian*'s response was that it could not stop the plaintiffs from withdrawing, but was not prepared to induce them to do so by paying any of their costs, or promising not to republish their allegations. It would want a significant contribution to its own costs – my brief fee of £30,000 would be appropriate – to emphasise its victory. Dick (whose fee was the same) said he would relay it – he was no longer instructed to act at the trial because of the conflict which had arisen between the plaintiffs. This was not some ploy to postpone the case until after the election? No, Dick assured me, and I believed him: it is one of the great advantages of the Bar that counsel never mislead each other. (They leave that sort of thing to solicitors).

Quite why the plaintiffs were self-destructing I could not tell. The discovery of the misleading of Heseltine had damaged Hamilton, but not Greer, who had most to lose from a withdrawal (his claim for £10 million for a start). What catastrophe had befallen them so suddenly? Greer maintains that he was advised his chances had slumped to zero because we discovered he had misled a Select Committee about the number of his secret 'commission' payments to Michael Grylls – he owned up to three, and we had found at least six in his books. Hamilton was furious with Greer, but then Greer hit the roof when he discovered that his co-plaintiff had apparently lied to Heseltine. At a conference on the Friday with their barristers and solicitor, the Hamiltons exploded with such disgust over Greer's 'culpability' that the lawyers found it professionally impossible to represent both – or either – of these clients, and so had to withdraw from the case. The tactical course for both plaintiffs, since a genuine conflict had erupted, was to obtain an adjournment (which the judge would have been obliged to grant) to instruct fresh solicitors and counsel or at least to take stock of their position. Once this long case had slipped from its October mooring in the busy court list it could not have been brought back until mid-1997, after an election at which Hamilton would certainly have been returned as MP for Tatton. The case would have stayed *sub judice*: there would have been no 'sleaze' headlines, no Downey Investigation, no Martin Bell (the BBC war reporter who won at Tatton) – and a lot more Tory MPs would have been elected. It remains one of the minor 'what ifs' of history: 'What if Hamilton and Greer had simply asked for their case to be adjourned?' (It need never have been brought again to trial, had Hamilton wished to avoid the expense of further action.) From their own accounts, it appears the plaintiffs fell out so badly that lawyers could not put them together again.

The fear in the *Guardian* camp over that dramatic weekend was that the plaintiffs would simply kick the case into touch by applying for an adjournment. Alan Rusbridger was champing at the bit: he wanted the trial to begin immediately, so all the evidence would emerge in open court. I had to tell him that since the plaintiffs' solicitors and counsel had withdrawn, the court would be certain to grant them a long adjournment to obtain new lawyers, so the trial would in all probability not begin until after the election. He winced. 'That would be the worst possible scenario.' Could it be prevented, perhaps, by offering some inducement: if they withdrew now rather than adjourned, the newspaper would not insist on claiming the costs run up by Geraldine's firm, or even my brief fee. Geraldine invited the plaintiffs to 'walk away' by paying the brief of my junior (Heather Rogers) which was £15,000. (This was bluff. Although it wanted some costs as a signal that the *Guardian* had won, what the paper was really playing for now was the right to publish the evidence it had prepared.) The plaintiffs' lawyers made desperate efforts to have Geraldine agree to lessen their clients' humiliation with apologies or corrections or statements in open court, but to no avail. By Monday afternoon they had capitulated, and agreed to signal the *Guardian*'s victory by publicly paying £15,000, the cost of spoiling Heather Roger's summer holiday.

I telephoned the judge to tell him that his trial for the morrow had been cancelled, and set out for the *Guardian*. It was an unprecedented night in the newsroom. Alan had chosen for the front page a large picture of Hamilton, under the headline 'A Liar and a Cheat'. The next eight pages summarised the evidence that the *Guardian* would have produced had the case gone ahead. This was a one-sided substitute for a trial, but the plaintiffs had brought it on themselves. They could have postponed the match, and they might actually have done better had they eventually played it. Instead, they had cut their own throats during the warm-up. But to everyone's amazement both Neil and Christine turned up in court the next day for the formal withdrawal, for all the world as if they had won. I heard groans when the judge described the *Guardian* as 'a responsible newspaper' which had 'published matters of constitutional and national importance'. Afterwards the MP posed in front of the Gothic towers of the High Court, his chin jutted out like one of its flying buttresses. Someone suggested a picture caption: 'You can't keep a bad man down'. The editor rejected it: 'The *Guardian* is *not* a tabloid newspaper.'

Britain is a nation beguiled by its own history. It clings to the illusion that it has the least corrupt Parliament in the world. As the *Daily Telegraph* put it, after the Hamilton saga: 'Anybody who knows anything about national politics in this country knows that, by and large, they are remarkably uncorrupt'. That depends on what you mean by corruption. Thirty per cent of MPs in the last Parliament accepted payment in return for 'parliamentary services': they described them as 'consultancy fees', but they were inducements to ask questions and meet ministers, not on behalf of constituents or on matters of national interest, but for the private interests which paid them. Over two-thirds – 450 MPs – were moonlighting with second jobs – as barristers, company directors, farmers, solicitors, consultants and even, incredibly, as parliamentary lobbyists. This, they said, gave them experience of real life, although one would hope they have that before they are elected. What it gave them experience of was real money, on top of a parliamentary salary which was more than three times the average wage, plus perquisites of a kind which most citizens can only dream about (free first-class travel, secretarial services, overseas trips, an additional £11,000 for having a constituency outside London). What emerged from Greer's aborted libel action was only a small part of one man's operation, a single case study made possible by the documents obtained through discovery. How many dozens of Al Fayed-type operations had gone on every year, through the agency of Parliamentary lobbyists? How many other clients were advised 'You need to rent an MP like you rent a London taxi' – and how often were lobbyists paid to do exactly that?

A committee chaired by Lord Nolan was set up as a result of the *Guardian*'s revelations, but the minds and bottoms of its members were firmly set in the green leather armchairs of the Gentlemen's Club. It recommended that MPs should continue to regulate themselves, for no better reason than that Parliament has always regulated itself. The addition of an investigator like Sir Gordon Downey to report to the Privileges Committee is not sufficient: he would not have reported into the 'cash for questions' case at all had the *Guardian* not agreed, after the collapse of the trial, to make formal complaints against the MPs and to supply most of Downey's evidence. Other advanced democracies have rejected the idea that MPs can be relied on to regulate themselves. They have established independent commissions, headed by a judge and staffed by skilled investigators, with a remit to investigate corruption allegations made against any public officials, from ministers and MPs to policemen and bureaucrats. Hearings are in public; witnesses who lie face prosecution for perjury, and high officials are not allowed the luxury of the privilege against self-incrimination. With an investigative machine of this calibre, errant MPs as well as ministers (over whom neither the Privileges Committee nor anyone else has jurisdiction) are much more likely to be detected: if found accepting bribes they are handed over for prosecution in the courts. The constitutional lesson of Neil Hamilton's case is that self-regulation of Parliament is as unsatisfactory as self-regulation of the press.

Sir Gordon Downey's Report, when released months after the election, was a comprehensive indictment of Neil Hamilton. It found the evidence that he received 'cash for questions' in brown envelopes from Al Fayed 'compelling'. He deliberately misled Heseltine and improperly hid a number of other financial interests from Parliament. But what was the status of Downey's report? Was he a judge, or merely an investigator for a committee of MPs – the Privileges Committee? Bizarrely, this committee then allowed the ex-MP to make a vicious televised attack, under parliamentary privilege, on Sir Gordon Downey and everyone else he blamed for his downfall. This was an unseemly occasion: how many other witnesses will now dare to come forward to accuse MPs, when they can be blackguarded like this for doing so? In December 1997 the Privileges Committee finally concluded that there could never be 'absolute proof' that Hamilton had been paid in brown envelopes, but endorsed Downey's finding nonetheless. The MP had shown 'a casualness bordering on contempt' for disclosure rules, and if he had been re-elected he would have deserved 'a substantial period of suspension from the service of the House'.

What this meant was that if Hamilton had been re-elected as MP for Tatton in 1997, he would in due course have been 'suspended' – but not forced to resign – for a period of six months or so. This would hardly have been a satisfactory result, for his constituents or for the public or for himself, but it is the only result that self-regulation, post-Nolan, is able to deliver. The moral, surely, is that 'voluntary self-regulation' of and by MPs should no longer serve as a substitute for legal regulation. Amongst the many reasons for reform would be fairness to MPs like Neil Hamilton, who has never had the evidence against him tested by cross-examination. In his case, this was a result of his decision to withdraw from the libel action, but it would have been fairer to him and better for all concerned if Al Fayed's allegations had from the outset been investigated and tried through the criminal process. In future, if MPs in Hamilton's position are to be given the day they deserve in court, they will have to be arrested on charges of receiving bribes and, if the evidence warrants it, placed on trial at the Old Bailey. If acquitted, they can go back to Parliament, and if convicted they should go to prison – for a period long enough to deter other MPs from similar temptations to act dishonourably.

Afterword: *The Justice Game*

> An advocate, by the sacred duty which he owes his
> client, knows in the discharge of that office but one
> person in the world, that client and none other. To
> save that client by all expedient means – to protect
> that client at all hazards and costs to all others,
> including himself, is the highest and most un-
> questioned of his duties; and he must not regard
> the alarm, the suffering, the torment, the de-
> struction which he may bring upon any other. He
> must go on, reckless of the consequences . . . even
> if his fate it should unhappily be, to involve his
> country in confusion for his client's protection.
>
> *Henry Brougham*

> Professional people have no cares
> Whatever happens, they get theirs.
>
> *Ogden Nash*

The truth about barristers is located at a mundane midpoint between the high-flown rhetoric of Lord Brougham (the advocate who defended Queen Caroline) and the master of the cynical sound-bite. It is precisely because barristers are well paid and immune to actions for negligence that they are meant to be psychologically prepared to stand up against the State on behalf of unpopular people and unpopular causes. I have never been convinced of this logic – as Gerald Gardiner said, 'I'd rather be a barrister on a miner's pay than a miner on a barrister's pay'. But note how the stars of the Bar, most adept at playing the justice game on behalf of others, skilfully avoid having to play it for themselves. They cling to their immunity from actions for negligence – an unjustified privilege which protects incompetents from being sued. They even suffer dilatory or dishonest solicitors who do not pay their fees, preferring to blacklist them rather than to sue for recovery. They do all they can to stay out of court because they know about the pitfalls of litigation. They know that justice is a game: they play it with other people's money and lives but never, if it can be avoided, with their own.

This is a fact, not a criticism. Barristers are, on the whole, dutiful in warning would-be litigants of the hazards. Our professional advice is invariably cautious and laden with warnings often couched in sporting odds which emphasise the risk. I adopt medical metaphors: litigation is like suffering a long if ultimately curable disease: malaria perhaps, where the temperature rises and falls, and long periods of inactivity are followed by feverish outbursts. Who would choose to endure it, in a life which is anyway too short? The defendant in a criminal trial cannot but fight the course, but the would-be plaintiff or defendant in a civil action who can settle for a small payment or apology has every reason to live to fight another day which may never come. Lawyers are not barkers at a fun-fair, urging naive players to roll up and claim their luck against the House. The best often go unrecognised because their genius is to keep their clients out of court rather than in it, or to produce solutions so acceptable that the problem is never heard of again.

The important point is that the justice game is not played for money but for people's rights and liberties. The first rule is don't play unless you have to. The second is play to win. And the third rule is that since winners often lose – in costs, in time, in irritation and mental fatigue – there must be more to victory than the pleasure of winning. There must be a moral.

As is well known, barristers have adapted their morals from Hackney carriage-drivers, who found it advantageous to the continuance of their monopoly to take anyone anywhere. Today, the 'cab-rank rule' is described as the kerbstone of the advocate's right to practise. It is said to have this salutary effect, that anyone – however evil, eccentric or unpopular – may find a professional to assist in asserting a legal right. But when such people are charged with criminal offences they usually qualify for legal aid, in which case there is no shortage of barristers anxious to defend them. The main virtue of the rule is that it protects barristers from unfair criticism for taking these unpopular cases: it reduces the amount of excrement through the letter-box.

The taxi-rank rule is of some constitutional importance. It originated in Lord Erskine's explanation to an Old Bailey jury as to why he accepted the brief to defend Tom Paine's *Rights of Man*, despite the fact that it cost him a lucrative retainer as adviser to the Prince of Wales. A cynic might say that Erskine accepted this brief so that he could boast about his own virtue in doing so: his famous speech is never read in full, because it is an epic of self-adulation, in the course of which he so condemns the book and its author (who had the foresight to flee to France) that he forgets to offer the jury any argument against convicting his client. But in the course of this speech Erskine stated the cab-rank rule in immortal language: 'From the moment that any advocate can be permitted to say that he will or will not stand between the Crown and the subject arraigned in the court where he daily sits to practise, from that moment on the liberties of England are at an end.'

This proud principle applies to all whose duty is to stand up to the State with professional skill on behalf of any wretch who obtains their services. That its constitutional importance needs emphasis was demonstrated in November 1997, when a barrister who happened to be married to the Prime Minister was wrongly criticised in the press for taking – in fact, for winning – a case enlarging the civil rights of convicted rapists. It may be difficult to explain why someone as clever as Cherie Booth QC should cudgel her brains on behalf of criminals – one day she might be instructed to argue for Myra Hindley's rights to be treated fairly by the Home Secretary – but unless we can face that prospect with equanimity there is little point in boasting about a legal profession independent of the State. Of course, the analogy between barristers and taxi-drivers cannot be pushed too far: for a start, we frequently carry indigent passengers free of charge. In other respects, our attitudes are similar to the cabbies I often hail: it's 'Sorry Guv, I'm just knocking off for lunch' or 'I won't take a fare south of the river'. (In other words it interferes with a vacation or is to be heard at the Inner London Crown Court.) So long as there are other, equally experienced drivers available, no problem of principle arises. What the rule guards against is barristers turning down cases in the area of their expertise because they dislike the defendant or the nature of the alleged offence.

There have been breaches of the rule – notably when the Bar Council itself stopped an English barrister from defending Nazis on trial at Nuremberg, and when no fewer than twenty-one QCs turned down briefs on behalf of the Old Bailey bombers in 1974. That was the time when one kindly judge, later a Law Lord, took a sufficient interest in my career to urge me, for its sake, never to accept a brief for a bomb trial: 'You don't want to become part of the alternative bar.' That was the mistaken mindset of his generation, and the miscarriages of justices it permitted have returned to haunt us all. It failed to recognise that it is the mark of a civilised society that persons accused of such evil should have the allegations against them tested with the utmost rigour.

I cannot forget my first call to the 'alternative bar', to advise an Irishman arrested for planting a bomb at West Ham underground station, killing a guard and endangering the lives of many commuters. It was in 1975, and the walk to his cell was through a corridor lined with Special Branch officers, their eyes full of contempt for a person and a profession determined to help an enemy, a few hours after the death of an innocent. It was under-standable, this righteous rage which has sometimes inflamed policemen to fabricate confessions or to beat suspects whom they believe (often correctly) to be guilty. It was also frightening. As I walked along the line I wanted to say to the nearest hard face, 'Look, we're on the same side really. I know you've risked your life capturing him' (he had a gun) 'and you are braver and more socially useful than I will ever be. But I've just got this small role to play in the process, to make sure that if he's put away, it's done fairly and squarely, OK?' They would not, by their looks, have understood; they knew I was going to advise an obviously guilty man to exercise his right to silence, which might make it marginally more difficult to convict, and they hated me for it.

This rage I had felt at West Ham against the defending lawyer translated into a general contempt for the adversarial system of justice: why bother about obeying the rules of trial, any more than obeying the rules of interrogation? The trial was a public relations wrap-up to the detective work of deducing guilt from association with Sinn Fein and from hand-swabs, even if these might also test positive from touching playing cards or cellophane around cigarette packets. Justice was not treated as the deadly serious game that it is, to be played by rules: cheating became acceptable so long as you were sure the defendants were guilty. The real problem about this 'noble cause corruption', which is obscured by films like *In the Name of the Father* with its travesty trial of the Guildford Four, was that the real thing seemed so fair. The judges were not biased, although no doubt they believed that Special Branch and the security services had found the guilty men. What they did not take on board – until forensic science came up with the ESDA test which could read electrostatically between the lines of old police pocketbooks – was the relationship between police rule-breaking (or the non-existence of rules for police to break) and miscarriages of justice.

Policemen and prison officers are more friendly now, and more fair: they have learned the hard way that lawyers who assist the enemy are actually assisting the justice system that the enemy aims to undermine. But it still can be difficult for young lawyers to come to terms with their professional duty in 'terrorist' cases. Many years later, in 1991, I took a pupil barrister to the committal proceedings for Dessie Ellis, the man who had made many of the IRA's explosive devices which caused mayhem on the mainland. He was the first Irishman to be formally extradited to stand trial in Britain, and the magistrate had been persuaded by a technical submission that there was no jurisdiction to try him here, so he would have to be set free. After the body search on leaving the court we walked back to my car, past armed police and alsatians and below the sharp shooters silhouetted against the roofs of overlooking buildings, and the pupil asked me nervously, 'Can you really sleep happily after that result?' I could, because it proved that the British State was fair enough to allow itself to be beaten at its own game.

Cases I could wish on other players usually involve freedom of expression, a principle of greater importance than the examples by which it must be defended. I had moral qualms over *The Guide to Self-Deliverance*, a 'do-it-yourself' suicide instruction manual issued to members of the Voluntary Euthanasia Society. The Attorney General sought to ban it, after forty-two people had died while following its advice – sometimes with the *Guide*, open and underlined, on the bed beside them. Suicide-lib is, I feel, a right for the over-nineties, or those with terminal illness, but by bringing the action the Attorney General had raised the stakes: if he failed, the

Guide could be sold in station bookstores to any depressed teenager temporarily taken hostage by his hormones. The action did fail, but I confess to sleeping more easily when the Society agreed with my advice and announced that rather than make the *Guide* a bestseller, it would confine distribution to its life members.

The most unpopular men I ever defended were from the Paedophile Information Exchange (PIE). They were not active paedophiles, but were certainly in the grip of a disease of the wrist which might be called graphophilia – an urge to correspond about child sex fantasies, at great length and in pornographical detail. PIE comprised a few dozen people: five were charged with conspiracy and the others were arrested and obliged to plead guilty to the minor offence of sending indecent material through the post. At the committal they were all, with one significant exception, called to give 'Queen's evidence'. I was revolted by their correspondence – yards and yards of infantile sexual fantasising in copperplate schoolmasterly hands. Nonetheless, I was a taxi prepared to ply for trade in such dark suburbs, and I cross-examined the procession of embarrassed men who had been permitted to plead to the minor charges in return for giving evidence against the others. The chief curiosity of the prosecution case was that everyone's favourite pen-pal, the hub of this daisy chain of pornographic penmanship, had not been arrested: for some unaccountable reason he was not a defendant nor called as a prosecution witness. The court was told that his name was Mr Henderson. I enquired no further: the rat-smelling antennae so vital for a defence counsel were not properly tuned. I failed to discover a classic British cover-up until after the trial, when police leaked to *Private Eye* the fact that it had been decided 'at a high level' that the man, whose name was not Henderson, should not be prosecuted or identified, because he had recently retired as the British High Commissioner in Canada after a long and distinguished career with MI6.

'If liberty means anything at all, it means the right to tell people what they do not want to hear,' said George Orwell – ironically, in an introduction to *Animal Farm* which Gollancz, his left-wing publishers, declined to publish lest it give offence to Stalin. The cases in this book are mostly about the right to tell people what most of them would never wish to see or read, or what 'they' –

officials Orwell calls 'the striped-trousered ones who rule' – do not want the people to hear. What is kept from the public, and what the public wish to be kept from, have this in common, that the law tends to be relied upon as the means of suppression. This book should serve as a warning to those who rely upon it: don't.

This is because Henry Brougham was right to this extent, that lawyers have no business truckling to 'they who must be obeyed', be 'they' ministers or security officials or secret policemen. A government enters court on terms equal to its enemies: other than in Singapore there can be no presumption of legality simply because an action has been done by officials of the State. In this book I have chosen cases to demonstrate how the law may humble the most powerful: governments here and abroad; the great departments of Whitehall; the security services; and wealthy private litigants ranging from the Bank of England to the Princess of Wales. It will not perform this function always or even usually, but it must always remain *possible* for law power to win over State power or private might, either through the upsets that the 'gang of twelve' are capable of causing or through independent prosecuters or judicial attention to principle. 'Justice' is not a result conforming to popular expectation, it is an objective judgment on the fairness of the procedures under which the case has been tried.

For this reason I am passionately in favour of the incorporation into British law of the European Convention on Human Rights, bedrock principles which recite the rules of the justice game. The Convention was drawn up in 1951 to serve both as a legal bulwark against the resurgence of fascism and as an articulation of civil rights being threatened by communist regimes in Eastern Europe. It embodies standards not so much fundamental as elemental, and the reason why so many of our laws and administrative practices have breached it is because we too often regard civil liberties as privileges to be granted at the discretion of the powerful rather than rights capable of assertion by members of the public. Enactment of the Convention will measurably improve the protection for individual freedom. It will enable full-blooded challenges to be made to the way discretionary power is exercised by ministers and officials, not merely by way of procedural review but from universal principles. It will improve the quality and comprehensibility of judicial decision-making, since arguments from first principles are apt to be more logical, realistic and understandable than those artificially constructed from the rag-bag of case-law precedents.

Legal commentators on the left have a knee-jerk antipathy to the notion of judges as guarantors of human rights. Their objections fail, at the end of the day, for want of any sensible alternative. The courts remain the only place where oppressive government action against individuals may be checked. The parliamentary opposition does not, by definition, have the numbers to intervene, short of a revolt by government back-benchers. MPs may harass and embarrass ministers over individual cases: they may call for explanations, but have no power to interfere further. The notion of Parliament as the sole guardian of liberty is risible: 3,000 pages of statutes and 2,000 separate statutory instruments receive Westminster's imprimatur each year, many of them without proper scrutiny or debate, their contents understood only by a handful of administrators and draftsmen. The media may take up particular cases of injustice, subject to their ability to obtain sufficient information and to the political allegiances of editors and proprietors. But trial by media – partial, simplistic and sensational – is no substitute for trials by judges, decided by the application of fundamental principles of law.

The law, after all, is a discipline which trains and controls those who apply it. When Convention principles become part of that law, they will be reflected in the attitudes of the law's disciples. The great majority of judges are at present white males from upper-middle-class backgrounds, but this will change as new generations with a more acceptable social, sexual and racial mix are appointed. In any event, incorporation of the European Convention does not foreshadow government by judges. It will simply mean equipping the most appropriate institution – the courts – with better principles and procedures for identifying and remedying abuses of power perpetrated against citizens by government departments. What the judiciary will not possess is power to strike down the sovereign Acts of an elected Parliament, but what it needs to have – because no other person or institution independent of govern-ment has it – is authority to ensure that decisions which affect the lives of people, taken by officials exercising the discretions given them by such Acts, are made and executed fairly, and consistently with human rights principles. This does not involve judges in deciding government policy, although it may involve them in ensuring that *as regards individuals*, the policy is implemented justly and humanely. There will be many conservative interpretations of the Convention and they will disappoint, but they will not damage existing rights. The likelihood is that after an initial period of uncertainty, decisions will emerge which will enrich the understanding of Convention guarantees by reflecting the spirit of liberty which appears so abundantly in British history, literature and political rhetoric, yet so circumspectly, at present, in British law. It may do something, in all countries where English precedents carry influence, to make up for the illiberal legal legacy bequeathed to our former colonies.

A Bill of Rights will be in tune with the progress made by the legal profession. I have set out the cases in this book chronologically to make the point that the justice game is much fairer than depicted by contemporary authors and television dramatists, who still portray it in a time warp, somewhere between the *Notable British Trials* series and an early episode of *Rumpole*. In those days the Old Bailey *was* a place of verbal torture, in which unfortunate members of the lesser orders were pulled to pieces by bullying, upper-class men in wigs and put down by caustic, terrifying judges. Its very atmosphere created an expectation of guilt, which successful defenders tried to dissipate by emotional but highly conventional appeals to the hearts of the hard-faced people of property who were the only class allowed to sit as jurors until 1973. Advocates have now shaped their styles to the cooler, more consumer-friendly spirit of the times. Gone are the pre-war histrionics of Marshall Hall and the bullying of Edward Carson, affectations which sound hollow in modern strip-lit courtrooms. Marshall Hall pulled off his notable victories in murder cases by cheap-jack appeals to the sentimental prejudices of propertied jurymen ('Look at her, Gentlemen. God never gave her a chance. Won't you?'). At a Crown Court in Snaresbrook or Acton today, young jurypersons would collapse in laughter if such an appeal were made – although they would be more likely than their predecessors to heed the plea if it were spoken with less bathos.

Yet pernicious pictures of forensic life live on in anthologies of what passes for legal wit and wisdom. Lawyer's anecdotes are rarely funny: they are usually about how grown men make jokes at the expense of the poor, the disabled and the inarticulate. The small boy who pulls wings off flies is practising for a career at the Bar. It is, indeed, at the expense of a small, poor and injured boy that the classic anecdote of forensic brilliance is told. The boy has been run over by a negligently driven tram, and the wealthy corporation responsible for his injuries have hired the much-admired advocate F E Smith to deny him compensation. 'FE', as he is affectionately known to his peers, coaxes the child to show the jury how high he can raise his arm after the injury, and then asks how high he could raise it before the injury – and of course the youthful arm is raised higher. This reparteedious story has been endlessly repeated over the past fifty years in law miscellanies and at legal dinners: a nursery trick, played to deny compensation to a boy who was run over by a tram through no fault of his own, it remains the paradigm forensic fable.

The justice system needs new fables, and certainly new anecdotes, to mirror all the changes that have been made to the game over the past quarter-century. Horace Rumpole served us well, although today he would be bankrupted by wasted costs orders and his face would not fit the glossy chambers brochure. His idiosyncratic independence was necessary at a time when the State would regularly trundle out what John Mortimer calls 'the great engine of the criminal law' to crush sinners and artists and dissidents. But that great engine, for all its smoke and noise, is not getting us very far or very fast either in processing juveniles so they will not reoffend or in convicting serious fraudsters or rapists or bent coppers. I meet colleagues from other countries who are 'special prosecutors', putting behind bars Mafia bosses and masters of the Wall Street universe, or who head commissions which catch by their white collars corrupt politicians and public servants and policemen. But in Britain, for all the half-baked ideas which come tumbling in profusion from Home Secretaries, you still have to be pretty stupid to end up in prison.

But that is another story, and a different book. The prison I remember most vividly was one I visited in Vietnam on a mission for Amnesty, in the countryside beyond Ho Chi Minh City (formerly Saigon). Our hosts hotly denied that it was a prison at all, but rather a 're-education camp'. It was full of broken men shuffling back and forth to a prison library stocked with the works of V I Lenin. The war had ended fifteen years before, and they had been held ever since: all had been officers of the South Vietnam Army, who had been guilty, we were assured, of brutal war crimes. The victors sincerely believed this, and it said something for the new regime that they had not been summarily executed. But it did not say enough. These suspects had never been tried, never given the possibility of proving their innocence. I knew better than to raise awkward questions in the presence of guards but I did ask, when we were out of earshot, whether they would have preferred a trial – with the death penalty if they lost – or fifteen years' detention. They all said, and genuinely I think, that they would rather have taken their chance on justice.

Practising law has taught me little more than that there are two sides to every argument and that the verdict will go against an argument which is good if the other argument is better. Never in twenty-five years have I heard a witness tell the whole truth (honest memory is always selective) and never have I seen a judge be totally fair, although many are as fair as their background and training and grumbling ulcer will allow. I have come to disbelieve defendants with gold taps in their bathroom and have learned that where there's smoke there's usually fire, although occasionally it comes from a smoke machine, and that even the smoking gun may have fingerprints on the handle which do not match the suspect's. After a string of wrongful convictions were uncovered a few years ago an admirable Chief Justice, Peter Taylor, went on television: he thumped the table and declared 'Justice is not a game!' That was when it struck me that we would do better to recognise that justice is the most serious and important game of all, and the best side will have a better chance of winning if its rules are precise and fair and obeyed. But what matters above all is that the result must never be a foregone conclusion. For all the grandiose descriptions that have been offered of the adversary system of trial, and for all the pomp and self-esteem that tends to affect its professional participants, it is the best method we have yet devised for giving the suckers an even break.

Chapter Notes

1. Who is Mr Abbie Hoffman?

Richard Neville provides an account of his life and crimes in *Hippie Hippie Shake* (Bloomsbury, 1995). C H Rolph's *The Trial of Lady Chatterley* was reissued by Penguin in 1990 in a commemorative edition, with a foreword by the author. And see G Robertson and J Carrick, 'The Trials of Nancy Young', *The Australian Quarterly* (June 1970), and Clavir and Spitzer (eds.), *The Chicago Conspiracy Trial* (Cape, 1971).

2. The Trials of *Oz*

The play *The Trials of Oz* was performed at the Aldwych Theatre in London, directed by Buzz Goodbody, January 1972; at the Anderson Theatre, New York (as a musical) directed by Jim Sharman, December 1972; and in the BBC 'Performance' series, directed by Simon Curtis, 1992. There was an instant book by Tony Palmer, *The Trials of Oz* (Blond and Briggs, 1971). The legal significance of the case is assessed by the author in *Obscenity* (Weidenfeld, 1979) and *Media Law* (third edition, Penguin, 1992). The Court of Appeal judgment is reported as *R v Anderson, Neville, Dennis and Oz Publications Ink Ltd*, 1972 1 QB 304. Michael Argyle's memoirs were published in the *Spectator* on 20 May 1995; the magazine's apology followed in its 17 June edition.

3. One of Our MPs is Missing

John Stonehouse tells his own story in *Death of an Idealist* (W H

387

Allen, 1975) and *My Trial* (Wyndam, 1975). The judicial account is *DPP v Stonehouse* (1978) AC 55. R D Laing and his fridge feature in *R D Laing: A Biography* by his son, Adrian (Peter Owen, 1984). The book about Kenneth Lennon is titled *Reluctant Judas* (Maurice Temple Smith, 1976).

4. Michael X on Death Row

The Michael X story is told by Derek Humphrey and David Tindal, *False Messiah* (Hart-Davis, 1977), and by V S Naipaul, *The Killings in Trinidad* (André Deutsch, 1980). Both works carry the easy condemnation of instant hindsight: a more balanced retrospective by Edward Pilkington, 'The Other Brother X', was published in the *Guardian* on 2 March 1993. The Privy Council decision in Michael's case is reported as *de Freitas v Benny* (1976) AC 239; its Noel Riley judgment is *Riley v Attorney General of Jamaica* (1983) 1 AC 719; while *Earl Pratt & Ivan Morgan v Attorney General of Jamaica* is at (1994) 2 AC 1. The position in Jamaica prior to *Pratt* is described in *Jamaica – the Death Penalty* (Amnesty, 1989). The description of hangings comes from evidence given by the Warden of San Quentin to the US Senate Judiciary Committee in 1968; a recent gruesome study of the execution business in the USA is Stephen Trombley's *The Execution Protocol* (Century, 1993). The best history of legal opposition to capital punishment is the optimistically entitled *The Abolition of the Death Penalty in International Law*, by William Schabas (Grotius, 1993).

5. Ferrets or Skunks? The ABC Trial

The ABC trial is the subject of a book by A (Crispin Aubrey), called *Who's Watching You?* (Penguin, 1980), and has been analysed by David Leigh in *The Frontiers of Secrecy* (Junction Books, 1980) and by David Hooper in *Official Secrets – the Use and Abuse of the Law* (Coronet, 1988). Jock Kane's allegations were the subject of 'World in Action' (ITV, 9 June 1980) and of a book *GCHQ: The Negative Asset* which remains injuncted from publication. E P Thompson's polemic against the Attorney General is republished in *Writing by Candlelight* (The Merlin Press, 1980).

6. *Gay News*: The Angel's Advocate

The best book on blasphemy is *Blasphemy: Verbal Offence against the Sacred, from Moses to Salman Rushdie*, by Leonard W Levy (Knopf, 1993). The *Gay News* trial is reported in a booklet by Nicolas Walter (who attended each day), published in 1977 by the Rationalist Press Association: *Blasphemy in Britain: The Practice and Punishment of Blasphemy and the Trial of* Gay News. The view from the Bench is to be found in Alan King-Hamilton's autobiography, *And Nothing but the Truth* (Weidenfeld, 1982), and from defence counsel's row in John Mortimer's autobiography, *Murderers and Other Friends* (Viking, 1994). The trial is the highlight of two of Mary Whitehouse's autobiographies, *A Most Dangerous Woman* (Lion Books, 1982) and *Quite Contrary* (Sidgwick & Jackson, 1993). She writes on homosexuality in *Whatever Happened to Sex?* (Wayland, 1977), and her tactics are analysed by Michael Tracey and David Morrison in *Whitehouse* (Macmillan, 1979). Whatever happened to *Gay News* is told in *Title Fight: the Battle for* Gay News, by Gillian Hanscombe and Andrew Lumsden (Brilliance Books, 1983). The author's argument for reforming the laws relating to both blasphemy and homosexuality are in *Freedom, the Individual and the Law* (seventh edition, Penguin, 1993). See also The Law Commission, *Offences Against Religion and Public Worship*, Working Paper No. 79, HMSO 1981: Report, HMSO 1985; *Whitehouse v Lemon and Gay News Ltd* (1979), A.C. 617; *Conegate v Customs and Excise Commission* (1986), 2 All ER 688; *R v Chief Stipendiary Magistrate, ex parte Choudhury* (1991), All ER 306 (the *Satanic Verses* case).

7. *The Romans in Britain*

The script of *The Romans in Britain* by Howard Brenton is published by Eyre Methuen (1981). Mary Whitehouse's diary features in Mary Whitehouse, *A Most Dangerous Woman* (Lion Books, 1982).

8. Invitation to an Inquest: Helen Smith

See *The Helen Smith Story* by Paul Foot (Fontana, 1983) and

Inquest: Helen Smith, The Whole Truth? by Gordon Wilson and Dave Harrison (Methuen, 1983).

9. The Prisoner of Venda

The report of the human rights mission to Malawi was published by the Law Society in 1992. Banda's rule is described by John Lwanda, *Kamuzu Banda of Malawi: A Study in Power and Paralysis* (Dudu Nsomba Publications, 1993). See also *Where Silence Rules: The Suppression of Dissent in Malawi* (Africa Watch, 1990). Dr Banda died in November 1997.

10. Show Trials

Francis Seow, Singapore's former Solicitor General, traces the 'Marxist conspiracy' in *To Catch a Tartar – A Dissident in Lee Kuan Yew's Prison* (1994). And see Asia Watch, *Silencing All Critics: Human Rights Violations in Singapore* (September 1989).

11. Fantasy Island

The facts stated in this chapter are based on findings of the Royal Commission, published as *Guns for Antigua*, by Louis Blom-Cooper QC (Duckworth, 1990). I have drawn additionally on the transcripts of the Commission's oral hearings and the exhibits submitted to it, and on the Hearings before the Permanent Sub-Committee on Investigations of the Committee on Governmental Affairs of the United States Senate, 12 and 13 September 1989 (*Structure of International Drug Trafficking Organisations*, testimony of Diego Viatara Salinas) and 27 and 28 February 1991 (*Arms Trafficking, Mercenaries and Drug Cartels*). Further details of Antiguan government corruption are to be found in the *Report to the Government of Antigua relating to Roydan Farm* by the law firm of Washington, Perito and Dubuc, a report not published by the Antiguan government. The Commission's Report should be compared with the decision of the Antiguan High Court in quashing one of its recommendations: *In an Application by Clyde S Walker* (Redhead J, 25 July, 1995) 'The Future of Colombia' by Gabriel García Márquez was first published in *Granta* magazine

(1989), and repeated in *News of a Kidnapping* (1997). The details of assassinations are found in *The Fight Against the Drug Traffic in Colombia* (office of the President, February 1990). No visit to Antigua is complete without reading Jamaica Kincaid, *A Small Place* (Penguin, 1988).

12. Come Up and See My Boggs

Contemporary accounts of the Old Bailey trial include Lawrence Wechsler, 'Onwards and Upwards with the Arts: Boggs Part 1' (*New Yorker*, 18 January 1988), 'Part II' (*New Yorker*, 25 January 1988) and Darcy Frey, 'Dow Jones's Man about the Commonwealth' (*The American Lawyer* Jan/Feb 1988, p. 143). *The Shock of the New* by Robert Hughes and *The Art of Paper Currency* by Martin Monestier (Quartet, 1983) served as textbooks for the trial. For Boggs and his more recent brushes with the Secret Service, see Timothy Sultan 'In Boggs we Trust', the *Spectator*, 13 May 1995.

13. Ali Daghir and the Forty Nuclear Triggers

For the author's more academic analysis of Daghir and other cases, see *Entrapment Evidence: Manna From Heaven, or Fruit of the Poisoned Tree?* The Criminal Law Review, November 1993. The Court of Appeal decision quashing the convictions of Ali Daghir and Jeanine Speckman was given on 25 May 1994. The Report by Congressman Gonzalez, *Nuclear Triggers Sting, Commerce Blunders and CIA Deception* was delivered to the US Congress on 18 February 1993. The US Government Treasury memorandum is dated 4 August 1989 and is headed 'Request for Foreign Travel – Operation Quarry'. Daghir's guilt was assumed by *Time* and *Newsweek* in their stories of his arrest: April 9, 1990. For a perceptive analysis of the case, as demonstrating that the functions of intelligence agencies and law enforcement are not compatible, see Nikos Passas and Jack Blum, 'Intelligence Services and Undercover Operations: The Case of Euromac' in Field and Pelser (eds) *Invading the Private: State Accountability and New Policing in Europe* (Dartmouth, 1998).

14. Friendly (*sic*) Fire

The plight of the 'friendly fire' parents was first identified by
Denis MacShane MP, *Friendly Fire Whitewash* (Epic Books,
1992). And see *Friendly Fire* by C D B Brian (Bantam, 1991).

15. UK Ltd: The Matrix Churchill Trial

The best account of the Matrix Churchill trial is the one David
Leigh wrote from the transcripts, with *actualité* supplied by
Richard Norton-Taylor: *Betrayed* (Bloomsbury, 1993). Paul
Henderson's autobiography, *The Unlikely Spy* (Bloomsbury,
1993), tells the victim's story. The Scott Report weighs over a
stone and comprises 1,806 pages plus an index and a CD-ROM:
*Inquiry into the Export of Defence Equipment and Dual-Use Goods to
Iraq and Related Prosecutions 1995*, HC115. For a cheaper read of
the purple passages from the Scott Report, see *Knee Deep in
Dishonour* by Richard Norton-Taylor, Mark Lloyd and Stephen
Cook (Gollancz, 1996). Scott's work is now being digested by
academics – see 'The Scott Report' (*Public Law*, Autumn 1996)
and *Under the Scott-Light: British Government seen through the Scott
Report*, eds Brian Thompson and F F Ridley (OUP, 1997). The
books on which I relied in preparing for the trial were *The Death
Lobby: How the West Armed Iraq* by Kenneth Timmerman
(Fourth Estate, 1992); *Unholy Babylon* by Adel Darwish and
Gregory Alexander (Gollancz, 1991); and, of course, *Republic of
Fear* by Samir al-Khalil – the book MI6 gave to Paul Henderson
as a way of telling him his life was in danger.

16. Diana in the Dock: Does Privacy Matter?

Part of this chapter was first published in the *New Yorker*,
September 1997, as 'Privacy Matters'. For a critique of media
self-regulation, see the author's *People Against the Press* (Quartet,
1983).

17. Cash for Questions?

David Leigh and Ed Vulliamy tell the *Guardian*'s story in *Sleaze –
The Corruption of Parliament* (Fourth Estate, 1997). Sir Gordon

Downey's Report, published by the Committee of Standards and Privileges is entitled 'Complaints from Mr Mohammed Al Fayed, the *Guardian* and Others against 25 members and former members' (House of Commons, Session 1997–98, Vol I, 2 July 1997). Hamilton's case is set out in Volume II of the appendices pp. 172–333. Ian Greer's version is *One Man's Word – The Untold Story of the Cash-For-Questions Affair* (André Deutsch, 1997). The final verdict of the Committee on Standards and Privileges, *Second Further Report: Mr Neil Hamilton*, was published on 5 November 1997.

Picture Credits
1 Popperfoto, 2, 3, *Oz* Magazine, 1971; 4 with permission of *Private Eye*; 5 © Times Newspapers Ltd (photo C. Travis); 6 Associated Press; 7 Andrew Wiard/Report; 8 Christopher Davies; 9 Laurence Burns, from the National Theatre production of *The Romans in Britain*; 11, © *Sunday Times* (illustration Phil Green); 12, by permission of Ron Smith; 13 Mirror Syndication International; 17 *The Observer*; 19 M. Peterson/Katz Pictures Limited; 20 The *Straits Times*; 21 © JS Boggs; 22 © M. Nichol; 23 NBC/Associated Press; 24 PA News (photo Louisa Buller); 25 Associated Press; 26 The *Independent* (photo John Voos); 27 © *Daily Mail*; 28 The *Independent* (photo Glynn Griffiths; 30 The *Guardian* (photo Martin Godwin).

Index